DRAWING ON STUDENTS' WORLDS IN THE ELA CLASSROOM

This book approaches English instruction through the lens of "figured worlds," which recognizes and spotlights how students are actively engaged in constructing their own school, peer group, extracurricular, and community worlds. Teachers' ability not only to engage with students' experiences and interests in and outside of school but also to build connections between students' worlds and their teaching is essential for promoting student agency, engagement, and meaningful learning. Beach and Caraballo provide an accessible framework for working with students to use critical discourse, narratives, media, genres, and more to support their identity development through addressing topics that are meaningful for them—their families, social issues, virtual worlds, and more.

Through extensive activities and examples of students writing about their participation in these worlds, this text allows educators to recognize how students' experiences in the classroom affect and shape their identities and to connect such an understanding to successful classroom practice. With chapters featuring effective instructional activities, this book is necessary reading for ELA methods courses and for all English teachers.

Richard Beach is Professor Emeritus at the University of Minnesota, USA.

Limarys Caraballo is Associate Professor of English Education at Teachers College, Columbia University, Deputy Executive Director at CUNY Graduate Center, and Research Fellow and Cyphers for Justice, and Founding Co-Director at IUME Teachers College, Columbia University, USA.

DRAWING ON STUDENTS' WORLDS IN THE ELA CLASSROOM

Toward Critical Engagement and Deep Learning

Richard Beach with Limarys Caraballo

NEW YORK AND LONDON

Cover image: Mindi Rhoades

First published 2022
by Routledge
605 Third Avenue, New York, NY 10158

and by Routledge
4 Park Square, Milton Park, Abingdon, Oxon, OX14 4RN

Routledge is an imprint of the Taylor & Francis Group, an informa business

© 2022 Richard Beach and Limarys Caraballo

The right of Richard Beach and Limarys Caraballo to be identified as author[s] of
this work has been asserted in accordance with sections 77 and 78 of the Copyright,
Designs and Patents Act 1988.

All rights reserved. No part of this book may be reprinted or reproduced or utilised
in any form or by any electronic, mechanical, or other means, now known or
hereafter invented, including photocopying and recording, or in any information
storage or retrieval system, without permission in writing from the publishers.

Trademark notice: Product or corporate names may be trademarks or registered trademarks,
and are used only for identification and explanation without intent to infringe.

Library of Congress Cataloging-in-Publication Data
A catalog record for this title has been requested

ISBN: [9781032160511] (hbk)
ISBN: [9781032155586] (pbk)
ISBN: [9781003246886] (ebk)

DOI: [10.4324/9781003246886]

Typeset in Bembo
by Newgen Publishing UK

CONTENTS

Author and Contributor Biographies   *vii*
Acknowledgments   *viii*

PART I
Overall Framing of Co-Authoring Practices
in Figured Worlds   **1**

1   Introduction: Students Co-Authoring Figured Worlds   3

2   Contextualizing Practices Through Components Constituting
Figured Worlds   26

3   Contextualizing Practices Based on Purpose, Norms,
Discourses, and Identities in School Worlds   49

4   Contextualizing Practices Using Genres and Media/Literature
in School Worlds   72

5   Co-Authoring Community Worlds   95

vi Contents

PART II
Students Co-Authoring Different Figured Worlds 117

6 YPAR as Figured World: Co-Authoring Identities,
Literacies, and Activism 119
Limarys Caraballo

7 Co-Authoring Peer Group Figured Worlds 142

8 Co-Authoring Extracurricular Worlds 163

9 Co-Authoring Sports Worlds 184

10 Co-Authoring Family Figured Worlds 206

11 Co-Authoring Workplace Figured Worlds 227

12 Co-Authoring Social/Digital Media Worlds 249

PART III
Implications for Teaching 273

13 Implications for Teaching: Bringing Students' Worlds into the
ELA Classroom 275

Index *289*

AUTHOR AND CONTRIBUTOR BIOGRAPHIES

Author Biography

Richard Beach is Professor Emeritus of Literacy Education at the University of Minnesota, Twin Cities. He is co-author of *Teaching Language as Action in the ELA Classroom* (*languaging.pbworks.com*) and co-editor of *Languaging Relations for Transforming the Literacy and Language Arts Classroom*. He is also co-author of *Teaching Climate Change to Adolescents: Reading, Writing, and Making a Difference* (*climatechangeela.pbworks.com*) and *Teaching Literature to Adolescents*, Fourth Edition (*teachingliterature.pbworks.com*). He served as a former president of the Literacy Research Association.

Contributor Biography

Limarys Caraballo is an associate professor of English Education and Curriculum at Teachers College, Columbia University, and is a member of the Doctoral Consortium Faculty in Urban Education at the CUNY Graduate Center. She is founding co-director of *Cyphers for Justice*, a youth-engaged research program that supports intergenerational participatory inquiry. Her research reframes deficit discourses about minoritized youth by amplifying their multiple voices, literacies, and identities.

ACKNOWLEDGMENTS

I would like to thank

- Ms. E, given that my research would not have been possible without her engaging classroom instruction and writing assignments, resulting in her students' quotes throughout this book.
- Limarys Caraballo for contributing her chapter to this book and for her ongoing feedback and interactions associated with this book project.
- Mindi Rhoades, Associate Professor of Teaching and Learning, The Ohio State University, for creating the book cover and two figures in this book.
- Karen Adler, Routledge editor, for all her support and encouragement for this book project.

PART I

Overall Framing of Co-Authoring Practices in Figured Worlds

1

INTRODUCTION

Students Co-Authoring Figured Worlds

This chapter posits the need to recognize how students construct or co-author their "figured worlds" through informal learning of different practices in community, peer group, extracurricular, sports, family, workplace, and social/digital media worlds. Providing students with opportunities to write and reflect about their practices in these different worlds in the ELA classroom contributes to their deeper learning. In writing and reflecting on their practices, students are contextualizing their use of languaging actions for enacting these practices for interacting with others; languaging actions that include emotions and embodied actions. This suggests the value of fostering "boundary-crossing" practices for bringing students' informal learning experiences in these different worlds into the classroom in ways that value the significance and worth of those experiences, leading to students' growth over time.

In writing a description of her peer group for her 12th grade English class, Laura noted how members of her group created a name for their group, "The Australian Voice Crackers:"

> When I was first introduced into the group, they were asking me what kind of music I listen to, so I said "Alternative" and listed off a couple of my favorite groups. ... Then they had asked where I come from, so I told them, 'Australia.' D. then shouts, "Why would you listen to the Australian Voice Crackers, they are awful!" It became an inside joke for a while then we changed it to our group name on Snapchat, so we've called ourselves that since then.

Laura values her participation in this group given that

> before I met these people, I was in a really tough place in my life. I hit rock bottom. So when they first invited me to a bonfire, I was a little anxious

DOI: 10.4324/9781003246886-2

about going, but I decided that it would be a good idea. I thought that I should probably get my life together and meet more people and try to fix myself up. I went, and they started to ask me to hang out with them more often, and I enjoyed being with these people. I told them what I was going through; they all mostly seemed to care at least a little bit.

They helped me get better, and they tried their best to understand. There were days where they knew I was sad or upset, and I wouldn't talk to them, but they would show up to my house and say, "Laura, tell us what's wrong, and we'll make it better." They made a huge impact on my life for the better. I would say I would call the people the love of my life just because I love them all a lot for being there for me and letting me talk to them about anything whenever I needed them.

Members of the group helped me order food at fast-food places and talk in front of strangers. Now, I can be more myself in class and out in public. They taught me to be myself and that nobody actually judges as much as I thought ... They are my little family of friends, and they are a lot greater than they come off as ... I'm glad they were so accepting of me and all my problems because, without their help, I'm not sure where I would be in my life right now, but I don't think it would be a good place. I really appreciate these people, and I think they should get more credit than they are given.

Laura describes how she and other peer group members co-authored their world as "my little family of friends." In addition, she portrays how, through participation in this world, she gained confidence in how to "talk in front of strangers."

Variation in Students' Engagement in School Worlds

Students' engagement in their school worlds often varies depending on the extent to which ELA teachers tap into their experiences outside of school worlds. In this book, given that experiences such as Laura's in her peer group world outside of school are essential for students' development, I posit the value of ELA teachers, as they often do, importing these experiences into the classroom to enhance students' engagement in school.

Recent research suggests students are often not engaged in school worlds. The YouthTruth project (2020, Spring; 2020, Fall; 2021, Spring) surveyed students across America about their perceptions of their experience in schools during the Covid pandemic. Only 42% of students in Spring, 2020 reported that their teachers made some attempt to learn about their lives outside of school. In Fall, 2020, that percentage declined to 30% but then increased to 43% in the Spring, 2021 survey. The results also indicated a decline in teachers' interest in students' non-academic identities, from 43% in Spring 2020 to 30% in Fall, 2020 and 28% in Spring, 2021.

While half of students perceived relationships with teachers as positive, only 31% experienced a strong sense of belonging to their school, and only 30%

experienced a sense of being a member of the school community, although that increased to 39% in Fall, 2020 and 43% in Spring, 2021.

While there were shifts across the three different surveys, and some of these results reflect the difficulties with switching to remote instruction during the pandemic, the overall results suggest that many students often do not necessarily experience a strong sense of connection or belonging with their school worlds. At the same time, students also have a strong sense of connection with being in their schools, something that they missed during the pandemic with only remote learning as an option.

A study of high school dropouts found that half of them indicated that they dropped out due to a lack of interest in their classes, given a lack of connections to their lived-world family and community experiences (Cohen & Smerdon, 2009). In addition, 70% noted that they were not motivated to learn, and two-thirds noted that they would have been more motivated given higher demands.

Students in another study noted their lack of engagement in school was related to how their learning revolved around a *knowing-that* acquisition of facts and information. Twenty-five students in an Irish school, ages 13 and 14, kept reflective journals and engaged in focus-group discussions of their engagement in their school relative to other worlds outside their school (Quinlan & Curtin, 2017). Only 24% indicated that they enjoyed learning in their school. Only 32% indicated that they enjoyed being in school, often due to lack of interest, leading to boredom based on perceptions of the content as not interesting or relevant to their lives.

During the pandemic, adolescents were often limited to virtual schooling, with fewer opportunities for face-to-face interactions with teachers and peers sharing their lives outside of school. They also had fewer opportunities to engage in school-sponsored sports or extracurricular activities. Jenny Radesky noted that a survey of parents found that their children as "remote learners had significantly higher hyperactivity, peer problems, defiance and sleep difficulties compared with children attending in-person school" (Bazelon, 2021, p. 58).

> On the other hand, Andrea Hunley noted that as a school administrator, I have never felt such a high level of energy around transforming education ... We're not going back to the way that things used to be. They have gained so much independence about what it means to be a learner. Some of the projects that kids have created while they were at home on remote learning have been incredible. We want to bring in more of that.
>
> *p. 61*

While the pandemic may have long-term negative effects on students, Hunley's comments suggest the need for teachers to acquire knowledge of students' experiences in their worlds, to draw on those experiences for instructional activities, and to enhance their engagement in their learning, the focus of this book.

6 Framing of Co-Authoring Practices

Students need to perceive their learning as having some relevance to their worlds outside the classroom, often related to perceptions of disparities between what they perceive as "book smarts" in school and their own "street smarts" associated with their daily experiences with issues of poverty, street culture, law enforcement, and unemployment in their communities, resulting in their critiquing the limitations of their school experiences (Fecho et al., 2020). As Mehta and Fine (2019) note, "schools need to become much more deeply attached to the world beyond their walls" (n.p.).

Alejandro Diasgranados, the District of Columbia 2021 Teacher of the Year, perceives his classroom as a two-way street for drawing on his students' experiences in worlds outside the classroom into his world (Torres, 2021). He notes that

> all students come to school with an abundance of cultural wealth. They are experts in their community and culture. These things are important to students and they should be able to remain important to students when they enter into our school buildings.
>
> *p. 21*

Making these connections then leads his students to address issues outside his classroom:

> They've seen how learning to write a simple persuasive essay isn't just an assignment we do every Friday, but how a persuasive essay can change a law or bring funding to our school or convince our principal to allow a teacher to loop up to the next grade.
>
> *p. 20*

Adolescents Co-Authoring Figured Worlds

Through participation in worlds outside the classroom, students are learning to actively co-author these worlds as "figured worlds," as shared "realm[s] of interpretation in which a particular set of characters and actors are recognized, significance is assigned to certain acts, and particular outcomes are valued over others" (Holland et al., 1998, p. 52). Figured worlds are constituted by:

- "Historical phenomena, to which we are recruited or into which we enter, which themselves develop through the works of their participants."
- "Processes or traditions of apprehension which gather us up and give form as our lives intersect them."
- "Social encounters in which participants' positions matter."
- "Activities in the usual, institutional sense. They divide and relate participants (almost as roles), and they depend upon the interaction and the intersubjectivity for perpetuation."

- "Relating actors to landscapes of action (as personae) and spreading our senses of self across many different fields of activity, but also by giving the landscape human voice and tone." (Holland et al., 1998, p. 41)

James Gee (2015) described a figured world as "a picture of a simplified world that captures what is taken to be typical or normal" (p. 114). Hartsfield and Kimmel (2010) note how figured worlds are constituted by actions based on "what people assume are appropriate ways to think, believe, act, and communicate (Gee, 2014)," actions "based on understandings influenced by our membership in social and cultural groups" (p. 444). They cite the example of one student's conception of the figured world of school in which parents exercise power by challenging the adoption of books perceived to be problematic, leading to censorship.

Rather than perceive these worlds as external entities "out there," the notion of figured worlds draws on the idea that people co-author these worlds as figured through their actions (Holland et al., 1998). For example, college students learned to engage in the figured world of romance, shaping their perceptions of academic versus social life based on discourses operating of that time (Holland & Eisenstat, 1990).While students were initially committed to focusing on academics, over time, many shifted to focusing more on concern about the need to establish romantic relations associated with the long-term goal of marriage.These students learned to participate in this normative (and often sexist) figured world of romance as

> populated by a set of agents (in the world of romance: attractive women, boyfriends, lovers, fiancés) who engage in a limited range of meaningful acts or changes of state (flirting with, falling in love with, dumping, having sex with) as moved by a specific set of forces (attractiveness, love, lust).
>
> *p. 52*

In contrast to the notion of worlds being "out there," adolescents collaboratively co-author their figured worlds

> through social interaction, and in them, people "figure" out who they are in relation to those around them. ... Through participation in figured worlds, people can reconceptualize who they are, or shift who they understand themselves to be, as individuals or members of collectives.Through this figuring, individuals also come to understand their ability to craft their future participation, or agency, in and across figured worlds.
>
> *Urrieta, 2007, p. 120*

Adolescents are co-authoring these worlds through relational, collaborative actions (De Jaegher & Di Paolo, 2007; Linell, 2016) within "passionate affinity-based spaces" through collaboration with others (Gee, 2017). Students learn to

8 Framing of Co-Authoring Practices

engage in collective action not as individual, independent actors but rather with and through others through use of consistent languaging actions (De Jaegher & Di Paolo, 2007; Linell, 2016) as members of communities, peer groups, extracurricular organizations, sports teams, families, workplaces, or media/online worlds.

Informal Learning as "Deeper Learning" in Figured Worlds

In participating in worlds outside the classroom, students engage in informal, relational learning as distinct from more formal learning in the classroom. One descriptor for informal out-of-school learning is in terms of

> passionate affinity-based learning [that] occurs when people organize themselves in the real world and/or via the Internet (or a virtual world) to learn something connected to a shared endeavor, interest, or passion first and foremost and then to others because of their shared affinity.
>
> *Gee & Hayes, 2011, p. 69*

This focus on relational learning shifts the prevailing focus on learning in schools as an autonomous, individual process to building relations with others in a figured world. For example, as students participate in the world of team sports, they learn to engage in the practices of learning types of plays and strategies for collaboratively interacting with other players, experiences they may then transfer into the classroom.

Through their experience in different worlds, adolescents acquire different notions of what it means to learn within and across different figured worlds; for example, learning certain practices in a workplace (Verhoeven et al., 2021). In some cases, they experience continuities across these worlds; for example, similarities in how they learn in school and how they learn in worlds outside of school (Bronkhorst & Akkerman, 2016). At the same time, they also experience discontinuities between their learning; for example, how their learning in a school arts program may bear little relationship with how they learn in their family world (Verhoeven et al., 2021). Some students also perceive a discontinuity between how they learn, noting a disparity between how school learning involves a focus on sitting passively at their desks, while learning in sports or playing music involves use of embodied actions.

An analysis of adolescents who were "hardly" engaged often perceived how they were more engaged with how they learned in worlds outside of school as distinct from their learning in school (Verhoeven et al., 2021). They also were more likely to be engaged in a peer group world with peers who were also not engaged in school. In contrast, adolescents who were "highly" engaged in school were more likely to perceive continuity between how their teachers and their parents perceived productive learning as devoting energy and time on schooling. Engaged students were also more likely to connect with peers who were also engaged in school.

This research suggests the importance of identifying those practices where students experience continuities across their different worlds in how they are experiencing and learning practices in worlds outside the classroom for enhancing what is described as "deeper learning" (Mehta & Fine, 2019; McTighe & Silver, 2020; Wergin, 2020). Students engage in deeper learning through being motivated based on a sense of purpose, engagement, community, and apprenticeship, things they may experience through engagement in worlds outside the classroom that they draw on for use in the classroom.

For example, students participating in extracurricular school theater programs experience "deep learning" given their high level of engagement through displaying competence to their audiences. Deeper learning also occurs when students' knowledge or beliefs are challenged, resulting in their revising their knowledge or beliefs. These challenges create a tension "between a perceived challenge to one's existing belief system on the one hand, and a perceived level of confidence in one's ability to create new meaning in that system on the other" (Wergin, 2020, p. 35). This "requires active, mindful agency of the sort that not only reacts to, but also seeks out new ways of being – ways that encourage us to step out of our comfort zones just far enough to allow our innate curiosity to take over" (p. 38).

In their analysis of a high school theater program, Mehta and Fine (2019) identified several positive elements contributing to students "deeper learning" associated with identity and creativity in the program:

- Purpose: Students had a clear sense of purpose driving their actions associated with achieving the goal of putting on a production.
- Student choice: The fact that students choose to participate in theater productions served to enhance their motivations.
- Community: Students experience bonding within the theater group, often identifying with the social positions of "theater kids," particularly students who did not identify with other peer groups or sports.
- Apprenticeship: Older students who had more experience in theater served as role models for younger students to socialize them into engagement in the production. (pp. 265–283).

ACTIVITY: STUDENTS DESCRIBING THEIR PARTICIPATION IN FIGURED WORLDS

Students could discuss or write about the different figured worlds they inhabit so that teachers can then generate activities for having them write and reflect on their participation in these different worlds. These activities could include having students recognize that these worlds are not simply "out there," but rather are collaboratively co-authored through their own actions, constituting unique worlds that are consistent with their identities, needs, beliefs, and knowledge; for example, that their family world is co-constructed through how family members interact with each other.

Co-Authoring Figured Worlds through Practices

A key concept in this book has to do with the notion of *practices*. Adolescents co-author figured worlds through their use of certain practices to "evoke the worlds to which they are relevant and position individuals with respect to those worlds" (Holland et al., 1998, p. 63). Their enactment of identities is "embedded in (social) practice and [is] itself a kind of practice" (p. 28).

Consistent with the notion of "communities of practice" (Wenger, 1998), students learn to employ certain practices as "building tasks" for enacting relations in those communities (Gee & Hayes, 2011; Rogers & Wetzel, 2013). They co-author a figured world as "a socially and culturally constructed realm of inter-pretation in which particular characters and actors are recognized, significance is assigned to certain acts, and particular outcomes are valued over others" (Holland et al. 1998, p. 52). Schatzki (2010) defines a practice as

> an organized, open-ended array of doings and sayings. This array is organized by a set of (1) action understandings, which combine abilities to perform actions, to recognize others' actions, and to respond to those actions, (2) rules, which are formulated directives, instructions, admonishments, and the like, (3) a teleological-affective structure, which embraces a range of ends, projects, actions, combinations thereof, and emotions that participants should acceptably pursue or exhibit, and (4) general understandings of matters germane to the practice involved.
>
> *Section on Ceremony and Ritual in chapter on The Dominion of Teleology*

Acquiring Practices as Ways of Doing/Acting

As students participate in a figured world, they acquire the use of certain practices for ways of doing/acting in an event or situation specific to a figured world. A practice

> means something a distinctive group of people does. Carrying out an experiment in a lab is a practice. Trading Yu-Gi-Oh! cards in a schoolyard is a practice. Writing a report on the local population for the city council is a practice ... Each practice makes use of a social language to help accomplish

Students Co-Authoring Figured Worlds **11**

a particular function or job. The learner must learn the practices (both understand them and want to do them).

Gee & Hayes, 2011, p. 62

Students acquire these practices over time by connecting past, present, and future actions to engage in practices by assessing how certain past actions result in a change in their present and future actions. For example, they develop the practice of commending others for their work through voicing positive comments for enhancing their relations with others. They then perceive this development as a trajectory or tradition for enacting roles/identities through interactions with others as well as a pathway for mediating resources for acquiring certain possible selves (Nasir et al., 2020).

Teachers employ a range of practices for engaging students in literacy learning. This includes "enabling practices" that serve to enhance students' sense of agency; for example, employing free/independent reading time and discussions contributing to students' enjoyment of reading (Frankel et al., 2018, p. 465). At the same time, teachers may also employ "constraining practices" associated with district-mandated testing or decontextualized strategy instruction that serve to limit or undermine student engagement in learning.

(Regarding having students employ the term "practices" to talk about their learning, I am concerned about whether students, particularly middle-school students, will readily understand and apply the meaning of "practices" as employed in academia. I therefore propose employing alternative language, involving using the words "ways of acting/doing things," in lieu of "practices" when working with younger students. I derive the words "ways of acting/doing things" from Bucholtz's (2015) notion of "ways of doing things" (p. 29) having to do with her discussion of enacting practices to help students focus on their use of their actions in figured worlds.)

Practices as Situated in Specific Social or Cultural Contexts in Figured Worlds

Practices are situated in specific social or cultural contexts or situations in figured worlds constituted by enacting social relations. In reflecting on the social institutional context of schooling related to ELA instruction during the pandemic and the need to have students experience supportive social relations, Antero Garcia (2021) called for a change in instructional practices. Given the need to move away from the practice of a competitive argumentation, he posits the need to "reframe writing practices—that still evaluate student growth—as sources for affirming the ideas students have rather than as reasons for casting vitriolic skepticism on an uncertain other" (p. 22). He also called for a shift toward the practice of drawing on students' experiences through their shared narratives. By then allowing "youth

12 Framing of Co-Authoring Practices

experience to guide the questions and hopes that students have about the world, we can reorient literature and nonfiction texts to better serve justice" (p. 23).

Students are more likely to want to acquire practices when they experience a sense of belonging to a world through practices defined as ways of knowing and being with others (Niemiec & Ryan, 2009). Through their supportive interactions with others, they develop a sense of relational agency, enhancing their abilities to co-author their worlds. For example, Laura's peer group members learned to interact with other members to enact a figured world based on shared comradery and support that provided her with a sense of belonging. Similarly, students who experience high degrees of belonging to their school world and experiencing a sense of affinity with their teachers are more likely to succeed in school and less likely to drop out (Korpershoek et al., 2020; Lohmeier & Lee, 2011).

Learning New Practices

Students learn to acquire new practices in figured worlds through interactions with others. When they experience positive uptake from those interactions—for example, receiving compliments for organizing political protests in their school—they then learn to perceive that practice as enhancing their sense of agency. At the same time, they may also experience "wobble" related to experiencing complications or uncertainty in their interactions (Fecho et al., 2005); for example, peers wondering about the purpose or value of engaging in a protest that might lead to a backlash from administrators/teachers and some peers.

Experiencing "wobble" leads to perceptions of the need for change in the use of practices through improvising or experimenting with alternative practices. Teachers also experience "wobble" when they recognize that their instructional practices are not engaging their students. Analysis of an ELA teacher in his initial years of teaching indicated that he drew on his previous ELA instruction that focused on teaching canonical, classic literature, which he found was not engaging for him as a student (Rubin & Land, 2017). "'And so I would do worksheets, like on Othello. I remember struggling through Othello over four or five weeks, you know? One play, and the kids struggling through it' (Interview, 10/7/15)" (p. 194). This led him to perceive the need to experiment with alternative methods of instruction.

As a gay, Latinx person with a largely Latinx student population, through participation in a book club with his own peers and a National Writing Project (NWP) summer workshop, he shifted to use of workshop instructional practices through the use of more current texts relevant to students lives, fostered responding to text as a social, interactive practice, and had students select their own writing topics and conferenced with them. In reflecting on the value of his participation in the NWP workshops, he noted how he changed

> "not just pedagogically, but also for myself, identifying as a writer ... getting to question everything, what is writing, what is reading. ... And that's what

[the change] is. It's identifying with the label [of workshop teacher] and pursuing it further." (Interview 10/7/15)

p. 196

Therefore, students and teachers benefit from reflecting on limitations of their current use of practices based on their experience of "wobble," leading to experimentation with alternative practices.

Drawing on Practices from Different Figured Worlds for Learning in the Classroom

Students learning to draw on practices from worlds outside the classroom involves the ability to engage boundary-crossing for making connections across practices in their different worlds. Within school worlds, engaging in integrative thinking involves making connections across different disciplines; for example, thinking about scientific evidence from climate change in an environmental science class as portrayed in a cli-fi novel in a literature class. Based on her experiences of teaching reading in her writing classes, Arlene Wilner (2020) noted that

> I have found that students find it easier to connect text with worlds than text with texts. Understandably so: abstracting and synthesizing ideas from multiple texts is generally more challenging than relating a text to one's own experience of the world.

p. 75

Teachers can foster integrated thinking by the use of "cultural modeling" (Lee, 2001; Lee et al, 2020). "Cultural modeling" involves tapping into how students perform practices through use of languaging actions in a world to have students replicate those languaging actions in a classroom world. For example, African-American students engage in using signifying practices in their community and peer group worlds associated with the use of African American Vernacular English (AAVE) (Lee, 2001). In teaching literature in English classes, teachers draw on students' experiences with these signifying practices to have students learn about the use of literary techniques and figurative language in literary texts. For example, students learn how the use of metaphoric language in hip-hop applies to understanding metaphoric language in literacy texts (Lee, 2001).

Students draw on practices that enhance their relational agency constituting making changes in their worlds (Raffo & Forbes, 2021). For example, a Mexican immigrant middle-school student, Eddy, participated in an after-school arts program that drew on his expertise as a break dancer in a professional dance community. He then served as an instructor for his peers for creating a dance performance requiring expertise in break dancing to "scaffold the movement of novices from the safe place of the workshop into new, unfamiliar public performance spaces" (Walker & Nocon, 2007, p. 185).

14 Framing of Co-Authoring Practices

Through this boundary-crossing experience, Eddy developed an enhanced sense of relational agency as someone who could enhance practices in a different world. The importance of students acquiring use of boundary-crossing practices suggests the value of supporting students from non-dominant backgrounds. This includes helping students "connect to larger networks of expertise and mature practice while providing them with opportunities to participate in expanded, horizontal—rather than hierarchical—systems that effectively recontextualized their competencies" (p. 193).

Adolescents' participation as "student historians" in the New York Historical Society Museum project enhanced their sense of relational agency through leading tours to help their peers understand the history associated with museum exhibits (Frosini, 2017). Through "open-mic" spoken-word performances, students experienced positive responses given how "'everyone has something important to say'" (Fisher, 2003, p. 127). A student in a musical performance noted "'we was like, "You like our song?" and that's how I'm meeting people. We sing our way to being friends'" (Kuntz, 2011, p. 28).

Teachers in the Queens School of Inquiry in Queens, New York, build a curriculum around ways to assist students from low-income families to succeed in school by drawing on their background experiences (O'Brien, 2016). The teachers were also addressing the challenge of how the income inequality in American society undermines students' sense of their future success, even if they experience positive learning in the school; for example, in terms of going on to and succeeding in higher education.

Through participation in addressing local community issues related to racial justice, students may begin to perceive themselves as having the agency to engage in collective action to address these issues in their community worlds.

ACTIVITY: CONTEXTUALIZING EXAMPLES OF THE USE OF PRACTICES IN WORLDS

Students could identify examples of certain practices as consistent ways of acting/doing things within a certain event or situation in their worlds. For example, they can identify that the practice of providing support for peers whom they perceive need support or providing advice to other players on their sports team leads to their being perceived as assuming a leadership role.

They can then reflect on how and why they value using these practices for interacting with others. For example, in the opening example of Laura's acquiring practices valued by her peer group, she recognized how the practices employed in her group, such as continually inviting her to participate with them and providing support for her to cope with her problems, served to boost her morale.

Contextualizing Practices as Languaging Actions

In contextualizing practices in events or situations, students are reflecting on their uses of language as actions for enacting these practices. Given that a primary focus of English language arts instruction involves the use of language and reflecting on language as action (Beach & Beauchemin, 2019), it is useful to consider how students enact practices through what is defined as *languaging* actions (Beach & Bloome, 2019; Linell, 2009). Languaging theory shifts the focus on language as a *noun* (concerning language as something to be accomplished or as a sense of competence) to languaging as a *verb*. The focus is then on the "doingness" and the activity of language that students and teachers are continually employing to enact relations (Linell, 2009), in which "language, action, and perception are seen as inseparable" (Jensen, 2014, p. 73). Languaging as action

> is the principal means used by people to maintain their social relationships: greeting one another in the lobby, chatting about life outside work during the breaks, telling stories about adventures and relationships and gossiping about shared friends on the way home.
>
> *Tusting, 2005, p. 41*

Focusing on languaging actions moves beyond traditional, formalist language instruction that assumes that students first need to acquire knowledge of grammar/usage rules to focus on enacting languaging actions for using practices co-authoring figured worlds with others. "There is not the world first, and then language that represents it; rather ... the world of objects, persons, and language are on the same plane—all are signs that interact and form new relations" (Leander & Rowe, 2006, p. 435).

Languaging as a Medium for Enacting Practices

Students use languaging to co-author their worlds with others. Languaging, therefore, serves as a *medium baked into* events in figured worlds for engaging in practices in those events. As a medium, languaging constitutes a world as "a socially and culturally constructed realm of interpretation in which particular characters and actors are recognized, significance is assigned to certain acts, and particular outcomes are valued over others" (Holland et al., 1998, p. 52). People employ languaging to enact or perform worlds through how they use languaging, through use of

> practices, stories, performances, and enactments that underlie (pre)ontological accounts. Languages/languaging are worlded through an innumerable array of heterogenous practices and artefacts.
>
> *Demuro & Gurney, 2021, p. 5*

16 Framing of Co-Authoring Practices

When students engage in enacting a world through languaging, they are already predisposed to employ it as the medium constituting that world in certain languaging actions. As Bertau (2014b) notes:

> Without a medium, we could not be self–other related selves. ... Hence, the medium language mediates the living individuals to each other, and by doing this it offers forms to the relation, forming its specific dynamics, enabling and constraining specific spacetimes as the between of the subjects.
>
> *pp. 527–528*

When students engage in a classroom discussion, high school debate, or a pep rally, they already know what kind of languaging to employ to participate in these events.

Through languaging as a medium, students learn to respond to others based on their actions and reactions. They learn to anticipate subsequent utterances or responses to previous utterances spread across time based on others' uptake from utterances (Bakhtin, 1984; Goffman, 1974).

> It's not that we have relationships, and we represent them in language; our relationships are constructed from the raw materiality of how we language connection and disconnection, opening up or closing down with each other. We talk relationships into being.
>
> *Beauchemin, 2019, pp. 24–25*

In Amber's group, members were employing languaging actions to enact supportive relations with each other.

ACTIVITY: CONTEXTUALIZING USE OF PRACTICES THROUGH LANGUAGING

To help students understand the concept of languaging as a medium for co-authoring figured worlds, students can discuss or write about a specific event/situation in their lives involving interactions with others or characters' dialogue in a literary text/movie. They then reflect on "What's going on here?" To do that, they identify how specific utterances serve as actions to enact specific relations constituting certain "in-between" meanings; for example, actions that serve to open up or close down relations with others, leading them to recontextualize the event/situation. For example, a student may realize that what they assumed was a friendly joke shared with their peers was actually offensive to one of their peers, leading to the need to recontextualize their interaction to apologize to the peer.

Languaging Actions as Emotions and Embodied Actions

Languaging actions also include enacting emotions and embodied actions. Languaging action as emotion mediates interactions by serving as the "grease" for languaging, evident in people "opening up" or "closing down" in interactions based on emotions and embodied actions (Lewis & Tierney, 2013; Jensen, 2014). These emotions such as envy, anger and empathy are located in the "in-between" relations (Bertau, 2014). These "in-between" meanings are enacted through facial expressions, eye contact, body positioning, gestures, intonation, etc. (Jensen, 2014).

Students experience emotions and embodied languaging actions through their everyday interactions in physical settings. Kate Murphy (2020) describes the use of embodied actions involved in everyday interactions through

> countless intuitive judgments—interpreting words, gestures and expressions and reacting appropriately. You've also got to get the timing and pacing right, as well as titrate how much to share and with whom. Social interplay is one of the most complicated things we ask our brains to do.
>
> *p.* 7

She notes how a lack of physical, face-to-face interactions during the Covid-19 pandemic results in a decline in employing these embodied actions.

> In normal circumstances, we get a lot of practice, so it becomes somewhat seamless. You don't think about it. But when you have fewer opportunities to practice, you get off your game. The surreal and clunky quality of virtual or masked interactions just makes matters worse.
>
> We underestimate how much we benefit from casual camaraderie at the office, gym, choir practice or art class, not to mention spontaneous exchanges with strangers … The privation sends our brains into survival mode, which dampens our ability to recognize and appropriately respond to the subtleties and complexities inherent in social situations.
>
> *p.* 7

This focus on embodied languaging actions suggests the importance of considering how the material, physical contexts of worlds shape participants' practice related to embodied actions. For example, in writing texts, students employ embodied practices, given how "writers use their bodies and the materials available to their bodies via the material world, to both create and to interact with textual artifacts" (Rule, 2019, p. 47).

ACTIVITY: CONTEXTUALIZING PRACTICES THROUGH USE OF LANGUAGING AS EMOTIONS/EMBODIED ACTIONS

To help students identify how languaging actions include emotions/embodied actions, they can discuss or write about a specific event/situation in which participants were expressing certain emotions. They could then reflect on how the expression of these emotions served to enact certain relations with others. For example, voicing anger about a peer's actions created an adverse relationship with the other based on the "in-between" meanings enacted through anger. Based on these examples, they could also reflect on examples in which they expressed emotions only as "inner speech" to themselves, as opposed to expressing emotions to others, as in cases of being reluctant to share those emotions with others.

Acquiring Languaging Through Exposure to Others' Languaging

Students acquire new ways of languaging through exposure to others' "external dialogue," leading to changes in their thinking as "inner dialogue" (Grossen & Salazar-Orvig, 2011). Based on exposure to others' "external dialogue," they acquire new "inner dialogue" for imagining and rehearsing interactions with others, resulting in the use of new "external dialogue" for languaging relations with others. They are therefore looping between "internal" and "external" dialogue, leading to growth in the use of languaging actions over time for enacting relational ways of being (Zittoun, 2014; 2017).

This looping process triggers an "inner dialogicality" as "inner dialogue with the object of knowledge—that is, thinking" (Zittoun, 2017, p. 132). At the same time, by being exposed to others as mirrors who voice alternative perspectives different from their own perspectives, students may experience tensions between these perspectives. They may then entertain alternative perspectives, resulting in their imagining new and different ways of relational being with others (Zittoun, 2017). For example, analysis of female students learning math found that students valued acquiring language for thinking about math problems:

> For example, Bobby helped Natalie by explaining, "if you don't know whole right, the plus—you have part plus part will give you the whole." ... "and whole minus part, it will give you the other part." At P3, Natasha's frustration from having to do everything "by our own" (Extract P3 group 2A) is extended by a later report of copying from her friend who "will teach us a bit."

Jones & Seilhamer, 2020, p. 11

Students also employ this looping process in their writing by drawing on and double-voicing others' voices (Bakhtin, 1984), as "external dialogue" for thinking about what to write. For example, they may quote other writers' perceptions on certain topics or issues. As Thompson and Wittek (2016) note:

> Even when students write ostensibly by themselves, they interact with culturally developed tools representing certain voices and their historical paths. ... As writers attempt to articulate their fragmented inner thoughts through speech or writing they enter a social world whereby both speaker and listener, or writer and reader, share the interaction and shape meaning according to the contexts that affect them. Writing can be seen as a psychological tool through which the writer translates and transforms the chaos of inner speech.
>
> *pp. 88–89*

Students Reflecting on Their "External Dialogue"

Students may also reflect on the limitations of their "external dialogue" for enacting relations with others, leading to recognizing the need to develop their languaging with others. In reflecting on how she acquired new ways of languaging relations with peers, Laura noted how, when members of her peer group initially reached out to help her, "I would try to shut them out. I'd be like, 'No, I don't want to talk to you today. I wanna be alone.' They'd be like, 'Laura, you can't be alone right now.'"

She then experienced her peer group's use of "external dialogue" as playful languaging actions associated with "really sarcastic joking ways. We're very forward about what we want with each other and stuff like that, but at the same time it's also a lot of joking around." She was initially "skeptical to trust them because I was like, 'I don't know if they're like this with everybody.' Then I realized that they do it out of love."

She describes how internalizing her peers' playful "external dialogue" led to developing her confidence in interacting with others, growth fostered by internalizing her peers' "external dialogue" to develop her "inner dialogue," leading to an increased sense of social agency in her "external dialogue":

> So before, when I had super bad anxiety I would shake in class. It would be really hard for me to talk in front of people. Just social situations were really difficult. This group of people became aware of my social anxiety and how bad it was and they helped me order food at fast food places and talk in front of strangers. Now, I can be more myself in class and out in public.

20 Framing of Co-Authoring Practices

Central to Laura's growth over time is her ability to reflect on her experiences of being alone and then draw on others' perspectives to enhance her interaction with others.

ACTIVITY: CONTEXTUALIZING USE OF "EXTERNAL DIALOGUE" FOR ACQUIRING "INNER DIALOGUE"

Students could discuss or write about their experiences with looping between "external dialogue" and "inner dialogue":

- Describe how you use your own "inner dialogue" in your everyday inter-action with others, as well as how you draw on others' "external dialogue" to construct multiple voices and perspectives for inclusion in your "inner dialogue."
- Have students describe or write about learning new languaging actions from interacting with others to then incorporate those actions as "external dialogue" for their own thinking as "internal dialogue" as well as new "external dialogue" with others.
- Support open-ended expression of alternative voices and perspectives in discussions through freewriting about their thoughts before or during a discussion to capture their "inner dialogue" for sharing in the discussion. Students could reflect on the voices and perspectives of their peers based on potential uptake from their languaging according to how discourses of race, class, and gender are shaping a discussion.
- Engage students in drama activities in which students adopt different voices and perspectives. For example, a student could describe how interacting with an English teacher's adoption of a feminist critical per-spective resulted in her acquiring novel ways of thinking about gender roles. They may then share her critiques of sexist practices she perceives in her peer group and family, resulting in changes in her sense of agency in fostering changes in her ability to influence others.

The Purpose of This Book

In this book, I posit the value of students importing their experiences outside of school in community, peer group, extracurricular, sports, family, workplace, and digital media worlds into the classroom. Through discussing and writing about these experiences, students are reflecting on how their evolving perspectives, beliefs, and identities shape the meaning of those experiences. To reflect on those experiences, they are posing the question, "From where do you read the world?" related to addressing questions such as:

- What are some experiences with people that shaped how you read the world, and what about those experiences had so much power?
- What language, words, or phrases have shaped how you read the world, and what about that language had so much power?
- How have the following influenced how you read the world: gender, sexuality, race, social class, religion, language, immigration, citizenship, dis/ability, body size, body image, neighborhood, school, and family structure?
- Would you like to change some of the ways you read the world? How might that be possible? (Jones & Woglom, 2015, p. 3)

In posing these questions, students are also considering how cultural practices valued in family, peer, and community worlds may differ from the cultural practices valued in school worlds (Ishimaru, 2019; Noguera & Syeed, 2020).

I also posit the need for students to learn to contextualize their use of practices based on components constituting participation in figured worlds: purposes, norms, discourses, identities, genres, and media/literature, the focus of Chapter 2. Throughout the book, I include recommended classroom activities to help students gain use of certain practices related to their learning to contextualize practices in their worlds based on purposes, norms, discourses, identities, genres, and media/literature.

In Chapters 3 and 4, I describe methods for helping students contextualize practices in the ELA classroom. The remaining chapters then provide examples of students from my research portraying and reflecting on their practices across community, peer group, extracurricular, sports, family, workplace, and social/digital media worlds.

Each of these chapters includes quotes from 12th-grade students enrolled in an English class in 2017 and 2019 taught by Ms. E in a suburban high school in the Upper Midwest. These students were part of a research study conducted by myself (Beach & Beauchemin, 2019; Beach & Caraballo, 2021a, 2021b). (All of the students from this research are identified using pseudonyms.) In this research, I analyzed the students' writing assigned by Ms. E about their experiences in different worlds, as well as interviewed students about their perceptions of their writing. The other group of students in this book included in Chapter 6, written by Limarys Caraballo, were participants in the Cyphers for Justice after-school YPAR projects in New York City.

The final chapter draws implications for teaching ELA based on the adolescents' experiences depicted in this book.

This book also has a website, *adolescentsworlds.pbworks.com*, which includes links, activities, and further readings for each of the book chapters.

Summary

In this introductory chapter, I posit the need to recognize how students construct or co-author their figured worlds through informal learning of different practices

22 Framing of Co-Authoring Practices

in community, peer group, extracurricular, sports, family, workplace, and social/digital media worlds. Providing students with opportunities to write and reflect about their practices in these different worlds in the ELA classroom contributes to their deeper learning. In writing and reflecting on their practices, students are contextualizing their use of languaging actions for enacting these practices for interacting with others; languaging actions include emotions and embodied actions. This suggests the value of fostering "boundary-crossing" practices for bringing students' informal learning experiences in these different worlds into the classroom in ways that value the significance and worth of those experiences, leading to student's growth over time.

References

Bakhtin, M. M. (1984). *Problems of Dostoevsky's poetics: Theory and history of literature* (C. Emerson, Ed. & Trans.). University of Minnesota Press.

Bazelon, E. (2021, September 12). Recovering from a broken school year. *The New York Times Magazine*, pp. 56–62.

Beach, R., & Beauchemin, F. (2019). *Teaching language as action in the ELA classroom.* Routledge.

Beach, R., & Bloome, D. (Eds.). (2019). *Languaging relations for transforming the literacy and language arts classroom.* Routledge.

Beach, R., & Caraballo, L. (2021a). Reflecting on languaging in written narratives to enact personal relations. *English Teaching: Practice & Critique, 20*(4), 521–533.

Beach, R., & Caraballo, L. (2021b). How language matters: Using ethnographic writing to portray and reflect on languaging actions. *Journal of Adolescent & Adult Literacy, 65*(2), 139–148.

Beauchemin, F. (2019). Reconceptualizing classroom life as relational-key. In R. Beach & D. Bloome (Eds.), *Languaging relations for transforming the literacy and language arts classroom* (pp. 23–48). Routledge.

Bertau, M. -C. (2014). Exploring language as the "in-between." *Theory & Psychology, 24*(4), 524–541.

Bronkhorst, L. H., & Akkerman, S. F. (2016). At the boundary of school: Continuity and discontinuity in learning across contexts. *Educational Research Review, 19*, 18–35.

Bucholtz, M., (2015). The elements of style. In D. N. Djenar, A. Mahboob, & K. Cruickshank (Eds.), *Language and identity across modes of communication* (pp. 27–60). De Gruyter.

Cohen, J. S. & Smerdon, B. A. (2009). Tightening the dropout tourniquet: Easing the transition from middle to high school. *Preventing School Failure: Alternative Education for Children and Youth, 53*(3), 177–184. doi:10.3200/PSFL.53.3.177-184

De Jaegher, H. & Di Paolo, E. (2007). Participatory sense-making: An enactive approach to social cognition. *Phenomenology and Cognitive Sciences, 6*, 485–507.

Demuro, E, & Gurney, L. (2021). Languages/languaging as world-making: The ontological bases of language. *Language Sciences, 83*, 1–13.

Fecho, B., Coombs, D., Stewart, T. T., & Hawley, T. S. (2020). *Novice teachers embracing wobble in standardized schools: Using dialogue and inquiry for self-reflection and growth.* Routledge.

Fecho, B., Graham, P., & Hudson-Ross, S. (2005). Appreciating the wobble: Teacher research, professional development, and figured worlds. *English Education, 37*(3), 174–199.

Fisher, M. T. (2003). Open mics and open minds: Spoken word poetry in African diaspora participatory literacy communities. *Harvard Educational Review, 73*(3), 362–389.

Frankel, K. K., Fields, S. S., Kimball-Veeder, J., & Murphy, C. R. (2018). Positioning adolescents in literacy teaching and learning. *Journal of Literacy Research, 50*(4), 446–477.

Frosini, F. (2017). An "I" in teen? Perceived agency in a youth development program. *Afterschool Matters, 25*, 29–37.

Garcia, A. (2021). Pedagogies of complicity: Perspective taking and healing. *English Journal, 111*(1), 21–24.

Gee, J. P. (2014). *An introduction to discourse analysis: Theory and method* (4th ed.). Routledge.

Gee, J. P. (2015). *Social linguistics and literacies*. Routledge.

Gee, J. P. (2017). *Teaching, learning, literacy in our high-risk high-tech world: A framework for becoming human.* Teachers College Press.

Gee, J. P. & Hayes, E. R. (2011). *Language and learning in the digital age*. Routledge.

Goffman, E. (1974). *Frame analysis*. Harvard University Press.

Grossen, M., & Salazar-Orvig, A. (2011). Dialogism and dialogicality in the study of the self. *Culture & Psychology, 17*(4), 491–509.

Holland, D., & Eisenstat, M. (1990). *Educated in romance: Women, achievement and college culture.* University of Chicago Press.

Holland, D., Lachicotte, W., Skinner, D., & Cain, C. (1998). *Identity and agency in cultural worlds*. Harvard University Press.

Ishimaru, A. M. (2019). *Just schools: Building equitable collaborations with families and communities.* Teachers College Press.

Jensen, T. W. (2014). New perspectives on language, cognition, and values. *Journal of Multicultural Discourse, 9*(1), 72–78.

Jones, S. A., & Seilhamer, M. F. (2020). Girls becoming mathematicians: Identity and agency in the figured world of the English-medium primary school. *Journal of Language, Identity & Education*. doi:10.1080/15348458.2020.1795862

Jones, S., & Woglom, J. F. (2015). From where do you read the world? A graphica expansion of literacies for teacher education. *Journal of Adolescent & Adult Literacy, 59*(4), 443–473.

Korpershoek, H., Canrinus, E. T., Fokkens-Bruinsma, M. & de Boer, H. (2020). The relationships between school belonging and students' motivational, social-emotional, behavioural, and academic outcomes in secondary education: a meta-analytic review. *Research Papers in Education, 35*(6), 641–680. doi:10.1080/02671522.2019.1615116

Kuntz, T. L. (2011). High school students' participation in music activities beyond the school day. *Update: Applications of Research in Music Education*, 30(1), 23–31.

Leander, K. M., & Rowe, D. W. (2006). Mapping literacy spaces in motion: A rhizomatic analysis of a classroom literacy performance. *Reading Research Quarterly, 41*(4), 428–460.

Lee, C. D. (2001). Is October Brown Chinese? A cultural modeling activity system for underachieving students. *American Educational Research Journal, 38*(1), 97–141.

Lee, C. D., Meltzoff, A. N., & Kuhl, P. K. (2020). The braid of human learning and development: Neuro-physiological processes and participation in cultural practices. In N. S. Nasir, C. D. Lee, R. Pea, & M. M. de Royston (Eds.), *Handbook of cultural foundations of education* (pp. 24–43). Taylor & Francis.

Lewis, C., & Tierney, J. D. (2013). Modeling emotions in an urban classroom: Producing identities and transforming signs in a race-related discussion. *Linguistics and Education, 23*(3), 289–304.

24 Framing of Co-Authoring Practices

Linell, P. (2009). *Rethinking language, mind, and world dialogically: Interactional and contextual theories of human sense-making.* Information Age Publishing.

Linell, P. (2016). On agency in situated languaging: Participatory agency and competing approaches. *New Ideas in Psychology, 42,* 39–45.

Lohmeier, J. H., & Lee, S. W. (2011). A school connectedness scale for use with adolescents. *Educational Research and Evaluation, 17,* 85–95. doi:10.1080/13803611.2011.597108

McTighe, & Silver, H. R. (2020). *Teaching for deeper learning: Tools to engage students in meaning making.* American Society for Curriculum and Development.

Mehta, J. & Fine, S. (2019, March 30). High school doesn't have to be boring. *The New York Times.* Retrieved from http://t.ly/Lvol

Murphy, K. (2020, September 1). We're all socially awkward now. *The New York Times* [Weblog post]. Retrieved from www.nytimes.com/2020/09/01/sunday-review/coronavirus-socially-awkward.html

Nasir, N. S., de Royston, M. M., Barron, B., Bell, P., Pea, R., & Goldman, S. (2020). Learning pathways: How learning is culturally organized. In N. S. Nasir, C. D. Lee, R. Pea, & M. M. de Royston (Eds.), *Handbook of cultural foundations of education* (pp. 195–211). Routledge.

Niemiec, C. P., & Ryan, R. M. (2009). Autonomy, competence and relatedness in the classroom: applying self-determination theory to classroom practice. *Theory and Research in Education, 7,* 133–144. doi:10.1177/1477878509104318

Noguera, P. A., & Syeed, E. (2020). *City schools and the American dream 2: The enduring promise of public education* (2nd ed.). Teachers College Press.

O'Brien, S. (2016). *Inside education: Exploring the art of good learning.* Routledge.

Quinlan, A., & Curtin, A. (2017). Contorting identities: Figuring literacy and identity in adolescent worlds. *Irish Educational Studies, 36*(4), 457–470. https://doi.org/10.1080/03323315.2017.1362352

Raffo, C., & Forbes, C. (2021). A critical examination of the educational policy discourse on/for school extra-curricular activities—A Deweyan perspective. *Oxford Review of Education, 47*(3), 301–315.

Rogers, R., & Wetzel, M. M. (2013). *Designing critical literacy education through critical discourse analysis: Pedagogical and research tools for teacher-researchers.* Routledge.

Rubin, J. C., & Land, C. L. (2017). "This is English class": Evolving identities and a literacy teacher's shifts in practice across figured worlds. *Teaching and Teacher Education, 68,* 190–199.

Rule, H. J. (2019). *Situating writing processes.* The WAC Clearinghouse.

Schatzki, T. R. (2010). *The timespace of human activity: On performance, society, and history as indeterminate teleological events.* Lexington Books.

Thompson, I. & Wittek, L. (2016). Writing as a mediational tool for learning in the collaborative composition of texts. *Learning, Culture and Social Interaction, 11.* doi:10.1016/j.lcsi.2016.05.004

Torres, C. (2021). Skills to change the world: An interview with Alejandro Diasgranados. *Council Chronicle, 31*(1), 20–21.

Tusting, K. (2005). Language and power in communities of practice. In D. Barton (Ed.), *Beyond communities of practice: Language, power and social context* (pp. 36–54). Cambridge University Press.

Urrieta, L. (2007). Identity production in figured worlds: How some Mexican Americans become Chicana/o activist educators. *The Urban Review, 39*(2), 117–144.

Verhoeven, M., Zijlstra, B. J. H., & Volman, M. (2021). Understanding school engagement: The role of contextual continuities and discontinuities in adolescents' learner identities. *Learning, Culture and Social Interaction, 28* (1), 1–17.

Walker, D., & Nocon, H. (2007). Boundary-crossing competence: Theoretical considerations and educational design. *Mind, Culture, and Activity, 14*(3), 178–195.

Wenger, E. (1998). *Communities of practice: Learning, meaning, and identity.* Cambridge University Press.

Wergin, J. F. (2020). *Deep learning in a disorienting world.* Cambridge University Press.

Wilner, A. F. (2020). *Rethinking reading in college: An across the curriculum approach.* National Council of Teachers of English.

YouthTruth (2020, Spring). Students weigh in: COVID-19: Aggregate report. [Online Web post]. Retrieved from http://youthtruth.surveyresults.org

YouthTruth (2020, Fall). Students weigh in, Part II: Learning & well-being during COVID-19. [Online Web post]. Retrieved from https://youthtruthsurvey.org/students-weigh-in-part2/

YouthTruth (2021, Spring). Students weigh in: Part III: Learning and well-being during COVID-19. [Online Web post]. Retrieved from https://youthtruthsurvey.org/students-weigh-in-part3/

Zittoun, T. (2014). Trusting for learning. In P. Linell & I. Markova (Eds.), *Dialogic approaches to trust in communication* (pp. 125–152). Information Age Publishing.

Zittoun, T. (2017). Symbolic resources and sense-making in learning and instruction. *European Journal of Psychology and Education, 32* (1), 1–20.

2

CONTEXTUALIZING PRACTICES THROUGH COMPONENTS CONSTITUTING FIGURED WORLDS

This chapter formulates a framework for understanding how students contextualize practices within their figured worlds based on the components of purposes, norms, discourses, identities, genres, and media/literature. Through learning to contextualize practices using these different components, students gain an understanding of how they are co-authoring their figured worlds through their own practices. Understanding the purposes for their use of practices helps them assess the value of use of their practices. Defining the norms and discourses operating in a world serves to determine the value and appropriateness of their practices for enacting certain identities. Students also learn to employ certain genres for use of practices as well as respond to media/literature portraying practices in a certain figured world.

The first chapter described how students acquire practices as ways of acting/ doing things in figured worlds through informal, deeper learning. This chapter raises the question of how students determine relevant practices to employ in events or situations in particular figured worlds.

Learning to Contextualize Practices

Students learn to contextualize practices in figured worlds for enacting relevant ways of acting or doing things for participation in a world. For example, learning to work as a barista at a Starbucks involves employing certain practices associated with interacting with customers in an efficient, friendly manner, practices acquired through training and emulating other baristas.

DOI: 10.4324/9781003246886-3

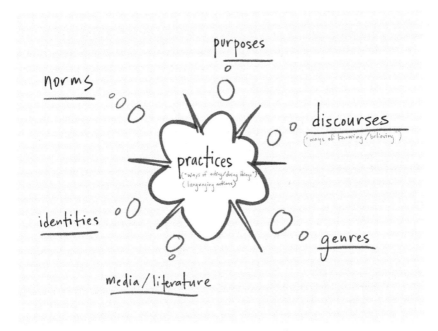

FIGURE 2.1 Students contextualizing components for engaging in practices in figured worlds

> We can learn some things about how to teach academic language and literacy practices in schools from these out-of-school, interest-driven cultures that use their own specialist styles of language.
>
> *Gee, 2017, p. 57*

By contextualizing practices within a specific world, students determine how to employ appropriate ways of acting/doing things consistent with different components of purposes, norms, identities, genres, media/literature, and discourses for co-authoring their figured world (see Figure 2.1). They do so given their need to be perceived as someone who is "with-it" in social events or situations as opposed to someone who is not "with-it" or is "out-of-it"—who lacks knowledge of how they should act or do things in an event or situation.

Developing Knowledge of Practices Over Time

How then do students learn to contextualize practices based on these different components? Students learn to contextualize practices by engaging in inquiry-based, problem-solving processes related to achieving certain purposes. To do so, they draw on previous practices associated with achieving similar practices in the past. For example, to achieve the purpose of pleasing others, they draw on

28 Framing of Co-Authoring Practices

the practice of languaging by commending others for their work, resulting in acquiring knowledge about the use of that practice (Yakhlef, 2010).

They then use this knowledge of past practices to contextualize present and future practices based on how one or more of the above components shapes the use of practices in specific events or situations. Finally, based on the discussion of languaging in Chapter 1, they contextualize these practices through "languaging thinking" (Newell et al., 2019). In "languaging thinking" students are reflecting on how they are using "language to provoke, facilitate, construct, enable, and fashion the thinking that teachers and students do" for creating relational spaces and time (Smith et al., 2018, p. 23).

As described in Chapter 1, Laura contextualizes her languaging practices to provide support for herself within the context of a peer group world as "my little family of friends, and they are a lot greater than they come off as … I'm glad they were so accepting of me and all my problems because without their help, I'm not sure where I would be in my life right now, but I don't think it would be a good place." By experiencing these supportive practices within her "family of friends," Laura can then apply these practices for experiencing supportive relations in future events or contexts.

To contextualize practices, students need to infer connections between practices in their classroom worlds and worlds outside the classroom. To foster making these connections, James Lang (2016) models the process of making connections in his literature class, leading to having his student inferring their connections:

> The other day, for instance, I used a Taylor Swift song to introduce students to the dramatic monologues of Robert Browning. In offering such examples, we can model the sorts of connections we expect of students. Finish the last class of the week five minutes early, and tell students that they can leave when they have identified five ways in which the day's material appears in contexts outside of the classroom. … In my class period on a Browning's monologue, for example, I might ask students to list five popular songs in which the "speaker" clearly does not represent the voice of the singer.
>
> *n.p.*

Students learn to contextualize practices through opportunities to engage in contextualizing these practices. In his book, *Small Teaching*, James Lang (2021) posits the centrality of practice itself for enhancing students' learning. He therefore devotes time during his college English classes, particularly at the end of classes, to have his students practice certain literacy practices. For example, he has students share their examples of formulating a thesis statement in response to a literary text. Having had students infer their intended audiences, he has them describe how they inferred those audiences for inferring their thesis statement.

Defining Purposes for Contextualizing Practices

As noted in Figure 2.1, students learn to apply different components for contextualizing their use of practices in figured worlds. Having a sense of *purpose* provides student adolescents with a vision or pathway for their future development based on their aspirations for the kind of person they want to be or what they want to contribute to the world (Burrow, 2021; Burrow et al., 2018). Having this sense of purpose then means that they may not be sidetracked with short-term setbacks or distractions.

Adolescents with a stronger sense of purpose are then less likely to take risks, given that they consider the long-term consequences of doing so. They are also more likely to report on positive events in their daily lives, experience higher levels of emotional autonomy from their parents, and are more likely to enact a stable sense of identity (Burrow et al., 2018).

> Having a sense of purpose also differs from having goals, given that goals might be thought of as intentions that can be accomplished, whereas we tend to think about purpose as an intentionality or life aim, meaning that it is always in front of you. For example, a goal of graduating. I can accomplish that goal. I can set a goal of getting a job, but a purpose might be something like being a caring father.
>
> *Burrow, 2021, n.p.*

Analysis of adolescents' daily diary recordings found that those with a stronger sense of purpose demonstrated higher levels of agency, self/adjustment-satisfaction, and sense of direction in their lives (Burrow & Hill, 2011).

Perceiving Classroom Activities Purposeful for Students' Lives

It is also important to consider the nature of purposes to employ practices related to advancing one's status or skills instead of making changes in society. For example, students may engage in purposes based on the former as "self-oriented motivation," related to "a desire to have a great career or enhance one's knowledge or abilities" (Lang, 2021, p. 198). In contrast, engaging the purposes driven by "self-transcendent motivation describes a desire to help other people, to change the world in some positive way, to make a difference" (p. 198).

A study of low-income high school students who planned to attend college found that those with higher self-transcendent purposes were more likely to enroll than those with higher self-oriented purpose levels (Lang, 2021; Yeager et al., 2014). It was also the case that college students with self-transcendent purposes devoted more time to reflecting on answering a challenging review question about how they would contribute to the world (Lang, 2021; Yeager et al., 2014).

In thinking about purpose related to engaging students in activities or projects for co-authoring worlds, students often contextualize purpose based on having positive uptake from audiences related to whether they have had a positive impact on making changes in those audiences. For example, students engaging in the Compose Our World curriculum *composeourworld.org/blog* perceived their activities as having a clear sense of purpose (Boardman et al., 2021). Students perceived their purposes for activities as based on having a clear connection to addressing a challenge or question. They also valued purposes that involved audiences other than simply their teachers and that involved producing a product such as a museum exhibit (Boardman et al., 2021, p. 15). In one unit, ninth-grade students experienced a sense of audience by creating exhibits for an interactive Museum of Humanity to address the question, "What does it mean to be human?" (Boardman et al. 2021, p. 20): *t.ly/vVzK*.

One group, whose theme was "standing up for what you believe in," explained that "minority protest … [such as] Black Lives Matter" is important because it offers people a means of standing up for their beliefs in an exhibit including a flag representing "the American way, the land of the free and how it all fails because of all the oppression"; a target referring "to police brutality and how Black people feel like a target"; and a scale. The label for the scale read:

> The scale is meant to represent the differences between what a minority has to do to be on the same level as a White person with the White people being the lightweight it takes less to push them up. And with minorities as the heavier weight, it takes more to push them up, just like in today's society.
>
> *p. 21*

Defining purposes also shapes students' use of languaging. In the Migrant Student Leadership Institute (MSLI) project, migrant students participated in the use of practices to make a change in their communities (Gutiérrez, 2008). In doing so, they employed languaging through the use of the subjunctive voice as in "might be" or "what if?" They also used modals, such as "could" or "would," and open-ended question-asking in ways that enhanced students' sense of agency. By framing their activities through this use of the subjunctive voice, students assumed that they could precipitate change through challenging status-quo practices.

Designing Activities or Projects Based on Purposes for Studying Worlds

In designing classroom activities or projects for students, it is useful to draw on features of the project-based framework from the Compose Our World (COW) curriculum design (Boardman et al., 2021), *composeourworld.org/blog*: purpose/

Components Constituting Figured Worlds **31**

authenticity, collaboration, iterative design, student emotions/care, and Universal Design.

Students need a sense of purpose associated with experiencing a sense of authenticity related to the motivation/desire to portray or address a certain aspect or issue that directly impacts their lives, such as racial justice. Students also need to know how to work collaboratively with peers to share and draw on each other's expertise in working together to support each other, something that is particularly important in conducting Youth Participation Action Research (YPAR) projects. Students engaging in YPAR projects employ a set of practices related to identifying problems/issues, examining related research, collecting information/data, and formulating ways to address these problems/issues, as described in Limarys's Chapter 6, in her description of the Cyphers for Justice projects.

As they are engaging in projects or activities, students need to reflect on whether and how they are achieving certain purposes, particularly in terms of their needs, motivations, and desires. The COW curriculum design also includes a focus on emotions related to CAPE: Caring about "the emotional needs of self and others," Advocacy in addressing systems of power, Perspective-taking in examining others' actions and motivations, and Empathy for "connecting the feelings of others" (Boardman et al., 2021, p. 73). The COW framework also draws on Universal Design for Learning (UDL) related to attending to student diversity and equity by providing students with choices in their learning and expressions and using alternative ways of representing their learning through multimodal options/genres.

ACTIVITY: CONTEXTUALIZING PURPOSES FOR ENGAGING IN PRACTICES IN FIGURED WORLDS

Students could discuss or write about their purposes associated with motivations or desires for employing practices in a certain figured world. For example, a group of students may be concerned about food waste in their school's cafeteria, leading to perceiving their purpose to help limit food waste as well as understanding how putting food in the garbage results in methane release in local garbage dumps. They may then organize a campaign to inform their peers and staff about the importance of composting uneaten food and distributing leftover food to local food banks.

Students in a school theater production could describe how they perceive the purpose for learning practices of projecting their voice/persona related to enhancing their performance as an actor. They may note that they achieved their purposes in parts of their performance, while, in other parts, they needed to revise their performance based on feedback from their teacher.

Contextualizing Practices Based on Adhering to Norms

Another important component for contextualizing practices involves how students use practices based on adhering to certain social or cultural *norms* in a figured world. Within a classroom figured world, adolescents perceive certain norms constituting appropriate or relevant languaging actions; for example, the extent to which they can challenge their teacher's perceptions. As a result, students pay attention to how teacher talk functions (upholding norms and rules, opening up content, [non]evaluating, maintaining conversational flow and coherence, inviting and supporting participation, probing thinking, providing sought-after language, and modeling dialogic dispositions) and responding accordingly (Boyd & Markarian, 2015, p. 278).

Within a figured world, people adhere to cultural norms as "dynamic and fluid, while also allowing for the past and present to be seen as merging, a continuum, or distinct, depending on how young people and their communities live race/ethnicity, language, and culture" (Paris & Alim, 2017, p. 8). For example, the meaning of practices associated with rap music derives from cultural contexts associated with non-dominant racial groups. These cultural practices are based on the historical legacies of Black, Latinx, Asian, Pacific Islander, and Indigenous peoples, given how new generations are redefining and enacting novel cultural practices in their communities.

Given the cultural meanings of practices, it is important to employ culturally sustaining pedagogy (CSP), particularly given the demographic shifts towards students of color being the majority of many school populations (Paris & Alim, 2017). CSP provides adolescents with resources for coping with how they are often marginalized in classrooms. For example, they may study how a history of White privilege and domination shapes the current lives of non-dominant peoples (Kirkland, 2013; Morrell, 2015).

Students also develop knowledge of norms by inferring how certain practices serve to achieve certain desired purposes in a particular figured world. For participating in roleplay activities, a student in my study, Marcus, identifies three norms for interacting with others in a roleplay with his peers.

- You have to acknowledge that this person is not the person you're used to talking to. So you can't assume things about them.
- The second one is kind of a rule of, "The other person is not me." So the first thing that you always want to do, unless you have a character reason for not doing this, is to assume that the other person is not going to react the same way that I would. So it gives you a certain level of caution when interacting with someone or something that's really unusual or alien.
- And the third thing is, you have to acknowledge that, regardless of the actions they take, this does not reflect back upon the person. You need to make sure that all of your players understand that anything that happens

out of the game stays out of the game, or that anything that happens in the game stays in the game.

Beach & Beauchemin, 2019, p. 152

Marcus's formulation of norms represents his sense-making awareness of how assuming a role entails employing practices of staying in one's role, differentiating the role from his identity, and maintaining boundaries between a roleplay versus one's lived world.

ACTIVITY: CONTEXTUALIZING PRACTICES BASED ON NORMS IN A FIGURED WORLD

Students can describe or write about the norms constituting their participation in an event or contest in a certain figured world. Their writing may include the use of narratives based on portrayals of deviations from norms associated with "events" (Bakhtin, 1993) to enhance "tellability" (Labov, 1997). They can reflect on how they learned whether they are adhering to certain norms/conventions as well as how they cope with violations of those norms/conventions. For example, students may describe how they acquired knowledge of norms constituting playing video games with their peers based on whether they were employing certain strategies in playing their game.

Contextualizing Practices Based on Discourses ("Ways of Knowing/Believing")

Discourses serve as ways of knowing/thinking—legal, scientific, psychological, religious/spiritual, economic, political, etc.—constituting practices in a figured world (Gee, 2011; Holland et al., 1998). Norman Fairclough (2003) perceives

> discourses as ways of representing aspects of the world—the processes, relations and structures of the material world ... different discourses are different perspectives on the world ... Discourses not only represent the world as it is (or rather is seen to be); they are also projective imaginaries, representing possible worlds that are different from the actual world, and tied into projects to change the world in particular directions.
>
> *p. 124*

People learn to employ big-D Discourses to define the value or worth of practices within a figured world (Gee, 2011). For example, through participation in the figured world of schooling, students acquire a Discourse of achievement emphasizing only certain kinds of academic performances constituting what it

34 Framing of Co-Authoring Practices

means to be a "good student" (Caraballo, 2012). In the social world of sports or the workplace, students may adopt a Discourse of competition based on a belief in the importance of winning (note: for the purpose of this book, I will use a small d for discourse that should be equated with Gee's big-d Discourse).

Enacting identities through discourses

Students construct their identities through adopting certain discourses as "identity tool kits" constituting certain ways of knowing and thinking for enacting identities in a figured world (Gee, 2011); for example, how they define themselves as a "track star" according to discourses constituting the world of sports.

Students employ certain practices consistent with discourses constituting social hierarchies within the school world for enacting identities as "nerds," "preps," "jocks," "goths," etc., through the use of languaging (Buckholz, 2015). For example, a high school student, Erich, enacts his "nerdy" identity through the use of languaging actions by employing "super standard English" as a relatively formal register lexis,

> as opposed to trendier and cooler intensifiers common among Bay City High School ... Together, these features exceed even the norms of standard American English. And hence, I term this speech style superstandard English; at Bay City High School, as elsewhere in American culture, this style is indexical of Nerdiness.
>
> *Buckholz, 2015, p. 38*

Discourses of race

Discourses of race serve to position students within social hierarchies in a figured world. For example, one teacher positioned an African-American male student in a classroom over time based on discourses of race, gender, and academic achievement associated with a "thickening" of his identity (Holland & Lave, 2001).

Positioning students as "unpromising" assumes that males, particularly males from non-dominant backgrounds, will not be as successful in the class as Whites and/or females (Wortham, 2006). White students in one study adopted a discourse of white privilege in a classroom discussion to critique other students' support of affirmative action programs (Beach et al., 2008). In adopting this discourse, they perceived affirmative action programs as denying Whites certain types of employment or access to higher education.

You can draw on Critical Race Theory (CRT) to have students examine how systematic racism shapes people's lives. To do so, students examine the historical development of how people construct racial identities as a category in ways that result in discrimination and diminution of those people (Delgado &

Stefancic, 2017; Ladson-Billings, 1998). A primary tenet of CRT is that race is a discourse constituting how governmental, legal, and economic systems enact practices regarding treatment of people. For example, how governments create policies related to not selling homes to Blacks in certain neighborhoods or banks not offering mortgages to Blacks to purchase homes (Sawchuk, 2021).

Organized critiques of teaching CRT in schools, resulting in protests at school board meetings, have charged CRT with positioning all Whites as racists, resulting in the assumption that White students will adopt negative self-perceptions. However, the primary focus of CRT is "an emphasis on outcomes, not merely on individuals' own beliefs, and it calls on these outcomes to be examined and rectified … the theory says that racism is part of everyday life, so people—white or nonwhite—who don't intend to be racist can nevertheless make choices that fuel racism" (Sawchuk, 2021, n.p.).

In defining the purpose for teaching CRT in the classroom, one social studies teacher noted that "I am trying to help all of my students understand the systemic nature of why people of color—particularly Blacks—are more likely to live in poverty, to struggle in school and to be incarcerated than people who are white" (Boegeman, 2021, p. A7). He provides students with a historical perspective on the development of systemic racism. Doing so involves

> an acknowledgment that racial disparities are a fact of history in this country, and that they continue to exist today … I've always told my students that in order to change the world, you first need to understand where that world comes from.
>
> *p. A7*

Discourses of social class

Adolescents may also reflect on how discourses of social class create hierarchies shaping their relations with others (Spratt, 2017). Underlying these class hierarchies is a discourse of meritocracy that distinguishes between the privileged "haves" who graduated from college to achieve economic success and the "have-nots" who lacked the economic or social capital resources to complete college—about two-thirds of American adults (Sandel, 2020).

George Packer (2019) defines meritocracy as "the system that claims to reward talent and effort with a top-notch education and a well-paid profession, its code of rigorous practice and generous blessings passed on down from generation to generation" (p. 58). This system

> has hardened into a new class structure in which professionals pass on their money, connections, ambitions, and work ethic to their children, while less educated families fall further behind, with little chance of seeing their children move up…. By kindergarten, the children of elite professionals are

36 Framing of Co-Authoring Practices

already a full two years ahead of middle-class children, and the achievement gap is almost unbridgeable.

p. 59

Within a meritocracy associated with accumulating markers of success, a study of upper-middle-class female adolescents found that they focused on building their portfolio or resume for their college applications, while working-class females were more likely to value fairness in interpersonal relationships (Gee et al., 2001). In describing her peers' discourses of class shaping their practices, a student in my study, Sandy, noted that

> They are upper-middle class, so their values were a little different than mine, and they didn't really match up. Language-wise they always seemed so tense. They were worried and looking about like oh, I have to get straight A's, and I have to be perfect, and I have to look pretty, and oh my gosh [I have] this presentation next week, and they're always so tense that it made me tense.

A case-study analysis of a working-class student in her college revealed a "mismatch between her primary discourse practices—for example, how she talked, wrote, and read—and the language and literacy practices that Empire [her college] rewarded" (Payne-Bourcy & Chandler-Olcott, 2003, p. 580). For example, her first-year composition course focused primarily on generating academic essays, without a focus on students' identity construction within and across different figured worlds that could have helped her examine the influence of social class on her identity construction.

Discourses of gender/sexuality

Discourses of gender/sexuality serve to reify stereotypical, essentialist differences between males and females based on the "statements 'Boys don't cry, girls finish their homework' and 'sugar and spice and everything nice, that is what girls are made of.' Each implies that gender is a richly inductive essential category and connects to the themes of likeability and competence" (Oyserman, 2019, p. 7).

In an analysis of a woman engaged in a support group for obese women, the woman perceived herself as weak and disadvantaged given her obesity (da Cruz & Bastos, 2015). She then adopted a discourse of gender associated with an assumption about women and body weight. Therefore, she is being positioned in the interviews through languaging as a certain kind of person based on discourses of body weight (da Cruz & Bastos, 2015). Rather than frame the woman's deficit self-perceptions as a function of her individual beliefs and attitudes, an "activist" languaging perspective considers how her self-perceptions are shaped by larger gender discourses shaping relations in interview contexts.

Discourses of gender also intersect with discourses of class. Early-adolescent females from lower-income British families coped with pressures to conform to a "popular girl" discourse in their peer group/school worlds in ways that conflicted with their home discourses associated with their socioeconomic status (Fisher, 2019). This required that they adopt a comprised stance based on a "middle-person" discourse that balanced assuming practices associated with higher-income family associations with a "popular girl" discourse with lower-income family associations that challenged the limitations of that discourse.

Ecological discourses

It is also the case that languaging reflects certain ecological discourses related to the need to connect with nature as reflected in the language and narratives used by certain peoples and/or Indigenous authors (Share, in press). For example, in Hawaii,

> there is a Hawaiian proverb which says *'O ke aloha 'aina ke kuleana i kakou a pau* - Love for the land is our privilege and responsibility. Hawaiian epistemology has a deep appreciation for richness and fullness of life beyond linear thinking. Hawaiians have a deep respect for all life forms, from the heavens, to the earth, to the land, to the sea ... When we say "Aloha 'Aina", we are acknowledging our connection and respect to the land and its people.
>
> *K. L. Hawkins, personal communication,*
> *September 21, 2020*

Unfortunately, this languaging may become extinct and fall out of use so that the ecological worldviews they represent are no longer articulated. "When a language dies, so much more than words are lost. Language is the dwelling place of ideas that do not exist anywhere else. It is a prism through which to see the world" (Kimmerer, 2013, p. 258).

ACTIVITY: CONTEXTUALIZING DISCOURSES RELATED TO RACE, CLASS, GENDER, OR ECOLOGICAL PERSPECTIVES

Students may engage in critical-inquiry activities about how their participation in figured worlds is constituted by adopting certain discourses related to race, class, gender, or ecological perspectives (Boyd, 2017). For example, students could discuss or write about how their practices associated with their race, class, and/or gender may be perceived as problematic in their school worlds, resulting in limiting their sense of agency in those worlds.

They could also discuss or write about how coaches and players on their sports teams subscribe to a discourse of "winning is everything" stance versus valuing what students gain from participation in sports regardless of whether their team is winning games or matches. They could then describe how differences in these stances influence players' attitudes towards playing; for example, how a "winning is everything" attitude leads players to engage in deviant or problematic play.

Contextualizing Identities in Figured Worlds

Adolescents also contextualize the use of practices for enacting certain *identities* as the "imaginings of self in worlds of action" in figured worlds (Holland et al., 1998, p. 5).

> "People tell others who they are, but even more important, they tell themselves and then try to act as though they are who they say they are."
>
> *p. 3*

As they participate in figured worlds, they are "figuring out" their identities within and across different worlds, given that "identities and the acts attributed to them are always forming and re-forming in relation to historically specific contexts" (p. 284). In some cases, this re-forming leads to "an individual portraying conflicting identities in diverging figured worlds" (Quinlan & Curtin, 2017, p. 459) through interactions with peers, parents, and teachers. While an adolescent may assume the social position of a resisting daughter within her family or peer group that values such resistance, she may adopt the identity of a compliant, dutiful student in the classroom. As one student noted about adopting a range of different identities related to the norms operating in her different worlds:

> I have many identities. I can sometimes have different personalities at times. ... Like at home I'm more of a crazy person, I start dancing around, but at school I'm more conservative. ... [I'm considered] like the loud African American. ... There's typical stereotypes that come up ... and I try to be funny and try to bring those out. (Interview)
>
> *Caraballo, 2019, p. 21*

Adolescents' degree of engagement in these worlds may vary depending on the extent to which they can display competence to their peers and adults, particularly through embodied actions through performances in music/bands, art, drama, and speech, as well as participation in sports or in the workplace as contrasted with adoption of limited roles in classroom worlds (Beach et al., 2015).

Enacting identities constituting personhood

Rather than thinking about identities as based on autonomous individuals, we can define identities according to the notion of personhood related to "what it means to be human together" based on how "we interact with each other" (Seymour et al., 2020, p. 15). Bloome and Faust define personhood as "a shared cultural and linguistic meaning for how 'person' as a category is defined including what kinds of persons exist, what inherent attributes a 'person' has, and how those attributes are distributed" (McCarthey et al., 2020, p. 62). People draw on these categories to

> "see" each other. How people begin to imbue meaning based on what they know or don't know about each other's collective histories. How one's knowledge about each other, or lack thereof, can create blinds spots that can have implications and consequences for the "who" and ultimately begin to structure social order.
>
> *Power-Carter & Zakeri, 2019, p. 223*

Students' enactment of their personhood determines how they "view their lives as inherently individual or collective; mature or developing; connected to others or distinct, capable of empathy, love mutuality, greed, selfishness, and self-centeredness or not capable of these" (Bloome et al., 2019, p. 236).

Adolescents enact personhood "through languaging—how people act and react to each other through their use of language (and related semiotic systems)" (Bloome et al., 2019, p. 236). For example, students who perceive themselves as a leader on their sports team may then focus on consistently providing support for other members of their team.

Contextualizing personhood according to norms

Adolescents also enact identities as personhood based on conforming to certain *norms* constituting practices as ways of acting/doing things related to adopting a certain identity *style* in how one acts in a certain world. Bucholtz (2015) defines style as engaging in

> practices of any kind using a range of stylistic features in both established and innovative ways. And because ways of doing things involve not only where people are but who they are, stylistic agents locate themselves and others in relation to culturally available social contexts as well as culturally available social types. Or to offer a more concise definition, style is a system of sociocultural positioning through modes of semiotic action.
>
> *p. 32*

For example, a student may enact their identity as "hip" through dress and use of rap as embodied languaging.

40 Framing of Co-Authoring Practices

At the same time, students may enact personhood for challenging how school norms often ignore "how context and/or diverse identities impact literacy teaching and learning" (Brownell, 2017, p. 253). For example, students discussed their experience of bullying practices in their high school located in a predominantly working-class African-American community (McCarthey et al., 2020). They challenged the school policies related to punishing students for bullying by contrasting their experience of bullying in their community's homes with administrators' perceptions of bullying in their school. While the students did not perceive bullying in a positive manner, they argued that expelling students for bullying in their school world only exacerbates the problem. They recognized how practices in community worlds transfer to their school worlds to enact personhood in these different worlds.

Students also enact personhood in school worlds based on their ability to employ literacy practices according to certain norms for completing tasks according to set, allocated, limited time periods associated with the concept of "time being" (Hikida, 2020, p. 199). Students who have difficulty adhering to these time limits may then be judged and positioned as "struggling" or "unmotivated," resulting in their acquiring a deficit sense of personhood based on certain moral norms constituting school practices.

Students also envision developing certain future possible identities by considering differences between hoped-for identities, expected identities, and feared identities (Roshandel & Hudley, 2018). For example, a student may envision a possible self as an actor based on receiving positive feedback on performing in a theater production or giving public speeches in a classroom (Roshandel & Hudley, 2018). Students participating in an after-school "School-to-Jobs" program that involved interactions with adults gained clarity in defining strategies for attaining possible selves in ways that enhanced their school engagement (Oyserman et al., 2002).

ACTIVITY: CONTEXTUALIZING PRACTICES FOR ENACTMENT OF IDENTITIES

Students could discuss or write about their enactment of identities across time and place through acquiring new practices, including imagining and adopting novel possible selves. Students could employ autobiographical narratives portraying a series of past events/situations in which they assumed certain roles/identities; for example, assuming the role of a sports team captain on their middle-school basketball team. They could then reflect on changes in their identities across these events/situations in time and space regarding development in their practices/genres evident in their languaging actions. They could also note how participation in a past event/situation led them to imagine their potential development of certain possible identities which may or may not have occurred.

Contextualizing Use of Genres as Social Action for Enacting Practices

While *genres* are often defined in terms of types of texts based on formalist text structure, i.e., the five-paragraph essay, narrative, or the mystery novel, a richer conception of genre perceives genres as typified ways of employing certain types of social actions (Miller, 1984; Martin & Rose, 2008). These genres include debates, protests, sonnets, discussions, reports, interviews, crime shows/films, speeches, documentaries, rap music, etc., constituting familiar practices constituting participation in a figured world (Bawarshi & Reiff, 2010). Engaging in a debate, interacting in a sales transaction in a store, or participating in social protest involves the use of certain prototypical practices. By acquiring knowledge of genre schema constituting certain typical actions, students then know how to participate in these worlds; for example, refuting claims in a debate.

To introduce her students to the notion of genre as social actions based on recurring, typical features, Jennifer Fletcher (2018) has her students view the YouTube video "Sir Mashalot: Mind-Blowing SIX Country Song Mashup" *youtube.com/watch?v=FY8SwIvxj8o* that portrays similarities between six different country songs. These videos all employ the same musical rhythm and chords as well as portraying meeting females who are sitting in or waiting to sit in a truck. Her students then identify similar words, phrases, musical structures, and subject matter using concept mapping.

She then has students examine similarities across texts of a certain genre based on the purposes for those genre features. For example, in reading introductions to academic books, students identify a preface, foreword, acknowledgments, and introduction for the purposes of framing the significance and contributions of the book within a particular subject matter or field.

For analyzing genre norms, she has students identify certain prototypical organizational features, language choices, and writer ethos, leading to applying those features to writing mock genres of an adventure story, horror story, obituary, diary, or Facebook page.

Contextualizing Worlds Based on Genre Knowledge

Students employ different genres for contextualizing the systematic use of shared practices constituting the familiar use of languaging actions in figured worlds. Within the world of a courtroom trial, participants employ the genres of interrogating witnesses, giving testimony, raising objections, instructing jury members, issuing verdicts, etc. Proposing a bill in a legislature involves formal, legal language, while a marriage proposal involves intimate, emotional languaging. Within a fast-food restaurant, customers and employees employ familiar, truncated interactions, while in an upscale "fine-dining" restaurant, they employ more elaborated verbal interactions. It is also the case that readers or audiences bring certain

42 Framing of Co-Authoring Practices

genre expectations to their responses to texts; for example, how they respond to characters' languaging actions in a comedy versus horror film (Ahn & Pena, 2021).

Students also draw on knowledge of discourses for contextualizing their use of certain genres (Lassen, 2016; Martin & Rose, 2008). Workers at a Starbucks coffee shop may adopt a discourse that "the customer is always right" as shaping genres of taking and receiving orders from customers. Citizens of a Danish city meeting to design more lower-carbon energy sources adopted sustainability and ecological discourses that shaped their use of genres of presentations, interactions, and reports constituting the meeting (Lassen, 2016). Participants' genre interactions revolved around recognizing the need to rethink and revise the status-quo discourse of energy production to generate clean energy alternatives.

One of the primary genres involves narratives. In writing their narratives, as illustrated by quotes from their narratives throughout this book, students in my study created narratives for making sense of their lives through how they construct identities according to adhering to or deviating from norms and discourses operating in a figured world. "Identity is primarily a narrative construction, based, however, on embodied experience in interaction with the environment" (Horsdal, 2012, p 65).

ACTIVITY: CONTEXTUALIZING USE OF GENRES FOR ENACTING PRACTICES

Students could identify uses of certain genres for contextualizing practices; for example, their use of narratives for sharing experiences about successes in their lives to project a positive self-image to others. They may also describe the use of genres specific to participation in certain worlds; for example, negotiating an agreement with parents related to deadlines for completing certain tasks or returning at certain times at night. They could then reflect on how they acquire the use of genres through observing others' use of genres related to enacting certain relations with others.

Media/Literature

Adolescents devote extensive time participating in media/literature worlds both outside and inside the classroom. Thirteen-to-eighteen-year-olds average 7 hours and 22 minutes of screen media daily (Rideout & Robb, 2019). In one study, 84% of adolescents indicated that they read blog posts/online news stories daily (Turner et al., 2019), while 45% of adolescents in another study noted that they were online "almost constantly" on their smartphones (Anderson & Jiang, 2018).

Adolescents employ media, including artifacts and literary texts, as "symbolic resources" to participate in practices for defining their identities (Zittoun, 2017).

Components Constituting Figured Worlds **43**

When students were asked about those symbolic resources they most valued, "about 25% of the respondents ... were interested in what could be called the 'school culture,' that is, reading novels, going to the theater, writing a diary'" (Zittoun, 2017, p. 8). In contrast, about 35% valued "youth culture" symbolic resources—for example, reading manga or playing video games that they perceive as not always valued in school worlds, a manifestation of disparities between school and their worlds.

Adolescents draw on media/literature to engage in "connected learning," defined as "how young people's actions, individually and collectively, intersect with key institutions in their lives and a wider array of media and communication possibilities open to them" (Ito et al., 2012, p. 264). They engage in connecting "home, school, community, and peer contexts of learning; support peer and intergenerational connections based on shared interests; and create more connections with non-dominant youth, drawing from capacities of diverse communities" (p. 264).

A connected learning framework "conceptualizes new literacies as a paradigm for expansive understandings of the nature and purposes of communication rather than a narrow signifier for technology. It focuses more on practices and enactment of agency than tools and normative academic indicators" (Mirra, 2019, p. 287). Students also draw on responses to literary texts as "connected reading" to infer applying portrayals of characters' practices for thinking about their practices and drawing on the lived-world practices for responding to characters' practices (Turner et al., 2019).

ACTIVITY: CONTEXTUALIZING USE OF MEDIA/ LITERATURE FOR ENACTING PRACTICES

Students can discuss or write about their use of media/literature for employing certain practices; for example, how they employ digital tools/social media to enact relations with others. For interacting with others on social media sites, they may describe how to portray certain events in their lives or photos/ videos of themselves or their experiences to portray their roles/identities to their audiences. They could reflect on the extent to which they are portraying only positive aspects of their identities to elicit certain responses, as opposed to any issues or challenges in their lives.

Responding To Literature/Media as "Text Worlds"

In responding to literature/media, students are enacting "text worlds" based on their knowledge of language to create the text as a world (Gavins, 2007; Gavins & Lahey, 2016). For example, they may respond to narrators' or characters' use

44 Framing of Co-Authoring Practices

of certain languaging actions through modal words such as "feel" or "think" that evoke students' related experiences of ways of knowing associated with enacting a certain world (Gavins, 2007). Text World Theory posits how students respond to texts for creating:

1. The discourse-world: the context in which reading takes place, which includes the situation of reading, and background information and knowledge brought to the event by the reader.
2. Text-worlds: these build up the fictional world in terms of time, location, characters and are developed through instances of actions and events. Text-worlds are constructed on the basis of textual cues and fleshed out by a reader's relevant background knowledge. Shifts in time and space trigger world-switches where readers' attention is diverted to a new set of actions and events (Mason & Giovanelli, 2021, p. 69).

For example, for teaching "The Red Wheelbarrow" (Williams, 1986), a teacher had students reflect on how they drew on their knowledge of certain words in the poem to construct visual illustrations of those words (Giovanelli, 2017). In responding to the poem, "A Jelly-Fish" (Moore, 1909), students created sketches of their meanings associated with specific words in the poem (Cushing, 2018). In her illustration, one student added

> a "blue background" and "spots of orange" [that] are not information found in the text itself, but are added in via her own background and schematic knowledge of oceans and sea creatures. She also draws on intertextual connections to help flesh out her own unique text-world, in her mention of "reaching to the stars", building deeper metaphorical connections that the poem evokes for her.
>
> *p. 16*

Engaging in these activities leads students to "reflect on the way that their own background knowledge contributes to building a text-world, [which] can be an empowering experience for young readers" (p. 15).

ACTIVITY: CONTEXTUALIZING MEDIA/LITERATURE AS "TEXT WORLDS"

Students could reflect on how they draw on their knowledge of languaging to infer the meanings of specific languaging in a media or literacy text as "text worlds." In doing so, they may apply related experiences associated with certain words; for example, experiences with jellyfish. They may also create illustrations or diagrams associated with how words evoke certain visual meanings to reflect on how they associate visual images with certain background experiences.

Summary

This chapter formulates a framework for understanding how students contextualize practices within their figured worlds based on the components of purposes, norms, discourses, identities, genres, and media/literature. Through learning to contextualize these practices, students gain an understanding of how they are co-authoring their figured worlds through their own actions. In the next two chapters, I describe ways of fostering students' contextualizing practices based on these components in the classroom.

References

Ahn, C., & Pena, E. (2021). Reality as genre. In J. Avila (Ed.), *Critical digital literacies: Boundary crossing practices* (pp. 13–34). Brill.

Anderson, M., & Jiang, J. (2018). *Teens, social media & technology 2018*. Pew Research Center. Retrieved from https://pewrsr.ch/2zImT64

Bakhtin, M. M. (1993). *Toward a philosophy of the act* (V. Liapunov, Trans.; C. Emerson & M. Holquist, Eds.). University of Texas Press.

Bawarshi, A. S., & Reiff, M. (2010). *Genre: An introduction to history, theory, research, and pedagogy*. Parlor Press.

Beach, R., & Beauchemin, F. (2019). *Teaching language as action in the ELA classroom*. Routledge.

Beach, R., Johnston, A., & Thein, A. H. (2015). *Identity-focused ELA teaching: A curriculum framework for diverse learners and contexts*. Routledge.

Beach, R., Thein, A. H., & Parks, D. (2008). *High school students' competing social worlds: Negotiating identities and allegiances in response to multicultural literature*. Erlbaum.

Bloome, D., Brown, A. F., Kim, M-Y., & Tang, R. J. (2019). Languaging personhood in classroom conversation. In R. Beach & D. Bloome (Eds.), *Languaging relations for transformation of the literacy and language arts classroom* (pp. 235–254). Routledge.

Boardman, A. G., Garcia, A., Dalton, B., & Polman, J. L. (2021). *Compose our world: Project-based learning in secondary English language arts*. Teachers College Press.

Boegeman, B. (2021, July 21). What critical race theory looks like in my social studies classroom. *Minneapolis Star Tribune*, A7. Retrieved from http://t.ly/CTQs

Boyd, A. S. (2017). *Social justice literacies in the English classroom: Teaching practice in action*. Teachers College Press.

Boyd, M. P., & Markarian, W. C. (2015). Dialogic teaching and dialogic stance: Moving beyond interactional form. *Research in the Teaching of English*, *49*(3), 272–296.

Brownell, C. J. (2017). Mandated curricula as figured world: A case study of identity, power, and writing in elementary English language arts. *English Teaching: Practice & Critique*, *16*(2), 252–267. https://doi.org/10.1108/ETPC-10-2016-0131

46 Framing of Co-Authoring Practices

Bucholtz, M. (2015). The elements of style. In D. N. Djenar, A. Mahboob, & K. Cruickshank (Eds.), *Language and identity across modes of communication* (pp. 27–60). De Gruyter Mouton.

Burrow, A. L. (2021, August 2). You 2.0: Cultivating your purpose. [Hidden Brain podcast]. Retrieved from https://hiddenbrain.org/podcast/cultivating-your-purpose/

Burrow, A. L., & Hill, P. L. (2011). Purpose as a form of identity capital for positive youth adjustment. *Developmental Psychology, 47*(4), 1196–1206.

Burrow A. L., Hill P. L., & Ratner K. (2018). Purpose. In R. J. R. Levesque (Ed.), *Encyclopedia of adolescence* (pp. 2993–3002). Springer. https://doi-org.ezp3.lib.umn.edu/10.1007/978-3-319-33228-4_368

Caraballo, L. (2012). *Constructing and negotiating identities-in-practice: Multiple identities, the enacted curriculum, and the figured world of achievement in a middle school English classroom* [Unpublished Doctoral Dissertation]. Teachers College, Columbia University.

Caraballo, L. (2019). Being "loud": Identities-in-practice in a figured world of achievement. *American Educational Research Journal, 56*(4), 1281–1317. https://doi.org/10.3102/0002831218816059

Cushing, I. (2018) 'Suddenly, I am part of the poem': Texts as worlds, reader-response and grammar in teaching poetry. *English in Education, 52*(1), 7–19, doi:10.1080/04250494.2018.1414398

da Cruz, C. A. G., & Bastos, L. C. (2015). Stories of an obese: Theory of positions and the discursive (re) construction of identities. *Ling.(dis)course, 15*(3). http://dx.doi.org/10.1590/1982-4017-150302-1415

Delgado, R., & Stefancic, J, (2017). *Critical race theory: An introduction* (3rd ed.). New York University Press.

Fairclough, N. (2003). *Analysing discourse: Textual analysis for social research.* Psychology Press.

Fisher, H. (2019). Managing the "popular girl" and "challenges at home" discourses at secondary school: The perspectives of 12-14 year old girls, predominantly from lower-income White British families. *Research Papers in Education, 35*(5), 548–573.

Fletcher, J. (2018). *Teaching literature rhetorically: Transferable literacy skills for 21st century students.* Stenhouse Publishers.

Gavins, J. (2007). *Text world theory: An introduction.* Edinburgh University Press.

Gavins, J., & Lahey, E. (Eds). (2016). *World-building: Discourse in the mind.* Bloomsbury Academic.

Gee, J. P. (2011). *How to do discourse analysis: A toolkit.* Routledge.

Gee, J. P. (2017). *Teaching, learning, literacy in our high-risk high-tech world: A framework for becoming human.* Teachers College Press.

Gee, J. P., Allen, A. R., & Clinton, R. (2001). Language, class, and identity: Teenagers fashioning themselves through language. *Linguistics and Education, 12*(2), 175–194.

Giovanelli, M. (2017) Readers building fictional worlds: Visual representations, poetry and cognition. *Literacy, 51*(1), 26–35.

Gutiérrez, K. D. (2008). Developing a sociocritical literacy in the third space. *Reading Research Quarterly, 43*(2), 148–164. https://doi.org/10.1598/RRQ.43.2.3

Hikida, M. (2020). Literacy and the time being. In D. Bloome, M. L. Castanheira, C. Leung, & J. Rowsell (Eds.), *Re-theorizing literacy practices: Complex social and cultural contexts* (pp. 197–208). Routledge.

Holland, D., Lachicotte, W., Skinner, D., & Cain, C. (1998). *Identity and agency in cultural worlds.* Harvard University Press.

Holland, D., & Lave, J. (Eds). (2001). *History in person: Enduring struggles, contentious practice, intimate identities.* University of New Mexico Press. Horsdal, M. (2012). *Telling lives: Exploring dimensions of narratives.* Routledge.

Ito, M., Gutiérrez, K., Livingstone, S., Penuel, B., Rhodes, J., Salen, K., … Craig Watkins, S. C. (2012). *Connected learning: An agenda for research and design.* Digital Media Literacy Research Hub.

Kimmerer, R. W. (2013). *Braiding sweetgrass: Indigenous wisdom, scientific knowledge, and the teachings of plants.* Milkweed.

Kirkland, D. E. (2013). *A search past silence: The literacy of young Black men.* Teachers College Press.

Labov, W. (1997). Some further steps in narrative analysis. *Journal of Narrative and Life History, 7* (1–4), 395–415.

Ladson-Billings, G. (1998). Just what is critical race theory and what's it doing in a nice field like education? *International Journal of Qualitative Studies in Education, 11*(1), 7–24.

Lang, J. M. (2016, March 7). Small changes in teaching: The last 5 minutes of class. [Weblog post]. Retrieved from http://t.ly/GFBa

Lang, J. M. (2021). *Small teaching.* John Wiley.

Lassen, I. (2016). Discourse trajectories in a nexus of genres. *Discourse Studies, 18*(4), 409–429.

Martin, J. R., & Rose, D. (2008). *Genre relations: Mapping culture.* Equinox.

Mason, J., & Giovanelli, M. (2021). *Studying fiction: A guide for teachers and researchers.* Routledge.

McCarthey, S., Duke, N. K., Bloome, D., Faust, S., García-Sánchez I. M., Stornaiuolo, A., & Alvermann, D. (2020). How can we study children's/youth's out-of-school experiences to inform classroom practices? *Literacy Research: Theory, Method, and Practice, 69,* 58–78.

Miller, C. R. (1984). Genre as social action. *Quarterly Journal of Speech, 70*(2), 151–176.

Mirra, N. (2019). From connected learning to connected teaching: Reimagining digital literacy pedagogy in English teacher education. *English Education, 51*(3), 261–291.

Moore, M. (1909). A Jelly-Fish. Poets.org. Retrieved from https://poets.org/poem/jelly-fish

Morrell, E. (2015). *Critical literacy and urban youth: Pedagogies of access, dissent, and liberation.* Routledge.

Newell, G. E., Thanos, T., Kwak, S., & The Ohio State University Argumentative Writing Project. (2019). Languaging the teaching and learning of argumentative writing in an 11-th grade International Baccalaureate classroom. In R. Beach & D. Bloome (Eds.), *Languaging relations for transforming the literacy and language arts classroom* (pp. 131–150). Routledge.

Oyserman, D. (2019). The essentialized self: Implications for motivation and self-regulation. *Journal of Consumer Psychology, 29*(2), 336–343.

Oyserman, D., Terry, K., & Bybee, D. (2002). A possible selves intervention to enhance school involvement. *Journal of Adolescence, 25*(3), 313–326. https://doi.org/10.1006/jado.2002.0474

Packer, G. (2019). When the culture war comes for the kids. *The Atlantic, 324*(4), 56–71.

Paris, D., & Alim, H. S. (2017). What is culturally sustaining pedagogy and why does it matter? In D. Paris & H. S. Alim (Eds.), *Culturally sustaining pedagogies: Teaching and learning for justice in a changing world* (pp. 1–21). Teachers College Press.

48 Framing of Co-Authoring Practices

Payne-Bourcy, L., & Chandler-Olcott, K. (2003). Spotlighting social class: An exploration of one adolescent's language and literacy practices. *Journal of Literacy Research, 35*(1), 551–590.

Power-Carter, S., & Zakeri, B. (2019). Examining our blind spots: Personhood, literacy, and power. In D. Bloome, M. L. Castanheira, C. Leung, & J. Rowsell (Eds.), *Re-theorizing literacy practices: Complex social and cultural contexts* (pp. 221–233). Routledge.

Quinlan, A., & Curtin, A. (2017). Contorting identities: Figuring literacy and identity in adolescent worlds. *Irish Educational Studies, 36*(4), 457–470. https://doi.org/10.1080/03323315.2017.1362352

Roshandel, S., & Hudley, C. (2018). Role of teachers in influencing the development of adolescents' possible selves. *Learning Environments Research, 21*(2), 211–228. https://doi.org/10.1007/s10984-017-9247-8

Sandel, M. (2020, September 6). The consequences of the diploma divide. *The New York Times*, Review section, p. 5.

Sawchuk, S. (2021, May 18). What is Critical Race Theory, and why is it under attack? [Weblog post]. Retrieved from http://t.ly/cTck

Seymour, M., Thanos, T., Newell, G. E., & Bloome, D. (2020). *Teaching literature using dialogic literary argumentation*. Routledge.

Share, J. (in press). *Ecowriting in every classroom*. DIO Press.

Spratt, J. (Ed.). (2017). *Wellbeing, equity and education: A critical analysis of policy discourses of wellbeing in schools*. Springer International Publishing.

Smith, P., Cheema, J., Kumi-Yeboah, A., Warrican, S. J., Alleyne, M. L. (2018). Language-based literacy differences in the literacy performance of bidialectal youth. *Teachers College Record, 120*(1), 1–36.

Rideout, V., & Robb, M. B. (2019). *The Common Sense census: Media use by tweens and teens, 2019*. Common Sense Media.

Turner, K. H., Hicks, T., & Zucker, L. (2019). Connected reading: A framework for understanding how adolescents encounter, evaluate, and engage with texts in the digital age. *Reading Research Quarterly*. Advance online publication. doi:10.1002/rrq.271

Williams, W. C. (1986). The Red Wheelbarrow. In *The collected poems of William Carlos Williams: Volume I, 1909–1939* (p. 224). New Directions Press.

Wortham, S. (2006). *Learning identity: The joint emergence of social identification and academic learning*. Cambridge University Press.

Yakhlef, A. (2010). The corporeality of practice-based learning. *Organization Studies, 31*(4), 409–430.

Yeager, D., Henderson, M., Paunesku, D., Walton, G., D'Mello, S., Spitzer, B., & Duckworth, A. (2014). Boring but important: A self-transcendent purpose for learning fosters academic self-regulation. *Journal of Personality and Social Psychology, 107*(4), 559–580.

Zittoun, T. (2017). Symbolic resources and sense-making in learning and instruction. *European Journal of Psychology of Education, 32*, 1–20. doi:10.1007/s10212-016-0310-0

3

CONTEXTUALIZING PRACTICES BASED ON PURPOSE, NORMS, DISCOURSES, AND IDENTITIES IN SCHOOL WORLDS

This chapter describes how students learn to contextualize practices based on the components of purposes, norms, discourses, and identities in school worlds. In contextualizing these components, students are determining how they are employing practices for enacting relations with others in a figured world (Beach & Bloome, 2019). In contextualizing purposes, students are inferring how their use of certain practices serves to achieve certain outcomes related to enhancing their sense of agency associated with their long-term vision of what they value in life (Kundu, 2020). In contextualizing norms and discourses, students are determining how their practices are consistent with the norms and discourses constituting a certain event or situation. In contextualizing identities, students are inferring how their use of practices serves to enact those identities for enacting supportive relations with others. Through their contextualizing, use of their practices leads to the development of their use of practices over time.

In the previous chapter, I described a framework for inferring how students can contextualize different components shaping the meaning of their practices in a figured world. Contextualizing entails framing practices in ways that shape the meaning of those practices in terms of adopting certain actions.

In this chapter, I focus on ways to help students contextualize the first four of these components: purposes, norms, discourses, and identities. Learning to contextualize these four components requires that students frame their practices in terms of components. For example, a student may frame their argument for changing their community's transportation system to move to increased use of buses using clean energy in terms of adopting a certain purpose as well as an ecological discourse of addressing the climate crisis.

DOI: 10.4324/9781003246886-4

50 Framing of Co-Authoring Practices

The next chapter will focus on contextualizing the remaining two components: genres and media/literature.

Contextualizing Purposes for Learning in Schools

In their analysis of instruction over a five-year period in 30 different schools, Mehta and Fine (2019) found that, when teachers provide students with a clear sense of purpose for activities, students tend to be more engaged. They also found that students were often more likely to experience a strong sense of purpose—what Mehta and Fine (2019) defined as "deeper learning"—when they were engaged in activities where they could display competence for audiences.

As noted in Chapter 1, in studying students participating in a school theater production, they found that students experienced a strong sense of purpose in having to think about reasons for use of certain practices in their theater production to achieve positive audience responses to their performances.

Students also had to reflect on reasons for selecting their roles in terms of how they would enact their roles given the unique traits and attitudes constituting those roles through use of languaging both in terms of voicing words and embodied actions.

They also recognized that they would need to work collaboratively with their peers to effectively interact with peers adopting other roles to portray the unique nature of relations between roles related to the underlying meanings of the play. Given that some students had more experience performing in plays, those students assumed the roles of mentoring other students with less experience to help them enhance their performances.

In creating activities for students based on portraying and reflecting on practices, students benefit from having some perceived *purposes* for engaging in those activities. Having a sense of purpose involves knowing the potential value or consequences of their participating in an activity in ways that may enhance their engagement. Students in the theater production were engaged, knowing that, through their performance, they may receive positive responses from an audience related to the quality of their performances.

Defining Purpose to Foster Deep Learning Through Relational Pedagogy

Formulating *purposes* for teaching to foster deeper learning involves the use of relational pedagogy to build supportive relations with students (Mehta & Fine, 2019). A relational pedagogy involves going beyond simply caring *about* students to caring *for* students (Carter Andrews et al., 2021). Rather than frame knowledge as predetermined content to be covered, a relational pedagogy recognizes that "our knowledge of the world is mediated by our relationships with those around us, particularly those to whom we are most attached" (Lysaker & Furuness, 2011, p. 187).

Formulating purposes based on students' change over time

One central purpose for schooling involves fostering adolescents' openness for change in their lives—that they have the potential to continually develop their identities (Bowen, 2021). While it is often assumed that learning change occurs primarily through schooling, it is also the case that students experience change through engagement in different worlds. They may change in their openness to embracing diversity through being in a diverse peer group or sports team, their sense of agency through their performance in a theater production or band performance, or their ability to interact with adults through serving adult customers in their coffee shop job. Teachers can tap into these students' abilities demonstrated in other worlds to help students gain a sense of their potential success in school worlds.

Teachers, parents, coaches, and workplace managers assume these mentoring practices to provide adolescents with support and encouragement that they have the potential to succeed in the future. In writing about his difficulties in high school as someone from a working-class family, Mike Rose (2012) noted how one English teacher recognized his potential and helped him gain admission to college; then, when he was struggling in his first year of college, how other English teachers worked individually with him on his writing, resulting in his success as a student.

Adopting relational pedagogy

Assuming these mentoring roles involves adopting a relational pedagogy approach. In this approach, students are acquiring knowledge about *how* one builds relations with others as a primary purpose for instruction (Beauchemin, 2019). As one teacher noted: "Teaching through relationships ... embeds formal knowledge in the world in which it actually belongs and from which it is born: that of the complex, historical, and social world of being human" (Goodman, 2015, n.p.). This involves creating activities that draw on students' experiences, interests, attitudes, and knowledge about their use of practices for enacting identities and building relations in different worlds—the focus of this book. Tapping into students' practices from worlds outside the classroom requires enacting relations with them to learn about those practices.

Fostering relational pedagogy by drawing on students' experiences in their different worlds shifts the focus from interactions based primarily on teacher/ student interactions to also include student-to-student interactions. By supporting students' interactions with their peers, contextualizing entails framing practices with their peers; teachers are inviting students to co-author their classroom with and through others as relational spaces. As they are valued by their peers through their interactions with others, they then develop a sense of relational agency, enhancing their sense of their abilities to co-author their worlds (Mitra & Serriere, 2012).

Teachers as Co-learners

Adopting a relational pedagogy also involves teachers adopting the *identity* of co-learner *with* students. When teachers share their own learning experiences with students, students are more likely to reciprocate by sharing their experiences with teachers. Students then perceive their teacher "as someone who merges self and teacher," bringing "him or herself into the teaching or into the relationships with students" (Kreber et al., 2007, p. 27).

For example, one English teacher noted "'When I read the newspaper; when I watch a movie, when I see an ad, I'm almost always thinking, at least in the back of my mind, "How might this fit into my teaching"'" (Mehta & Fine, 2019, p. 336). This teacher perceives the *purpose* of his teaching in the school world as "part of the real world; it's the real world for me and them for much our lives—I want to make it vital to their experience as human beings (p. 337).

Students are also more likely to perceive the benefit of relational pedagogy given how they may perceive a focus on relations as enhancing their development over time. As Hedegaard (2011) notes:

> People *learn* when their activities change their social relations in a practice and thereby give them possibilities for new activities. *Development* occurs when a person's learning takes place *across* institutional practices and changes the person's relation qualitatively across all the practices in which the person participates. (italics added)
>
> *p. 12*

For example, prior to her interactions with peers as described in Chapter 1, Laura was coping with a sense of loneliness. When she began interacting with her peers, they perceived the need to help by sharing their concerns with her, saying, "'Laura, tell us what's wrong, and we'll make it better.'" Through engaging in this practice of her peers providing assistance, Laura experienced how they were "being there for me and letting me talk to them about anything whenever I needed them."

Ms. E's Purposeful Use of Relational Pedagogy

Ms. E notes how her students respond positively to her use of relational pedagogy through her talk with them about their writing, noting that her students comment,

> "I was so surprised that you read my things, and that you bring things up about it in class." I'll read their narratives, and then we'll talk about things, and there's certain kids I know based on what they wrote, that they want it shared or they don't. So I'll be like, "Okay, well, you know what I'm talking

Purpose, Norms, Discourses, and Identities **53**

about because you had that coach." And they're like, "Oh yeah!" So then you start referencing things that they wrote about, and it makes them feel loved and appreciated about what they wrote about, or why it was good. And they're completely shocked that somebody not only liked what they wrote but remembered it. I like stories. I like to read them, and I like to tell them. And it makes me like the people when I know their story.

She also described the importance of being consistent in her interactions with students

so that they know exactly who I am. I'm exactly the same. But other teachers have this strange robotic persona where they don't let their guard down ever because they don't want to lose control. So part of the way that I control them is through not being controlled. I really do like them. I love them. Little things they do make me feel really good.

She is also open to students engaging in alternative embodied actions in her classroom. She cites the example of students performing a play when "they put the costumes on, and they're running around the room hitting each other with swords; they're reading and having fun. I think I almost got fired the other day because I had them up on my teacher's desk pretending it was a balcony, and they decided because I said it was okay." When one of her students asked her to give her a hug, she first responded that "'I shouldn't be hugging students.'"

And she then said, "'I need a hug.'" After she did that, "'the other students all started hugging and it was this mob, it was funny. Lately I've decided; I didn't used to hug kids. There was a senior boy who looked like he'd been crying and I was like, 'Man, do you need a hug?' And he was like, 'Yeah, actually I could really use a hug right now.' So I hugged him, and the other kids were like, 'Aww!' And then they started hugging and they were like, 'Here's a hug for you bro.' So they don't get that, I think, a lot."

ACTIVITY: REFLECTING ON PURPOSES CONSTITUTING FORMAL VERSUS INFORMAL LEARNING

Students are more likely to experience relational pedagogy through the use of informal as opposed to formal learning activities. Students could contrast purposes for constituting their formal classroom learning practices and their informal learning in worlds outside the classroom through responding to the following questions:

- What kinds of literacy practices might be unusual or even weird to see in school?

- Why do you think certain kinds of literacy are accepted in school and others aren't?
- Who do you think decides which kinds of literacy are appropriate for school and which aren't?
- Why do you think schools focus only on certain types of literacy practices? What are some benefits of focusing only on these types? What are some drawbacks? (Speciale & Bartlett, 2020, p. 230)

Contextualizing Norms Constituting Use of Practices in School Worlds

Teachers and students also contextualize their classroom activities based on adhering to certain *norms* constituting certain consistent, defined uses of practices in a classroom for achieving certain purposes. For example, you may establish a norm that students need to listen carefully to their peers in discussions. By adhering to that norm, students may then perceive the value of doing so as contributing to their empathizing with their peers' perspectives.

For setting norms in her classroom at the beginning of each year or semester, Cait O'Connor (2021) has her students formulate community agreements that "allow students to build a set of expectations for themselves, the students who are there every day, and hold each other accountable for those expectations as they get to know each other better" (n.p.), *t.ly/NzBT*. To do so, students identify and rank those values that they believe should inform their agreement related to, for example, respect, friendship, integrity, loyalty, etc. Students' agreements include the practices of "using kind words, giving everyone's opinions space, prioritizing impact over intention, not interrupting, and not embarrassing people if they make mistakes" (n.p.). Rather than having to conform to artificial school-imposed rules, which often don't work, students are creating their own set of norms based on their shared values.

Students also experience norms associated with informal learning activities such as playing digital games as distinct from norms associated with more formal classroom interactions (Hung et al., 2012). For example, in learning to play basketball, students adhere to the norm of learning to coordinate their play in relation with other players based on the norms of the value of collaborative "team play." Analysis of students' informal learning in basketball versus formal learning in mathematics classes found that students experienced higher levels of engagement in basketball than in learning mathematics related to differences in their purposes for learning (Nasir & Hand, 2008).

In examining use of language in school worlds, it is also important for students to address certain language ideologies related to adopting a prescriptive versus descriptive approach to language use (Wolfram, 2019). Rather than perceive

Purpose, Norms, Discourses, and Identities **55**

prescriptive versus descriptive approaches as a binary, an alternative analysis involves considering "'who prescribes for whom, what they prescribe, and for what purposes'" (Cameron, 1995, p. 11) (quoted in Wolfram, 2019, p. 62). People positing a descriptive approach value *variation* in language use across different worlds; for example, variation in use of dialects across different communities or regions. In contrast, people who posit a prescriptive approach value *uniformity* or standardization in language use across different worlds based on adherence to norms or rules associated with "proper English."

It is also the case that norms constituting prescriptive perspectives on language use reflect certain social hierarchies; for example, assumptions about use of "proper English" are often equated with racial and class hierarchies (Metz, 2019)—students' use of African-American Vernacular English (AAVE) or use of language by students from lower-income homes may be perceived as not "proper English." Students could reflect on the reasons for these assumptions about language norms based on larger notions of who has power in society.

To have his students respond to examples of language variation, Mike Metz (2019) plays short audio clips from characters' speech in movies to then have students identify the characters' attributes associated with race/ethnicity, class, gender, and age based on their language. Students then reflect on how they may apply certain stereotyped norms to inferring these attributes; for example, associating characters with "foreign" accents with "the other." They can then step back and reflect on how they derived certain prescriptive norms from exposure to judgements by teachers, parents, and/or peers, as well as critiquing the limitations of these norms.

ACTIVITY: CONTEXTUALIZING NORMS FOR USE OF PRACTICES

Teachers can provide students with specific prompts to foster reflection about their adherence to norms constituting practices in certain worlds. Ms. E had students use narrative and ethnographic writing to portray their actions for achieving certain purposes in specific events or activities in their lives (Beach & Caraballo, 2021a; Beach & Caraballo, 2021b). For example, she asked her students to reflect on their ethnographic writing by providing them with some specific reflection prompts to have them reflect on their practices related to purposes, norms, identities, and discourses:

1. How would you describe how the specific ways of talking or communicating in your group served to create positive or negative relations with others in your group?

2. How would you describe how the specific ways of talking or communicating in your group served to create positive or negative relations with peers outside this group?
3. How would you describe the degree of ethical concern and/or trust in the group for others and/or others outside the group evident in people's interactions and the language you have already identified that the group uses?
4. How do others perceive your group in your school or community? How would you describe how figures of authority and/or other groups trust your group more or less than other groups?
5. What are some ways of talking or acting in your group that influence these other groups or people's perceptions of your group? (Beach & Caraballo, 2021b, p. 143)

Contextualizing Discourses Constituting Practices in School Worlds

Students and teachers also contextualize practices in school worlds based on *discourses* as certain ways of knowing/believing in their school worlds. These discourses often revolve around "achievement" based on standardized test scores that measure regurgitation of know-that information versus knowing-how practices (Caraballo, 2019). Based on their test scores, students may be identified as a "struggling reader" even though they are avid readers of graphic novels (Moje & Ellison, 2016).

These discourses then shape instructional practices. Given the need to enhance "low-ability" students' test scores, teachers in lower-track ELA classes often employ less group work, slower-paced instruction, and limited comprehension instruction as a prerequisite to the discussion of complex ideas (Hodge, 2019). Teachers may also employ "helicopter teaching," where they overly specify practices based on step-by-step completion of specific tasks (Kittle & Gallagher, 2020). In contrast, students in small, advanced AP classes engage in critical-thinking practices, while students in larger remedial classes may be engaged in more skill-drill learning experiences that limit their sense of agency to engage in critical thinking (Hodge, 2019).

For working with students who are having difficulty reading, it is important to avoid describing them as "struggling" or "low-ability" readers, labels that only serve to reify negative self-perceptions (Hall et al., 2010). These discourses also include problematic cultural construction of adolescents as immature, unsophisticated, lacking agency, and even irresponsible, resulting in the imposition of strict disciplinary norms in schools (Lesko, 2012).

A more productive relational pedagogy approach involves creating supportive relations through continually providing students with engaging activities for them to demonstrate success over time; for example, having them build their reading interests through choosing texts they enjoy and sharing that enjoyment with peers and yourself. They then begin to perceive responding to texts as *relational reading*—thinking about how a peer or you may value their sharing what they learned from reading a text as something a peer or you may benefit from.

Ms. E challenged discourses of "helicopter teaching" by creating supportive relations with students in which teachers treat adolescents as co-learners. She also created activities that allow students to demonstrate agency associated with acting as mature adolescents with a sense of agency. In my interviews with students, they consistently appreciated how Ms. E perceived them as people from whom she could learn about their lives as capable students.

Positioning of Students Based on Discourses of Race, Class, and Gender

Another challenge in school worlds is that students are also positioned in school worlds in problematic ways based on discourses of race, class, and gender, as described in Chapter 2. Teachers may also adopt discourses to ascribe to superficial, stereotypical perceptions of students' cultural practices from non-dominant communities as inferior to and even competing against assumed academic literacies (García-Sánchez & Orellana, 2019). Students from non-dominant communities also acquire valued funds of knowledge in family and community worlds that may not necessarily be also valued in school worlds (Heath, 1983; Moll & González, 2004).

This suggests the need for teachers to acquire knowledge of and draw on students' lived-world practices consistent with the cultural practices in those worlds to redefine and broaden traditional notions of academic literacies. This entails finding out

> what kids do when they are not in school: who they talk with; where they go; what games they play; what they read, write, listen and view … youth do engage in rich and complex practices every day. They play, read, write, talk and work with their peers and families, using language (often multiple linguistic varieties) to do a wide range of things including to entertain, argue, compare, contrast, and take action in the world. They observe and participate in a wide range of relationships, activities, and tasks. They learn from that engagement.
>
> *García-Sánchez & Orellana, 2019, pp. 19–20*

Discourses of Race

Students often experience disparities between the literacy practices valued in family, community, and peer group worlds versus literacy practices in school worlds (Kirkland, 2013). Analysis of school assessments is often developed based on prior knowledge constituting life in White, middle-class cultures in ways that are not valued in non-dominant family worlds (Kirkland, 2013). Moreover, these assessments also assume that the test-takers will consistently perceive and respond to test items in the same, identical manner based on responses to autonomous, decontextualized texts as opposed to responding to and creating texts within familiar cultural contexts.

Students may also resist their positioning based on race. Mexican-American adolescent females in a California high school who were often assigned to vocational-track classes identified how they resisted being positioned in deficit ways through challenging and resisting in their classes through voicing their own alternative perspectives grounded in their lived-world experiences (Bettie, 2014).

Discourses of Class

Middle-class to upper-middle-class students may have certain advantages in schools given discourse of schooling that values the use of standardized tests and analytic essay writing as based on a discourse of achievement (Caraballo, 2019). These students often frame their participation in school practices based primarily on demonstrating potential future success related to college admissions (Gee & Crawford, 1998).

Students from lower-income families may also experience disparities between the practices valued in school worlds versus their family worlds (van Galen & Noblit, 2007). They may then perceive how they are positioned as outsiders given the assumption that they lack practices or agency associated with middle-class to upper-middle-class school practices; for example, of not being motivated to strive to achieve high grades or to be popular within the school culture.

Discourses of Gender

While female students may be demonstrating superior academic performances relative to males, they may still be perceived as lacking certain practices associated with STEM and/or computer worlds (Smagorinsky, 2017). At the same time, male adolescents often experience a lack of interest in reading certain texts in school versus a higher interest in reading about topics related to their engagement in video games, sports, or certain hobbies (Smith & Wilhelm, 2002).

Students also engage in practices constituting their gender identity based on participation in discourses of gender. As part of a report based on their narratives

Purpose, Norms, Discourses, and Identities **59**

about moving across different countries, one female co-author described how, in moving from Germany to Texas as an adolescent, she had to create

> a figured world in which she had to become someone else in the context of what was valued in that particular school culture. Texas was very different from Germany. I had to learn to read the figured world of how girls wore more makeup and teased their hair. They performed femininity in very different ways than the girls in Germany.
>
> *Wiggins & Monobe, 2017, p. 164*

She noted that having to conform to these different cultural norms results in how you lack a real sense of self because your survival depends on molding yourself to the context, rather than the context being just one aspect of your identity. When people are positioned in survival mode, they are not engaged in self-making, but rather limited to varying degrees of accepting, rejecting, or negotiating the identities being offered to them.

> *p. 166*

ACTIVITY: CONTEXTUALIZING PRACTICES BASED ON DISCOURSES CONSTITUTING PRACTICES

Students could write about or discuss their participation in different practices as shaped by certain discourses associated with the beliefs or ways of knowing shaping practices in different courses and/or interactions with specific teachers, peers, events, or activities. For example, they could contrast their learning experiences across different classes based on differences in disciplinary discourses in which they were engaged in one class but not another class. Students could identify specific events that served to either engage or not engage them in these classes and reasons for their engagement or lack of engagement.

Contextualizing Identities in School Worlds

Learning in a school world also involves acquiring practices for enacting the *identities* of students through how they position themselves in relation to their teachers and peers (Green et al., 2020). In one study, "seventy-two percent of students stated that they feel that in school they have to 'act in a certain way' and they do not always feel like themselves the way they do outside of school" (Quinlan & Curtin, 2017, p. 465).

A student who positions themselves or is positioned by their teacher as a "good student" employs those practices constituted by their school world with that identity. For example, one seventh-grade female student, Leslie, conforms to

60 Framing of Co-Authoring Practices

the norms of a traditional school world to enact a fixed, institutional "good student" identity.

> Leslie wears the school uniform, including the argyle shirt, in the clean, pressed form reminiscent of retail management; she is performing good student as designed by the school board and department store.
>
> *Urbanski, 2016, p. 60*

She also consistently completes assignments based on conforming exactly to the desired result without questioning the value or worth of an assignment.

Given how the "good student" identity is valued in schools, students may perceive themselves in deficit ways as not being a "good" or "smart" student (Quinlan & Curtin, 2017). One student noted how "'the smart kids in my class are really smart, and sometimes when I find what we are doing in class hard I know that they find it easy … this makes me feel like the stupid one, and I get embarrassed'" (Quinlan & Curtin, 2017, p. 464). Another student noted how he felt "'much more comfortable outside of school because I hang around with people who make me feel good about myself … I can express myself more, and I am definitely chattier outside of school'" (Quinlan & Curtin, 2017, p. 465). Another student noted that when she is outside of school, she is

> with people who are like me, we are not too smart, but we love walking around town talking about clothes and music. These things just aren't as important in school. The textbooks and in English the learning of poems and plays are more important, and I find that too hard. You just can't do whatever you want … well first off there are school rules, these rules don't apply outside of school.
>
> *Quinlan & Curtin, 2017, p. 467*

As a result, students perceive themselves as outsiders who no longer belong to their school world (Urbanski, 2016).

Over time, however, students in my study did develop a sense of belonging to school worlds—coping with challenges, setbacks, or failures served to enhance their development related to their enhanced sense of agency for dealing with these challenges, setbacks, or failures.

Enacting and Drawing On Students' "Funds of Identity"

Adolescents also enact identities by drawing on "funds of identity" derived from worlds outside of school (Esteban-Guitart et al., 2019). The concept of funds of identity draws on the notion of "funds of knowledge" acquired from students' family and community cultural experiences (Moll & González, 2004). For example, in a Latinx family world, students acquire knowledge of how to translate

Purpose, Norms, Discourses, and Identities **61**

English into Spanish for parents who may not be fluent in English, a practice constituting a supportive fund of identity (Orellana & García-Sánchez, 2019). Teachers can then draw on this practice as a fund of identity to have these students also serve as translators for peers who may still be learning English.

> This suggests the value of teachers conducting an inventory of students' backgrounds to expand both the teacher's and peers' understandings of the different perspectives, experiences, beliefs, values, and languages that young people bring to the classroom [as well as tapping] into what young people are reading and writing outside of school and [recognizing] young people's proficiency with reading and writing in out-of-school domains.
>
> *Moje & Ellison, 2016, p. 32*

The notion of funds of identity presupposes that identities are constituted by a toolbox of "symbolic resources" that serve to help people to make sense of their practices (Zittoun, 2006). "For a child, it might be a doll they play with every day; for an adult it might be their marriage, the Catholic Church or work" (Esteban-Guitart et al., 2019, p. 162).

This focus on funds of identity suggests the value of importing resources from worlds outside of school for use in school through "boundary crossing" activities (Akkerman & Bakker, 2011). For example, a high school visual arts teacher positioned herself and her students in her art class as "artists" related to variations in their level of experience or ability as artists (Green et al., 2020). For one student, Maya, whom she positioned as "inexperienced," the teacher altered her interactions with the other students in the class to provide her with assistance. In listening to Maya's self-reflections, she revoiced Maya's languaging to reiterate issues in the student's use of "'thick lines' and 'dark shading'" in her drawings in a manner that positioned her as "inexperienced" (p. 137).

> Through this discursive process, the teacher positions Maya as an example of an artist whose work the group can learn from, even if the artist is inexperienced in describing her process or using expected discourse—including allusions to drawing processes and practices, some of which Maya had missed given her point of entry into the class.
>
> *p. 137*

Enacting Identities Constituting Belonging to School Worlds

Students in my study developed a sense of belonging to school worlds over time based on acquiring an increased sense of agency (Beach et al., 2015). In response to the prompt, "the lessons we take from *obstacles we encounter* can be fundamental to later success. Recount a time when you faced a *challenge, setback, or failure*. How did it affect you, and what did you learn from the experience?" Tanya described

62 Framing of Co-Authoring Practices

her negative experience in middle school in which she "never went a year without an F, Ds or Cs. All I wanted was to succeed and be 'smart' like other kids I knew. These setbacks and many others have become my biggest asset."

Since seventh grade, she had been enrolled in math support classes, leading to her developing "a love for the subject [that] taught me to always ask questions and be patient. I will always be thankful for those teachers who helped me reach my goals." After doing well in ninth and tenth grade, in which "my hard work and perseverance were finally paying off," she then again experienced a decline in her grades in her junior year, creating stress for her as "the worst time in my life thus far." She then drew on her

> many setbacks that I was able to use ... to help move myself forward. At my lowest points when I was crying and I felt like I just couldn't, I would remind myself that I'd get through this and that things had to come down before they could come up. Experiencing all these setbacks has allowed me to learn from them and grow as a person. I'm not afraid to fail. If I do I know I will be able to pick myself back up.

By identifying those practices that enhanced her sense of belonging in her school world, Tanya recognized how the use of productive practices served to enhance her success in school.

ACTIVITY: REFLECTING ON ENACTING IDENTITIES IN SCHOOL WORLDS

Students could discuss or write about their experiences of being socialized or mentored to acquire identities in school worlds. They may describe specific events or situations in which teachers made explicit the norms or discourses constituting practices valued in an activity or classroom. For example, they may note how a teacher, in giving an argumentative writing assignment, provided specific criteria for assuming a persona that would result in audiences perceiving that persona as credible.

Students may also describe tensions between their adoption of practices constituting their identities in their school world versus practices constituting identities in their other worlds. For example, they may note that, in engaging in an activity of conducting research on a topic in a school world, they needed to be concerned about whether they were conforming to their teacher's criteria for conducting effective research. They could then contrast that experience with conducting their own research related to acquiring information online on how to play a video game in which they generated their own criteria associated with their particular purposes or needs.

Students' Identity Development Over Time

As they move within and across school worlds, students develop their identities based on employing turning point practices leading to their success in school (Nasir et al., 2020; Wortham & Reyes, 2015). This development involves learning through acquiring

> memories, competencies, key formative events, stories, and relationships to people and places. It also provides material for directions, aspirations, and projected images of ourselves that guide the shaping of our trajectory going forward. In other words, the journey incorporates the past and the future in our experience of identity in the present.
>
> *Wenger-Trayner et al., 2015, p. 19*

In an interview with myself, Marla noted, in writing her admissions essay, that, given that the colleges she was applying for "really pride themselves on having like a wide variety of people and views ... I'm showing that I'm willing to consider them and learn about them [and that] would be really important to those colleges and important to me." She now realizes that in "having a conversation you can learn from the other person and that's like a good thing and not a bad thing." At the same time, she also noted how reflecting on changes in her practices took

> a really long period of time for me to change. But it was like people just saying things that like really made sense and I was, like, that it really makes sense to me, but that's not what I was taught. I was getting really frustrated that there are these two sides, that really does make sense. I slowly started to be like, well, maybe I should go with more of what I'm thinking now than what I was taught. That took me a really long time to change.

Socialization of Students' Identities in School Worlds

Students also develop identities as new members of school worlds, as peripheral participants who then become regular members of a world in an apprenticeship process (Lave & Wenger, 1991; Rogoff, 1994). Adolescent African-American students were socialized to become active members of a Black Sunday school world through activities that involved working directly with adults using shared practices (Peele-Eady, 2011).

As they move through their events in a specific world, students formulate pathways or trajectories based on experiencing certain positive experiences across events related to adopting identities. For example, a high school student, Jill, attended college with the purpose of majoring in engineering. However, because she did not have access to role models or resources associated with engineering, she switched to a business major and, given enhanced role models

64 Framing of Co-Authoring Practices

and resources, she did well in that major (Nasir et al., 2020). Analysis of one student perceived to be continually challenging status quo norms led to creating a pathway based on perceiving her as a discipline problem, resulting in her alienation from the classroom (Wortham & Reyes, 2015). However, later in the school year, as both she and the teachers shifted their perceptions, the teacher adopted a more supportive positioning in ways that enhanced her engagement in the classroom.

In describing her experience in middle school and the first two years of high school, Ana noted that she continually struggled, leading to her mother's belief that "'I believed in you thinking that you would change someday, but I guess I was wrong.'" Based on her mother's assessment, she "changed my entire lifestyle; I stopped acting like a fool and started putting time into my work," resulting in a marked increase in her academic performance evident in her receiving A grades in her courses.

Donald described how he had difficulty assuming responsibility for his work in school. In recognizing the limitations of blaming others for low grades in school, he shifted his focus to developing self-initiative, given his belief that

> a person's will is what defines them. I define will as the ability to push oneself and to embrace the shortcomings one has. Since my sophomore year, I've focused almost solely on improving my will, forcing myself to take the hard road, not just coast through my life.

In portraying turning-point events in their schooling experience, these students highlighted the importance of learning to alter their perceptions of their ability to succeed in school, resulting in improvements in school.

Shifting from Elementary to Middle to High School to College

When students transition from elementary to middle school, as early adolescents, they undergo major psychological and social changes (Cohen & Smerdon, 2009). If they are developmentally behind their peers, they may experience stress in their peer relations and in their academic performance (Erickson et al., 2013). Analysis of 14,000 students' transition from eighth grade in a middle school to ninth grade in high school found that they had lower grades and fewer friends than students who remained in eighth and ninth grade in the same school, experiences that have adverse psychological/physical health and academic effects during all of their high school experience (Felmlee et al. 2018).

Students who have strong friendship networks are more likely to experience success in these transitions, given that they may no longer be relying on their family for support (Bagwell & Schmidt, 2011). It is also the case that having strong peer relations in high school versus social isolation is a key factor contributing

Purpose, Norms, Discourses, and Identities **65**

to social capital related to both academic and economic success (Shi & Moody, 2017). Students moving from being the oldest in eighth grade to now being the youngest in ninth grade can no longer assume leadership roles (Felmlee et al., 2018). On the other hand, for some students, being in a new high school space can have positive effects related to opportunities to create new identities and relations.

In moving from high school to college, students experience interactions with a wider range of people than in high school, resulting in broadening of their perspectives. Marcus noted how

> being in college has exposed me to people who have extremely different beliefs than myself. I'm meeting people who are engineers, liberal arts majors, people from across the world, across the country. People who I never would've met outside of this environment. I've become a lot more aware of how people view the world. The way I view the world is very different from other people. I think, especially in recent times, one of the things I've had a lot of interesting discussions with people about is racial inequality.

This suggests the value of educators in middle and high schools within a district, as well as college educators, formulating plans and activities to provide support for students navigating this transition and coordination of a shared curriculum, as well as mentoring for new ninth grade students in high schools prior to and during the beginning of ninth grade.

Shifting Across Different School Cultures

Students also experience challenges when they move between different types of school cultures. Alandra described her experience with the same group of 20 students over a period of nine years in a small private school located in Kansas, including her closest friend. However, when she moved to her current community, and started at a middle school, she moved from

> a class of 20 to a class of 300, and recognized the cliques right away. For the first year, I came home crying every day and found it really hard to talk to new people; it was impossible for me to bond with the kids at my new school. Because of that, I had to learn how to be more dependent on myself rather than the people around me.

Where in her private school, "everyone had the same beliefs and wore the same uniforms. It was different to hear opinions that were not in agreement to my own, and I realized how much the clothes you wear can separate one person from the other." Given these challenges, "I gained a new knowledge of the world around me and going into my second year of public school I became more outgoing. I was beginning to build relationships with my classmates." The fact that she was "having to start over, I am able to build even stronger connections with the friends I have today. I also learned how to adjust to new situations: I believe that the experience made me a better person and who I am today."

ACTIVITY: STUDENTS CONTEXTUALIZING PRACTICES FOR MOVING ACROSS GRADE LEVELS OR BETWEEN DIFFERENT SCHOOL CULTURES

Teachers can have students write about or discuss their experiences of moving from elementary to middle school and/or middle school to high school or across different school cultures related to the challenges or difficulties as well as the positive aspects of their transitions. They could describe events or incidents associated with experiences of lack of or strong affiliation with their new school based on missing or having connections or bonds with teachers or peers supporting their transition. They may note how certain teachers helped them address issues associated with acquiring alternative practices, for example, homework completion policies, in their new school, as well as how certain peers served as mentors to share their own transition experiences.

They may also describe similarities or differences in the practices between schools based on certain norms, beliefs/discourses, and purposes shaping a school. For example, students may describe how their middle-school administrators and teachers were open to deviations from norms or rules, while administrators and teachers in their high school adhered to strict observance of norms or rules.

Coping with Specific Learning Challenges in School Worlds

Students also wrote about their experiences coping with specific learning challenges that require them to engage in learning how to readjust their practices to cope with these challenges. Ruth described her experience in the fifth grade of being diagnosed as having dyslexia, resulting in her being assigned to an individual education plan (IEP). As a result, in sixth grade, she was assigned to a specially designed English course for students with IEPs.

However, rather than focusing on literacy practice, which was her "main struggle," the class focused on grammar and writing. "I was already pretty good at that stuff so the class felt pointless." In seventh grade, she was assigned to a social studies class for IEP students with a similar focus, so that she then "had two

English classes. One class, easy and wasted time; the other, no idea what was going on. That's when I decided that in eighth grade I was not going to take any more special classes."

Given her struggling, negative middle-school experience, she began to lose her motivation to engage in high school, given the difficulty of

> getting started on work and staying on task made the dream of good grades nearly impossible. I visited some therapists and doctors because I thought I had ADD. Turns out, I was right. They prescribed me medication for it. Once we found the right dose, I found motivation again, and my grades started to look better. With this extra motivation, I found alternative ways of getting work done. I used audiobooks for English and new study habits to help me get started and acquire better time management.

She also experienced increased motivation in her art classes, given the benefits of being "able to show off a complete piece instead of a half drawn sketch. I finally am a successful artist rather than a distracted doodler." She also benefited from being "head captain" of the school's marching band, allowing her to

> prove that I am capable of being responsible and better at time management. Doing small jobs and chores are also so much easier. I have finally gotten the motivation to get all of my life together. I am a more productive person. I've also learned that being dyslexic actually does give me some special abilities. I'm able to read upside down and backward.

Marcus also experienced difficulty reading words in elementary school. In fourth grade, his reading teacher, Ms. P, recognized that he was dyslexic, given how he had difficulty processing text, leading to an additional medical diagnosis that he had attention deficit disorder (ADD) "so my short-term memory fails me more often than not." Ms. P also helped him focus his attention on moving across text, given that

> I couldn't readily go from line to line to line, especially when with small texts what she did is she recognized that and she started making it so like, or she made me this little window that was one line wide.

From this experience, he recognizes how "learning how to learn has been a challenge throughout my life. I don't always think in an orderly way. My thoughts often jump around and when I'm tired numbers can still trick me. However, now I accept myself." He perceives his elementary school experience as involving "a whole lot of learning about myself learning or learning how to function in a more academic environment where I really needed to learn, which was helpful."

ACTIVITY: CONTEXTUALIZING CHALLENGES IN LEARNING PRACTICES

Students can describe or write about their experiences learning practices across time based on adopting certain pathways, including how veteran members socialized them as new members into a world. For example, students could note how, as new members of their school's speech/debate team, they benefited from observing how veteran members engaged in formulating arguments designed to achieve positive audience uptake.

Students could also describe how they drew on practices from familiar worlds to cope with learning challenges in new worlds. For example, students may note how they apply the practice of assuming different roles for their school's theater production to having to adjust to adopting different, unfamiliar roles in their workplace world. They may then reflect on how in adopting different roles in a theater production they had support from their theater director, while in their workplace world, they received little training on how to assume their roles for interacting with others.

Summary

In this chapter, I described how students learn to contextualize practices based on the components of purposes, norms, discourses, and identities in school worlds. I posit that students are more likely to learn to do so through adoption of a relational pedagogy approach that focuses on the use of practice for enacting relations with others, as well as drawing on practices from other worlds to enhance their learning in school worlds. I also discuss how students learn to acquire new practices as they move across grade levels, contributing to their growth over time.

In the next chapter, I discuss how students learn to employ practices through the use of genres and media/literature.

References

Akkerman, S. F., & Bakker, A. (2011). Boundary crossing and boundary objects. *Review of Educational Research, 81*(2), 132–169.

Bagwell, C. L., & Schmidt, M. E. (2011). *Friendships in childhood and adolescence.* Guilford Press.

Beach, R., & Caraballo, L. (2021a). Reflecting on languaging in written narratives to enact personal relations. *English Teaching: Practice & Critique, 20*(4), 521–533.

Beach, R., & Caraballo, L. (2021b). How language matters: Using ethnographic writing to portray and reflect on languaging actions. *Journal of Adolescent & Adult Literacy, 65*(2), 139–148.

Beach, R., Johnston, A., & Thein, A. H. (2015). *Identity-focused ELA teaching: A curriculum framework for diverse learners and contexts.* Routledge.

Purpose, Norms, Discourses, and Identities **69**

Beauchemin, F. (2019). Reconceptualizing classroom life as relational-key. In R. Beach & D. Bloome (Eds.), *Languaging relations for transforming the literacy and language arts classroom* (pp. 23–48). Routledge.

Bettie, J. (2014). *Women without class: Girls, race, and identity.* University of California Press.

Beach, R., & Bloome, D. (Eds.) (2019). *Languaging Relations for transforming literacy and the language arts classroom.* Routledge.

Bowen, J. A. (2021). *Teaching change: How to develop independent thinkers using relationships, resilience, and reflection.* John Hopkins University Press.

Cameron, D. (1995). *Verbal hygiene.* Routledge.

Caraballo, L. (2019). Being "loud": Identities-in-practice in a figured world of achievement. *American Educational Research Journal, 56*(4), 1281–1317. https://doi.org/10.3102/0002831218816059

Carter Andrews, D. J., Richmond, G., & Marciano, J. E. (2021).The teacher support imperative: Teacher education and the pedagogy of connection. *Journal of Teacher Education, 72*(3), 267–270.

Cohen, J. S. & Smerdon, B. A. (2009).Tightening the dropout tourniquet: Easing the transition from middle to high school. *Preventing School Failure, 53*(3), 177–184.

Erickson, J., Peterson, R. L. & Lembeck, P. (2013, May). *Middle to high school transition. Strategy brief.* Student Engagement Project, University of Nebraska. Retrieved from http://k12engagement.unl.edu

Esteban-Guitart, M., Lalueza, J. L., Zhang-Yu, C., & Llopart, M. (2019). Sustaining students' cultures and identities. A qualitative study based on the funds of knowledge and identity approaches. *Sustainability, 11*(12), 3400. Retrieved from http://dx.doi.org/10.3390/su11123400

Felmlee, D., McMillan, C., Inara Rodis, P., & Osgood, D. W. (2018). Falling behind: Lingering costs of the high school transition for youth friendships and grades. *Sociology of Education, 91*(2), 159–182. doi:10.1177/0038040718762136

García-Sánchez, I. M., & Orellana, M. F. (Eds.). (2019). *Language and cultural practices in communities and schools: Bridging learning for students from non-dominant groups.* Routledge.

Gee, J. P., & Crawford, V. (1998).Two kinds of teenagers: Language, identity, and social class. In D. Alvermann, K. Hinchman, D. Moore, S. Phelps, D. Waff (Eds.), *Reconceptualizing the literacies in adolescents' lives* (pp. 225–245). Erlbaum.

Goodman, S. (2015, February 25). The importance of teaching through relationships. [Weblog post]. Retrieved from www.edutopia.org/blog/importance-teaching-through-relationships-stacey-goodman

Green, J. L., Brock, C., Baker, W. D. & Harris, P. (2020). Positioning theory: Its origins, definition, and directions in education. In N. S. Nasir, C. D. Lee, R. Pea, & M. M. de Royston (Eds.), *Handbook of cultural foundations of education* (pp. 119–140). Routledge.

Hall, L. A., Burns, L. D., & Edwards, E. C. (2010). *Empowering struggling readers: Practices for the middle grades.* Guilford Press.

Heath, S. B. (1983). *Ways with words: Language, life, and work in communities and classrooms.* Cambridge University Press.

Hedegaard, M. (2011). A cultural-historical approach to children's development of multiple cultural identities. In M. Kontopodis, C., Wulf, & B. Fichtner (Eds), *Children, development and education: International perspectives on early childhood education and development* (pp. 117–134). Springer.

Hodge, E. M. (2019). "Common" instruction? Logics of ability and teacher decision making across tracks in the era of common standards. *American Educational Research Journal, 56*(3), 638–675. doi:10.3102/0002831218803328

70 Framing of Co-Authoring Practices

Hung, C-M, Huang, I., & Hwang, G-J. (2014). Effects of digital game-based learning on students' self-efficacy, motivation, anxiety, and achievements in learning mathematics. *Journal of Computers in Education, 1*(2–3),151–166. doi:10.1007/s40692-014-0008-8

Kirkland, D. (2013). *A search past silence: The literacy of Black males.* Teachers College Press.

Kittle, P. & Gallagher, K. (2020). The curse of "helicopter teaching". *Educational Leadership, 77*(6), 14–19.

Kreber, C. (2007). What's it really all about? The scholarship of teaching and learning as an authentic practice. *International Journal for the Scholarship of Teaching and Learning, 1*(1), 1–4. doi:10.20429/ijsotl.2007.010103

Kundu, A. (2020). *The power of student agency: Looking beyond grit to close the opportunity gap.* Teachers College Press.

Lave, J. & Wenger, E. (1991). *Situated learning: Legitimate peripheral participation.* Cambridge University Press.

Lesko, N. (2012). *Act your age!: A cultural construction of adolescence.* Routledge.

Lysaker, J. T., & Furuness, S. (2011). Space for transformation: Relational, dialogic pedagogy. *Journal of Transformative Education, 9*(3),183–197. doi:10.1177/1541344612439939

Mehta, J. & Fine, S. (2019). *In search of deeper learning: The quest to remake the American high school.* Harvard University Press.

Metz, M. (2019). Principles to navigate the challenges of teaching English language variation: A guide for nonlinguists. In M. D. Devereaux & C. C. Palmer (Eds.), *Teaching language variation in the classroom: Strategies and models from teachers and linguists* (pp. 69–75). Routledge.

Mitra, D. L., & Serriere, S. C. (2012). Student voice in elementary school reform: Examining youth development in fifth graders. *American Educational Research Journal, 49*(4), 743–774. https://doi.org/10.3102/0002831212443079

Moje, E. B., & Ellison, T. L. (2016). Extended—and extending—literacies. *The Journal of Education, 196*(3), 27–34.

Moll, L. C., & González, N. (2004). Engaging life: A funds of knowledge approach to multicultural education. In J. Banks & C. McGee Banks (Eds.), *Handbook of research on multicultural education* (2nd ed.), (pp. 699–715). Jossey-Bass.

Nasir, N. S., de Royston, M. M., Barron, B., Bell, P., Pea, R., Goldman, S. (2020). Learning pathways: How learning is culturally organized. In N. S. Nasir, C. D. Lee, R. Pea, & M. M. de Major (Eds.), *Handbook of cultural foundations of learning* (pp. 195–211). Routledge.

Nasir, N. S., & Hand, V. H. (2008). From the court to the classroom: Opportunities for engagement, learning, and identity in basketball and classroom mathematics. *Journal of the Learning Sciences, 17*(2), 143–179. doi:10.1080/10508400801986108

O'Connor, C. (2021, August 24). Using Community Agreements to start the year strong. [Weblog post]. Retrieved from www.edutopia.org/article/using-community-agreements-start-year-strong

Orellana, M. F., & García-Sánchez, I. (2019). *Language and cultural processes in communities and schools: Bridging learning for students from non-dominant groups.* Routledge.

Peele-Eady, T. (2011). Constructing membership identity through language and social interaction: The case of African American children at Faith Missionary Baptist Church. *Anthropology & Education Quarterly, 42*(1), 54–75.

Quinlan, A., & Curtin, A. (2017). Contorting identities: Figuring literacy and identity in adolescent worlds. *Irish Educational Studies, 36*(4), 457–470. doi:10.1080/03323315.2017.1362352

Rogoff, B. (1994). Developing understanding of the idea of communities of learners. *Mind, Culture, & Activity, 1*(4), 209–229.

Rose, M. (2012). *Back to school: Why everyone deserves a second chance at education*. New Press.

Shi, Y., & Moody, J. (2017). Most likely to succeed: Long-run returns to adolescent popularity. *Social Currents*, *4*(1), 13–33.

Smagorinsky, P. (2017). Misfits in school literacy: Whom are U.S. schools designed to serve. In K. A. Hinchman & D. A. Appleman (Eds.), *Adolescent literacies: A handbook of practice-based research* (pp. 199–214). Guilford Press.

Smith, M. W., & Wilhelm, J. D. (2002). *Reading don't fix no Chevys: Literacy in the lives of young men*. Heinemann.

Speciale, T. J., & Bartlett. L. (2020). Building student awareness of literacy practices: Anthropological perspectives. *Journal of Adolescent & Adult Literacy*, *64*(2), 226–230.

van Galen, J. A. & Noblit, G. W. (Eds.). (2007). *Late to class: Social class and schooling in the new economy*. SUNY Press.

Urbanski, C. D. (2016). *Untangling urban middle school reform: Clashing agendas for literacy standards and student success*. Teachers College Press.

Wenger-Trayner, E., Fenton-O'Creevy, M., Hutchinson, S., Kubiak, C., & Wenger-Trayner, B. (2015). *Learning in landscapes of practice: Boundaries, identity, and knowledgeability in practice-based learning*. Routledge.

Wiggins, J. L., & Monobe, G. (2017). Positioning self in "figured worlds": Using poetic inquiry to theorize transnational experiences in education. *Urban Review*, *49*, 153–168. doi:10.1007/s11256-016-0386-5

Wolfram, W. (2019). Language awareness in education: A linguist's response to teachers. In M. D. Devereaux & C. C. Palmer (Eds.), *Teaching language variation in the classroom: Strategies and models from teachers and linguists* (pp. 61–66). Routledge.

Wortham, S., & Reyes, A. (2015). *Discourse analysis beyond the speech event*. Routledge.

Zittoun, T. (2006). *Transitions: Development through symbolic resources*. Information Age Publishers.

4
CONTEXTUALIZING PRACTICES USING GENRES AND MEDIA/ LITERATURE IN SCHOOL WORLDS

This chapter describes ways of having students contextualize the use of genres and media/literature to employ certain practices in school worlds. Students employ genres associated with systematic ways of engaging in discussions or in conducting research methods as well as using narrative and ethnographic writing to portray their use of practices in different worlds, as illustrated throughout this book. Students also respond to portrayals of characters' practices in media/literature as "symbolic resources" to experience critical perceptions of norms and discourses constituting characters' practices in figured worlds, leading to their inferring connections to their own lived-world practices and to then critically reflect on those practices.

In this chapter, I describe methods for engaging students in contextualizing their use of genres and media/literature for co-authoring practices in school worlds. A primary focus of this book involves drawing on students' experiences from their different worlds to illuminate their classroom literacy experiences, an approach similar to methods employed in the Compose Our World project, *composeourworld.org* (Boardman et al., 2021). ELA teachers often do ask students to connect their responses during or after responding to literary or media texts to their own lived-world experiences; for example, how, in reading about Esperanza's concerns about practices in her community world in *The House on Mango Street* (Cisneros, 1991), they describe their concerns about their own community world.

At the same, teachers could also have students describe experiences in their world prior to responding to a text based on certain anticipated practices portrayed in the text so that, having done so, they could be thinking about those related experiences as they are reading or viewing the text. Inferring connections with related experiences both after and before responding to a text creates a two-way

DOI: 10.4324/9781003246886-5

Genres and Media/Literature **73**

synergy that values the relevancy of students' experiences for expanding the meaning of texts.

Recontextualizing Practices From Different Worlds in School Worlds

As they are drawing on related experiences with practices from other worlds, teachers can also have students go beyond simply describing those experiences to also reconceptualize those practices from new and different perspectives, as illustrated by Figure 4.1.

Recontextualizing practices from events in other worlds involves having students reflect on those events through their discussions or writing based on applying alternative perspectives associated with the use of genres or media/literature. For example, in responding to Esperanza's critiques of common, problematic practices in her neighborhood, students may then critically reflect on practices in their own neighborhood; for example, resorting to gun violence to settle disputes. Through recontextualizing practices, students then critique the limitations of those practices, leading to changing or improving the use of those practices.

Teachers can invite students to share their experiences from worlds outside the classroom as connected to the uses of genres or responses to media/literature through demonstrating an interest in students' lives outside of school. For example, one ELA teacher valued the need to "'see students first as people' and she went out of her way to talk to students, to attend their performances and games, and to show them in little ways and big ones that she cared about them" (Mehta & Fine, 2019, p. 244). Ms. E had students use ethnographic and narrative writing, as described below, to have her students portray and reflect on events as portrayed in their worlds outside the classroom and learn more about students' lives to build personal connections with them.

She also had students infer connections between their responses to media/literature as "symbolic resources" (Zittoun, 2017) for portraying and reflecting on their practices for enacting relations with others and leading to change for enacting alternative identities (Hobel et al., 2019). Zittoun (2017) describes how

> symbolic resources have outcomes: they can participate in a person's identity transformation; they can also function as knowledge, or invite the person to

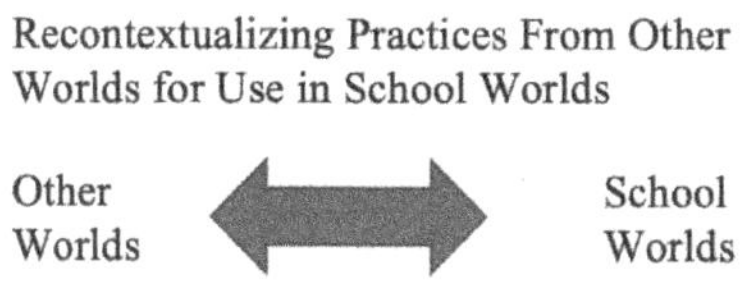

Recontextualizing Practices From Other
Worlds for Use in School Worlds

Other
Worlds

School
Worlds

FIGURE 4.1 Recontextualizing practices from other worlds for use in school worlds

74 Framing of Co-Authoring Practices

look for specific skills and pieces of knowledge; and third, and overall, they participate in the person's sense-making and elaboration of experience.

p. 7

From experiencing imaginative use of languaging as symbolic resources, students are "making connections across actual and narrative worlds, often revising self in the process" (Lysaker & Wessell-Powell, 2019, p. 180).

Learning to Use Different Genres Across Different Worlds

Within their school world, students discover that they need to employ different genres across different worlds—that writing literary criticism in their English classes may not apply to writing lab reports in their chemistry class. They may also discover the need to employ different variations in their use of academic languaging across different classes, suggesting the importance of inviting students to employ playful language. For example, in an assignment on learning to employ academic language, one student employed playful language, resulting in his instructor criticizing his use of playful language and in his diminished sense of his identity as a writer (Piekut, 2019).

Students may also have difficulties in transferring their use of genres across different worlds. One student, Daniel, who developed the use of a writing genre associated with his experience in the military, found that this genre did not transfer to his writing in school (Hobel, 2019).

Daniel wants to structure and store knowledge in the same way he did in the military. He has another sense of words than the teachers. For him, it is not important to use different voices and concepts in different disciplines. In the same way as he did in the army, when writing, he wants to describe, but he does not invest energy in appropriating the discourse of the subjects.

p. 115

In attempting to apply his writer identity enacted in the military to his school world, Daniel is reluctant to entertain new ways of knowing and thinking in his school world. This suggests the need to help students such as Daniel by engaging them in activities that invite them to experiment with alternative ways of knowing and thinking, for example, by having them adopt different characters' perspectives in a role-play activity.

Fostering Discussions as Genres in School Worlds

One primary genre for participation in school worlds involves the use of discussions. Participating in discussions as a genre involves the use of certain consistent languaging actions associated with posing and responding to questions. Classroom discussions often involve the use of teacher-centered interactions based on the use of the IRE ("initiate," "react," "evaluate") genre (Mehan, 1979), in which students respond to teacher questions with short answers. In contrast, a more productive, alternative practice involves asking open-ended questions with no predetermined response, leading to more elaborate responses and ideally supporting relational, collaborative responding (Beach & Beauchemin, 2019). For example, beginning a discussion with open-ended engagement questions invites students to draw on their own related experiences to connect with a topic or text (Beach et al., 2021).

It is also important that students perceive their contributions to discussions not as definitive statements but rather as exploratory, tentative "passing theories" (Kent, 1993) related to the use of open-ended think-alouds (Beck, 2018). Adopting a tentative, dialogic stance associated with "throwing out ideas" invites peers to reciprocate by sharing their own "passing theories," leading to collaborative exploration of ideas.

Students may also be more actively engaged in small group discussions in which they themselves can chart the direction and focus for sharing ideas through assuming identities as facilitator, leader, scribe, devil's advocate, connector, and summarizer (Harvey & Daniels, 2009). In these small group discussions, they can pose their own questions using heuristics such as The Critical Response Protocol based on the following questions:

- What are you noticing?
- What did you see that makes you say that?
- What does it remind you of?
- How do you feel?
- What questions does the "text" raise for you?
- What did you learn? (Beach et al., 2010, p. 27).

Given their experiences with remote learning during the pandemic, students largely became accustomed to engaging in online discussions using Zoom, *zoom. us*; Skype, *www.skype.com*; WebEx, *www.webex.com*; Microsoft Teams, *tinyurl.com/ zzoon4o*; or Google Meet, *meet.google.com*; as well as Google Hangouts, for iOS, *tinyurl.com/tbuaaos*, or Android, *tinyurl.com/j5mfdd4*.

Students can also use online sites such as Share Board; Fring: Video Calls + Chat; BT Chat HD; ooVoo Video Chat; Vtok: Google Talk Video; FaceTime; ClickMe Online Meetings; GoToMeeting; and Adobe Connect for iOS. Teachers can also use Skype for connecting with schools throughout the world, *www.t.ly/aHfN*; as well as ePals, *www.epals.com*; Youth Voices, *youthvoices.net*; and TakingitGlobal, *www. tigweb.org*, to set up connections for students to communicate with other students in different parts of the country or world.

Engaging in "Critical Conversations" in Discussions

Teachers can also engage students in "critical conversations" to foster students' critical inquiry about their use of practices in their worlds (Schieble et al., 2020). For example, they may note that in responding to portrayals of women characters in a novel, they adopted a feminist critical perspective (Appleman, 2015) to critique stereotypical portrayals of those characters.

Teachers can also support students' willingness to voice alternative perspectives and emotions by soliciting their expressions of emotions and needs by having them respond to the following questions:

- How does this experience differ from my own?
- What can I learn from listening in this moment?
- What emotions am I experiencing as I listen?
- How much do I know about this experience? What questions do I need to ask to learn more? (Schieble et al., 2020, p. 59).

For example, in a course on multicultural literature related to issues of institutional racism and White privilege, White students from low-income families expressed resentment about affirmative action programs (Beach et al., 2008). They assumed that these programs supported students of color in ways that precluded them from receiving support for attending college.

However, the teacher for this course and another student in the course, who were both from working-class families, challenged these perspectives based on the need for affirmative action programs to support students of color who might not otherwise attend college. As a result, some students voiced their critiques of affirmative action and modified their perspectives over time during the course. Through their voicing alternative perspectives, students changed their perspectives in ways that challenged their resentment about affirmative action programs.

Engaging in "Languaging Thinking Practices"

Engaging in "critical conversations" involves students using "languaging thinking practices" by stepping back to reflect on and make explicit *how* they are thinking about an issue or topic in response to the prompt, "How did you think about this?" (Kim & Bloome, 2021). In reflecting on their practices in specific events, students are answering the question, "'What is it that's going on here?'" (Goffman, 1974, p. 8). Or, in having students reflect on their languaging in formulating arguments, students may respond to the question, "'In argument, how do we go further?'"

For example, in addressing a problem, a student may note that "I was thinking last night that I should analyze the problem by dividing it into parts and then synthesizing those parts later." Sharing this thinking then leads to others sharing their

Genres and Media/Literature **77**

own or similar ways of thinking within a social context. Students then value these ways of thinking so that they then value the social benefits of explicating sharing their thinking through their interactions (Bloome & Beauchemin, 2016).

In reflecting on his problematic performance on his ski team, a student in my study, Tim noted how, in his races, he was using his internal "languaging thinking practice" to continually

> compare myself to the top skiers on our team. I always thought that if I wasn't getting to their level of skiing, I wasn't improving. I would become angry or sad that I wasn't reaching those heights. Even if I was improving, I didn't realize or didn't care because it wasn't good enough to be at the top.
>
> I had forgotten that I should focus on myself and that the improvements that I had made were still very important. Sometime after starting my third year on the team, I realized that this wasn't a healthy nor good mentality to have. It was damaging to have a mindset where I would feel upset for not being able to reach where the top skiers are. They have skied much longer than I have and put in much more work than I have.

Here, Tim is reflecting on how he was thinking about his performance based on attempting to compare himself with the "top skiers on our team," resulting in his negative self-perceptions.

ACTIVITY: ENGAGING STUDENTS IN CRITICAL THINKING PRACTICES

Students can engage in critical-thinking practices by sensing certain issues, topics, or events in their lives or texts that lead to students wanting to share their concerns about these issues, topics, or events. This requires supporting students who may be reluctant to share their concerns publicly, as well as creating a space where students are comfortable voicing competing perspectives on an issue, topic, or event. Teachers can also provide students with certain critical stances, such as a feminist or Critical Race Theory framework, that provide students with a way to frame their critiques in larger discourses.

Students can also employ "languaging thinking practices" (Kim & Bloome, 2021) to reflect on *how* they are thinking about their languaging related to participation in certain social events or situations, particularly for addressing problems or issues. For example, in a class discussion in which they are formulating arguments related to sharing ideas about addressing racial discrimination in their community, students may reflect on how their own racial identities and experiences shape their perceptions of racial discrimination.

Explaining How to Employ Practices to Others

Another example of using a genre related to learning in the classroom involves formulating explanations on how to employ certain practices with peers or family members. For example, as a member of a soccer team, a player notices how other players prematurely attempt to score goals as opposed to first passing the ball to other players to set up a play for scoring a goal. She may then explain to these players the need to set up a play rather than prematurely attempt to score a goal.

Therefore, explaining the use of practices involves contextualizing practices based on making explicit the *purposes* for using those practices—for example, the purpose of setting up a play to score a goal. It also involves addressing certain *discourses* as ways of knowing/believing as misconceptions or false beliefs about using certain practices; for example, the belief that one needs to shoot a ball quickly to the goal to score a goal, as opposed to setting up a play to score a goal.

These models are so deeply ingrained that we are not consciously aware of them. Self-explanation forces us to step back and see our existing models. Once we have done so, then we can see what needs fixing, and engage in meaningful repair and revision in light of the new information we have been presented (Lang, 2021, p. 141).

Teachers can draw on students' experiences of explaining practices in lived worlds to have them engage in self-explaining *how* they are using practices for responding to or writing a text by synthesizing those practices in their own words (Lang, 2021). For example, students may explain to a teacher in a writing conference *how* they thought about imagining their audience in writing a letter to the school newspaper as "languaging thinking processes" (Kim & Bloome, 2021).

Engaging in self-explaining enhances students' understanding in responding to texts. In one study, eighth-graders were asked to read brief passages from a high school biology textbook about the human circulatory system and were prompted to self-explain what they were learning after each sentence they read, versus students who just read the passages without self-explanation. (Chi et al., 1994; Lang, 2021). Students who engaged in self-explaining demonstrated higher levels of understanding than students who did not engage in self-explaining. Students also benefited from self-explaining to their peers, given how they had to contextualize their explanation based on considering their peers' prior knowledge (Chi et al., 1989; Lang, 2021).

Employing Specific Research Practices as Genres for Studying Figured Worlds

For engaging students in studying practices in their figured worlds, teachers have students employ specific research practices as genres for studying their figured worlds. Students engaged in the Cyphers for Justice project as described in Chapter 6 learned to employ research methods associated with YPAR (Youth

Genres and Media/Literature **79**

Participatory Action Research) projects for studying issues or challenges in their worlds. (For examples of practices from the ToolsForChange (TfC) project, see *tools4changeseminar.com project* (Tobin & Feit, 2020).

Posing Questions

To engage in studying practices in their worlds, students pose specific questions that serve to frame their collection of information or data through observations, interviews, surveys, audio/video recordings, etc. In posing questions, it is important that they be open-ended questions as well as having a genuine interest in addressing a specific issue or topic. For example, given their concern about racial injustice in their school, students may pose the question regarding the extent to which their Black versus Caucasian peers have been arrested and the nature of charges associated with those arrests.

Reviewing Relevant Related Research or Experiences

Given their question(s), students may then need to conduct a review of published research to identify methods others have used to address similar questions(s), as well as the results of their research. For example, they may find other research related to arrest rates for Black versus Caucasian students in schools, particularly in terms of differences in the demographic makeup of those schools.

Determining Research Methods

Students then need to determine how they will collect relevant data or information to address their questions in which they "think and act like a detective" (Tobin & Feit, 2020, p. 42). This includes determining the type of research methods they want to employ—surveys, case studies, observation, interviews, etc.

It is important to consider the criteria for youth conducting YPAR research in light of criteria for assessing traditional academic research, which is also highly contested. Academic research has traditionally been judged for publication in peer-reviewed journals based on definitiveness associated with validity and reliability of data analysis, which are constructs based on conventions of quantitative research. Qualitative researchers have long challenged the relevance of validity and reliability in research that involves participants' authentic experiences, perspectives, and understandings of personal, social and/or institutional phenomena and argued for trustworthiness as the standard for naturalistic inquiry (Lincoln & Guba, 1986).

YPAR research is often, though not always, qualitative or a mix of qualitative and quantitative (mixed methods, such as Fine et al., 2004) and is often related to problem-based inquiries that entail adopting an open-ended stance of uncertainty and incompleteness (Bettencourt, 2018). Youth adopting a more open-ended, critical inquiry stance may then be open to identifying their participants' and

80 Framing of Co-Authoring Practices

their own alternative perspectives without necessarily assuming that they need to resolve differences in these perspectives, given the need to achieve definitive findings.

Youth researchers and collaborative teams are also often continually reflecting on their processes as they are conducting their research to remain open to changing their methods, given perceptions that challenge their preconceptions (Bettencourt, 2018). Engaging in this type of disciplined inquiry helps to convey the sense of trustworthiness necessary for their audiences to understand how they attempted, in an honest manner, to explore the complexities of the phenomenon they were studying.

Collecting Data or Information

Based on their question(s) and research methods, students then collect data or information through surveys, observations, interviews, text analysis, etc. One of the challenges in conducting interviews is the need for both the interviewee and interviewer to establish a sense of trust between themselves to feel comfortable sharing their thoughts. To address these challenges, in conducting interviews with participants, students can employ OARS techniques involving asking **o**pen-ended questions, providing **a**ffirmation for their perspectives, engaging in **r**eflective listening to restate the interviewee's answers, and **s**ummarizing what one learns from their answers (Miller & Rollnick, 2002).

Four students from diverse backgrounds in a Philadelphia high school observed and recorded information about how their teachers' and peers' use of language related to their attitudes toward language/dialect differences (LeBlanc, 2018). They found that strict adherence to Standardized English as the set norm in their school by teachers and peers led to deficit perspectives of their own language/ dialect use. By investigating where language and literacies were marked in their neighborhoods, churches, homes, schools, and classrooms in Philadelphia, the boys demonstrated how notions of Standard English prevailed in part because of narratives about imagined futures of jobs, globalization, classroom discipline, and morality (LeBlanc, 2018, p. 9).

Using Writing to Reflect on Practices in Figured Worlds

In writing about their experiences in different worlds through the genres of narratives or ethnographic writing, students in my study were using their writing to reflect on the meaning of their practices in figured worlds (Beach & Caraballo, 2021a; 2021b). Students may also use their writing to reflect on how changes in their practices have enhanced their sense of well-being. As previously noted, having recognized the limitations of his comparing himself to other members of his ski team, Tim wrote about the need to stop comparing himself with others on the team to appreciate how he himself improved in his skiing ability over time.

I became aware of how far I have come and the difference between my first and third year on the team. I also started to become a lot happier because of this. I didn't have that burden in my mind where I was constantly conflicted. I had a new stance on myself in the sport which later transferred over into my everyday life. I compared myself to other people less and less and this has made my skiing and life more enjoyable.

By taking action to address the limitation in comparing himself to others, Tim is using his reflection to take action to change his ways of being/acting, resulting in improving his performance. College student graduates participating in the Meaningful Writing Project, *meaningfulwritingproject.net*, perceived their writing as helping them gain certain insights into their practices and gained a sense of agency through their writing (Eodice et al., 2017; Williams, 2017).

Use of Ethnographic Writing for Portraying Practices

One type of writing for studying the use of practices in figured worlds involves using small-scale "mini-ethnography" studies. (For methods of engaging in ethnographies of language use, see School Kids Investigating Language in Life and Society, *www.skills.ucsb.edu*). By observing and noting participants' use of certain practices, students identify consistent patterns in their use of these practices based on adhering to certain norms within events or situations.

As described in Chapter 3, students in Ms. E's 12th grade ELA classes engaged in "mini-ethnography" studies of their participation in different worlds based on different components (Beach & Caraballo, 2021a). Based on the prompts described in Chapter 3, students were asked to reflect on their practices based on purposes, norms, identities, and ways of knowing/believing in certain activities, events, or traditions.

I analyzed students' reports in 2017 and 2019 as well as interviewing students about their writing related to their perceptions of what they learned from their analysis of certain worlds (Beach & Caraballo, 2021a, 2021b), reports contained throughout this book. In writing their "mini-ethnographies," students identified certain consistent patterns in their interactions that enhanced their relations. Mark noted how members of his peer group participate in a weekly meeting to share experiences and engage in playing an online game:

> Every Friday night the group of five guys logs onto the voice chat app, Discord. We all joke around and talk about how our week at school had gone. This gathering had developed into a tradition for us over time. During these Friday night gatherings, we'd then log onto Rainbow Six Siege and get ready to practice our strategies and play some ranked. Ranked is the name of the game mode where two teams try to beat each other and are very competitive. This is important to our group as it shows if our practice

has been paying off for us and tells us what we need to improve upon. This helps us connect as friends and develop our communication skills.

One essential aspect of their ethnographic writing involves bracketing out their presuppositions or assumptions about practices in an event or context. By doing so, students are more open to perceptions that may challenge their presuppositions or assumptions, just as anthropologists recognize the need to bracket out their Western cultural assumptions when studying practices in Third World countries. For example, in observing a car body shop consisting of only male employees, Renee recognized the need to bracket her gender assumptions that these employees would assume traditional masculine practices. She noted that

> observing this place was such a great experience because it gave me an understanding that there's always more than the eyes see. All of the people working in the shop might have all been men, but they treated each other as if they were family. It was clear that they all had respect for one another and they also had respect for each of their profession. When people think about auto body shops they probably think about the rude men and how awkward the place can be, but in this shop, there's a whole different vibe.

Use of Narratives for Portraying Practices

Students in my study also wrote narratives portraying their practices (Beach & Caraballo, 2021b). In writing their narratives, students were using their narratives for the *purpose* of making sense of events in their lives; for example, recalling specific events relating to how they made improvements in their playing a sport.

Sharing narratives with others also serves the purpose of building relations with others. In an interview with myself, Ms. E noted that her initial assignments involving writing personal narratives and analysis of peer group languaging are designed to

> build relationships with kids. They write about themselves a lot. By the time the first trimester is over, my relationship with them is sometimes profoundly greater than the relationships they have with other teachers ... That builds a level of trust. They tell me things that they might not tell another person ever.

Narratives revolve around portrayals of how certain practices conform to or deviate from *norms* operating in a particular world as contributing to a narrative's "tellability" (Labov, 1997). Rather than share the relatively ordinary event that "I drove to school today," a student may dramatize that event by noting that "While I was driving to school today, another car passing in their lane in the opposite direction almost hit me," contributing to making the narrative event worth telling.

In creating narratives, students also portray their *identities* as certain "kinds of persons" (Holland et al., 1998, p. 60) through how they employ languaging to interact with others. Students in one project created a book in which they included "collage, drawing, comics, painting or even writing. The objective is to create their own narrative of "who I am", "what defines me", or "the most important things in my life" (Esteban-Guitart et al., 2019, p. 6).

Students portray how they perceive themselves as becoming certain kinds of persons based on connecting past actions to future imagined selves related to changes in their ways of knowing/believing (McAdams, 2015). They are also reflecting on the development of certain attitudes or ethics, given how they "are not creating a merely random identity, rather, they are actively narrating themselves relative to a moral ideal of what it is to be a good person" (Rymes, 2001, p. 498).

Use of Narratives to Portray Identities

Based on the notion of "showing versus telling," students also portray their identities through the use of languaging associated with certain practices constituting their identities (Linell, 2009). Ms. E encouraged her students to employ dialogue in their narratives to portray their practices. She cited the example of a student's narratives in which she used "dialogue and how the whole paper wasn't narrative; it was dialogue. Like it was almost like reading a play. So adding dialogue to these narratives really changed the level of interest that we had in reading them."

She also has students portray how their languaging varies according to context, citing the example of interacting "with your youth group leader at church. Are you going to talk to them like you talk to your friend in the locker room? And they're like, 'No!' And I say, 'Okay, so we know when we talk to other people, we change how we talk.'" She also stresses the importance of the use of accurate descriptive details in their writing associated with a sense of honesty. She cites the example of "'There's a bear outside your window and you need to describe the bear. So what kind of bear is it? Is it a panda bear, polar bear, large hairy gay man?' So it's that honesty that they kind of return to you. You're honest with them, they're honest with you."

Methods for Teaching Narrative Autobiographical Writing to Portray Identities

In writing narrative autobiographies, students often create a laundry list of events during their past lifetime, resulting in superficial portrayals of those events. In contrast, students benefit from focusing on and fleshing out one or two specific past events in some detail through actions and dialogue to explore how they have grown or changed. When writing about past events, students need to think about what they were like in the past and how they can portray the earlier perspectives and identities. To select these events in their lives, students can create a timeline and then focus on a key moment when they were coping with certain problems or issues.

Students could read examples of autobiographical narratives or memoirs such as *I Know Why the Caged Bird Sings* (Angelou, 2010) or *Between the World and Me* (Coates, 2015). For examples of short autobiographies, they can read *We Are Here to Stay: Voices of Undocumented Young Adults* (Kuklin, 2019). This collection includes writing by nine undocumented adolescents coping with the threat of being reported to legal authorities (for a unit with writing about adolescents coping with adversities, see *bit.ly/366wlwp* (Ford, 2019)).

To acquire specific information about these past events, students can interview people who knew them in the past and talk about their prior perceptions (for examples of interviews with people on the StoryCorps site and podcast, see *www.storycorps.org/stories*). They can also find photos of themselves, mementos, or documents from the time period to evoke memories of their actions or beliefs. In addition, teachers often have students create maps of the home or neighborhood where they grew up and mark sites of significant events that could be addressed in their writing.

ACTIVITY: USING ETHNOGRAPHIC AND NARRATIVE WRITING ABOUT PRACTICES IN STUDENTS' WORLDS

Students can engage in ethnographic and narrative writing about their practices in their worlds, as illustrated by writing by Ms. E's students in the remaining chapters. To foster this writing, you can share published examples, as well as examples of your own students' writing. You can also have students reflect on their portrayals of certain types of languaging actions constituting practices.

For example, in our research on the most frequent types of languaging actions in their ethnographic writing, we found that students most frequently portrayed and reflected on "references to connections, understandings, collaboration, and support for others" (Beach & Caraballo, 2021a, p. 143), an indication of the importance of using languaging for enacting relations with others (Beauchemin, 2019). We also found a similar focus in students' reflections on types of languaging action in their narrative writing (Beach & Caraballo, 2021b).

Using Writing to Portray Norms and Discourses Constituting Figured Worlds

Adolescents can also use their narrative writing to portray how their practices represent adherence to certain *norms* and *discourses* constituting their worlds. In doing so, they are showing how people are employing ways of knowing shaping

Genres and Media/Literature **85**

their practices in a world (Yagelski, 2009). For example, students may portray how certain social and cultural norms of their school or community based on a conservative discourse limit the ability of that community to address problems in the community.

In one project, students from seven high schools conducted research on issues facing their community. They used Google Docs and the GroupMe chat app to share their findings with each other, as well as with members of the community, and to propose changes for addressing these issues; for example, communicating with school administrators about issues of equity in funding and support of sports and extracurricular activities across their different schools (Marciano & Warren, 2019).

Through adopting a critical stance through their writing about the discourses operating in a particular figured world, students recognize the need to challenge status quo cultural practices in that world. Undergraduate female students reflected on the value of engaging in collaborative writing about their employment opportunities in Qatar, given its traditional gendered discourses regarding women in the workplace world (Scotland, 2020). One female student, Aisha, noted that

> I have always been against equality between men and women because every person has their own role in life. However, it is not right that women get paid less than men despite having the same qualifications. Men and women should get paid the same.
>
> *p. 269*

Writing her paper led Aisha to change her mind about the value of working: "'Before writing our term paper, I did not accept the idea that women should be able to work, but after writing the essay and talking with my group, I am thinking about working after I graduate'" (p. 269). Another student, Ghalya, wrote about the need for husbands to support their wives' right to work. She noted that "'now I realize that also I need my husband to support my working. My husband should agree to my working before we are married. This should not be a problem'" (p. 269).

Using Media/Literature as "Symbolic Resources"

Students also draw on their use of media/literature as "symbolic resources" for making sense of events in their lives (Zittoun, 2017). For example, they may

> not only listen to a song for the esthetic experience it provides but [also] because it allows one to feel closer to a friend abroad. It is through these complex semiotic and often emotional dynamics that these cultural elements can be said to make sense to the person in a specific situation.
>
> *Zittoun, 2017, p. 5*

For example, a female student who seeks to marry someone whom her parents oppose decides to resist her parents through drawing on texts such as *Titanic* or *Romeo and Juliet* or on certain songs about romance to imagine alternative ways of thinking about her challenge (Zittoun, 2006). In responding to *Real Women Have Curves* (Lopez, 1996) and *Between the World and Me* (Coates, 2015), students became aware of how power relations shaped their lives in ways that enhanced their sense of agency outside the classroom (Gordon, 2019). One student noted that "in this class, I have learned so many things, which in my opinion, now in the future I am going to change the law with immigration issues" (interview, May 3, 2017, p. 17).

Students benefit from having a clear sense of *purpose* for engaging in media/literature to acquire the use of certain practices. They often value the use of media/literature for their own personal purposes more than for doing schoolwork. While the use of media/literature texts for homework was perceived as something they were required to do by their school world, students perceived reading newspapers as something they valued for their understanding of current events in their community worlds (Laursen, 2019).

Students are also more likely to experience a clear sense of purpose by engaging in activities where they assume an active identity. In participation in a theater production of the play *The Servant of Two Masters* (Goldoni, 1961), students experienced a clear sense of purpose based on considering ways to engage their audiences through their participation in rehearsals (Mehta & Fine, 2019). This required the student directors, stage managers, costume designers, actors, and adult advisers to coordinate their practices based on shared, common goals. Assuming these different roles contributed to assuming leadership associated with directing their peers to acquire certain practices. One student described her thoughts that "'I'm the director; I'm in this leadership position; I need to step up,' and I learned how to kind of get over myself, and be a leader" (p. 276).

Students also experienced a different sense of time between being in their classes versus being on stage. In their classes, students experienced time as codified, while in extracurriculars or sports, they experienced time as open-ended and related to the experience of flow (Csikszentmihalyi, 1990). As one student noted about being in class, "'I'm checking the clock every ten minutes. In costumes, I'll get there at 3:00. It'll suddenly be six o'clock'" (Mehta & Fine, 2019, p. 267).

Participation in the theater production required a key element of deep learning—performing in an innovative, creative manner, in ways that go beyond the focus on analysis in classrooms. One student noted that "I think analyzing can only go so far. … Whereas creation, you can make whatever you want" (p. 301).

Drawing on Norms and Discourses in Use of Media/literature

Students also draw on media/literature to learn how to adhere to certain *norms* or *discourses* constituting people's or characters' practices operating in a certain world;

Genres and Media/Literature **87**

for example, how characters in a detective novel employ practices of investigating crime in the world of law enforcement.

Attending to Norms in Using Media

In communicating with each other online, adolescents frequently employ "text-speak" or "teenspeak" as languaging that is frequently perceived as deficient or inadequate use of language, representing a decline in adolescents' literacy standards (Thurlow, 2007). These critiques fail to recognize how adolescents contextualize their use of this languaging for interacting with peers, consistent with their meta-linguistic awareness of certain social norms, so that, in other contexts, they will resort to different languaging styles. Adolescents employ this languaging that "is not meant to be for, or necessarily about, adults. As a young person quoted in one article put it: 'It's a teen-to-teen thing.'" (Thurlow, 2007, p. 224).

Knowing how and when to employ certain language styles requires students' awareness of social norms constituting their use of media in a particular world. In texting a grandparent, they may then not employ "text-speak," given their awareness of interacting with a different audience.

Critiquing the Use of Discourses Constituting Responses to Literature

Adolescents also draw on responses to characters in media/literature to critique how discourses of race, class, and/or gender are shaping their own participation in worlds. Elsa, a ninth-grade Mexican immigrant, in responding to *The House on Mango Street* (Cisneros, 1991), was critical of the fact that another male student in her discussion group voiced the notion that "'all Hispanics have an attitude problem'" (p. 58). When the other student indicated that "'some Hispanics have a problem'," she responded to him, "'Not the whole race! You can't go around judging all Hispanic people just because one person is mean to you'" (p. 58).

On the other hand, she also noted that "race has nothing to do with it" (p. 58), a reflection of her "conflicting notions about her own identity regarding racism—she believes: *Racism is imposed* and *Racism is an individual choice*. She saw racism as some-thing inherited, or taught by other—an imposed piece of one's identity" (p. 59).

Elsa challenged the gender stereotypes and racial stereotyping of "all Hispanics"; at the same time, she adopted a discourse that "all human beings are seen as fun-damentally the same and differences are simply illusions" (p. 61). "This lack of acknowledgment of the power structures points to the need for critical literacy facilitation to do more instruction about social systems and structures prior to and in conjunction with the critical literacy practices" (p. 62).

Students also use their experience with media/literature to reimagine their own worlds by engaging in the practices of recognition, recontextualization, social imagination, and narrative imagination (Lysaker & Wessel-Powell, 2019).

88 Framing of Co-Authoring Practices

Recognition involves drawing on personal experiences to connect with related experiences in their own lives; for example, an older brother reading about a portrayal in a novel of an older brother interacting with other family members. *Recontextualizing* involves inferring connections between their lived-world experiences and portrayals of experience in a text. Inferring these connections may then lead to recontextualizing those lived-world experiences; for example, the older brother applying a new perspective on his family relations. *Social imagination* involves students imagining novel, alternative ways of being in their own lives; for example, imagining themselves playing on a sports team in college. Students may then employ their *narrative imagination* to create narratives in which they imagine themselves engaged in future ways of being in different worlds.

Teachers can have students respond to media/literature in ways that verify their ability to reimagine their worlds through their responses. For example, Ms. Nelson was teaching *Things Fall Apart* (Achebe, 1995) in her 11th grade English class as part of a unit on different "Ways of Seeing" (Seymour et al., 2020). She was concerned that her students were overly dependent on her to provide them with certain interpretations of the novel. She noted in an interview that "what I really wanted was for my students to see each other as authorities of a text and as valued stakeholders in the conversation" (p. 38). This required her to "create new spaces in my classroom—spaces that by design would help them discover on their own that they needed to reposition themselves into different viewpoints in order to unpack and build complex arguments" (p. 38).

To "re-position" her students, she asked them to respond to these questions in the beginning of the unit: "'What is a text's subtext? How is it [subtext] working on you?'" "'How does language work to challenge and reinforce cultural power?'" In posing these questions, she is focusing on having her students "recognize that the author of the text is constructing a social relationship with them and that they are responding to the social relationship by how they take up the subtext [based on] how the subtext is 'working on you?'" (pp. 39–40).

Contextualizing Media/Literature from a Critical Race Theory Perspective

Students also benefit from contextualizing media/literature in historical contexts from a Critical Race Theory perspective. Adopting this critical race perspective challenges the historical perspective of neoliberal multiculturalism that "images a picture that over time racial minorities have to fight less and if they fail in society it is solely due to an individual's fault" (Coles, 2019, p. 18). For example, students may infer connections between how a history of White privilege and domination shapes the portrayals of non-dominant characters within similar contemporary worlds (Kirkland, 2013; Morrell, 2015.

Through adopting a Critical Race Theory perspective, Black high school students often identified historical forces shaping Black people's lives (Coles, 2019). One student attributed Black people's economic status to how this economy, it's like based off of wealthy white men. Like it's not that many Black people 'cause they not giving them any opportunities 'cause of like the past with what Black people went through, what we went through. So, we don't have as much opportunities as white people.

Coles, 2019, p. 17

As part of the study, students also drew images portraying their perspective of racism. One student included the image of the KKK in his image as a

symbol of violence because they were a violent group, they acted out of hate through violence on Black communities in the South and so it connects to racism, because they for one were racists; and also like, they were driving Black people out of their homes and building crosses.... And then just like over the course of history, they just been known for like eradicating groups of people, like aborigines in Australia or sub groups in Asia ... all because they just white and they just mad cause they are white.

p. 19

Another female Black student drew a "Body Map," in which she listed for the outside of her map: "Ghetto, Loud, Lazy, Avg Philly Girl, Dumb, and Goofy. On the inside of her Body Map, how she views herself, she listed: Intelligent, Hard-Working, Dedicated, Beautiful, Funny, Baddie (read attractive), Fortunate, Mother, and Strong" (p. 24), a rejection of negative perspectives of Black adolescent females.

Adopting a critical analysis of the evolution of practices over time focuses on the influence of hegemonic, dominant practices, including binaries of school versus non-school figured worlds. Critiquing practices from a cultural or historical perspective involves what Carol Lee (2001) describes as "cultural modeling." For example, in responding to media through sampling different fragments and memes of media messages, students may engage in remixing them to portray their ambivalence about the complexities of these often mixed messages (Gutiérrez et al., 2017). For instance, in responding to hip-hop videos, they may portray both the social justice discourses as well as the sexist discourses portrayed in these videos.

ACTIVITY: ENGAGING STUDENTS IN REIMAGINING THEIR WORLDS THROUGH RESPONDING TO MEDIA/ LITERATURE

Teachers can have students draw on their responses to media/literature to reimagine their own worlds by drawing on the norms/discourses in a text to then recontextualize their own worlds based on those norms/discourses. Given the importance of teaching about the climate crisis in the ELA classroom

90 Framing of Co-Authoring Practices

(Beach et al., 2017; 2019–2020), in responding to the novel *Dry* (Shusterman & Shusterman, 2019), which portrays an adolescent main character's future world of Los Angeles suffering from drought due to climate change, students may reimagine their own community both in the present and in the future coping with a similar lack of water. In recontextualizing their own world, they may consider the potential effects of drought and ways to adapt to a world with little water.

Constructing Identities Through Responding to Media/literature

Students also construct their *identities* based on their use of media/literature practices as symbolic resources; for example, when a student described herself as a "newspaper lady" based on her daily reading of newspapers (Laursen, 2019, p. 458). In a figured world, certain

> characters (for example, newspaper ladies) act in a certain way (for example they read newspapers every day) in accordance with a specific storyline. In this way, the narrative aspects are given prominence in the understanding of social meaning and identity making … as resources in their social meaning-making and identity processes when positioning themselves in relation to one another and to different discourses about literacy.
>
> *pp. 458–459*

In some cases, students perceived "reading as a strong semiotic identity resource that is connected to perceptions of their sense of belonging to current and future communities" (p. 474). In participating in the theater production noted above, students experienced being "around the arts, liberal political and social values, inclusion of minorities and gay students, and love of theater" (Metha & Fine, 2019, p. 272). As a member of a theater community, students acquired identities for working effectively with others through languaging interactions; for example, they learned how to voice respect to peers for their successful contributions or performances.

ACTIVITY: CONTEXTUALIZING IDENTIFICATION WITH CHARACTERS IN MEDIA/LITERATURE

Students could reflect on whether or not they identify with certain characters in media/literature related to their own sense of identity. They may note reasons for identifying or not identifying with a character based on their affinity with the character's practices or their resistance to practices they perceive to be unethical or misguided. For example, in giving a book talk about *Confessions of a Serial Kisser* (Van Draanen, 2008), a student talked about his strong interest in how the main character was trying to define her own identity as a struggling high school student as related to his struggle in defining his identity based on developing his own identity through enhancing his identity as a reader (Frankel, 2016). While his teacher defined the identity of being a good reader as acquiring literacy practices related to reading comprehension, the students perceived being a good reader as related to enacting certain personhoods.

Summary

In this chapter, I described ways of having students contextualize the use of genres and media/literature to employ certain practices in figured worlds. Students in my study used narrative and ethnographic writing genres to portray their use of practices in different worlds, as illustrated throughout this book. Students also benefit from responding to portrayals of characters' practices in media/literature to infer connections to their own lived-world practices.

References

Achebe, W. (1995). *Things fall apart*. Everyman's Library.

Angelou, M. (2010). *I know why the caged bird sings*. Virago.

Appleman, D. (2015). *Critical encounters in high school English: Teaching literary theory to adolescents*. Teachers College Press/National Council of Teachers of English.

Beach, R., Appleman, D., Fecho, B., & Simon, R. (2021). *Teaching literature to adolescents* (4th ed.). Routledge.

Beach, R. & Beauchemin, F. (2019). *Teaching language as action in the ELA classroom*. Routledge.

Beach, R., Campano, G., Edmiston, B., & Borgmann, M. (2010). *Literacy tools in the classroom: Teaching through critical inquiry in Grades 6–12*. Teachers College Press.

Beach, R., & Caraballo, L. (2021a). How language matters: Using ethnographic writing to portray and reflect on languaging actions. *Journal of Adolescent & Adult Literacy, 65*(2), 139–148.

Beach, R., & Caraballo, L. (2021b). Reflecting on languaging in written narratives to enact personal relations. *English Teaching: Practice & Critique, 20*(4), 521–533.

Beach, R., Share, J., & Webb, A. (2017). *Teaching climate change to adolescents: Reading, writing, and making a difference*. Routledge/National Council of Teachers of English.

Beach, R., Share, J., & Webb, A. (Winter 2019–2020). Climate change in the classroom: A natural part of English language arts. *American Educator, 43*(4), 18–22. www.aft.org/ae/winter2019-2020/beach_share_webb

Beach, R., Thein, A.H., & Parks, D. (2008). *High school students' competing social worlds: Negotiating identities and allegiances in response to multicultural literature*. Erlbaum.

92 Framing of Co-Authoring Practices

Beck, S. W. (2018). *A think-aloud approach to writing assessment: Analyzing process & product with adolescent writers.* Teachers College Press.

Beauchemin, F. (2019). Reconceptualizing classroom life as a relational key. In R. Beach & D. Bloome (Eds.), *Languaging relations for transforming literacy and language arts classrooms* (pp. 23–48). Routledge.

Bettencourt, G. (2018). Embracing problems, processes, and contact zones: Using youth participatory action research to challenge adultism. *Action Research, 18*(2), 153–170. doi:10.1177/1476750318789475

Bloome, D., & Beauchemin, F. (2016). Languaging everyday life in classrooms. *Literacy Research: Theory, Method, and Practice, 65*(1), 152–165.

Boardman, A. G., Garcia, A., Dalton, B., & Polman, J. (2021). *Compose our world: Project-based learning in secondary English language arts.* Teachers College Press.

Chi, M. T. H., Bassok, M., Lewis, M. W., Reimann, P., & Glaser, R. (1989). Self-explanations: How students study and use examples in learning to solve problems. *Cognitive Science, 13*(2), 145–182.

Chi, M. T. H., DeLeeuw, N., Chiu, M.-H., & LaVancher, C. (1994). Eliciting self-explanations improves understanding. *Cognitive Science, 18*(3), 439–477.

Cisneros, S. (1991). *The house on Mango Street.* Vintage.

Coates, T-N. (2015). *Between the world and me.* Spiegel & Grau.

Coles, J. A. (2019). The Black literacies of urban high school youth countering antiblackness in the context of neoliberal multiculturalism. *Journal of Language and Literacy Education, 15*(2), 1–35.

Csikszentmihalyi, W. (1990). *Flow: The psychology of optimal experience.* Harper & Row.

Eodice, M., Geller, A. E., & Lerner, N. (2017). *The Meaningful Writing Project: Learning, teaching and writing in higher education.* Utah State University Press.

Esteban-Guitart, M., Lalueza, J. L., Zhang-Yu, C., & Llopart, M. (2019). Sustaining students' cultures and identities. A qualitative study based on the funds of knowledge and identity approaches. *Sustainability, 11*(12), 3400. Retrieved from http://dx.doi.org/10.3390/su11123400

Fine, M., Roberts, R. A., & Torre, M. E. (2004). *Echoes of Brown: Youth documenting and performing the legacy of Brown V. Board of Education.* Teachers College Press.

Ford, C. (2019, October 29). Build Your Stack: Memoir and reading choice. National Council of Teachers of English. Retrieved from https://ncte.org/blog/2019/10/build-stack-memoir-reading-choice

Frankel, K. K. (2016). The intersection of reading and identity in high school literacy intervention classes. *Research in the Teaching of English, 51*(1), 37–59.

Goffman, E. (1974). *Frame analysis: An essay on the organization of experience.* Harvard University Press.

Goldoni, F. (1961). *The servant of two masters.* Heinemann.

Gordon, C. T. (2019). Trusting students' voices in critical English education. *Journal of Language and Literacy Education, 15*(1), 1–33.

Gutiérrez, K. D., Cortes, K., Cortez, A., DiGiacomo, D., Higgs, J., Johnson, P., ... Vakil, S. (2017). Replacing representation with imagination: Finding ingenuity in everyday practices. *Review of Research in Education, 41*, 30–60, doi:10.3102/0091732X16687523

Harvey, S., & Daniels, H. (2009). *Comprehension and collaboration: Inquiry circles in action.* Heinemann.

Hobel, P. (2019). Young adults' school writing experiences. In E. Krogh & K. S. Jakobsen (Eds.), *Understanding young people's writing development: Identity, disciplinarity, and education* (pp. 106–120). Routledge.

Holland, D., Lachicotte, W., Skinner, D., & Cain, C. (1998). *Identity and agency in cultural worlds*. Harvard University Press.

Kent, T. (1993). *Paralogic rhetoric*. Associated University Press.

Kim, M-Y., & Bloome, D. P. (2021). When thinking becomes a topic of classroom conversations: Languaging thinking practices in a high school English classroom. *Research in the Teaching of English, 56*(2), 177–199.

Kirkland, D. E. (2013). *A search past silence: The literacy of young Black men*. Teachers College Press.

Kuklin, S. (2019). *We are here to stay: Voices of undocumented young adults*. Candlewick.

Labov, W. (1997). Some further steps in narrative analysis. *Journal of Narrative and Life History, 7*(1–4), 395–415.

Lang, J. M. (2021). *Small teaching*. Wiley.

Laursen, H. P. (2019). Likes and loathing in the middle time: How adolescents time–space their figured literacy worlds. *Cambridge Journal of Education, 49*(4), 457–476. doi:10.1080/0305764X.2018.1556607

LeBlanc, R. J. (2018). Those who know and are known: Students using ethnography to interrogate language and literacy ideologies. *Journal of Adolescent & Adult Literacy, 61*(5), 489–499.

Lee, C. (2001). Is October Brown Chinese? A cultural modeling activity system for underachieving students. *American Educational Research Journal, 38*(1), 97–141.

Lincoln, Y. S., & Guba, E. G. (1986). But is it rigorous? Trustworthiness and authenticity in naturalistic evaluation. *New Directions for Program Evaluation, 30*, 73–84.

Linell, P. (2009). *Rethinking language, mind, and world dialogically*. Information Age Publishing.

Lopez, J. (1996). *Real women have curves*. Dramatic Publishing Company.

Lysaker, J. & Wessel-Powell, C. (2019). Comprehending as "a manner of living." In R. Beach & D. Bloome (Eds.), *Languaging relations to transform instruction in the literacy and language arts classroom* (pp. 172–192). Routledge.

Marciano, J. E., & Warren, C. A. (2019). Writing toward change across youth participatory action research projects. *Journal of Adolescent & Adult Literacy, 62*(5), 485–494.

McAdams, D. P. (2015). Three lines of personality development: A conceptual history. *European Psychologist, 20*(4), 252–264.

Mehan, H. (1979). *Learning lessons*. Harvard University Press.

Mehta, J. & Fine, S. (2019). *In search of deeper learning: The quest to remake the American high school*. Harvard University Press.

Miller, W. R., & Rollnick, S. (2002). *Motivational interviewing: Preparing people for change* (2nd ed.). Guilford Press.

Morrell, E. (2015). *Critical literacy and urban youth: Pedagogies of access, dissent, and liberation*. Routledge.

Piekut, A. (2019). Narratives in student writer development: Practices and potentials. In E. Krogh & K. S. Jakobsen (Eds.), *Understanding young people's writing development: Identity, disciplinarity, and education* (pp. 121–143). Routledge.

Rymes, B. (2001). *Conversational borderlands: Language and identity in an alternative urban high school*. Teachers College Press.

Schieble, M., Vetter, A., & Martin, K. M. (2020). *Classroom talk for social change: Critical conversations in English language arts*. Teachers College Press.

Shusterman, N., & Shusterman, J. (2019). *Dry*. Simon & Schuster.

Scotland, J. (2020). Using texts which address local issues to create a discursive space within an undergraduate writing course. *Journal of Language, Identity & Education, 19*(4), 260–274. doi:10.1080/15348458.2019.1655425

Seymour, M., Thanos, T., Newell, G. E., & Bloome, D. (2020). *Teaching literature using dialogic literary argumentation*. Routledge.

Thurlow, C. (2007). Fabricating youth: New-media discourse and the technologization of young people. In S. Johnson & A. Ensslin (Eds.), *Language in the media* (pp. 213–233). Continuum.

Tobin, W., & Feit, V. (2020). *Student research for community change: Tools to develop ethical thinking and analytic problem solving*. Teachers College Press.

Van Draanen, W. (2008). *Confessions of a serial kisser*. Knopf.

Williams, B. T. (2017). *Literacy practices and perceptions of agency: Composing identities*. Routledge.

Yagelski, R. P. (2009). A thousand writers writing: Seeking change through the radical practice of writing as a way of being. *English Education, 42*(1), 6–28.

Zittoun, T. (2006). *Transitions: Development through symbolic resources*. Information Age.

Zittoun, T. (2017). Symbolic resources and sense-making in learning and instruction. *European Journal of Psychology and Education, 32*, 1–20.

5
CO-AUTHORING COMMUNITY WORLDS

This chapter describes activities for students studying practices they employ in community worlds of youth organizations/clubs, geographical communities, and environmental communities. These practices include enacting identities and adhering to norms constituting participation in community worlds, as well as critiquing the discourses of race, class, and gender shaping practices in these community worlds. Students can conduct research on issues or problems facing their own communities through identifying reasons for and collecting data on certain issues and problems, leading to making changes in their communities. These practices enhance their sense of agency associated with making change. Students may also employ certain genres, such as use of rap, as well as responding to literature portraying community issues or problems.

The remaining chapters in this book focus on students' participation in different worlds beyond their school worlds, beginning with community worlds.

Of the different worlds discussed in this book, the notion of community worlds is the most amorphous, given different notions of what constitutes a community. While the notion of community is typically associated with participation in neighborhoods, towns, suburbs, cities, states, or countries, later in the chapter, students' reflections on their participation highlight their experience of a sense of community in local face-to-face and online clubs or organizations.

Communities as "Communities of Practice"

Consistent with the notion of "communities of practice" (Lave & Wenger, 1980), students experience a sense of community when they participate in a group of people who share a common sense of *purpose* driving the use of practices in a

DOI: 10.4324/9781003246886-6

community. Members of a community also subscribe to certain *norms* and *discourses*, leading to defining their *identities* as community members, often through their use of *genres* or *media/literature*. For example, they may experience a sense of community by participating with a group of neighbors to lobby for planting more trees in their neighborhood to address the climate crisis. Therefore, participating in and being a part of a community involves social practices for engaging in actions (Peele-Eady & Moje, 2020).

Central to the concept of community is that members of a community or affinity group strive to achieve a common purpose, even though members may not all agree on the practices for achieving that purpose (Peele-Eady & Moje, 2020). For example, they may perceive the need to address racial justice issues in their community related to their perceptions of the disproportionate arrests of Black youth by police and reports of uniformed police officers in their school engaging in problematic relations with Black youth. They may then determine that addressing these issues requires an organized effort associated with creating a community world whose members share the same commitment to achieving a shared goal, even if they do not agree on practices for doing so.

They then need to identify those practices that are most likely to assist them in achieving their purposes. Defining how their practices achieve certain purposes involves determining the norms constituting what they consider to be appropriate legal practices within their community regarding how and why police officers should or should not arrest adolescents.

Communities of practices also revolve around shared literacy practices, what Fisher (2005) describes as "Participatory Literacy Communities" (PLCs), in which students may engage in literacy practices of "spoken word poetry, open mic events, bookstore events, writers' collectives, and book clubs" (p. 117). These PLCs are "organized outside of work and school settings or they are alternative and supplementary spaces for learning. PLCs are *chosen spaces*" (Fisher, 2005, p. 117). In these spaces, adolescents may learn to employ languaging actions through the use of "words rethinking worlds" (Shor, 1992) based on "pushing the boundaries of literacy" (p.118). Engaging in PLCs involves the practice of drawing on popular/ youth culture/media languaging actions, with performance through spoken word/rap (Fisher, 2005).

It is important that adolescents' community practices and practices associated with non-dominant/low-income communities be valued in school worlds, given the assumption that students from non-dominant/low-income communities lack certain academic literacy practices equated to "(white) middle-/upper-class monolingual and monoculture practices and cultural funds of knowledge" (García-Sánchez & Orellana, 2019, p. 11).

Drawing on students' experiences in their community worlds serves as a bridge between school and their communities and challenges these deficit notions of students' practices in community worlds as conflicting with practices valued in school worlds (García-Sánchez & Orellana, 2019). The extent to which community-world practices are valued in school worlds depends on how academic literacy practices are defined in ways that include these practices. For example, students in Black communities acquire intricate literacy practices associated with hip-hop/rap performances that teachers may or may not draw on for creating classroom writing, literary responses, or drama activities.

Communities as Youth Organizations/Clubs

Adolescents acquire practices through participation in community organizations or clubs (Peele-Eady & Moje, 2020):

- YMCA/YWCA, Boy/Girl Scouts, 4-H, etc., as well as their local church/ religious organizations designed to support adolescents (Penuel, 2020). Other organizations include the
- Gay-Straight Alliances (GSAs) designed to provide support for LGBTQ youth (Poteat et al., 2016), including the practice of sharing videos online for educating others about LGBTQ experiences.
- The Futures Project in a Los Angeles high school that provides low-income adolescents working with UCLA faculty to engage in social inquiry projects (Oakes & Rogers, 2006).
- The Padres y Jóvenes Unidos project in Denver that addresses disciplinary practices impacting non-dominant students in Denver schools (Annamma et al., 2019; Penuel, 2020).

Adherence to Shared Norms and Discourses

These organizations/clubs often revolve around adherence to shared *norms* and *discourses* constituting memberships in these organizations/clubs. One example of a community organization is the 4-H organization, with six million nationwide members who subscribe to certain norms and discourses codified by the "Five C's" (caring, character, competence, confidence, and connection) (National 4-H Council, 2019).

Analysis of adolescents' participation in 4-H found relatively high levels of a sense of purpose in life, contributing to drawing on practices from their 4-H experience for use in other aspects of their lives (Burrow et al., 2020). These practices include "getting outside of their day-to-day lives and thinking about how they can give back to others, [which] really kind of drives them and gives them that sense of purpose" (p. 16). One adolescent noted how, in participating in dairy cow judging,

> people think you know it's just about cows, but it's much more than that. You have to be able to problem-[solve]; you have to be able to debate on your feet, and come up with reasons quickly. So you're learning those life

98 Framing of Co-Authoring Practices

> skills, so you're learning those life skills through a topic you're familiar with and are passionate about.
>
> *p. 15*

Another noted the value of their experience in 4-H camps as

> an environment where people encourage each other, and they know if they try something and they don't do a good job that there's so many people who are there to help them and to guide them to be better. And so, they're more likely to try things out of their comfort zone.
>
> *p. 16*

Adolescents also engage in organizations designed to address issues in their community. Nine adolescents in Detroit engaged in a Photovoice project to document instances of racial segregation in their neighborhoods as part of a Michigan Youth Policy Fellows (MYPF) supportive team (Aldana et al., 2016). They acquired methods of taking photos to portray issues of segregation in the Detroit area; for example, portraying disparities between resources in the Detroit schools versus suburban schools. They also discussed issues of race, affirmative actions, and academic disparities between Blacks and Whites. One participant noted to his urban and suburban peers that:

> Even the #1 school in the Detroit Public School district lacks resources. For example, Detroit schools are given new buildings so you will have a new bathroom with no soap or new library with rows of bookcases and no books.
>
> *p. 351*

This led participants to define connections between school funding and neighborhood/regional wealth versus poverty.

They also addressed issues of segregation in both urban and suburban schools, where, even though there was integration in suburban schools, they noted that there was still segregation in the lunchroom or in ability-grouped classes. One Asian-American adolescent noted how she could perceive the disparities between different communities related to income levels, leading her to perceive the need to become more active in addressing these income disparities. At the end of the project, the MYPF team created an art exhibit portraying their photos and writing where they served as tour guides sharing their perceptions of the exhibit with visitors from their community.

Mentoring and support for engaging in community worlds

One major benefit of participation in community worlds is that adolescents also experience mentoring for engaging in pathways for acquiring certain practices.

For example, through the support of the Linked Learning Alliance, *linkedlearning. org*, employers and community organizers provide adolescents from non-dominant communities in California with pathways into organizations and workplaces. The Big Brothers/Big Sisters organizations also provide mentoring to help adolescents acquire practices for interacting with and learning from adults outside their families or schools.

The GripTape, *griptape.org*, project involved adolescents designing their learning activities outside of school (Burrow et al., 2020). Adolescents were provided with financial support to design their own projects based on their particular interests and related to a framework involving having courage and curiosity, engaging in research, working with a community, brainstorming and applying ideas and solutions to address their challenge, and achieving certain results.

Analysis of a 2018 cohort found that adolescents developed positive mindsets and agency through engaging in their projects related to setting goals and reflecting on achieving those goals and perceiving themselves as successful learners outside of school (GripTape, 2019). As one participant noted, "I really care about this project so I go out of my way to talk to people and figure it out … for me it is about going out and getting it for myself" (p. 8).

As part of a course on social change at San Jose State University taught by Scott Myers-Lipton (2018), students acquire a range of practices associated with engaging in organized campaigns to make a change in their communities. Students learn to identify issues that need to be addressed by talking with members of communities regarding their perceptions of problems facing their community.

For taking community action to make a change, students learned about "power over" for counter-acting against individuals or organizations seeking to limit change, resulting in the need to develop their "power over" to challenge those attempted limitations. They also learned about "power with" for working collectively with others to collaboratively share power to make decisions for taking action (Myers-Lipton, 2018, p. 52).

In 2012, when a student in the course was working in an after-school program, she discovered that children in the program were putting snacks in their backpacks to take to their homes. As they shared with her, their parents were not earning enough to purchase food, leading her to propose to Myers-Lipton the need for a campaign to increase the minimum wage in San Jose, resulting in the Campus Alliance for Economic Justice project. Students in the course then conducted research to find that when cities raised their minimum wages low-wage workers could then pay rent or buy food and discovered how that increased spending stimulated the local economy.

As a result of intensive organizing and an effective media campaign, the students convinced the city council to put the issue on the ballot in San Jose. Sixty percent of the voters supported an increase in the minimum wage from $8 to $10 an hour, one of the highest one-time minimum-wage increases in America at that time.

Challenges with Community-based Youth Organizations Related to Purpose

Adolescents may also experience certain challenges in participating in after-school "enrichment"/community-based educational organizations (CBES) designed to provide adolescents from non-dominant families with support for coping with challenges in their lives (Baldridge, 2019, 2020).

One of the challenges with these programs involves how certain *purposes* for these programs shape the nature of participation in them. On the one hand, these programs attempt to assist adolescents with activities that bolster their sense of agency, given the challenges they face in their daily lives shaped by systemic racism and income inequality. Adolescents in these programs often create stronger bonds with the adults running these programs than with their teachers, even though they are often not perceived as functioning as educators (Heathfield & Fusco, 2016; Brion-Meisels et al., 2020).

On the other hand, adult leaders may experience tensions related to the purposes of their programs. Consistent with deficit discourses of adolescence, they may assume that they need to remediate adolescents based on

> a response to the perceived individual and cultural "deficits" of young people instead of emphasizing systemic racism, class subjugation, and other forces of domination. Therefore, these spaces exist as affirming and humanizing spaces of resistance and containers to "fix" minoritized youth.
>
> *Baldridge, 2020, p. 619*

This focus on remediating adolescents in these programs is often framed in terms of larger neoliberal discourses of individualism, choice, competition, and standardization as a means for addressing assumed adolescent "deficits" as opposed to a focus on challenging institutional racism and income inequality (Baldridge, 2019, 2020).

As a result, these programs are often under pressure to function more like schools, based on neoliberal discourses for "remediating" adolescents related to deficit discourses. In her research of one program in the Midwest, Baldridge found that the staff was often frustrated by the lack of a focus on interrogating racial justice or sexism shaping adolescents' lives. They often experienced pressure from administrators of these programs to not focus on these issues, given how such a focus may impact program funding. She identifies this tension as a paradox, given how the programs "have the potential to address issues of racial justice or sexism but can also simultaneously reify deficit narratives that blame youth for their academic and social position within society" (p. 622). As a result, "youth workers too can embody all of these logics and enact contradictory actions through their engagement with youth" (p. 623).

ACTIVITY: CONTEXTUALIZING PRACTICES IN COMMUNITY YOUTH ORGANIZATIONS

Students could discuss or write about their experiences in community youth organizations or clubs based on their practices through participation in these worlds. They could note how they perceived the value of acquiring these practices consistent with the norms operating in an organization and how those practices contributed to achieving certain purposes that they valued; for example, learning how to work collaboratively with other members of the organization. They could also describe how adult brokers or mentors helped them acquire these practices through modeling or providing supportive feedback.

Geographically Based Community Worlds

Adolescents also participate in geographical community worlds of their neighborhood, suburb, town, city, state, or country. It is important to define the meanings of these geographical worlds as involving more than just place or time, in terms of different historical, emotional, spiritual, or intellectual meanings constituting participation in a community world (Peele-Eady & Moje, 2020). For example, members of American society subscribe to certain norms and discourses associated with notions of democracy and individual freedom in ways that differ from beliefs and values operating in a dictatorship.

Students can also engage in critical inquiry about challenges and issues in their local community. One example of such a project is the Sustainable Democracy Project (SDP) located in the Dr. Albizu Campos Puerto Rican High School (PACHS) in Chicago, designed to support students who have dropped out of high school (Schultz, 2017). In this project, students examined reasons for issues in their community, leading to addressing these issues.

In another project, middle-school students employed their writing to describe their emotions related to perceived issues of injustice in their community (Hogan, 2016). Students identified issues of

> feminism and racial discrimination in particular community neighborhoods, prevalence of misinformation regarding immigrant and un(der)documented narratives, school climate/bullying, teacher approaches to sensitive topics (which evolved from a teacher's proud display of a confederate flag), and a need for an LGBTQ alliance at the middle school level.
>
> *Hogan, p. 39*

Students then generated final reports as oral presentations to specific audiences—faculty, coaches, teachers, parents, community leaders, and/or peers.

There is also a need to expand the focus on communities to include global contexts requiring the adoption of "critical global literacy" related to a cosmopolitan understanding of global cultural norms and discourses (Hull & Stornaiuolo, 2014; Yoon et al., 2018). Adopting global, cosmopolitan perspectives involves engaging in "boundary-crossing where an individual deliberately and consciously pushes against society's ideological constraints" (Gutiérrez, 2018, p. 94). Gutiérrez quotes Rogers Hall (Hall & Jurow, 2015) in relation to how challenging traditional boundaries leads to "'consequential learning as the re-organization of people's participation in social practices that allows them to be recognized as competent and valued participants in dynamic and contentious networks of practice' (Personal communication, October 13, 2017)" (p. 25). The fact that students in rural schools may have less exposure to multicultural, global perspectives than in urban schools suggests the value of providing these students with multicultural perspectives through literature or media (Brown, 2021). Having students in a rural school respond to and write about multicultural literature set in global contexts resulted in these students adopting more global perspectives (Brown, 2021).

ACTIVITY: ADDRESSING ISSUES OR CHALLENGES IN GEOGRAPHIC COMMUNITY WORLDS

Students can describe or write about their participation in geographic community worlds by identifying certain issues or challenges facing their local communities and examining ways to address those issues or challenges, ideally with a group of peers. This includes interviewing local residents to ascertain their perspectives on these issues or challenges as well as investigating the barriers to addressing those issues or challenges (Myers-Lipton, 2018). Students may then formulate some possible remedies to present to residents or local officials that may result in a potential change in the status quo. In formulating these remedies, they will include both reasons for taking action and the potential benefits.

For example, I interacted with teachers and students in a middle school to study issues facing an urban neighborhood in St. Paul, Minnesota. These issues included gentrification resulting in residents not being able to afford to live in certain sections of the neighborhood, increases in crime, lack of public spaces for young people to interact with each other safely, etc. Students engaged in field trips to interview neighborhood residents, business owners, and government officials. Students then created presentations, including photos and recordings of interviews for sharing with the school and parents.

Addressing the Climate Crisis in Environmental Worlds

Related to the need to adopt global perspectives (Brown, 2021; Yoon et al., 2018), adolescents perceive themselves as facing a problematic future associated with negative effects of the climate crisis related to increased temperatures, droughts, wildfires, hurricanes, flooding, sea rise, etc. (Beach et al., 2017; *climatechangeela. pbworks.com*).

Adolescents are highly concerned about climate change effects. In a Washington Post-Kaiser survey, six out of seven youth ages 13 to 17 expressed the belief that "human activity is causing climate change;" four out of five called it a "crisis" or "major problem" (Males, 2019). Research on adolescents' brain development suggests that adolescents are more likely to think about long-range innovations necessary to address climate change than older generations.

Youthful thinking across multiple dimensions is better at imagining innovative policies to adapt to future contingencies; elder thinking is suited to resolving the practicalities. That is why elder-dominated media and leaders fixate on the short-range dollars-and-cents costs of change, while the climate-strike youth focus on the long-term price of inaction (Males, 2019, n.p.).

Inspired by Greta Thunberg, a Swedish adolescent who had assumed a leadership role in addressing climate change, adolescents engage in youth organizations focused on fostering sustainability practices in their school or community. They also engage in political actions to push for changes in policies regarding energy production, transportation, urban design, agriculture, etc. (For examples of activities, see *http://t.ly/tSvY*.) For example, adolescents organized the Zero Hour organization *thisiszerohour.org*, the Sunrise Movement, *www.sunrisemovement.org*, and Our Climate, *ourclimate.us*, to actively lobby for changes in local and national policies related to climate change.

Adolescents also participated in "global climate strikes" in 2019 and 2020 (*globalclimatestrike.net*). A portrait of an 18-year-old leader of the Zero Hour organization portrayed how she devotes her time to organizing protests or meeting with politicians (Jarvis, 2020). Educators and students organized Schools for Climate Action, *schoolsforclimateaction.weebly.com*, to teach and organize lobbying at the local and national levels. Students in St. Louis Park High School formed a club focused on climate change issues to then create a report card in which they graded their local city government on addressing different environmental/sustainability issues and then presented that report card to their city council for their responses.

One example of an internship program related to participation in environmental worlds is the Urban Explorers project (Bang et al., 2009). Participants adopted the perspective of Indigenous community members that related to perceiving plants, animals, the land, and humans as synonymous with their discourses, as opposed to a traditional Western science perspective that may not perceive these components as synonymous (Penuel, 2019). Students also contributed their writing of narratives, poetry, and essays to the book *Writers on Earth* (*writetheworld.com/writers_on_earth*).

Adolescents engaged in the Educational Video Center organization, *evc.org*, for young people in New York City created a documentary about lead poisoning and toxic mold in New York City's 400,000-resident public housing system (Goodman, 2020). The documentary portrays one of the adolescents, whose asthma was caused by the "silent killers" in her family's living environment.

Adolescents in an after-school job-training program created a documentary, Green Grease Guzzlers (*t.ly/FxDs*), about the conversion of a small diesel bus to use cooking oil for fuel, which then became a mobile media center to show videos at outdoor events (Corwin, 2020).

Adolescents in Oakland, California created technology platforms to address issues of health, access to food, and environmental justice in low-income neighborhoods in the city (Akom et al., 2016). They participated in visiting and analyzing 30 retail food/liquor outlets to map and identify the nature of the food options available in these outlets as well as collect notes and images of these outlets.

Given that they found a lack of healthy food options in these neighborhoods, they recommended that these store outlets stock more organic/locally grown fresh produce at affordable prices and that farmers' markets be located and advertised in or near these neighborhoods.

ACTIVITY: CONTEXTUALIZING PRACTICES IN ENVIRONMENTAL WORLDS

Students could discuss or write about participation in organized efforts related to addressing and taking action on environmental justice and climate change effects (for examples, see *t.ly/XT84*). They could read reports or cli-fi literature portraying climate change effects and discuss or write about their direct experience with droughts, fires, heat due to rise in temperatures, hurricanes, sea rise, extreme weather events, etc.

They could also note how they participated in local efforts to engage in recycling, reduced meat consumption, reduction of energy use, use of public transportation, etc. They could also advocate for changes in larger systems related to a shift from fossil fuel to clean energy production, transportation, housing/building design to reduce heat emission, agriculture, urban planning, health care, legal/political organizations, etc. For example, they could study issues of location of fossil-fuel plants in low-income neighborhoods related to the effects of emissions on health issues in those neighborhoods or the design of streets in their towns or cities related to the need to reduce traffic, encourage the use of bicycles/walking, and planting of trees.

Enacting Identity Practices in Community Worlds

Adolescents also construct their *identities* as community members through employing practices valued in certain communities; for example, the use of "insider language," clothing/apparel, physical actions, etc., that mark their membership in a community. For example, a group of Latinx adolescents living in Detroit identified with their local Detroit community through wearing "a Detroit Tigers baseball cap in red, white, and green, and remarking, as one young man did, 'It's like it's both parts of us. We are from Mexico, but we are also from Detroit.'" (Peele-Eady & Moje, 2020, p. 232).

Adolescents enact identities through their languaging related to uses of regional dialects or language constituting membership in community worlds. Two White adolescent females adhered to discourses constituted by the use of "Appalachian English" in a rural Appalachia high school as contrasted with formal, standard English (Slocum, 2019). One of the two students, Chayla, embraced the fact that she employed "country" speech versus "proper" or "city" speech for enacting an identity in resistance to school norms. She also interacted with another student, Tracy, who was new to the school, regarding adopting "country" speech to enact peer relations in a manner that served to critique *norms* and *discourses* associated with valuing "proper English" in the school world.

In an interview, Chayla noted that "'People here talk about the way I talk. I like the way I talk. So, I'm mean, I guess I take on that [stereotype]. Or, like, we're the redneck, and stuff, but I mean, I embrace it!'" (Slocum, 2019, p. 290). Tracy, as an outsider, perceived how the school norms and discourses around "proper" speech undermined her peers' sense of agency. "'A lot of kids in there I know aren't going to college because they feel like they can't. And they just don't try. So, I think it has a lot to do with growing up here.'" (p. 292).

ACTIVITY: REFLECTING ON LANGUAGING FOR CONSTITUTING COMMUNITY IDENTITIES

Students could describe or write about how their use of certain language or dialects serves to define their identification with certain geographical communities; for example, their use of African-American Vernacular English (AAVE) as residents of a Black neighborhood, or use of Spanglish as members of a Latinx community. Students could then reflect on how they learn to vary their use of language or dialects across different social and cultural contexts; for example, learning to employ standard English in their school classes, while using alternative language or dialects in their peer group or family worlds.

106 Framing of Co-Authoring Practices

Using Ethnographic Research to Study Issues in Community Worlds

Teachers can also collaborate with students in conducting ethnographic studies of issues and practices in their local communities, as did Ms. E's students through their "mini-ethnography" projects described in Chapter 4.

Students could identify issues facing their local communities by interviewing or conducting surveys of residents. For example, residents may perceive a need for more public mass transit in their community, given the need to reduce dependency on car transportation to lower emissions. They can then determine the extent to which residents actually use mass transit and whether they would use it given the increased availability of mass transit. They could also interview local authorities regarding policies on mass transit and potential funding for increased mass transit.

Students could then import what they learned as funds of knowledge about their communities into the classroom (Moll & González, 2004). Teachers and students in an Australian school engaged in projects involving studying the uses of different languages and the use of multimodal communication employed in the school through recording findings in language diaries and conducting recorded interviews (D'warte, 2019). Students created maps to portray different languages for "drawing and labeling the ways they were reading, writing, talking, listening, and viewing with different people in different places in their everyday worlds" (p. 224). As one student noted:

> My friends and I learned more about our language and we talked about what we do; we change it up all the time. It (mapping) gets you to draw and talk about your language and it feels kind of interesting because it feels like that people want to know about you and your language and stuff. It made me think about what I do and how I can think about this more when I have to do English work.
>
> *p. 224*

Through engaging in this collaborative research, teachers acquired new insights into their students' languages, leading to their recognition of the limitation of "abstract or fixed versions of the linguistic and culturally situated practices of communities" (p. 226). Teachers then focused on "transcultural and translingual competencies [that] were foregrounded in lessons examining how language and literacies worked and shifted across and around practices, communities and countries and worked to achieve a widening range of purposes for a variety of audiences" (p. 226).

Students may research examples of other similar efforts in communities to address other issues to reach out to some teachers or community members who share their concerns about these issues, based on adopting a culturally sustaining instructional perspective (Paris & Alim, 2017). To address the issue of arrest rates in their community, they may interview any peers who may have been arrested...

They may then gather some relevant data regarding arrest rates, regarding the nature and reasons for their arrests, and collect any video portrayals of such arrests. Based on their findings, they may then generate a report to share with their school's administration/school board and their city council.

Students Gaining Agency through Participation in Community Projects

Through their participation in these projects, adolescents experience an enhanced sense of agency related to their ability to address and make change in their communities. In a drama program in New York City, Public Works (*http://t.ly/dPZq*), adolescents acquired acting practices from mentor actors, resulting in performing in a musical version of a Greek myth or a Shakespeare play in Central Park during the summer (Heath et al., 2019). Through participation in this project, they gained a sense of agency and self-efficacy given that

> they had never before been needed nor had they been so persistently and generously offered help in getting to where they needed to be. For many participants, rehearsals marked the first time in their lives that they knew someone cared where they were because they were needed elsewhere for good reasons. Thus, regular on-time appearances became the norm for participants.... They now realized they were developing positive social and conversational skills centered on the here and now and the future and no longer on their failures of the past. [This led to] acceptance of an "I can do this" attitude leading them to take classes in other fields, seek job training, and apply with confidence for jobs.
>
> *pp. 255–256*

Analysis of the project found that participants adhered to the following learning principles:

- Adults and youth work side by side toward developing, creating, and assessing projects and performances.
- Talk consistently circles around interpretation of trends and patterns and the need to see challenges as learning opportunities.
- On-going work, day by day, must always lead to an annual public performance, exhibition, or outcome reviewed by external critics.
- Sites of learning must exist across years and be operated by personnel who have a steady presence and the capacity to recruit external supporters and promoters.
- No one is rejected from participation except those who would, for one reason or another, present a threat to others engaged in the enterprise.
- Acceptance among creators, young and old, of strengths and challenges of all participants is a given basis for co-existence, as is recognition of different talents, energies, and ways of facing the world. (Landay & Heath, 2021, pp. 105–106).

108 Framing of Co-Authoring Practices

Six adolescents identified as The Chicago Youth Fulfillment Demonstrators (CYFD) engaged in a project examining how housing instability shaped homeless members of a drop-in center in a Chicago church, leading to their creating a report to share with the drop-in central staff (Aviles & Grigalunas, 2018). Users of the center experienced being turned away when the center was "at capacity," resulting in issues concerning their safety when they had to roam the local neighborhood before they had access to the center. The six adolescents became highly engaged in their research, as evident in one member creating

> a Facebook page to share information she was uncovering through her research to raise awareness and understanding among her Facebook network. Towards the end of the workshops, another female youth, who had exhibited much curiosity about the educational process of obtaining her GED and/or high school diploma, made the decision to enroll in an alternative high school diploma program.
>
> *p. 234*

Adolescents with migrant farmworker family backgrounds participated in the Migrant Student Leadership Institute (MSLI) in Los Angeles (Gutiérrez, 2018). As part of that project, adolescents created written statements that they performed orally to their peers, instructors, and counselors regarding their experiences as migrants/immigrants within the larger context of participation in their communities and families.

In a project as part of a drama program at Central High School in St. Paul, Minnesota, students create their own original plays based on researching issues of social justice associated with race, class, and gender (Landay & Heath, 2021; Mandell & Wolf, 2003). They then perform their plays for their school and/or community to share their portrayals of these issues, leading to peers or community members addressing these issues.

ACTIVITY: CONDUCTING STUDIES OF COMMUNITY WORLDS

Students can conduct studies of their participation in community worlds based on practices of identifying specific issues that need to be addressed and reasons for these issues, posing research questions, determining relevant research methods, gathering and analyzing information and data, and generating results. As illustrated in Limarys Caraballo's Chapter 6, in conducting these studies, students need to consider interacting with a range of participants to acquire alternative perspectives on an issue. They may also

> examine how their own membership or allegiance to a particular neighborhood, town, suburb, or community and a community organization serves to define their identities related to certain norms or discourses associated with a community.

Drawing on Community Genre Practices for Use in School Worlds

Based on the notion of "cultural modeling," Carol Lee (2006) draws on African-American students' use of *genres* such as raps valued in their peer group/neighborhood communities for teaching the use of metaphoric language in literary texts. Students in communities with multiple languages engage in the genre of translating language for their parents (Reynolds & Orellana, 2019). Students may also reflect on how their practices in their community worlds contribute to learning in their school worlds (Lee et al., 2020). Building on their practices in their community worlds assumes "that learning happens everywhere, every day—not just in school—[and] can go a long way toward countering 'deficit' ideas about non-dominant communities" (García-Sánchez & Orellana, 2019, p. 19).

In one classroom functioning as a PLC, a teacher, Joe, drew on students' experiences of rap/hip-hop genres from their local community to engage students in spoken word performances (Fisher, 2005). Students were engaged with their classroom performances as well as "listening for the words that incite and inspire" (p. 128). In this classroom,

> literacy was a practice; for example, the "read and feed" system in Joe's class depends on everyone making contributions by a) sharing their writing and b) actively listening in order to give constructive feedback to other members of the community.
>
> *p. 128*

Students can assume leadership roles related to addressing issues in their school associated with transferring their participation in larger issues in their community to their school world. Alex Miles, a Black senior at Twin Cities Academy, assumed an active role in the school's Racial Justice Club. Members of the club discussed the racial disparities in the school administrator's disproportionate disciplinary treatment of Black versus White students, including an incident in which he was suspended for adopting a "'a threatening pose.'" (Cruzen, 2020). He then organized a school walkout in 2017 and met with local law enforcement and city representatives regarding policies impacting local Black people. At an event in which he received an award for his work, Alex noted that "'For a long time, we've been misunderstood in this country. And we've just got to practice loving each other.'" (n.p.).

110 Framing of Co-Authoring Practices

Teachers and students also employ genres as problem-solving activities to identify issues and challenges facing their community; for example, youth violence, public transportation, unemployment, sexually transmitted diseases, etc. Teachers then contact local community organizations who provide students with information about their issue or challenge and serve as mentors to assist students. For example, one project involved the issue of food deserts in their community related to the lack of fresh/nutritious food. The school's assistant principal worked in the local Puerto Rican Cultural Center (PRCC) to invite the students to address this issue. They were concerned that "'part of the issue of a food desert is that there's an overabundance of high-fat and high-calorie food, but that's very low in nutrition … because this leads to obesity'" (Schultz, 2017, p. 77). The assistant principal also had students grow vegetables in gardens and a greenhouse that serve as a basis for sofrito, a basic Puerto Rican food, leading students to participate in the project.

Students in the project also created online portfolios (SDP's) to document their learning for both community members and their teachers (Schultz, 2017). The use of portfolios did itself serve as a challenge, given how, as one teacher noted,

> The rubric I use was an ever-changing debate among community partners, staff, and myself. Everyone had an opinion, and I had to figure out what was the best for the students and me, and keep it in line with the history of PACHS. Many times, I doubted myself and my efforts because the SDP does not lend itself to immediate, quantifiable results of student improvement.
>
> *Schultz, 2017, p. 83*

This teacher's concern with assessment again reflects the issue in school worlds related to the larger tension of a neoliberal discourse of accountability for "achievement" versus fostering meaningful learning experiences for students.

Students experience various practices within and across school and community worlds that limit or support their development of their identities based on employing practices leading to their success in school (Wortham & Reyes, 2015).

ACTIVITY: EMPLOYING GENRES FOR ENGAGING IN CRITICAL INQUIRY ABOUT FIGURED WORLDS

Students could identify a particular problem or issue facing their community to then employ discussion or research genres described in Chapter 2 to engage in critical-inquiry research to investigate ways to address these problems or issues; for example, higher temperatures in their low-income neighborhoods due to lack of trees, and traffic leading to adverse health effects. Based on their investigations, they could then generate some solutions to addressing these problems or issues; for example, planting more trees and reducing traffic in their neighborhoods.

Employing and Critiquing Media/Literature Related to Community Worlds

As previously noted, "Participatory Literacy Communities" (PLCs) support students' performance of their writing to achieve positive uptake from audiences, enhancing their sense of competence (Fisher, 2005). These PLCs are "organized outside of work and school settings or they are alternative and supplementary spaces for learning." Through their performances, students are not only engaging their audiences, but they are also using their performances to envision imagined community worlds, for example, performing a poem portraying future community with reduced carbon emissions in ways that improves their community members' health.

Students could examine how media/literature represent community worlds based on portrayals of the *discourses* shaping practices in those worlds. For example, the notion of Manifest Destiny, formulated in the 1840s, posited the notion that White Americans should expand westward to assume control of the Western territories through the removal of Native Americans. This discourse of Manifest Destiny was portrayed in Daniel Boone or Davy Crockett stories and Western/cowboy Hollywood movies based on religious, moral, and capitalist discourses justifying this westward expansion (Slotkin, 1973). It also ignored the need to preserve natural resources such as rivers and lakes, leading to the current issues with lack of water in the entire Western region.

The Facing History and Ourselves Project, *www.facinghistory.org*, involves students in critically examining historical events to explore how perceptions of and narratives about those events shape their current community worlds. Students in Tanya Hodge's tenth grade Humanities class at South High School, Minneapolis, engaged in a unit on "What is the United States of America's Story?" (Hodge, 2019), in which they were asked to address two of the following questions:

- What does it mean to be American Me?
- How does one define one's self within the larger expectations of society?
- How does culture shape the lens through which we view our society?
- How do American literature and history help to define our view of the United States today?
- What are the ways that people are truly free in the United States? What are the ways in which people are prisoners? (Beach & Beauchemin, 2019, p. 134).

In this unit, students address these questions through responding to texts such as "The Danger of a Single Story" (Adiche, 2009). Students then need to critique how narratives such as those reflecting the Manifest Destiny control of the West have negative consequences. Students then recognize how stories enact power, given how Adiche "did not have a single story of America" (Hodge, 2019, p. 10),

112 Framing of Co-Authoring Practices

leading to the realization that "we realize that there is never a single story about any place." (p. 10).

They also read excerpts from numerous texts, including *There There* (Orange, 2018), about Native Americans in the Bay Area and Abraham Rodriquez's (1992) *The Boy Without a Flag: Tales of the South Bronx*. They also read Jose Angel Villablongo's (1992) poem "In the Good Old U.S.A.," which ends with "'Today, I am no longer ashamed./I am proud of being Afro-Puerto Rican./I am proud of my heritage, my language/my brillo hair, and my name'" (p. 328). Students then created their own live performance or video spoken-word poem enacting their own community world identity based on these readings.

Students could also critique how local news broadcasts often portray urban communities as crime-ridden as a means of engaging audiences through drama- tizing events for a larger suburban audience (Gorski, 2013). One analysis of media representations of Black males found that a prevailing portrayal connected Black males with social problems of poverty, criminality, and unemployment, with only limited positive representations related to sports, music, and physical achievement (The Opportunity Agenda, 2011).

Given how they are often portrayed in the media in deficit ways, Black and Latinx adolescents employed arts to address the issue of gentrification of their urban neighborhood resulting in evictions of low-income families of color and increased police harassment (Wright, 2020). The adolescents created theater productions based on their analysis of these issues to share their own personal experiences of coping with these issues; for example, their experience of being frisked by police. They also collected data to determine that security guards had expelled one-third of adolescents from a new local shopping mall and public park.

Participants engaged in creating a "real skit" portraying an experience with injustice in which police stopped them on their way to school (Wright, 2020). They then enacted in an "ideal skit," in which they portrayed an imagined alter- native just world. In that world, a police officer engages in a friendly, supportive conversation in which he tells them that he won't ask them for their ID and that his role is to provide protection.

Students could also examine how narratives represent and reflect the discourses and social genres constituting identities in community worlds (Mirra, 2020). In her ethnographic analysis of conservative people in Southwest Louisiana who had lost jobs in the fossil-fuel industry and, as a result, held low-income jobs, Hochschild (2020) identified how people adopted a "right-wing deep story" that positions them as

> waiting in line for the American dream that you feel you very much deserve. It's like waiting in a pilgrimage, and the line isn't moving. Your feet are tired. You feel you are properly deserving of this reward that's ahead. And the idea is, you don't begrudge anyone in this right deep story. You're not a hateful person. But then you see—the second moment of the right-wing

deep story—somebody cutting ahead of you. Why are they getting special treatment?

n.p.

These "deep stories" reflect discourses associated with "what you feel about a highly salient situation that's very important to you. You take facts out of the deep story. You take moral precepts out of the deep story. It's what feels true … They're dreamlike and are told through metaphor" (Hochschild, 2020, n.p.).

ACTIVITY: CRITIQUING MEDIA/LITERATURE REPRESENTATIONS OF COMMUNITY WORLDS

Students could critique how media/literature represent their community worlds (see also activities in Chapter 12 on media representations of worlds). They could critique how television news often highlights incidents of crime associated with urban neighborhoods based on an implied cause-and-effect relationship between those neighborhoods and crime. They may also examine shared narratives of the history of key events in their communities; for example, narratives of how their neighborhood has coped with a high number of shootings or issues of the decline in housing values or lack of employment in their neighborhoods. They may also create narratives of positive examples of development or growth in their neighborhoods through members participating in neighborhood development projects.

Summary

This chapter described activities for students studying practices they employ in community worlds of youth organizations/clubs, geographical communities, and environmental communities. These practices include enacting identities and adhering to norms constituting participation in community worlds and critiquing the discourses of race, class, and gender shaping practices in these worlds.

By conducting YPAR and ethnographic research on issues in these worlds, students understand these practices associated with their participation in their own worlds (Marciano & Warren, 2018). In Chapter 6, Limarys Caraballo describes specific examples of adolescents engaged in YPAR projects for studying their community and school worlds.

References

Adichie, C. N. (2009, July). *The danger of a single story* [Video]. Ted Conferences. Retrieved from http://t.ly/xXuS

114 Framing of Co-Authoring Practices

Akom, A., Shah, A., Nakai, A., & Cruz, T. (2016). Youth Participatory Action Research (YPAR) 2.0: How technological innovation and digital organizing sparked a food revolution in East Oakland. *International Journal of Qualitative Studies in Education, 29*(10), 1287–1307. doi:10.1080/09518398.2016.1201609

Aldana, A., Richards-Schuster, K., & Checkoway, B. (2016) Dialogic pedagogy for youth participatory action research: facilitation of an intergroup empowerment. *Social Work with Groups, 39*(4), 339–358. doi:10.1080/01609513.2015.1076370

Annamma, S. A., Anyon, Y., Joseph, N. M., Downing, B., & Simmons, J. (2019). Black girls and school discipline: The complexities of being overrepresented and under studied. *Urban Education, 54*(2), 211–242.

Aviles, A. M., & Grigalunas, N. (2018). "Project awareness": Fostering social justice youth development to counter youth experiences of housing instability, trauma and injustice. *Children and Youth Services Review, 84*, 229–238.

Baldridge, B. J. (2019). *Reclaiming community: Race and the uncertain future of youth work.* Stanford University Press.

Baldridge, B. J. (2020). The youthwork paradox: A case for studying the complexity of community-based youth work in education research. *Educational Researcher, 49*(8), 618–625.

Bang, M., Medin, D., & Cajete, G. (2009). Improving science education for Native students: Teaching place through community. *SACNAS, 12*(1), 8–10.

Beach, R., & Beauchemin, F. (2019). *Teaching language as action in the ELA classroom.* Routledge.

Beach, R., Share, J., & Webb, A. (2017). *Teaching climate change to adolescents: Reading, writing, and making a difference.* Routledge.

Brion-Meisels, G., Fei, J. T. & Vasudevan, D. S. (Eds.). (2020). *Building youth-adult partnerships in out-of-school time settings.* Information Age Publishers.

Brown, A. (2021). *A mixed methods approach to initiating a critical global literacy curriculum in the rural high school English/language arts classroom.* [Unpublished Doctoral dissertation]. Saint John's University.

Burrow, A. L., Ratner, K., Porcelli, S., & Sumner, R. (2020). Does purpose grow here? Exploring 4-H as a context for cultivating youth purpose. *Journal of Adolescent Research*, 1–30. doi:10.1177/0743558420942477

Corwin, J. (2020). Green Guerrillas Youth Media Tech Collective: Sustainable storytellers challenging the status quo. *Journal of Sustainability Education, 23*. Retrieved from http:t.ly/9UBU

Cruzen, I. (2020, December 31). After witnessing growing racial tensions, Twin Cities Academy senior got to work to make things better. *Minneapolis StarTribune*. [Weblog post]. Retrieved from http://t.ly/1BHX

D'warte, J. (2019). Exploring, thinking, and learning about languages and literacies with young people in super-diverse Australian classrooms. In I. M. García-Sánchez & M. F. Orellana (Eds.), *Language and cultural practices in communities and schools: Bridging learning for students from non-dominant groups* (pp. 213–230). Routledge.

Fisher, M. T. (2005). From the coffee house to the school house: The promise and potential of spoken word poetry in school contexts. *English Education, 37*(2), 115–131.

García-Sánchez, I. M., & Orellana, M. F. (2019). Introduction: Everyday learning: Centering in schools the language and cultural practices of young people from non-dominant groups. In I. M. García-Sánchez & M. F. Orellana (Eds.), *Language and cultural practices in communities and schools: Bridging learning for students from non-dominant groups* (pp. 1–24). Routledge.

Goodman, S. (2020). Teaching for environmental justice at the Educational Video Center. *Journal of Sustainability Education, 23*. Retrieved from http://t.ly/iMxD

Gorski, P. C. (2013). *Reaching and teaching students in poverty: Strategies for erasing the opportunity gap.* Teachers College Press.

GripTape. (2019). *GripTape: Youth-driven learning: Summary of findings: Learning Cycle III.* Retrieved from http://t.ly/BxlH

Gutiérrez, K. D. (2018). Social design-based experiments: A proleptic approach to literacy. *Literacy Research: Theory, Method, and Practice, 67*, 86–108.

Hall, R., & Jurow, A. S. (2015). Changing concepts in activity: Descriptive and design studies of consequential learning in conceptual practices. *Educational Psychologist, 50*(3), 73–189, doi:10.1080/00461520.2015.1075403

Heath, S., Bellino, M. J., & Winn, M. (2019). Adaptive learning across the life span. In N. S. Nasir, C. D. Lee, R. Pea, & M. K. de Royston (Eds.), *Handbook of the cultural foundations of learning* (pp. 247–260). Routledge.

Heathfield, M., & Fusco, D. (Eds.). (2016). *Youth and inequality in education: Global actions in youth work.* Routledge.

Hochschild, A. R. (2020, October 18). The deep stories of our time. [Podcast]. In *On Being with Krista Tippett*. Retrieved from http://t.ly/tHw3

Hodge, T. (2019). *What is the United States of America's story? Humanities 2 unit.* South High School.

Hogan, J. J. (2016). Troubling a "cultured hell": Empowering adolescent voices through youth participatory action research. *Voices from the Middle, 24*(2), 39–41.

Hull, G. A. & Stornaiuolo, A. (2014). Cosmopolitan literacies, social networks, and "proper distance": Striving to understand in a global world. *Curriculum Inquiry, 44*(1), 15–44.

Jarvis, B. (2020, July 21). The teenagers at the end of the world. *The New York Times Magazine.* Retrieved from http://t.ly/at2A

Landay, E., & Heath, S. B. (2021). Hard-won joy: Equity through collaboration. *Theory Into Practice, 60*(1), 103–112.

Lave, J. & Wenger, M. (1980). *Situated learning: Legitimate peripheral participation.* Cambridge University Press.

Lee, C. D. (2006). "Every good-bye ain't gone": Analyzing the cultural underpinnings of classroom talk. *International Journal of Qualitative Studies in Education, 19*(3), 305–327.

Lee, C. D., Nasir, N. S., Pea, R., & de Royston, M. M. (2020). Reconceptualizing learning: A critical task for knowledge-building and teaching. In N. S. Nasir, C. D. Lee, R. Pea, & M. K. de Royston (Eds.), *Handbook of the cultural foundations of learning* (p. xvii). Taylor & Francis.

Males, M. (2019, December 18). How youth have changed the climate movement. *YES! Media.* Retrieved from http://t.ly/4NNw

Mandell, J., & Wolf, J. (2003). *Acting, learning, and change: Creating original plays with adolescents.* Heinemann.

Marciano, J. E., & Warren, C. A. (2018). Writing toward change across youth participatory action research projects. *Journal of Adolescent & Adult Literacy, 62*(5), 485–494. doi:10.1002/jaal.921

Mirra, N. (2020). A quality of imagination: Young people show us "what's next" in ELA. *Voices from the Middle, 27*(4), 9–11.

Moll, L. C., & González, N. (2004). Engaging life: A funds of knowledge approach to multicultural education. In J. Banks & C. McGee Banks (Eds.), *Handbook of research on multicultural education* (2nd ed.). (pp. 699–715). Jossey-Bass.

Myers-Lipton, S. (2018). *CHANGE! A student guide to social action.* Routledge.

116 Framing of Co-Authoring Practices

National 4-H Council. (2019). Grow true leaders campaign media resource center. https:// 4-h.org/about/leadership/national-4-h-council/

Oakes, J., & Rogers, J. (2006). *Learning power: Organizing for education and justice*. Teachers College Press.

Orange, T. (2018). *There there: A novel*. Knopf.

Paris, D., & Alim, H. S. (2017). What is culturally sustaining pedagogy and what does it matter? In D. Paris & H. S. Alim (Eds.), *Culturally sustaining pedagogies: Teaching and learning for justice in a changing world*. (pp. 1–21). Teachers College Press.

Peele-Eady, T. B., & Moje, E. B. (2020). Communities as context for learning. In N. S. Nasir, C. D. Lee, R. Pea, & M. K. de Royston (Eds.), *Handbook of the cultural foundations of learning* (pp. 230–247). Routledge.

Penuel, W. R. (2020). Promoting equitable and just learning across settings: Organizational forms for educational change. In N. S. Nasir, C. D. Lee, R. Pea, & M. M. de Royston (Eds.), *Handbook of cultural foundations of learning* (pp. 348–364). Routledge.

Poteat, V. P., Calzo, J. P., & Yoshikawa, H. (2016). Promoting youth agency through dimensions of gay–straight alliance involvement and conditions that maximize associations. *Journal of Youth and Adolescence, 45*(7), 1438–1451.

Reynolds, J. F., & Orellana, M. F. (2009). New immigrant youth interpreting in white public space. *American Anthropologist, 111*(2), 211–223. doi:10.1111/j.1548-1433.2009.01114.x

Rodriguez, A. (1992). *The boy without a flag: Tales of the South Bronx*. Milkweed.

Rose, M., & Baumgartner, F. R. (2013). Framing the poor: Media coverage and U.S. poverty policy, 1960-2008. *Policy Studies Journal 41*(1), 22–53.

Schultz, B. D. (2017). *Teaching in the cracks: Openings and opportunities for student-centered action-focused curriculum*. Teachers College Press.

Shor, I. (1992). *Empowering education: Critical teaching for social change*. University of Chicago Press.

Slocum, A. (2019). Exploring identity through literature and language: Adolescents' identity positioning in rural Appalachia. *Journal of Language, Identity & Education, 18*(5), 283–296. doi:10.1080/15348458.2019.1612749

Slotkin, R. (1973). *Regeneration through violence: The mythology of the American frontier 1600–1860*. Wesleyan University Press.

The Opportunity Agenda. (2011). Media representations and impact on the lives of black men and boys. Retrieved from http://t.ly/5qel

Villablongo, J. A. (1992). In the good old U.S.A. In M. M. Gillan & J. Gillan (Eds.), *Unsettling America: An anthology of contemporary multicultural poetry* (p. 328). Penguin Books, 1994.

Wortham, S., & Reyes, A. (2015). Discourse analysis beyond the speech event. Routledge.

Wright, D. E. (2020). Imagining a more just world: Critical arts pedagogy and youth participatory action research. *International Journal of Qualitative Studies in Education, 33*(1), 32–49, doi:10.1080/09518398.2019.1678784

Yoon, B., Yol, O., Haag, C. Simpson, A. (2018). Critical global literacies: A new instructional framework in the global era. *Journal of Adolescent and Adult Literacy, 62*(3), 205–214.

PART II

Students Co-Authoring Different Figured Worlds

6

YPAR AS FIGURED WORLD

Co-Authoring Identities, Literacies, and Activism

Limarys Caraballo

This chapter describes adolescents' use of practices through participation in the Youth Participatory Action Research (YPAR) Cyphers for Justice project as itself a figured world for studying issues and problems facing their schools and communities. Through use of these practices, such as formulating questions and collecting/analyzing data, adolescents acquired a sense of purpose related to assuming identities associated with collaboratively making change as well as learning to critique discourses constituting practices in their schools and communities. They also learned to employ genres such as hip-hop/spoken-word poetry for portraying their perceptions of worlds and benefitted from interactions with adult mentors and peers for collaboratively conducting their research in ways that apply to learning in all of their worlds.

> I am certainly thankful for YPAR.... With this research, I was able to find out more about myself and why I started denying my culture at a young age—but this research process also made me more appreciative of my culture and my roots.
>
> *Michaela, group reflection, May 2016*

In this chapter, I discuss the purposes and practices that guide and sustain co-authored youth worlds centered in research, art, and activism, in which youth construct identities as agents of change as they engage in critical social action in their communities. While academic conventions typically characterize students as achievers based on standardized test scores and the internalization of the dominant academic knowledge and conventions implicit in the curriculum, this chapter documents after-school and community spaces, such as the YPAR program described below, as co-authored worlds. I draw from my previously published

DOI: 10.4324/9781003246886-8

research on identities-in-practice and recent co-authored work on the Cyphers for Justice (CFJ) program. In CFJ, students engage in arts and activism via social action, youth culture, and participatory research, to demonstrate how youth experience more expansive opportunities to explore important languaging actions and relations (Caraballo & Lyiscott, 2018; Caraballo, 2016; Caraballo & Filipiak, 2021). Informed by a conceptualization of identities as constructed in figured worlds, I describe how YPAR engagements, often situated in co-curricular figured worlds, can inform how educators and students conceptualize their relations in classroom contexts.

Youth-Engaged Spaces as Co-Curricular Figured Worlds

Classrooms and schools are inherently evaluative contexts (Jackson, 1994), particularly amidst increasing standardization and accountability. A classroom may be examined as a figured world in which discourses of achievement (i.e., normalized expectations about how to "be" a high-achieving student) become more overt. Students are characterized as achievers when they pass standardized tests, learn "mainstream academic knowledge" (Banks, 1993), and master the dominant "culture of power" (Delpit, 2006) implicit in the enacted curriculum—the curriculum jointly created by students and teachers during instruction (Snyder et al., 1992).

Beyond the explicit curriculum, the "official" course of study (Britzman, 1989; Eisner, 1985), the enacted curriculum is what students and teachers experience in the classroom as a figured world of achievement, in which discourses produce and regulate certain behaviors as acceptable and unacceptable. Discourses also "create 'social positions' (perspectives) from which students are 'invited' (summoned) to speak, listen, act, read and write, think, feel, believe, and value in certain characteristic, historically recognizable ways, combined with their styles and creativity" (Gee, 1996, p. 128). In other words, these discourses, or ways of conceptualizing achievement in education, inform how students position themselves and interact with, resist, and respond in their academic environments.

The figured world is also the dynamic and discursive context in which students construct multiple identities among and across multiple axes of differentiation (e.g., race, ethnicity, gender, class, ability, etc., as in Braidotti, 1994). Among various interrelated identities-in-practice (Caraballo, 2011), youth's experiences as students factor significantly into constructing and negotiating their multiple identities. As a collaborative space that disrupts typical power relations between youth and adults, and between educators and learners, a figured world could be described according to Homi Bhabha's (1994) notion of the *third space*, which he theorizes to be a hybrid temporal space, a "liminal moment of identification" (p. 185). For Bhabha, the "third space is the space of hybridity itself" (Fahlander, 2007, p. 23), where identities are re/negotiated and interrogated; we conceptualize the YPAR seminar as a third space of "agency that negotiates its own authority" (p. 185). Bhabha's temporal and liminal concept of the third space offers a theoretical basis for a kind of hybrid space in which multiple identities and literacies as researchers, educators, and students might be re-negotiated.

This chapter highlights this type of intentional space, underscoring the identities, literacies, and languaging actions that the participants constructed in a unique YPAR context. Youth and adult allies were all apprenticed into new roles in relation to their chosen action research projects. As educators, researchers, graduate students, and teaching artists in the program, we referred to ourselves as *adult allies* in order to acknowledge the power relations between "adults" and "youth." These power relations can never be completely erased, but, by positioning ourselves deliberately as allies rather than "teachers," we named our desire to de-center traditional dynamics between educators and learners. YPAR disrupts dominant understandings of who gets to identify and "practice" being an educator, learner, knower, and/or agent of change. These understandings allow the possibility of a collaborative space where the co-construction of critical knowledges and pedagogies of pluralism (Morrell, 2008) blurs (though never eliminates) some of the boundaries of agency and identity between students, teachers, researchers, and participants.

YPAR as a Figured World

One of the earliest studies to document Participatory Action Research (PAR) with youth argues for the power of "engaging in a process that positions youth as agents of inquiry and as 'experts' about their own lives" (McIntyre, 2000, p. 126). Noguera (2009) underscores the significance of YPAR in education by arguing that, in "most research into policy and school reform initiatives, particularly in education, youth are treated as the passive objects" whose "experiences, perceptions, and aspirations" are often overlooked by those who are responsible for identifying and "fixing" educational problems (p. 18). In addition, my scholarship has focused on the ways in which youth and educators construct identities in relation to their involvement with Cyphers for Justice (CFJ), a YPAR program in which youth and educators construct identities as researchers, activists, artists, and as learners. At the time of this writing the stakes are even higher for all schools and in society—the tragedy and anxiety of the COVID-19 pandemic, learning to teach remotely, struggles against voter suppression, the ongoing fight against endemic racism, and vicious diatribes and senseless legal challenges against critical race theory (Sawchuck, 2021).

Many educators are returning to classrooms in uncertain circumstances, unsure of the resources for teaching and students' well-being after many have faced isolation and loss during the pandemic. Nonetheless, teachers and administrators have worked tirelessly with/for their students, and many students have demonstrated incredible resourcefulness and taken advantage of the disruption in the status quo to innovate and support others (Carter-Andrews et al., 2021; Marciano, 2020).

So, a central question is how can educators and students build together in schools from and with what we have learned and experienced? How can we heal and recover from the anxiety and exhaustion induced not just by the pandemic but the ongoing fight against White supremacy, xenophobia, racism and prejudice, anti-Asian hate, and antiblackness? In the increasingly high-stakes context of teaching today, it is crucial for educators and their students to engage in collaborative inquiries to address these issues that affect all, most directly.

Building upon culturally responsive approaches to addressing the complexity of social inequalities, particularly in relation to the role of home languages and literacies in a more expansive knowledge of culture, culturally sustaining pedagogies (CSP) challenge educators and researchers to address the marginalization of nondominant languages and literacies in order to better meet the needs of students and work to sustain the rich and multiple identities and literacies that they already possess (Paris, 2012). In this sense, YPAR projects can engage students and their teachers in rigorous research inquiries as part of a radical effort to broaden the field's understanding of inquiry-based knowledge production. This effort is led not just by scholars in academic institutions but also by students and teachers who directly experience the educational contexts that scholars endeavor to understand.

Like PAR, YPAR represents "a new paradigm, a challenge to existing epistemologies, and, thereby, a competing (or complementary) entry into the political economy of knowledge production" (Noffke, 1997, p. 307). Thus, YPAR is both a method of research that is committed to expanding who is invited/permitted to conduct and disseminate research and also a pedagogical framework based on a conception of teaching and learning through collaborative inquiry. Morrell traces the roots of PAR and YPAR to Brazilian educator Paulo Freire, who argued that meaningful transformation and change must occur in collaboration with everyday people who make a "conscious effort to disrupt or call into question this paradigm of knowledge production" (2006, p. 67).

The Figured World of YPAR as a Context for Critical Participation

This chapter draws from a larger IRB-approved qualitative study of the experiences of high school students and preservice teachers in the context of Cyphers for Justice (CFJ), an after-school critical social research program. CFJ is hosted by the Institute for Urban and Minority Education (IUME) at Teachers College, Columbia University, and the College Now program at Queens College of the City University of New York (CUNY). Since 2012, this after-school seminar has brought together one or two annual cohorts of preservice teachers, teaching artists, and teacher educators with 12 to 18 high school students who seek to design and implement a series of semester-long critical social research projects focused on educational issues. One cohort is awarded college credit as part of a dual-enrollment program, and the other follows a typical co-curricular after-school club model. Both cohorts engage with qualitative research methods and digital media tools, hip hop, and spoken word to think through and present research findings.

A broad aim of the CFJ program is to apprentice youth as critical social researchers through culturally sustaining (Paris, 2012) practices that affirm their dynamic literacy identities. CFJ apprentices high school youth and educators as critical researchers through the use of hip hop, spoken word, digital literacy, and critical social research methods. Our approach disrupts dominant understandings of who gets to identify as and "practice" being an educator, knower, or agent of change and allows the possibility of a collaborative space where the co-construction of critical knowledges and pedagogies of pluralism (Morrell, 2008) blurs (though never eliminates) some of the boundaries of agency and identity between students, teachers, researchers, and participants.

CFJ builds upon Gutiérrez's (2008) use of Bhaba's concept of third space, defined above, to frame a "transformative space where the potential for an expanded form of learning and the development of new knowledge are heightened" (p. 152). Data sources include audio session recordings, interviews, field notes, and student artifacts. Students' and preservice teachers' narratives are analyzed as part of an ongoing iterative process (Bogdan & Biklen, 2007) to examine how the students' and teacher candidates' YPAR experiences informed their perceptions about literacies, social change, and social justice.

The CFJ program initiates the inquiry process by first cultivating a context of critical participation. In framing the space for the critical social research seminar, one of the main objectives of the adult allies was to create a brave space (Arao & Clemens, 2013), a generative third space for critical participation. We sought to accomplish this by incorporating the multiple identities and literacies of the youth and by situating our work within critical awareness of key sociocultural issues. Situated at the nexus of our research and teaching of qualitative research, the seminar is at once centered on the qualitative research process *and* on the cultivation of culturally sustaining literacy practices that readily reflect the cultural and generational realities of youth participants (Paris & Alim, 2014).

Our attention to developing and sustaining the rhetorical and linguistic modes of hip-hop writing, spoken word, and digital literacy is directly connected to our commitment to disrupting hierarchies through the YPAR process. By incorporating students' multiple identities and literacies, we sought to normalize the presence of youth culture alongside, rather than subordinate to, a dominant academic culture. As one example of this, in an effort to tap into student schemas and generate ideas and emotions for suggested YPAR topics, we utilized the hip-hop culture tradition of the cypher (Lyiscott, 2019). The art of creating a cypher is a hip-hop cultural practice that is rooted in West African traditions. The art form is a rhythmic dialogue, a sacred circle, marked by an exchange of ideas or witty banter, usually crafted extemporaneously. Within the context of hip-hop pedagogy, this form is utilized for exercises in creative expression, free association, tapping into student schema, inclusivity, and attending to group dynamics (Caraballo & Lyiscott, 2018; Hall, 1996; Kirkland, 2013).

In addition to having the opportunity to relate to their teachers and peers more personally, youth are encouraged to take a stand. For example, in response to one facilitator's question—"What is it that you refuse to be silenced about?"—one student responded "racism, and how people are in denial" about its existence in our society. Such a critical stance supports our ongoing reflection on how youth and educators construct their identities and literacies as researchers and position themselves as agents of change in the interest of social-justice-driven work toward educational equity.

Languaging Identities and Discourses in the Figured World of CFJ

According to Kumashiro (2000), students and teachers construct perceptions of themselves and others in relation to hierarchies of knowledge and power that become manifest in the academic curriculum. In contrast, CFJ provides an opportunity to construct identities as researchers and agents of change. As Joweria shared, the adult allies reminded her constantly of the "voice that I had as a researcher, thinking about my identity as a researcher. They reminded me that the teacher's knowledge is not the only knowledge … kept reminding me that the knowledge I bring to the table is important, that I have my own cultural lens and that is important when I communicate" (Caraballo & Cyphers for Justice Youth, 2020).

Given the primary focus on practices (as noted in the model in Chapter 2), I highlight CFJ projects that examine those practices constituting identities and discourses in certain figured worlds. I use a practice theory approach to knowledge and identity construction as the theoretical lens to examine such experiences among the youth who participate in CFJ. I conceptualize CFJ as a figured world in which students negotiate their identities in the context of the "collective imaginings" of a group that seeks to center their voices and experiences; for instance, as raced, classed, gendered, abled persons (Holland et al., 1998, p. 49). As an intergenerational youth and educator development program, CFJ is a third space that offers participants the possibility of constructing new identities, such as Joweria did.

From a Bahktinian perspective, the "authoring self" or "self-in-practice" is the interface between an individual's past experiences, discourses, and practices and those to which they are exposed in the present. To understand the self in a sociocultural context, it is necessary to consider the self or person with their current positionality (Holland et al., 1998). Persons "develop through and around the cultural forms by which they are identified, and identify themselves, in the context of their affiliation or disaffiliation" with cultural, racial, ethnic, etc., forms and practices (p. 33). Positionality, in turn, is understood in terms of the persons' position in a figured world. Therefore, a youth's self-in-practice experiences knowledge construction as mediated by past learning experiences as well as their positionality in relation to the research process. As Trevor shared during a group reflection after completing the CFJ program, "Cyphers for Justice was the first time I realized I could do research, you know, outside of high school."

Within the paradigm of a practice approach, conceptualizing identity as a social and contextual construction has theoretical roots in social identity theory (Penuel & Wertsch, 1995; Stephan & Stephan, 2004). That theory posits that the self is composed of multiple identities based on group memberships such as gender, race, ethnicity, peer groups, etc. (Stets & Burke, 2000). I conceptualize "identity construction" as the process through which students create, negotiate, reconcile and operationalize their multiple identities and multiple selves (Hemmings, 2000) in their sociocultural context (Penuel & Wertsch, 1995). Due to the manifold ways in which these group memberships may be constructed, identities-in-practice are situated in particular figured worlds, such as CFJ.

In conducting YPAR projects, students benefit from engaging in collaboration involving the practices of sharing different ideas or perspectives on the nature of the issue or challenge and how to address the issue or challenge. This includes being open to negotiating alternative ways of conducting their project in ways that value differences in perspectives so that students value each other's ideas. Engaging in YPAR projects also presupposes that, based on the findings of their research implying problems or issues, youth will push for the need to take collective actions to address these problems or issues. For example, according to Murphy and Smith (2020), teacher Matt Colley helped his ninth-grade students in English and history classes take part in a *Take Action Project* for engaging in civic action to address issues of concern to his students. He provided his students with optional genres to advocate change by using petitions, posters, flyers, infographics, presentations, oral histories, etc., focusing specifically on the use of petitions. When youth engage in YPAR projects, they often draw on their cultural practices to examine issues most relevant to them. For example, students in the CFJ program draw on hip-hop culture, using languaging from a youth culture perspective (Caraballo et al., 2020).

Constructing and Leveraging YPAR Identities, Practices, and Languaging Actions

I propose that participatory research, grounded in the catalytic nature of YPAR, leads to the co-construction of critical knowledges that can in turn reframe the question of what counts as knowledge in the school curriculum. The data collected in connection with the CFJ program, since its inception in 2012, suggests that youth incorporate various literacies and languaging actions, including poetry, hip-hop bars, protests, public service announcements, and presentations to stakeholders, in order to communicate the findings of their research as well as articulate their experiences and perspectives. According to Charmaz (2011), "grounded theory begins with gathering data but relies on the moving back and forth between data gathering and analysis" (p. 166). I use grounded theory open coding to allow themes to "arise from the researcher's interaction with the data" (p. 165). Furthermore, my narrative approach to data analysis (Moen, 2006; Richardson, 2000; Charmaz, 2011) informs how texts (whether they be interview transcripts or student writing) are interrelated, nonlinear narratives produced within continuously shifting relations (Walkerdine, 2007). Building upon these alternative critical approaches, I share examples of the experiences and knowledge production of students, teachers, and communities engaged in YPAR, positioning them as agents of social change. In the sections that follow, I highlight some of the identities, practices, and languaging actions that youth and adult allies constructed and leveraged in the context of their participation in CFJ.

Constructing Identities as Researchers

Gloria's recollection and initial impressions and assumptions about activism remind us of how deeply enmeshed our identities are in the work that we do. These identities informed Gloria's research in CFJ, which she joined as a ninth-grader in high school, as they do eventually in her college classes and activist work. In a recent co-authored article, she explains how, even as a young student, she was "already campaigning for social and community change through [her] actions" but did not yet have a language or a sense of self in relation to this work:

> Part of that mental disconnect between my actions and an activist identity was due to the institutionalized perception of activism in schools; activists present and past were only brushed upon in class, the depths and contexts of their battles irrelevant to the curriculum, and their causes were painted as far-off and distant, removed from the everyday life of students. Activism in school was and is still told from a Western-centric narrative, ensuring the erasure of my people's history from American textbooks, and barely, if ever, addressing the systemic oppression of BIPOC and its lingering consequences. All of this and more is further perpetuated by the hegemonic structure of classrooms, where teacher voice is constantly valued over student voice.
>
> *Yeom et al., 2020, p. 492*

However, these identities as researchers must not be generalized, as youth and adult allies constructed their own in the context of their experiences with CFJ. While several CFJ participants sought ways to continue their research after the program had ended, some youth felt more comfortable participating as youth board members, or continuing to assist with the programs, serving as peer mentors, but did not necessarily want or need to continue with their original research projects. For example, Antoine chose not to continue working on his project or sharing his research in professional development workshops and other similar opportunities. Yet his self-reflection on his experience with YPAR and CFJ suggests that he constructed an identity in this figured world that led him to develop practices and engage in languaging in very particular ways, with deep impacts on his future relations and interactions with others beyond CFJ.

> [CFJ] allowed me to get together with a group of my friends, to actually talk, not just about the things going on in the latest rap song, but about other things—things that make us who we are, basically ... our personalities, trouble at home, what we are going through. It also helped me not just talk to my friends, not just give them recommendations, but also to listen. It gave me confidence to speak to other people because we had to interact with a lot of different people, different age groups in CFJ, and also becoming aware of things happening in our world. Commonly you don't see people of such different backgrounds in just one setting. So to bring them all into one setting to express ideas, challenging others' ideas to strengthen them even more, that's what really brought out the difference of CFJ.

When I asked about how his participation in the project may have impacted his relationships with other people, Antoine noted that

> it also helped me be closer to my family, actually. It brought me closer to family, doing more things together, such as card games, all of those things we used to do together in CFJ, like when we started to create those raps, starting with one word on the board and creating the rest [of the story] ourselves. I actually did that with friends about a month ago.

Antoine's positive perceptions of his participation in CFJ outside of his school world demonstrate the need to recognize how youth are continually learning through participation in different figured worlds—not only in school worlds but also in community, peer group, extracurricular, sports, family, workplace, and digital/media worlds as described in this book. With the examples that follow, I document the kinds of learning that occur in this figured world to highlight practices that could also support a culturally sustaining teaching stance to foster deep learning and critical engagement in secondary classrooms.

Rethinking Activism

As Richard Beach discussed in Chapter 4, engagement in collaborative research can be very generative for youth and the educators that work with them, leading to the nurturing of practices that invite engagement, supporting construction of identities as agents of change, and fostering critical consciousness of our society. In the CFJ program, this process begins with youth engaging in activities, such as

128 Students Co-Authoring Figured Worlds

Freirean culture circles, that challenge all of us beyond our comfort zones (Lyiscott et al., 2020).

For example, two CFJ members, Bella and Jonathan, explored the concept of youth oppression, which they defined as "the experience of repeated, widespread, and systematic injustice." In responses to surveys collected from classmates at their school, they found that young people report dealing with racism, sexism, bullying, favoritism, etc., both in their working environments and in schools where many viewed youth oppression as an act of "adultism." In a presentation on their research to a group of preservice and in-service teachers, Bella and Jonathan challenged their audience to reflect on their peers' experiences of feeling judged or shamed by their teachers. In this sense, activism may be defined as inciting others to critical self-reflection to examine the ways in which we, as adult allies and/or educators, may be inadvertently perpetuating marginalizing discourses about youth.

A second approach to broadening ideas about activism involved promoting awareness of problematic discourses in society and popular media. Youth researchers sought to expose pervasive discourses in society, more broadly, that can be quite toxic to children and youth. For example, in their CFJ YPAR project, Agatha and James examined "rape culture" among youth, reflecting how media representations influence practices associated with a rape culture (Buchwald et al., 2005). They were interested in studying how rape culture fosters "prevailing social attitudes [that] have the effect of normalizing or trivializing sexual assault and abuse." In their project, they addressed the questions:

1. How does rape culture impact young people?
2. How do youth perceive masculinity and femininity?
3. How does popular media contribute to rape culture?

Agatha and James surveyed 50 high school students on the effects of popular music and found that 90% of students indicated that they believed that music does promote male dominance and violence towards women while, at the same time, 90% indicated that they still listen to this music. They cited the example of the song "Blurred Lines" by Robin Thicke "that was literally the number one song of the summer. It got so many plays, but it has so much misogynistic language just put into it." They recommended that teachers have students "think critically about actions/media" related to how the media plays a "role in rape culture, [to] think about how you can deconstruct the negative stereotypes and take action." In this sense, activism was defined as promoting awareness of a dynamic that is so deeply enmeshed in popular culture that it would otherwise be overlooked.

Third, as part of our intergenerational work as adult allies and youth board members, we engaged in a series of inquiry discussions to explore what it means to have an impact after participating in CFJ. We recently published an article about our findings (Yeom et al., 2020), where we explored how our identities as artists, activists, and researchers continue to grow given our circumstances—recognizing this is different for every person and inherently situated in particular figured worlds. After their initial experiences with YPAR, youth who have served as youth board members in CFJ after completing the program as high school students have continued to construct identities as activists, scholars, and artists, in very different ways. For Jordon, this meant thinking about how he could make a difference in his community:

> Prior to Cyphers, I witnessed issues that plagued my community and had a passion to help people, but I felt powerless to do anything. When I joined CFJ, I was happy to meet people my age who shared similar values. We all wanted to help others, and CFJ taught us that when working together, anything is possible.
>
> *Caraballo et al., 2020, p. 8*

Genre as Action: From Research Question to Spoken Word

During any given semester, the CFJ cohorts develop various interconnected research projects that are interrelated in their focus on educational and social justice but that also lead to individual inquiries and produce uniquely creative artefacts such as poems, raps, and other media. The youth's research is grounded in and enriched by the exploration of hip-hop and digital literacies in the context of weekly seminars, and, rather than developing their performances *after* completing the research, creative expression is embedded throughout the inquiry process, conceptualizing writing/composing, in itself, as a method of inquiry rather than just a way to report findings (Richardson, 2000).

As part of the weekly YPAR sessions, the students explored the tenets and artistry of hip-hop along with learning the basic elements of qualitative research—how to develop research questions, design a study and write protocols to collect data via surveys, interviews, photovoice, and other methods, and analyze their findings—and youth research and social action, illustrating "the interrelatedness of leveraging multiple literacies toward engagement in critical social action" (Caraballo & Hill, 2014, p. 8). Although each inquiry had a different trajectory, findings, and implications, each team's data analysis reflects the experiences and knowledge production of the students, teachers, and communities most directly involved.

In a recent CFJ-sponsored professional development workshop for teachers, Mijin Yeom, who taught YPAR methods in the College Now cohort of Cyphers for Justice, described the research process to about 35 workshop participants, who ranged from preservice to early career teachers, as follows. The youth presenters begin by identifying relevant problems in education that are of interest to them. It could be a moment or experience where they felt frustrated or isolated, or not, but the inquiry is grounded in an issue or experience that is, by their own admission, of great relevance and/or importance to them. Once their issue or problem has been identified, there are several prompts and activities that encourage each research team to explore the possible root causes of each issue. Then, they draft a vision statement that imagines what changes could be possible as a result of their research and activism. Next, they draft a mission statement that articulates what the youth would like to accomplish with their research, and then they outline specific goals to guide the work of the group or team.

Having reached some shared understandings about their topic, each team begins to design a research study. The youth draft the research questions that will guide their inquiry by asking broad, as well as specific, questions about their topic—questions whose answers would help them to address their goals and mission. As part of their research design process, youth are also learning about various data collection methods, from interviews and focus groups to surveys or photovoice protocols (Bettencourt, 2020; De los Rios, 2017). They consider what would be the best kind of data to collect, how to analyze it, and to whom they should direct their findings and recommendations for action. And then, perhaps most importantly, there is a performative aspect of youth's experience in CFJ, grounded in youth and hip-hop culture and embedded throughout the research process. Teaching artists facilitate workshops of different rhetorical modes to support youth researchers' multiple literacies, from performing spoken word (aka. spittin') to digital representations, in sharing their research.

For example, Michaela, Nia, and Tiana turned frequently to poetry as they explored their experiences with colorism, an issue they experienced personally in their communities, in which standards of beauty and class status were linked to having lighter skin. Their research sought to raise awareness of this problem to prevent younger children from growing up to mimic these ideals. Their mission was "to promote self-love and encourage people to be proud of their backgrounds and envision a community where young people are more accepting and knowledgeable of each other's cultures."

After interviewing 80 students in their neighborhoods (50 high school and 30 elementary students) and analyzing the data they collected, their findings suggested that students seemed to normalize discriminatory remarks previously made about them and didn't feel comfortable talking about race with other students. All of the participants had claimed to be comfortable in their own skin but then favored Eurocentric attributes when describing themselves and others. As they were analyzing their data, Nia wrote and performed multiple drafts of a spoken-word poem to share with her group and others during our work sessions.

> The problem is far from fixed We got little black girls constantly claiming that they're mixed Self-denial ingrained in a little child's brain when they're put in an environment where color ain't the same.

Strokes of **BLACK** emphasize the sorrow on a woman's face. The tears she cries for her trans sisters whose lives go away violent and unnoticed.

BROWN shades that color the faces of a crowd marching for the rights they were denied from the beginning of time.

RED smudges from the smoke of a bonfire to commemorate those tough spirits that survived the hardships forced on them.

ORANGE specks that light a dark path that many venture down for themselves and others.

YELLOW streaks in a sunrise on the days the world seems a little more welcoming than the generation before.

GREEN arches that salute how far we've come and how far we still have to climb.

BLUE squares that make up ballots that propel the dreams of many fighting their way out of the shadows.

PURPLE streaks for the walls of a dreary school building to brighten the minds of the children who can't decide what community they belong to.

More **COLORS** for more pride, our identities are us and we are infinite. And, liberation is what we will name the painting that illustrated our story from the back of this parade to the front.

FIGURE 6.1 Marissa shared her "Emotional Coloring" poem, evocative of the colors of the Pride flag, when she presented her research on the experiences of LGBTQ+ youth

In a group reflection about the research and performance process, Nia shared emphatically: "If someone asked me to explain something, I could be like, 'OK, well, I think that the root of this problem is …' But no, if you told me, "I want you to explain by spittin'," I will spit it to you and you will understand it."

Similarly, Marissa, who conducted an anonymous survey of 50 students in two high schools in her city, learned that LGBTQ+ people of color are very unlikely to find sources of support in schools and often feel isolated from various social groups. Having conducted some historical research on the role of queer people of color in the gay rights movement, and the intersection of issues related to race/ethnicity, gender identity and sexual orientation in schools, she hoped to amplify the experiences of queer youth of color. As she prepared a research presentation to share with educators, she wrote poetry and created a visual representation to convey her perspective and raise awareness (see Figure 6.1). The weaving together of youth's overlapping research and artistic investigations honors the interrelatedness of research, art, self-expression and social action (Yeom et al., 2020).

Discourses, Purposes, and Practices with/in YPAR

Consistent with the components discussed by Richard Beach in Chapter 2, youth may be driven to this kind of deep critical engagement by *purposes* associated with the motivation to address issues or problems they perceive as posing challenges to their world(s). I share the following extended examples to highlight how

132 Students Co-Authoring Figured Worlds

youth researchers engage with a variety of discourses and practices, such as in the media or among their peers, to achieve their own goals and purposes via YPAR.

In one example, CFJ youth researchers Wynter and Ellie came together despite coming from very different cultural backgrounds, social circles, and grade levels at their school. Wynter, an African–American sophomore whose family had lived in Harlem all of their lives, joined forces with Ellie, whose family had recently moved to New York City from Denmark for her father's new job. Both had been troubled by the way their friends discussed body image, particularly young women. Their study sought to explore (1) when and how often young women feel pressure to live up to an ideal body image; and (2) what they see as the biggest factor for where these ideas of body image come from. Their study was conducted in two phases: the first, a survey administered to 65 high school juniors. The survey asked questions ranging from "Describe/draw your ideal body type" to "How often do you experience or witness insecurity about body image?" and "How often do you experience these insecurities?"

The second phase consisted of interviews with a subset of those who responded to surveys. The 14 students (11 female, three male) interviewed were part of a convenience sample, peers whose schedule overlap made interviews possible. The interviews offered an opportunity to ask students to elaborate on questions similar to those they had answered previously in the survey. Because audio recording was not possible nor appropriate in a bustling school environment, interviewees' responses were written as spoken to ensure accuracy in reporting the data. The survey results that Wynter analyzed during the first phase of her study indicated that 84% of 65 respondents (both male and female) believed there is a single ideal image for women in society. The remaining 16% felt that there were various "ideal" images, depending on culture, race, age, body type, etc. An overwhelming 84.6% also reported experiencing insecurity about their own bodies more than once daily. A smaller percentage, 24.6%, reported feeling constantly insecure about their bodies.

Seeking to explore further and improve the trustworthiness of her study, Wynter and Ellie conducted interviews with a subset of the survey respondents. Their data analysis focused on emerging codes related to media messages regarding female body image, ideals about beauty, and notions of self-acceptance. A key theme throughout the data was how the media seemed to inform what was considered ideal in terms of female body image, as exemplified in one female participant's comment during an interview:

> I think girls do feel pressured [by the media]. They want to be accepted and media pushes them to want to be accepted. Like with rappers having certain girls in their videos. They see that and want to be like those girls. Young girls idolize and make role models out of video vixens because they see the money and fame.

In a similar comment, another female interviewee stated that

> as a gender it's hard to feel accepted when the media puts this image of what beauty really is and then boys and girls everywhere have that image in their head and when someone doesn't live up to that ridiculous standard, they're not [considered] beautiful.

While most respondents believed that there was pressure from the media for women to look a certain way, no one really knew where these media messages really originated.

Echoing concerns and questions about gender and body image in the YPAR seminar discussions, youth have many concerns about race and are frustrated by their experiences of prejudice and racism. The role of race in encounters with law enforcement was prominent for the six African-American male participants Trevor interviewed among friends, family, and community. Several codes and themes emerged from all six of the interviews. The most urgent is the idea that there is no "real scientific reason why Blacks die" disproportionately at the moment of apprehension by police. All of his interviewees had been affected by, or lived with someone who was directly affected by, police excessive force. Their responses conveyed the belief that the high incidence of casualties among young Black males goes unchecked because, as one participant (a veteran employed as a security guard) expressed: "there's no consequence when a cop kills a Black person because our lives are expendable and they've always been expendable." In the same vein, he questioned the public narrative about crime in neighborhoods of color, countering that the higher number of arrests is "not because Blacks commit more crime. It's because there is more policing in urban areas." Similar to the findings from participatory action research studies in other New York City neighborhoods, high rates of arrest seem to be associated with racial profiling and other forms of aggressive policing such as those promoted by initiatives such as *Stop and Frisk* and *Broken Windows* policing (Stoudt et al., 2012).

A second general area of consensus in the interview data pertained to how the danger at the intersection of racism and police brutality might be addressed. All participants came up with a similar response to this issue: police need to know the community that they are policing. Citizens should feel like the police are in their communities to serve and protect, not to "search without warrants, or harass." Their perspectives have implications for law enforcement and community activism. When police begin to increasingly work in their own communities, where community is defined as sharing similar values and experiences with respect to skin color, culture, class, and/or neighborhood, communities of color may begin to feel that a police presence is meant not to antagonize but to serve and protect. Similarly, zero-tolerance policies often criminalize youth within academic contexts and pave their way to the school-to-prison pipeline.

134 Students Co-Authoring Figured Worlds

Wynter's and Trevor's findings in relation to very different issues have similar important implications for how educators can engage with youth's experiences of difficult personal circumstances as well as their interactions with policies and consumption of media sources that frame their experiences. As critical scholars have argued, there is an urgent need for a critical media pedagogy (Morrell et al., 2013) that will equip youth with critical literacy tools (Caraballo & Lyiscott, 2018). Students need these tools for their critical participation in today's society, particularly in light of the ubiquitous use of technology and presence of mainstream and social media via the Internet (Alexander, 2006). Given the prevalence of concerns about race and gender, in particular, that came up in the YPAR seminars, implications for educators include incorporating these experiences into the curriculum and offering opportunities for students to engage in discussion about the issues that they encounter within and beyond school walls.

Co-Authoring Learning Environments

CFJ youth poured themselves into their YPAR work in the fall of 2020, in the midst of the pandemic—they gathered information among peers and teachers, examined their own perspectives, and made recommendations for educators based on findings. But even more important than the results and specific recommendations that educators received from the youth during their presentation and collaborative sessions with preservice teachers are the practices and collaborative approaches that they modeled, which stood in stark contrast to the hierarchical institutional practices that many of them had experienced in their own schools.

Bhavishya and Aleemah conducted their CFJ YPAR project on the school-to-prison pipeline as an example of how community worlds impose certain practices onto school worlds. They examined how these practices undermine how schools should "create a positive program that helps students understand worldly issues and how to deal with them [so that] youth live and participate in a community free of punishment." They posited that, as a reflection of zero-tolerance policies adopted in schools since the 1990s, schools often do not create a positive space free of punishment. Steeped in a discourse of institutionalized racism, these practices result in students from disadvantaged backgrounds being 5.8 times more likely to be incarcerated than Whites in a prison system that is often operated by the government and for-profit corporations.

Based on a survey of their peers, they found that all had been through a metal detector, and half of those who took it also witnessed racial discrimination in school. These practices create a school-to-prison pipeline as "a cycle through which students are pushed out of schools and into prisons and penitentiaries. And it's basically a process of criminalizing youth and putting them into law enforcement cycles." They recommended that schools not contact police for small misdemeanors, implement mental health check-ups, give students a voice in their education, make lessons relevant to current problems, and value students' opinions, perspectives, and beliefs.

As Will stated in his own research presentation on student *and* teacher engagement before and during the COVID-19 pandemic, both educators and learners need to collaborate and consider the other's perspective in order to promote the type of learning environments that can best meet everyone's needs. The goal of his research project was to promote opportunities for students "to engage with how their curriculum should be organized and determined, using their own perspectives," so he interviewed teachers and students before and during remote learning to better understand how each felt about their learning environment. His findings suggested that "teachers and students are seeking similar changes in their classroom environment"; students did not feel that their voices were considered in the curriculum, and teachers, especially, experienced tensions between what they were "supposed" to teach and what/how they *wanted* to teach or thought they should (Caraballo, 2018).

Youth voices, experiences, and perspectives are often overlooked because expectations around decontextualized "best practices" in curriculum, pedagogy, and assessment often lead to more teacher- or administrator-driven academic contexts. Also, while the theory and practice of culturally responsive and sustaining pedagogies have been increasingly well received by educators and policymakers (e.g., see the New York State Culturally Responsive-Sustaining Education Framework, 2018), the policies and practices, lack of resources, and racial injustice that perpetuate inequities and support White supremacy are deeply embedded in our social and educational institutions (Love, 2019). These effects have been exacerbated by endemic racism and the coronavirus pandemic.

In Practice: Fostering Critical Participation in Youth Worlds

Amidst continuously shifting demographics, educators are being challenged to adopt more dynamic approaches to teaching and learning that reflect the literacies and cultures of racially and linguistically diverse classrooms, while stakeholders are tasked with preparing students for success in 21st-century work, civic and social contexts. In the face of significant systemic obstacles to justice and equity, youth research and civic engagement projects, such as YPAR, promote collaboration between students and educators toward effective mechanisms for centering and responding to the needs, concerns, and interests of youth toward building more just and inclusive learning contexts. In this chapter, I have argued that educators can use the situated literacies, languaging, and practices nurtured in youth-engaged spaces as critical tools with which to address the power relations inside and outside the YPAR space.

Ongoing interviews and field notes from meetings with adult allies in CFJ indicate that teachers see a connection between their collaborative work with students in the YPAR seminars and their ideas about mainstream classroom

136 Students Co-Authoring Figured Worlds

instruction. Our approach to YPAR draws from critical sociocultural theories and cultural studies, framing identities and literacies as constructed in the context of practice within a figured world (Caraballo, 2011; Holland et al., 1998). Based on that understanding of the interrelatedness of identities and cultural worlds, the CFJ program actively seeks to foster a figured world of critical participation that supports participants' identities, practices, literacies, and languaging as researchers and agents of change. As Gloria, a CFJ alum, reflected in our co-authored article on her experience with YPAR,

> I was suddenly equipped with a more culturally and racially aware literary lens. I became more aware of the intersections between class and race within literacy, both textually and audibly. For example, when reading articles with my peers, I frequently consider socioeconomic and racial aspects that wouldn't have crossed my mind before Cyphers. Is this article about hydraulic fracking simply about public vs. corporate interests? Or is there also a disparity between how indigenous people and other folks are impacted? Did the author take those divides into account?
>
> *Caraballo et al., 2020, p. 8*

Similarly, educators can transform the school curriculum to nurture students' civic and media literacies across disciplines by developing their ideological, institutional, interpersonal, and internal lenses for critically understanding social and educational injustice (e.g., see Bell, n.d.). One aspiring teacher, Yeila, after working with youth on their projects for a semester, shared that her experiences with YPAR had challenged her to expand her perspectives regarding her students and her teaching:

> This experience means a huge change in how I look at my work not only as a … teacher but also as researcher … I learned … that true education is situated within a reciprocal relationship between the community, the classroom, and the university. I have realized that learning is not a one-way action—that teachers can learn from their students in the same way students learn from their teachers, based on experiences, mutual interaction, and respect for other people's opinions.

More broadly, in terms of the inquiry process, what may begin as an investigation of a specific topic can lead to a much more nuanced understanding of the relationship between the researcher and the research process, as well as a common commitment to educational justice issues. As one CFJ youth researcher, Joweria, noted after collecting her data,

> You have to sit down and say to yourself: "What is it that stands out? What is common in all of the answers that you got?" So you have to be careful not

to leave anything out, but you also have to be able to pick up a theme that is common in all of the data that you collected … that was kinda hard, but it also showed how we all … share the same problems.

Caraballo & Filipiak, 2021, p. 437

As demonstrated in all of the examples from their CFJ projects, young people drew upon their rich languaging and socialization practices as resources in constructing agentive identities as researchers, activists, and engaged citizens. As another youth researcher, Mia, shared in a group reflection,

I came here and there were people thinking like me, asking questions, who were doing poetry, and I was like, this is amazing! And you don't [typically] get a place where youth have power, a place where you can state your ideas and no one is saying "OK, now back to the subject"!

In particular, the cultivation of critical digital literacies in their YPAR work afforded youth the opportunity to identify and respond to barriers in their educational and social contexts and create new and humanizing spaces. As Joweria shared after presenting at a conference, "I don't know, I just feel free in this course. In this research. It makes me feel good because it doesn't matter how I say it" (Caraballo & Filipiak, 2021, p. 438).

The students' experiences with the YPAR curriculum and its disruption of traditional adult-centric hierarchies and epistemologies made visible those opportunities for learning and social action that youth found most compelling and affirming. Access to experiences such as YPAR is particularly impactful for urban youth from historically marginalized populations, whose rich experiences, identities, and literacies are often excluded in traditional and increasingly standardized educational contexts. Therefore, creating spaces in which students and teachers may engage in dialogue and critical analysis on key social and educational issues challenges educators to work collaboratively with youth in ways that support and promote culturally sustaining (Paris, 2012) curricular and pedagogical stances. Creating these spaces also facilitates students' construction of identities and literacies as researchers and agents of change—all in the interest of educational equity and social justice.

ACTIVITY: WHERE DO WE GO FROM HERE?

Many educators feel inspired to incorporate youth-engaged research into their teaching practice—some feel overwhelmed by the possibility. Regardless of where teachers stand, incorporating youth research into their practice is not about adding a project to the curriculum or starting an after-school club (although both could be starting points, under certain conditions). There is no single way to implement or facilitate participatory research with youth, and the most important factor has little to do with the activity or project and more to do with broadening our assumptions about who can do empirical research, what counts as knowledge, and how to disrupt some of the power dynamics between educators and learners as well as individuals, communities, and institutions.

If interested in centering youth research in practice, teachers may want to start by:

1. Reading about different approaches to youth research and activism: YPAR Hub, *yparhub.berkeley.edu*; Public Science Project, *publicscienceproject.org/about/history*; Council of Youth Research, *idea.gseis.ucla.edu/projects/the-council-of-youth-research*; and The Bushwick Action Research Collective, *bushwickactionresearch.org*; see also books on participatory action research: Buckelew & Ewing (2019), Chevalier & Buckles (2019), Edwards-Groves et al. (2019); and, for research methods, YouTube Research Shorts: *www.youtube.com/c/ResearchShorts*.
2. Asking some of the young people in your school or community what issues they care about, what questions they have, and where they feel heard and valued. What ideas do they have? What changes would they like to see?
3. Recruiting like-minded adult allies with whom to collaborate. Youth research is incredibly rewarding but also laborious. Initiatives work best and are most effective when they are supported by collaborative teams and/or communities!

References

Alexander, B. (2006). Web 2.0: a new wave of innovation for teaching and learning? *Educause Review, 41*, 32–44. www.educause.edu/ir/library/pdf/ERM0621.pdf

Arao, B., & Clemens, K. (2013). From safe spaces to brave spaces. In L. M. Landreman (Ed.), *The art of effective facilitation: Reflections from social justice educators* (pp. 135–150). Stylus Publishing.

Banks, J. A. (1993). The canon debate, knowledge construction, and multicultural education. *Educational Researcher, 22*(5), 4–14.

Bell, J. (n.d.). The four I's of oppression. YouthBuild USA. Retrieved from www.morningsidecenter.org/teachable-moment/lessons/challenging-stereotypes-michael-brown-and-iftheygunnedmedown

Bhabha, H. (1994). *The location of culture*. Routledge.

Bogdan, R. C., & Biklen, S. K. (2007). *Qualitative research for education: An introduction to theory and method*. Pearson.

Braidotti, R. (1994). *Nomadic subjects: Embodiment and sexual difference in contemporary feminist theory*. Columbia University Press.

Britzman, D. P. (1989). Who has the floor? Curriculum, teaching, and the English student teacher's struggle for voice. *Curriculum Inquiry, 19*(2), 143–162.

Bettencourt, G. (2020). Embracing problems, processes, and contact zones: Using youth participatory action research to challenge adultism. *Action Research, 18*(2), 153–170.

Buchwald, E., Fletcher, P. R., & Roth, M. (Eds.). (2005). *Transforming a rape culture* (Rev. ed). Milkweed.

Buckelew, M., & Ewing, J. (2019). *Action research for English language arts teachers: Invitation to inquiry.* Routledge.

Caraballo, L. (2011). Theorizing identities in a "just(ly)" contested terrain: Practice theories of identity amid critical-poststructural debates on curriculum and achievement. *Journal of Curriculum and Pedagogy, 8*(2),155–177.

Caraballo, L., & Hill, M. (2014). Curriculum-in-action: Cultivating literacy, community, and creativity in urban contexts. *English Leadership Quarterly, 37*(1), 5–11.

Caraballo, L. (2016). Students' critical meta-awareness in a figured world of achievement: Toward a culturally sustaining stance in curriculum, pedagogy, and research. *Urban Education, 52*(5), 585–609. doi:10.1177/0042085915623344

Caraballo, L. (2018). Multiple literacies as culturally sustaining pedagogy in English language arts. In A. T. Costigan (Ed.), *An authentic English language arts curriculum: Finding your way in a standards-driven context* (pp. 156–183). Routledge.

Caraballo, L., Comrie, J., & Tsang, G. (2020, Jan/Feb). Cyphers for Justice: The role of beyond-school literacies in developing critical thinking and social awareness. *Literacy Today, 39*(1), 8–10.

Caraballo, L. & Cyphers for Justice Youth (2020, July). *Plenary session: Cypher as pedagogy: Critical epistemology and Cyphers for Justice. Reimagining Education Summer Institute (RESI)* [Conference session]. Teachers College, Columbia University, New York, NY.

Caraballo, L., & Filipiak, D. (2021). Building futures: Youth researchers and critical college-going literacies. *Review of Education, Pedagogy, and Cultural Studies, 42*(5), 427–450. doi:10.1080/10714413.2021.1874852

Caraballo, L., & Lyiscott, J. (2018). Collaborative inquiry: Youth, social action, and critical qualitative research. *Action Research, 18*(2), 194–211. doi:10.1177/1476750317752819

Carter Andrews, D. J., Richmond, G., & Marciano, J. E. (2021). The teacher support imperative: Teacher education and the pedagogy of connection. *Journal of Teacher Education, 72*(3), 267–270.

Charmaz, K. (2011). A constructivist grounded theory analysis of losing and regaining a valued self. In F. J. Wertz, K. Charmaz, L. M. McMullen, R. Josselson, R. Anderson, & E. McSpadden (Eds.), *Five ways of doing qualitative analysis: Phenomenological psychology, grounded theory, discourse analysis, narrative research, and intuitive inquiry* (pp. 165–204). The Guilford Press.

Chevalier, J. M., & Buckles, D. J. (2019). *Participatory action research: Theory and methods for engaged inquiry.* Routledge.

Culturally Responsive-Sustaining Education Framework (NY-CRS). (2018). Retrieved from New York State Department of Education: www.nysed.gov/common/nysed/files/programs/crs/culturally-responsive-sustaining-education-framework.pdf

De los Rios, C. (2017). Picturing ethnic studies: Photovoice and youth literacies of social action. *Journal of Adolescent & Adult Literacy, 61*(1), 15–24.

Delpit, L. (2006). *Other people's children: Cultural conflict in the classroom.* The New Press.

Edwards-Groves, C., Olin, A. & Karlberg-Granlund, G. (Eds.). (2019). *Partnership and recognition in action research.* Routledge.

Eisner, E. (1985). *The educational imagination*. Macmillan Publishing.

Fahlander, F. (2007). Third space encounters: Hybridity, mimicry, and interstitial practice. In P. Cornell & F. Fahlander (Eds.), *Encounters | Materialities | Confrontations: Archaeologies of social space and interaction* (pp. 15–41). Cambridge Scholars Press.

Gee, J. P. (1996). *Social linguistics and literacies: Ideology in discourses*. Taylor and Francis.

Gutiérrez, K. D. (2008). Developing a sociocritical literacy in the third space. *Reading Research Quarterly, 43*(2), 148–164.

Hall, S. (1996). Introduction: Who needs identity? In S. Hall & P. DuGay (Eds.), *Questions of cultural identity* (pp. 1–17). Sage.

Hemmings, A. (2000). Lona's links: Postoppositional identity work of urban youths. *Anthropology & Education, 31*(2), 151–172.

Holland, D., Lachicotte, W., Skinner, D., & Cain, C. (1998). *Identity and agency in cultural worlds*. Harvard University Press.

Jackson, P. (1994). Life in classrooms. In B. Moon & A. S. Mayes (Eds.), *Teaching and learning in the secondary school* (pp. 155–160). Routledge.

Kirkland, D. (2013). *A search past silence: The literacy of young Black men*. Teachers College Press.

Kumashiro, K. (2000). Toward a theory of anti-oppressive education. *Review of Educational Research, 70*(1), 25–53.

Love, B. L. (2019). *We want to do more than survive: Abolitionist teaching and the pursuit of educational freedom*. Beacon Press.

Lyiscott, J. J. (2019). *Black appetite. White food. Issues of race, voice, and justice within and beyond the classroom*. Routledge.

Lyiscott, J. J., Caraballo, L., Filipiak, D., Riina-Ferrie, J., Yeom, M., & Lee, M. A. (2020). Cyphers for Justice: Learning from the wisdom of intergenerational inquiry with youth. *Review of Education, Pedagogy, and Cultural Studies, 42*(5), 363–383.

Marciano, J. E., Peralta, L. M., Lee, J. S., Rosemurgy, H., Holloway, L., & Bass, J. (2020). Centering community: enacting culturally responsive-sustaining YPAR during COVID-19. *Journal of Multicultural Education, 14*(2), 163–175.

McIntyre, A. (2000). Constructing meaning about violence, school, and community: Participatory action research with urban youth. *The Urban Review, 32*(2), 123–154.

Moen, T. (2006). Reflections on the narrative research approach. *Qualitative Methods, 5*(4), 1–11.

Morrell, E. (2006). Critical participatory action research and the literacy achievement of ethnic minority groups. In J. V. Hoffman, D. L. Schallert, C. M. Fairbanks, J. Worthy, & B. Maloda (Eds.), *55th yearbook of the National Reading Conference yearbook* (pp. 1–18). National Reading Conference.

Morrell, E. (2008). Six summers of YPAR: Learning, action, and change in urban education. In J. Cammarota & M. Fine (Eds.), *Revolutionizing education: Youth participatory action research in motion* (pp. 155–187). Routledge.

Morrell, E., Duenas, R., Garcia, V., & Lopez, J. (2013). *Critical media pedagogy: Teaching for achievement in city schools*. Teachers College Press.

Murphy, S. M., & Smith, M. A. (2020). *Writing to make an impact: Expanding the vision of writing in the secondary classroom*. Teachers College Press.

Noffke, S. E. (1997). Professional, personal, and political dimensions of action research. *Review of Research in Education, 22*, 305–343.

Noguera, P. (2009). Foreword. *New Directions for Youth Development, 123*, 15–18. doi:10.1002/yd.311

Paris, D. (2012). Culturally sustaining pedagogy: A needed change in stance, terminology, and practice. *Educational Researcher, 41*(3), 93–97. doi:10.3102/0013189X12441244

Paris, D., & Alim, H. S. (2014). What are we seeking to sustain through culturally sustaining pedagogy? A loving critique forward. *Harvard Educational Review, 84*(1), 85–100.

Penuel, W. R., & Wertsch, J. V. (1995). Vygotsky and identity formation: A sociocultural approach. *Educational Psychologist, 30*(2), 83–92.

Richardson, L. (2000). Writing: A method of inquiry. In N. K. Denzin & Y. S. Lincoln (Eds.), *Handbook of qualitative research* (2nd ed.) (pp. 923–948). Sage.

Sawchuck, S. (2021, May 18). What is Critical Race Theory, and why is it under attack? *Education Week* [Weblog post]. Retrieved from www.edweek.org/leadership/what-is-critical-race-theory-and-why-is-it-under-attack/2021/05

Snyder, J., Bolin, F., & Zumwalt, K. (1992). Curriculum implementation. In P. W. Jackson (Ed.), *Handbook of research on curriculum* (pp. 402–435). MacMillan.

Stephan, W. G., & Stephan, C. W. (2004). Intergroup relations in multicultural education programs. In J. A. Banks & C. A. M. Banks (Eds.), *Handbook of research on multicultural education* (2nd ed., pp. 782–798). Jossey-Bass.

Stets, J. E., & Burke, P. J. (2000). Identity theory and social identity theory. *Social Psychology Quarterly, 63*(3), 224–237.

Stoudt, B. G., Fox, M., & Fine, M. (2012). Contesting privilege with critical participatory action research. *Journal of Social Issues, 68*(1), 178–193.

Walkerdine, V. (2007). *Children, gender, video games: Towards a relational approach to multimedia.* Palgrave Macmillan.

Yeom, M., Caraballo, L., Tsang, G., Larkin, J., & Comrie, J. (2020/21). Reimagining impact: Storying youth research, arts, and activism. *Review of Education, Pedagogy, and Cultural Studies, 42*(5), 482–503. doi:10.1080/10714413.2021.1874850

7

CO-AUTHORING PEER GROUP FIGURED WORLDS

This chapter describes students co-authoring peer group worlds based on their shared use of languaging practices for interacting with each other. They employed these practices to achieve the purposes of enacting identities within their groups in ways that enhanced their sense of group coherence and belonging. They also adhered to certain group norms and discourses constituting certain shared uses of languaging for enacting relations with other group members based on a sense of shared trust. Students also portrayed how they bonded through the use of shared texts or media and employed "insider language" to foster a sense of group exclusivity. At the same time, they also experienced coping with challenges and conflicts between groups, requiring that they act together cohesively. Students can also respond to portrayals of peer group practices in literature by connecting those portrayals to their own lived-world peer group practices.

Adolescents engage in peer group figured worlds using these different components to enact practices. Many adolescents are continually interacting with their peers, developing friendships essential to their wellbeing. While some peer groups consist of relatively tight, close, familiar members, other peer groups are loose, less-definitive groups with evolving, tenuous, short-term relations. I drew on the students' descriptions of their participation in peer groups related to how they contextualized their purposes, norms, discourses, identities, genres, and media/literature for enacting practices in their groups.

Employing Practices in Peer Groups for Achieving Certain Purposes

Students acquire the following practices for achieving *purposes* associated with valuing participation in peer groups through their participation in peer groups.

DOI: 10.4324/9781003246886-9

Co-Authoring Peer Group Figured Worlds **143**

Members of peer groups are more likely to be engaged in a group when they share a common *purpose* driving use of practices in that group (Van Bavel & Packer, 2021). They then adopt a group *identity* as members of that group related to how they perceive themselves as contributing to those common purposes. For example, as illustrated by Laura's group described in Chapter 1, members of a peer group may agree to meeting one day a week at the same time and place for the purpose of sharing their experiences and providing support for each other, enacting the group identity of being supportive peers.

Experiencing a Sense of Belonging through Peer Group Participation

As reflected by Laura's experience of receiving support from her peers, one primary practice involves providing members with a sense of belonging as valued members of a group. Assad described how being a member of her Somali peer group provides her with a "feeling of belonging" through engagement in practices and beliefs associated with Somali culture.

> In this group, I've been taught the importance of faith and knowing where you came from. Having respect for myself and growing to be someone worthwhile. Being in this kind of group has made me the woman I am today and hope one day I can evolve to be something greater than that.

This sense of belongingness enhanced students' perceiving the value of how other members of a peer group can help them develop over time, as was the case with Laura's group helping her change. Allen described how participating in the shared practice of use of humorous languaging encouraged him to become more outgoing to develop

> from the shy introverted person I used to be, to the annoying loudmouth chirping nut I am today. It forced me to become someone who wasn't afraid of joking and messing around, and it also forced me to become uncomfortable. I changed from someone who was more quiet and into breaking the rules/laws, into a better person. This will keep my mind open, and realize how everyone is going through struggles of their own. I love how they taught me how to help someone else out, just because you can, and should.

In his reflections on his group, Allen noted

> how simple actions are able to be magnified ... a small action can be laughed at, pointed out, questioned, made fun of, etc. When we do this, it shows how our group is able to build off of one another.

144 Students Co-Authoring Figured Worlds

He contrasts languaging in his group as being more supportive of his developing personhood than his languaging "in the classroom [where] nobody can really fully be themselves. You're stopped by the actual structure of the class, the other students, the teacher, and the rules."

Adolescents are continually engaged in informal, casual interactions in school hallways, lunchrooms, bus rides, carpooling, social events, attending concerts/ movies, etc., as well as through social media, in ways that serve to enhance adolescents' relations. They may then value these informal, familiar practices more than the formal learning practices that occur in school worlds.

A study of 13-to-17-year-old female students found that their use of these supportive languaging actions/verbal comments had a positive influence on their social and emotional development (MacPherson et al., 2016). Members also perceive peer groups as a space for sharing personal information about their lives that they may not wish to share with parents or teachers, such as recounting their experiences engaging in problematic situations or seeking advice on coping with these situations.

The fact that adolescents value the support they receive from their peers is reflected in research indicating that adolescents' use of supportive languaging in peer groups has a more substantial influence on their development of personhood than their classroom interactions (Tuggle et al., 2016). In addition, peer group participation in shared-leisure, out-of-school interactions through phone talk, social networking, playing video games, or going to movies were more likely to enhance relationship satisfaction than in-school interactions (Carlson & Rose, 2010).

Given the low-stakes, casual nature of these informal interactions, adolescents may then be willing to adopt different practices based on a sense of shared cultural *norms*, resulting in the development of identities through the use of certain languaging actions in these interactions. Assad valued her participation in her Somali peer group, given how

> the specific ways we communicated in our group served to create positive relations within our group because many social norms in our Somali culture are derived from Islamic tradition, and that is similar to other Islamic countries. The common way to greet someone is to say Assalamualaikum ("God bless you"). Also, in our generation of Somali people, it's common to say "say Wallahi" after everything that's surprising, which means "say I swear to God."
>
> *Beach & Beauchemin, 2019, p. 28*

Students develop a sense of trust in their peers by relying on peers to share knowledge about local events and news as well as give personal advice, particularly when they perceive their peers' knowledge is valid or truthful (DeSteno, 2015). They also experience trust when their peers are consistently responsive to their needs and concerns across time (DeSteno, 2015; Reis et al., 2017). They can

Co-Authoring Peer Group Figured Worlds **145**

then predict that the other will not betray them or renege on their commitments (Hommel & Colzato, 2015; Reis et al., 2017)—that they mean what they say. When they experience a lack of trust in their peers, they are then reluctant to share knowledge about themselves with peers (Nepal et al., 2011).

Recognizing Peer Group Members' Unique Traits and Perspectives

Students also wrote about or described in interviews how they valued their peers' unique traits and perspectives within their group related to how they contribute to a group's vitality.

Michelle describes how, in sharing their experiences during their car rides, they "learn the different ways we all think. We all know when something is wrong, when someone is tired, or if someone is bouncing off the walls for no reason. When we all realize this, we just go along with it, no questions asked." She notes how the group "bonded over and grew closer from" assisting with each other's problems, given that "we all know each other's past drama and have learned that we never wanted to be treated like that again, hence why we created this carpool of our own." As a result, "we have learned to grow from each other. Not only grow separately but grow together, as a group. Through being together, we have all learned that what we have together is more powerful than any pain any of us have ever experienced when we were not a group."

Prior to her participation in the group, her "confidence levels were very low, and I felt as if no one even liked me. After hanging out with only these girls, they showed me that I can be completely myself, which has made me more confident than I have ever felt before." Based on the support she receives from the group, "I only want to surround myself with people who are not only similar to me but love who I am as a person. They also introduced me to the fact that whether I'm around someone random, or someone that I've known for ten years, that I should just be my goofy, caring self."

Michelle's experience in this peer group demonstrates the value of having a support group in which members enjoy each other's company through humorous interactions. Members can also assist other members in coping with issues in their lives, given that they know about the history of each other's issues. Michelle also notes that she has acquired a sense of personhood through her languaging with her peers (Bloome et al., 2019) related to "who I am as a person ... my goofy, caring self."

In an interview, she noted that "I don't want to be surrounded by people who are going to make me feel like I can't act like myself around them." Rather, she wants "to surround myself with people who are not always similar to me but love, but love who I am as a person." Within her group, she "feels so loved; like they for sure made me feel happier and better about coming to school."

At the same time, adolescents acquire practices involving being included as group members or being excluded from peer groups. Analysis of narrative accounts of peer group exclusion by 682 adolescents found that 90% had experienced exclusion, primarily in school contexts, associated with five categories of actions involved in being excluded: ignoring, disqualifying, insulting, blaming, and creating new rules (Sunwolf & Leets, 2004).

Students also experience practices resulting in conflicts within and across peer groups, in some cases due to languaging miscommunications or misunderstandings. One challenge in experiencing these conflicts is that students had difficulty knowing how to react spontaneously, given the unpredictable nature of tense, unfolding conflicts in their interactions with peers (Roth, 2014). In having to make split-second decisions as events unfold within their group, they may not know whether those decisions will be productive in addressing or preventing a conflict.

Engaging in Shared Activities or Projects

Students also noted how they benefited from forming groups for the practice of engaging in certain shared activities or projects that provided them with a sense of purpose for their interactions. Betsy noted that, as a fifth-grader, she and two peers founded a sumo wrestling club competition in the school parking lot, contrary to their school's policy. She noted how "secret sumo became the token sport of the fifth grade. It was like our community of kids duking it out in the parking lot before school. It was beautiful. Nothing could ever beat us down."

In reflecting on this activity, Betsy noted how she and her peers created "a community that included students of different ages, genders, cliques, and backgrounds. We took something as boring as waiting in the parking lot before school and made it fun." She also noted that she and her other two peers were "happy around each other, trusted them, and had mutual respect. I have had the blessing to share the same relationships with friends in high school."

ACTIVITY: CONTEXTUALIZING PRACTICES FOR PARTICIPATING IN PEER GROUPS

Students could discuss or write about their group members' practices that serve to support their peer group, as evident in their use of specific languaging actions. For example, they may note how members are willing to support members coping with problems in their lives by inviting them to openly share their problems.

They may also observe how, when group members engage in the practice of proposing an activity/project, for example discussing going on a bike ride, that other group members, rather than rejecting that proposal, are willing to modify or negotiate alternative options for engaging in the activity. They may also portray instances of a group agreeing to achieve a shared purpose driving an activity/project. For example, working on a project to raise money to support a homeless peer serves to motivate or, in some cases, to not motivate their engagement in that activity/project.

They could also describe enacting shared *purposes* for use of practices for forming their groups related to participation in a shared activity/project, as was the case with Betsy's sumo wrestling group. For example, students may describe how members of their face-to-face or social media group share a common interest as fans of a sports team, creating or responding to specific movie/video genres, participating in outdoor activities, engaging in political action, etc. For these activities/projects, students may be more likely to bond together when they value the purpose driving their activity/project.

Enacting Peer Group Practices Based on Norms and Discourses

Adolescents also employ practices in peer groups based on adhering to *norms* and *discourses* shaping their practices. They are sensitive about how they should act to maintain the memberships, status, and/or popularity within a group given their identity as a group member. Detra identified primary *norms* underlying adopting *identities* for shaping interactions in her group:

> Rule of the group: "Be a parrot within the parrots." To us, this means that we have to talk during our meetings as it is necessary to open up so the others can help if necessary because one of us might relate to what the other is going through. I feel like we are respected by our other friends and I don't think everyone ever in school knows of our friend group. We talk and feel comfortable with one another because we have opened up to the other.

They are also aware of how group members subscribing to certain ways of knowing/believing is associated with how certain practices are valued or not valued in their group, such as the importance of keeping in touch with members experiencing difficulties or issues in their lives.

Norms and Discourses Constituting Race, Class, and Gender Peer Group Membership

Adolescents also adopt different norms or discourses based on their peer group membership related to race, class, or gender. For example, students in White focus groups often draw on discourses of race to employ general labels such as "the Hispanics" or "the Black kids," while Black and Latinx students were more likely

148 Students Co-Authoring Figured Worlds

to perceive racial-ethnic groups as including students involved with other groups as well as recognizing these other groups more in terms of diversity within those groups (Crabbe et al., 2019).

Students may also define their peer group allegiances or membership based on social class. Students from middle-to-upper-middle-class family backgrounds may align with more "conventional" groups, while lower-income families align themselves with "unconventional" groups.

As noted in Chapter 2, upper-middle-class female peer group members employed languaging associated with displaying academic success related to school achievement based on enacting "portfolio shape-shifting" identities (Gee et al., 2001). In their conversations, they shared experiences related to being valued as successful according to markers of school success in terms of earning good grades or being perceived as popular participants in school functions. In contrast, females from lower-income families focused their conversations on their relations with peers and family members outside of school as salient to their identity construction.

Adolescents are also socialized to adopt certain peer group practices based on gender. For example, members of a female peer group may value the use of practices related to sharing their personal lives with each other (Way, 2013). Members of a male peer group may value practices associated with being perceived as "cool" related to enacting certain masculine practices (Way, 2013). Male members may also assume that, as they move into adulthood, based on a discourse of individualism and autonomy, they should be able to cope with challenges in their lives on their own. As one participant in the study noted, "'Now I'm a man, I need to take care of myself and not rely on others'" (Way, 2013, p. 210).

At the same time, it is important not to essentialize these gender differences based on certain gender stereotypes; for example, that females and males consistently adopt certain set practices, given how female and male adolescents may adopt a range of alternative practices that defy these stereotypes (Butler, 2006). This is particularly important for providing support for gay adolescents; for example, by fostering gay students' portrayal of the exploration of their experiences through their writing (O'Daniel & Mikulec, 2020).

Voicing Emotions as Languaging Actions Shaping Peer Relations

Students described events in which they voiced emotions as languaging actions that shaped their experience of conflicts with peers (Lewis & Tierney, 2013). Harry described an instance where he and a peer, E, were hiking in the woods after they thought they had tied up their canoe at a certain spot on a lake; Harry and E return to where they assumed they had left their canoe only to not find their canoe. When E noted that he'd asked Harry to tie up the canoe, Harry can't recall doing so, leading to their arguing over whose responsibility it was to "tie up the boat, both denying we had anything to do with the catastrophe at hand. Our anger soon turned into sadness and despair, as we realized how serious our predicament actually was."

After attempting to brainstorm for several hours about how they could return on the river to their camp, they then heard a clunking noise in the distance, only to discover their canoe at a different spot from where they had assumed they had tied it up.

> After our mini brawl out at sea, we both looked at each other in the eyes and again started to laugh hysterically. We couldn't contain ourselves as we paddled. Eventually, we made it back to the houseboat, where E's parents were waiting for us.

In reflecting on this event, Harry noted that "things me and E said to each other provoked strong emotions in each other. We fought a bit, and became distant until we learned the truth. Because of the conflict, our relationship grew stronger."

During unfolding events leading to conflicts, adolescents may experience languaging emotions that exacerbate the conflict. However, after the intensity of these unfolding emotions subsides, their conflicts may lead to reconciliation. These events demonstrate how emotions as languaging actions can serve to enact and defuse conflicts, illustrating the need for adolescents to know how to then cope with those emotions to achieve reconciliation.

ACTIVITY: CONTEXTUALIZING PRACTICES RELATED TO NORMS/DISCOURSES CONSTITUTING PEER GROUP PRACTICES

Students could discuss or write about practices associated with adhering to or violating norms or discourses in a peer group. These practices may include:

- Identifying and contextualizing emotions shaping relations or conflicts in unfolding events related to identifying reasons for those emotions leading to addressing those emotions, for example, reasons for participants' anger with others, to achieve reconciliation in an event.
- Making split-second decisions in unfolding events/situations in ways that require an intuitive sense of determining appropriate actions. This sensemaking draws on the group's norms for coping with previous related events/situations.
- Noting how participants were able to stand back from an event to determine how a history of previous conflicts triggers a current conflict so that, based on analysis of reasons for those previous conflicts, parties can achieve some resolution based on addressing those reasons.

Ms. E's Students' Survey Perceptions of Norms and Discourses Constituting Peer Group Practices

Ms. E also had students reflect on how certain norms and discourses shape their practices based on their peer group status/popularity within their school world. Previous research documents how peer groups such as the "jocks" may be perceived as relatively high in popularity in their school worlds, but not necessarily high in terms of academic performance, perceptions associated with "geeks" (Crosnoe, 2011; Eckert, 1989). Depending on the socioeconomic status of a school, "preppies" may be perceived in a positive or negative light, while other groups such as "druggies" may be perceived as outliers or deviant within a school world.

In her study of peer groups in one Bay Area high school, Bucholtz (2011) found that the White preppies were "the institutionally most powerful white students at the school; they were well known and highly visible, often holding prestigious roles within elite extracurricular activities such as the student newspaper and the student council" (p. 44). In contrast, alternative peer groups "stood in opposition to the conformity and conservatism associated with mainstream students. Such teenagers often operated outside the institutional structure of the school and reveled in challenging its authority" (p. 44).

At the same time, members of both groups shared common aspirational and academic goals, while the non-conventional groups were more critical of an obsession with the need to achieve popularity. Bucholtz also found that Black students' use of hip-hop practices served to enhance their status, given how hip-hop was perceived as highly popular for all groups in the school.

At the same time, in her study, adolescents also often disavowed the practices of categorizing or classifying themselves as not capturing the complexities of their identities.

In 2019, Ms. E had her students complete rating forms associated with their perceptions of the importance of certain factors shaping their perceptions of popularity in their school world (see Table 7.1).

In response to the statement "my being perceived as popular by my peers in school," 83.3% indicated that "being perceived as popular" was either a "1" ("less

TABLE 7.1 Students' perceptions of the importance of factors shaping their identities (n = 54)

My being perceived as popular by my peers in school is: Less important (42.6%) Important (40.7%) Neutral (7.4%) Somewhat important (9.3%) Most important (0%)
My being perceived by others based on how much money I'll earn in life is: Less important (25.9%) Important (38.9%) Neutral (18.5%) Somewhat important (16.7%) Most important (0%)
My perception of peers' popularity depends on how they dress or the car they drive. Strongly disagree 33.3% Disagree 37% Neutral 16.7% Agree 11.1% Strongly Agree 2%

important") (42.6%) or a "2" ("important") (40.7%), with 0% indicating "most important." The majority, therefore, did not perceive being popular as important within their school world, although some of their perceptions may be due to conceptions of the meaning of "popular" as having relatively negative connotations.

In response to the statement "my perception of peers' popularity depends on how they dress or the car they drive," 70.3% either strongly disagreed (33.3%) or disagreed (37%), with only 13.1% either agreeing/strongly agreeing. This suggests that students do not perceive social class status markers related to their families' wealth or social class, as reflected in their clothing or the type of car they drive, influencing their peers' popularity.

Similarly, when asked to rate the importance of "my being perceived by others based on how much money I'll earn in life," 64.8%, or about two-thirds, rated the importance of earning money as a "1" ("less important") (25.9%) or a "2" ("important") (38.9%), with no one rating this as "most important." This suggests that financial earning related to class status was less salient for this group of students.

In response to the statement "how students talk depends on who they hang out with," 55.5% either agreed (37%) or strongly agreed (18.5%), a reflection of the importance of how they perceive specific language registers as markers of peer group identity/membership—although 18.5% responded as "neutral." This suggests that through engagement in certain peer groups, members acquire use of a certain "insider language" (Madsen et al., 2015) constituting membership in a peer group.

These survey results are somewhat consistent with Bucholtz's (2011) findings, given how certain peer groups do not necessarily perceive being popular as necessarily desirable, as well as how, despite the fact that the school is located in a middle-to-upper-middle-class suburb, markers related to class status were perceived as less salient.

ACTIVITY: DISCUSSING OR WRITING ABOUT PERCEPTIONS OF PEER GROUPS IN A SCHOOL

Students could discuss or write about their perceptions of different categories of peer groups in their school based on differences related to popularity, academic focus, and deviation from school norms. For example, they may identify groups such as the "Populars," "Jocks," "Good-Ats," "Fine Arts," and "Brains" (Crabbe et al., 2019), as well as categories unique to their own school culture. They may identify their categories for these groups and practices most valued in these groups, leading to noting their allegiances to or lack of connections with these groups.

Students can also create a graph or map for visually placing their groups as related to other groups based on these criteria. For example, on a

152 Students Co-Authoring Figured Worlds

continuum of high versus low popularity, the "Populars" or "Jocks" may be placed towards the upper end of a continuum. In contrast, the "Druggies" or "Goths" may be placed on the low end of the continuum.

They could also reflect on experiences of being included or excluded from participating in a group given how they are judged as "fitting in" or "not fitting in" to a group given that group's status or standing within the school's hierarchy.

Students could then assess the benefits and liabilities of these group hierarchies within their school world based on their analysis. For example, on the one hand, they may note that some groups serve as a home for students who perceive themselves as outsiders within the school culture. Yet, on the other hand, they may also perceive these groups as excluding students, resulting in a segregated school world undermining building relations across differences.

Adopting Identities in Peer Groups

Adolescents also adopt certain *identities* within peer groups associated with personhood by being valued for engaging in certain practices by other group members to make positive contributions to the group. They may assume a leadership role by providing a group with a sense of direction or delegating responsibilities to group members. They may also contribute their knowledge or expertise to help their group address certain problems or issues.

By assuming these identities, group members experience a sense of belongingness relative to perceiving themselves and being perceived as a valued, contributing group member. Detra notes how the identities she assumed in her group served to complement other members' identities:

> Our roles are what make us perfect together. We balance each other. E looks mean but when one gets to know her, she melts hearts. Her smile is contagious and can light up a whole room.
>
> E is the selfless person in the group. N is the rude ass goof. When we all see him, our first instinct is to laugh. His clownery is on a whole 'nother level. He's also clingy in a cute way.
>
> Z shows up when he wants to show up and he's like E, however, I don't believe that his smile can light up a whole room.
>
> J is the fact bringer and anime superfan. She can talk about anime constantly. She's also sassy and doesn't know when to shut up.
>
> M and S are such cuties. S doesn't come early to school so we never really have time to bond.

Me and A are the stylish people in the group. I'm more of the stylist and fashion advice consultant. I am the mother of the group as I feed them and listen to their problems.

Yolanda describes how members of her group assume identities based on their contributions to the group:

S, the mom. S would do anything for us. She takes care of us and makes sure we stay out of trouble. She cares when nobody else seems to.

We have E, the freshie. I've been best friends with her longer than the squad existed. Since my sophomore year and her freshman year.

We have S, the driver, and the party animal. S always drives us everywhere. I can't recall a time she didn't drive us. She is a major party animal.

It is hard to categorize myself; I think I would be the emotionally unstable one and comic relief. I always am on the verge of a breakdown, especially when one messes with my ice cream.

I was kind of like a comic relief. Like I'm really good at making everyone laugh. I said one of them was a mom cause she really is. And then the other one is actually a mother. No, no, no. Like just a mom. That's my role.

Detra and Yolanda are perceiving how the different members of their peer groups each enact certain unique practices constituting their identities in ways that benefit their groups.

Assuming Identities for Influencing Others' Actions

Students also assume *identities* related to employing practices for engaging in "push," to influence others to engage in certain activities or events (Ende & Everette, 2020). For example, group members may attempt to organize a peer group to protest a school problem, requiring that students know how to employ languaging to obtain others' agreement to participate.

For example, Allen describes how his peer group is organized around participation in traditions of "poker night, Halloween night, and other big traditions. They're so impactful that no member will ever forget about this group even if they wanted to." For Halloween, members of the group pose for a photo on a local golf course hole and hold a race around the course.

He describes how members of his peer group are

unconsciously pushing each other to be better. There is so much competitiveness in the gang that makes each member strive to improve. If one person is really good at one aspect, everyone tries to reach the level the top dog is at.

154 Students Co-Authoring Figured Worlds

At the same time, group members may adopt identities involving their peers attempting to "pull" them into engaging in an activity. Engaging in pulling languaging requires persuading their peers of the value of participating in an activity or recognizing the value of being included as a group member (Ende & Everette, 2020).

Allen notes how participation in the group

> has shaped my personality and how I act in society. I will continue to stay determined and motivated to always be improving, whether that is physical or mental skills [and this] has taught me to support every single person when they are struggling.
>
> One time during the summer the gang went to one of the member's cabins. When it was really late one night, gazing at the stars, the group had a compliment circle where we all complimented each other on the things we love about each individual.
>
> My group of friends has shown me that there's people who think and act like me. So I've slowly been able to start being more extroverted.

Allen's peers employed languaging that not only served to enhance his sense of belonging within the group. They also modeled that use for languaging to enhance his ability to interact with others so he was "being more extroverted."

ACTIVITY: CONTEXTUALIZING PRACTICES FOR ADOPTING IDENTITIES IN PEER GROUP WORLDS

Students could discuss or write about how they adopted certain *identities* related to contributing to or influencing others in their group; for example, assuming a leadership role in their group to "push" other members to employ certain practices or their experiences of being "pulled" into participating in a group.

Students could also describe or write about how individual group members assume particular identities related to contributing their expertise in certain practices/genres to the overall group. Students could also discuss or write about their experiences of being socialized into a group as a new member by understanding the group's practices associated with certain purposes, norms, narratives, media/genres, and discourses.

Use of "Insider Language" for Enacting Peer Group Relations

Students also noted how they enact these practices within peer groups through the use of "insider language" (Madsen et al., 2015) known only to group members as a means of enacting exclusive relations between members, language that often involves the use of humor or parody.

Allen describes how the use of "insider language" is central to his group's interactions, given that

> the tone of speech is rarely serious. This includes mostly speaking in jokes, slang, accents, and imitations. Jokes are made about anything and everything. Jokes seem to flow in and out constantly. The more random and unorthodox the jokes, the better.

He describes how for members, "as speakers, the goal is to get the point across in as few words as possible, and this is really noticeable with this group. 'One-hundred percent' (the name of the group's text group chat) is shortened to 'hundred p,' and 'doubletree' (a hotel they hang out and swim at because one member's dad is part of the staff) is shortened to 'dub tree' or even just 'the tree.'"

Allen also notes how members of his peer group are continually generating new words "so other people don't really know what we're saying sometimes. We also use different words because they are just fun to say out loud." He cites an example of the use of the word, "clei," as a "synonym for bad, awful, terrible, or inferior. The gang constantly makes fun of each other whenever we are together. So, someone would say something like, 'You are so clei at this game.'" The group also created the word "'Chrester,' which is essentially a roast that means they only go to church on Christmas and Easter."

Engaging in this anachronistic "insider language" led him to assume the identity of "someone who wasn't afraid of joking and messing around, and it also forced me to become uncomfortable. I changed from someone who was more quiet and into breaking the rules/laws, into a better person."

Marvin described how his peer group, the "Animal Kingdom," uses

> nicknames and other inside jokes to separate us from others. We are a big mixing pot when it comes to having style, taking inspiration from anything and everything around us … everyone is given a nickname, for the most part, that includes animal names such as rhino or the dragon warrior.

Members of his peer group also used languaging through "a secret handshake that only members of the kingdom know. The handshake consists of many different claps and snaps and is used every time we see each other whether in school or outside of school."

Marla describes her peer group's languaging as based on a "discombobulated dialect that has made deciphering it a long and tedious task. Although their speech is daunting to follow, they have clearly laid out roles for their members and granted them titles to fit accordingly. Their speech seems to be a collage of seemingly completely different words and phrases." An instance that was recorded between two members followed something like this: "I'm about to Dairy Queen myself right off a roof. Though certain sayings will stay unique to particular members, everyone can understand and respond in their own manner."

She notes that the practice of voicing insults actually has a positive influence, given that "when people who you care about and care about you mock parts of you, it's impossible to think of them as things to feel bad about. Things I was self-conscious about suddenly became something I feel comfortable to joke about."

Marla attributes her development to participate in the group:

> Because of them, I feel much happier and am willing to share my thoughts without the fear of being mocked. Having a mix of people who share common interests and interests far from my own has allowed me to expand my views on communication. I am now able to talk to people I do not know and my social pool has expanded and allowed me to find new connections.

She also notes how each "individual member fulfills the roles given to them by the rest. Their behavior is reliable. They are also reliable in their meetings which occur every morning before school in the same location."

These students' use of "insider language" that only members comprehend serves to create an exclusive group identity, enhancing their sense of belonging.

Much of the students' use of "insider language" consists of humor and parody that serve to mitigate against being overly serious in their interactions as a means of enjoying each other's company. Mason described his group's use of "insider language" through "double-voicing" (Bakhtin, 1981) or parody of different registers or accents, noting how, in

> Junior year, this group spoke in a British tone and accent for nearly three weeks. Yelling out "Look at his trainers, yeah!!!" and "Whatup bruv?," was starting to become part of their normal vocabulary. They really try to play the part by morphing their faces, and really trying to change their voice.

Students acquire practices constituting participation in the figured world of romance (Holland et al., 1998). In Bill's narrative, "The Royal Request," he and his peers describe elaborate plans for issuing an invitation to his peer at the beginning of a class to go the school's homecoming ball:

> As he enters the classroom, he rehearses what he anticipates will happen
> "First, I will put my crown on, grab the bouquet of flowers in one hand, and in the other go over my lines. Then, N will carry the scroll into the room to make the announcement, right after J, my other accomplice, blows a trumpet to get the class's attention. Once N gets done making the announcement, I will walk in and say my lines, asking M to homecoming."

At the same time, he wonders, "What if J or N mess up? What if I mess up? What if I am so nervous, that I throw up all over the people in the first row? What if M says no?" That last one scares me.

In the beginning of class, "J walks in to blow the trumpet. Do-do-do-dooo!"

Then N walks in and unravels the scroll and clears his throat, "Huh-huh. Here ye! Here ye! Shalt M rise for a few words from thy King!" he declares, in a booming voice.

"Okay, it's showtime," I think to myself. My hands are shaking and I feel a single bead of sweat fall through my hand.

As I enter the room, a few girls exclaim, "Ahhhs" while some of my friends yell, "Atta way B!"

"M," I cry out, "I have searched hither and thither to find my Queen, and I have found thee. Will you accompany me to Homecoming?" "Yes! Of course!" M says.

As I hear this, a wave of relief washes over me as now I can relax. Still shaking, I give her a hug as our spectators erupted in claps and cheers.

As I give M a hug goodbye and we all start to go our separate ways, I finally relax now that the proclamation has been announced and the recipient has accepted the invitation to the ball later that month."

In this narrative about this unfolding event, Bill is co-authoring the figured world of romance (Holland et al., 1998) through parodying, or "double-voicing," (Bakhtin, 1981) certain language registers/dialects, double voicing a "royal," Elizabethan register as in "'Here ye! Here ye! Shalt M rise for a few words from thy King!'" and "'I have searched hither and thither to find my Queen, and I have found thee.'" Bill and his peers' use of an Elizabethan register reflects their awareness of how language itself serves to enact the event contextualized within the figured world of romance.

ACTIVITY: CONTEXTUALIZING USE OF "INSIDER LANGUAGE" FOR ENACTING IDENTITIES IN PEER GROUPS

Students could describe or write about their use of "insider language" unique to their peer group associated with how that language functions to enact a sense of exclusivity for their group. In describing specific words or phrases, they could describe the origins of this languaging; for example, how they acquire certain words/phrases through parodying or "double voicing" (Bakhtin, 1981) language from popular culture/media texts, performers/ groups, or song lyrics in ways that draw on certain meanings or memes constituting the meaning of peer group figured worlds, as was the case with

158 Students Co-Authoring Figured Worlds

> the derivation of Laura's "Australian Voice Crackers" group. They could also describe how they perceive their use of "insider language" for enacting exclusivity as well as a sense of play in their group to enhance group bonding.

Adolescents' Use of Genres and Media/Literature for Enacting Peer Relations

Adolescents also enact peer relations through the use of genres and media/literature. For example, one popular online social genre involves social responses to YouTube videos. One of the most popular YouTube videos for adolescents is Let's Play YouTube, *www.youtube.com/user/LetsPlay*, where adolescents share their experience playing games such as Minecraft (Dezuanni, 2020). (For a video by Michael Dezuanni (2021) on his research on "peer pedagogies" involved in creating Let's Play Minecraft videos, see *t.ly/UyCT.*) (For one example of a video, where Gemini Tay (2021) describes creating an island using Minecraft over the period of 100 days, and which had over three million views, see *t.ly/hh4s*).

Based on his research, Dezuanni posits that the appeal of these videos as a social media genre constituting what he describes as "peer pedagogy" derives less from participants providing instructions on playing games and more on their sharing their personal experiences playing the games, interaction with other members of their group, and sharing personal information about themselves as a means of appealing to their viewers.

Ms. E also had students share their responses to media/literature for discussions of practices constituting their own peer relations. Students inferred connections between the conflicts between Ralph's and Jack's peer groups in *Lord of the Flies* (Golding, 1997) with experiences of conflicts in their own lives. These conflicts between Ralph and his two supporters, Piggy and Simon, and Jack's group revolve around a lack of trust between the two groups. They each had competing notions of how to survive on the island in order to be rescued, where Ralph and his two peers stress the importance of maintaining a signal fire while Jack's group is more focused on hunting food.

In the novel, Ralph distrusts Jack, given his failure to respond to Ralph's requests regarding maintaining the signal fire. Sharon cites the example in *Lord of the Flies* in which Ralph "is not happy that Jack has let the fire go out. Ralph tries to tell Jack that meat is not their highest priority and that getting rescued is." Their conflict results in "Ralph's trust in Jack [starting] to diminish at this point and their relationship worsens." She compares Jack's languaging actions with her peers not doing "the thing that they were supposed to do. Their reactions served to limit my trust in them."

Deborah compares the growing conflict between Ralph and Jack with her experience of peers not providing her with consistent support when "I became

Co-Authoring Peer Group Figured Worlds **159**

closer with someone that they didn't like. They showed me that they were not true friends because they gave up on me, just like the boys gave up on the fire. They lost my trust because they abandoned me for petty reasons."

Assad describes how when the boys first were on the island, Piggy began asking questions as to their location "but nobody really speaks as they don't really know each other and trust hasn't been established." She compares the boys' not having relevant information about their location with her own experience of moving to her community and being excluded. She was "confused with my surroundings and asking questions with my peers, but nobody would speak to me as there was no trust established and little 6th graders didn't like strangers."

Comparing portrayals of peer group conflicts in *Lord of the Flies* to their own experiences with peer conflicts led students to identify reasons for these conflicts, often having to do with a lack of trust between peers (Stommel, 2016). Students noted the impact of lack of consistency of support across time, failing to resolve conflicts, exclusionary actions, and need for emotional support related to enacting trusting relations.

ACTIVITY: CONTEXTUALIZING PRACTICES IN MEDIA/LITERATURE PORTRAYALS OF PEER GROUP CONFLICTS

Students could respond to portrayals of peer group conflicts in media/literature by identifying the nature of and reasons for those conflicts. They could then infer connections to similar conflicts in their own lives, noting reasons for those conflicts and attempts to achieve some reconciliation. For example, in responding to the conflicts between families in *Romeo & Juliet* and *West Side Story*, students could identify similar conflicts between families or groups in their own lives, such as conflicts between candidates of political parties vying for election.

Drawing on Peer Group Practices for Use in the ELA Classroom

How can teachers draw on the use of these practices from students' peer group worlds in the ELA classroom? As noted in Chapter 4, students can write about their peer group experiences to reflect on their use of practices portrayed in their ethnography writing (Beach & Caraballo, 2021a) and their narrative writing (Beach & Caraballo, 2021b).

Teachers can also support the development of a free-reading program in which students interact with each other in ways that build relations. Students select their books to read and then share their responses to those books through book talks or interacting informally with peers about their experiences reading those books.

For example, four eighth-grade teachers in a middle school created a program for an entire school year. Students devoted class time to voluntary reading of self-selected young adult literature that appealed to them at their own pace (Ivey & Johnston, 2013).

The teachers did not employ quizzes or comprehension questions to determine students' understanding of their reading, but rather focused on fostering peer group social sharing of responses to the books. Observations of the student and end-of-the-year interviews with 71 students found that they were often highly engaged with reading about adolescent characters coping with challenges similar to challenges in their own lives (Ivey & Johnston, 2013). Students also engaged in book-talk and informal recommendations to their peers.

In their groups, students valued sharing their responses with other students who read the same book. "'Me and Layla were reading the books at the same time, so we would talk to each other about it, and then I would have to go back and reread or whatever and figure out what they were trying to say'" (p. 261). They also shared responses with peers with whom they had no relationship, leading to creating new friendships. "'We both read that, and we talked about how much we liked it, and now we're really good friends'" (p. 262) and "'we really weren't that close before, but it turns out we both had an experience in that book, and we bonded over that'" (p. 262). Students also created stronger relations with their teachers. "'They're talking to me as if they're readers and I'm a reader, so we're on an equal playing field. It's no longer teacher and student. We're the same'" (p. 262).

Students also identified changes in their ability to empathize with others' perspectives associated with considering their peers' perspectives. One student noted that "'I thought [*Destroying Avalon* by Kate McCaffrey] was really good, really sad at the end. But it just makes you think about, to pay attention to how people react, to pay attention to how they're feeling about stuff.'" (p. 262). They also shared how they became "'more open-minded because of the stuff I read ... more open-minded and more willing to listen'" (p. 264). Students also assumed social agency through noticing how their peers benefited from books they recommended those peers to read.

Summary

This chapter described how adolescents co-author peer group worlds based on their shared use of practices for languaging interacting with each other. One critical practice constituting peer relations revolves around the importance of adolescents' need for trust in each other established through their languaging. Students also portrayed how they bonded through the use of shared texts or media and employing "insider language" to foster a sense of group exclusivity. At the same time, they also experienced coping with challenges and conflicts between groups, requiring that they act together cohesively.

References

Bakhtin, M. (1981). Discourse in the novel. In M. Bakhtin, *The dialogic imagination: Four essays* (M. Holquist, Ed.; C. Emerson & M. Holquist, Trans.; pp. 259–422). University of Texas Press.

Beach, R., & Beauchemin, F. (2019). *Teaching language as action in the ELA classroom.* Routledge.

Beach, R., & Caraballo, L. (2021a). How language matters: Using ethnographic writing to portray and reflect on languaging actions. *Journal of Adolescent & Adult Literacy, 65*(2), 139–148.

Beach, R. & Caraballo, L. (2021b). Reflecting on languaging in written narratives to enact personal relations. *English Teaching: Practice & Critique, 20*(4), 521–533.

Bloome, D., Brown, A. F., Kim, M-Y., & Tang, R. J. (2019). Languaging personhood in classroom conversation. In R. Beach & D. Bloome (Eds.), *Languaging relations for transforming the literacy and language arts classroom* (pp. 235–254). Routledge.

Bucholtz, M. (2011). *White kids: Language, race, and styles of youth identity.* Cambridge University Press.

Butler, J. (2006). *Gender trouble: Feminism and the subversion of identity.* Routledge.

Carlson, W., & Rose, A. J. Activities in heterosexual romantic relationships: Grade differences and associations with relationship satisfaction. *Journal of Adolescence, 35*(1), 219–224.

Crabbe, R., Pivnick, L. K., Bates, J., Gordon, R. A., & Crosnoe, R. (2019). Contemporary college students' reflections on their high school peer crowds. *Journal of Adolescent Research, 34*(5) 563–596.

Crosnoe, R. (2011). *Fitting in, standing out: Navigating the social challenges of high school to get an education.* Cambridge University Press.

DeSteno, D. (2015). *The truth about trust: How it determines success in life, love, learning, and more.* Plume.

Dezuanni, M. (2020). *Peer pedagogies on digital platforms: Learning with Minecraft Let's Play videos.* MIT Press.

Dezuanni, M. (2021, July 13). Learning with Minecraft Let's Play videos: Peer pedagogies on digital platforms. [Video]. YouTube. Retrieved from http://t.ly/UyCT

Eckert, P. (1989). *Jocks and burnouts: Social categories and identity in the high school.* Teachers College Press.

Ende, F., & Everette, M. (2020). *Forces of influence.* American Society for Curriculum & Development.

Gee, J. P., & Allen, A. R., & Clinton, R. (2001). Language, class, and identity: Teenagers fashioning themselves through language. *Linguistics and Education, 12*(2), 175–194.

Golding, W. (1997). *Lord of the flies.* Penguin.

Holland, D., Lachicotte, W., Skinner, D., & Cain, C. (1998). *Identity and agency in cultural worlds.* Harvard University Press.

Hommel, B., & Colzato, L. S. (2015). Interpersonal trust: An event-based account. *Frontiers in Psychology.* Retrieved from https://doi.org/10.3389/fpsyg.2015.01399

Ivey, G., & Johnston, P. H. (2013). Engagement with young adult literature: Outcomes and processes. *Reading Research Quarterly, 48*(3), 255–275.

Lewis, C., & Tierney, J. D. (2013). Mobilizing emotion in an urban classroom: Producing identities and transforming sign in a race-related discussion. *Linguistics and Education, 24*(3), 289–304.

MacPherson, E., Kerr, G., & Stirling, A. E. (2016). The influence of peer groups in organized sport on female adolescents' identity development. *Psychology of Sport and Exercise, 23*(1), 73–81. doi:10.1016/j.psychsport.2015.10.002

Madsen, L. M., Moller, J. S., & Karrebeck, M. S. (2015). *Everyday languaging: Collaborative research on the language use of children and youth.* De Gruyter.

Nepal, S., Sherchan, W., & Paris, C. (2011, January 3). *STrust: A trust model for social networks. 2011IEEE 10th International Conference on Trust, Security and Privacy in Computing and Communications, 2011* [Paper presentation]. Changsha, China, pp. 841–846. doi:10.1109/TrustCom.2011.112

O'Daniel, K., & Mikulec, E. (Eds.). (2020). *Writing out of the closet: LGBTQ voices from high school.* Dio Press.

Reis, H. T., Lemay, E. P., & Finkenauer, C. (2017). Toward understanding understanding: The importance of feeling understood in relationships. *Social and Personality Psychology Compass, 11*(3), Article e12308.

Roth, W.-M. (2014). *Curriculum*-in-the-making: A Post-constructivist perspective.* Peter Lang.

Stommel, J. (2016). Trust, agency, and connected learning [Weblog post]. Retrieved from www.t.ly/IL03

Sunwolf, & Leets, L. (2004). Being left out: Rejecting outsiders and communicating group boundaries in childhood and adolescent peer groups. *Journal of Applied Communication Research, 32*(3), 195–223. https://doi.org/10.1080/0090988042000240149

Tay, G. (2021, April 4). I spent 100 days in Minecraft Skyblock. [Video]. YouTube. Retrieved from http://youtube.com/watch?v=tqFC2uGxRu0

Tuggle, F. J., Kerpelman, J., & Pittman, J. (2016). Young adolescents' shared leisure activities with close friends and dating partners associations with supportive communication and relationship satisfaction. *Journal of Leisure Research, 48*(5), 374–394.

Van Bavel, J. J., & Packer, D. J. (2021). *The power of us: Harnessing our shared identities to improve performance, increase cooperation, and promote social harmony.* Little Brown Spark.

Way, N. (2013). Boys' friendships during adolescence: Intimacy, desire, and loss. *Journal of Research on Adolescence, 23*(2), 201–213.

8

CO-AUTHORING EXTRACURRICULAR WORLDS

This chapter describes how students employ certain practices through their participation in extracurricular activities (ECAs) in ways that enhance their sense of agency and belonging. Students experience a strong sense of purpose related to experiencing a sense of belonging as well as displaying competence for audiences; for example, through playing in a band. Students also acquire use of certain norms associated with acquiring languaging actions employed in certain ECAs; for example, norms for giving speeches as a member of a speech team. Students also adopt practices related to enacting their identities. For example, through their participation in performing in a band or giving speeches, they are able to display competence to others in ways that bolster their identities.

Adolescents in my study engaged in a number of different ECAs related to or housed in their high school; for example, taking part in the school band, speech team, dance/cheerleading team, or school clubs. Through their participation in these school ECAs, students gain a sense of agency based on how they are perceived for their performances, often through effective languaging. They also experience a sense of belonging as contributing members to the ECA. They also acquire practices in these ECAs through effective mentoring by adult leaders. Through these experiences, they develop a stronger sense of identity over time as someone who has certain specific practices valued by others, practices that they can apply for use in other worlds.

Purposes Related to Benefits of Participating in ECAs

Adolescents develop the use of practices in ECAs for building relationships, collaborating with others, engaging in teamwork, enacting change, and acquiring communication, conflict management, and leadership skills (Mancha & Ahmad,

DOI: 10.4324/9781003246886-10

164 Students Co-Authoring Figured Worlds

2016). In one study, students identified different purposes related to these benefits of engaging in ECA activities. For example, they noted how they gained practices of setting goals, managing time, assuming responsibilities, regulating emotions, creating new peer relations, fostering loyalty and intimacy with peers, learning collaboration practices, taking leadership roles, taking and giving feedback, acquiring communication skills, and learning to network with adults (Dworkin et al., 2003).

Adolescents participating in 120 organizations over a ten-year period that included theater and arts-based programs found that they benefited from being perceived as resources for and taking responsibilities for achieving success, as well as from receiving useful feedback from mentors and peers, including problem-posing "what-if" questions (Heath & Soep, 1998).

Through participation in the school band, Jennifer described her experience as a novice when she started playing in the school band, leading to her experiencing relations with other band members.

> The first day of marching band, I thought I was a goner. We got handed a folder with around thirty songs, and they wanted us to memorize them. I immediately thought that there was no way I was going to do this. I didn't know this at the time, but I actually was going to be successful in memorizing the music. The things that not only made me successful with memorizing the music, but also successful in finding myself, were the different words we used, the uniforms we got to wear, and drum circle. Marching band changed who I am today, and changed, for the better, who I will be in the future. I think this is because I found people who I could relate with, and everyone was so welcoming.

Through their performances as part of the band, giving speeches, or performing as members of a dance/cheerleading team, students are "displaying competence" to audiences (Csikszentmihalyi & Larson, 1984). They then receive positive feedback for their performances, bolstering their sense of agency related to perceiving themselves as highly competent; for example, in delivering speeches that move their audiences. Jennifer recalled how

> during my last season of marching band, I had a solo. It is very uncommon for a trombone to have a solo. I was so excited for it. I would most certainly not have been able to do this four years ago. Just the thought of playing solo in front of hundreds of people terrified me. It still did terrify me, but the difference is that I didn't let my shyness overcome me. I am so thankful that marching band broke me out of my shell of shyness.

Students who played in a school band also benefited from responses from audiences outside of school worlds (Kuntz, 2011). As one band member noted, "'We sing in the street. Me and my friend, [name], we was walking home and

Co-Authoring Extracurricular Worlds **165**

we was like, singing and we was like, "You like our song?" and that's how I'm meeting people. We sing our way to being friends'" (Kuntz, 2011, p. 28). Students also noted how they valued playing in the school band, which they perceived as a "'family'" and a "'a home away from home' ... They talked about the return of alumni every football season. People came back to see what is happening and reacquaint with old friends" (p. 28).

Students participating in the Barrio Writers ECA summer writing program, with ten chapters in Texas and California, produce writing related to issues in their lives associated with social change for reading aloud to their local community as well as publication in an anthology (Olson Beal et al., 2019).

Perceiving themselves as highly competent through audience feedback results in their perceiving the need to continue improving their practices. Students increased in confidence through participation in an after-school film club (Chapin et al., 2018. As one student noted,

> I've improved in my acting. So before I went to film club, I was very nervous and I did this nervous laugh. After film club, I actually got better at everything, like confidence, I'm not worried to be in front of the camera, I'm not scared.
>
> *p. 12*

Students also acquired the ability to adopt other's perspectives through collaboration on scriptwriting and experienced autonomy not found in their classrooms.

Formulating Purposes for Participation in ECAs

Because students choose to participate in ECAs voluntarily, they then derive their *purposes* for employing practices given their motivation and desire to engage in ECAs. For participating in speech contests, students define purposes on how to gain their audiences' identification with their positions or stances. For performing for audiences at sports events, members of the school band or cheerleading team engage in practices that will appeal to audiences attending these events. In contrast, in the classroom, students are engaging in practices to achieve goals/outcomes formulated primarily by a teacher. While some students, particularly successful students, may value these goals, others may not, particularly if they are not interested in the topics, issues, or texts they are studying.

Extrinsic versus Intrinsic Purposes

One issue related to their perceptions of their purposes is the extent to which students engage in ECAs simply for the *extrinsic* purpose of building their resume/portfolio for college admissions versus for their *intrinsic* value associated with their personal development (Dell'Antonia, 2019). To reflect on the latter intrinsic value, students could identify how ECA activities contribute to their sense of flow, enhancing their sense of self-efficacy and positive affect (Burdick, 2011).

Several students in my study described their experiences as members of the school band, dance, cheerleading teams, and robotics and Karate clubs employing practices involving coordination with other team members for performing for audiences.

Students also noted how playing in the band served as a "'healing mechanism' ... 'I think if you're sore about something, doesn't really matter what ... you can sit down with music and it makes it better, to an extent of course'" (Kuntz, 2011, p. 29). They also value how playing in the band was part of a tradition in which they served as mentors for younger siblings or other peers to play in the band, resulting in their perceiving their participation as a lifelong endeavor.

In describing her experience playing in the school band, Martha noted how

> being a part of the marching band gave me a sense of belonging and helped me find a positive group of friends who help make me feel better about myself rather than make me feel worse. I trust the people in my group of people because they treat me like an equal and we don't bully one another or put each other down about being excited about band because we all feel the same way about it. Marching band comes with new vocabulary, flashy uniforms, and memories that will last forever.

It is often the case that a purpose for participating in ECAs is framed to enhance students' engagement in school worlds. Participation in ECAs may contribute to enhanced academic performance (Blomfield & Barber, 2011; Brown & Larson, 2009). However, critiques of this research on the academic benefits of ECA participation note that the evidence for a causal connection between ECA practices and school is often defined primarily in terms of individualistic cognitive benefits (Shulruf, 2010). This research suggests the need for an alternative perspective for analysis of how students' affective, transactional practices with peers in ECAs enhance their relational agency in ways that improve their participation in school worlds (Bradley & Conway, 2016; Dworkin et al., 2003; Raffo & Forbes, 2021).

Students' Sense of Belonging through Participation in ECA's

Students' engagement in ECAs is related to an enhanced sense of school *belonging* (Brown & Larson, 2009), often due to how students create new peer relations through their involvement in ECAs (Dworkin et al., 2003). Participation in ECAs is particularly beneficial for adolescents from schools with a lower socioeconomic status. They may not have certain advantages present in other worlds, resulting in their increased participation in ECAs associated with their school worlds.

One study compared 1,504 eighth- to tenth-grade students in schools with a lower socioeconomic status related to their participation in ECAs. Those students who did participate were more likely to have a more positive social self-concept and self-worth than those who did not participate (Blomfield & Barber, 2011). It was also the case that students who experienced specific positive experiences in their ECAs enhanced their sense of self-worth. One explanation for these results is that, for students in schools with a lower socioeconomic status, having the opportunities for positive engagements in ECAs becomes more salient than for students from higher socioeconomic backgrounds.

Students can also experience a sense of belonging through engagement in participating in ECAs with peers. Middle-school students experienced high levels of engagement in after-school ECA programs based on their intrinsic motivation and concentrated effort as contrasted with their lack of engagement in homework completion (Shernoff & Vandell, 2008). Based on their analysis of students' engagement in ECAs in high school, Mehta and Fine (2019) found that

> what was powerful about extracurriculars is that students were supported in leading their learning. They were taking responsibility for teaching others and gradually becoming the ones who upheld the standards of the field. The more we can create similar opportunities in core subjects—giving students the freedom to define authentic and purposeful goals for their learning, creating opportunities for students to lead that learning, and helping them to refine their work until it meets high standards of quality—the deeper their learning and engagement will be.
>
> *n.p.*

One reason for adolescents' enhanced sense of engagement in ECAs involves their acquiring practices as "critical capacities foundational to success at any endeavor" (Intrator & Siegel, 2014, p. 17). Acquiring these practices motivates students to continue to acquire practices for "learning how to work through failure and success" so that participants were engaged through "doing an activity rather than learning about it" (p. 47).

ACTIVITY: CONTEXTUALIZING PURPOSES FOR FORMULATING PRACTICES IN ECAS

Students could discuss or write about how formulating purposes for practices in ECAs involves engaging audiences through specific languaging actions. For example, members of a cheerleading team may perceive the purpose of using certain cheers to elicit fans' cheers during a game. They could then compare how they can draw on formulating purposes for practices in ECAs with inferring purposes for classroom practices. For example, students may perceive the purpose of rehearsals for a performance in their theater club to engage audiences as similar to formulating purposes for their writing to engage their teacher.

Use of Brokers to Support Acquiring Practices in ECAs

Students gain a sense of purpose for gaining new practices through support from teachers, adults, and/or peers who function as brokers to assist students in acquiring these practices (Hung et al., 2012). They do so by helping students articulate and clarify their thinking.

Peers or adults, therefore, assume an essential role in modeling and facilitating languaging actions associated with engaging in ECAs. Students participating in an after-school "School-to-Jobs" program that involved interactions with adults gained clarity in defining strategies for attaining possible selves in ways that enhanced their school engagement (Oyserman et al., 2002).

One example of brokers assuming an important role is events in the Public Works drama program in New York City over a six-year period. Adolescents from low-income communities worked with adult artists, leading to performances of a play to the public (Heath et al., 2020). Participants indicated that they had never before been needed nor had they been so persistently and generously offered help in getting to where they needed to be. For many participants, rehearsals marked the first time in their lives that they knew someone cared where they were because they were needed elsewhere for good reasons. Thus, regular on-time appearances became the norm for participants (Heath et al., 2020, p. 255). As a result, adolescents developed

> positive social and conversational skills centered on the here and now and the future and no longer on their failures of the past [and] acceptance of an "I can do this" attitude leading them to take classes in other fields, seek job training, and apply with confidence for jobs.
>
> *p. 256*

Their experience reflects how certain apprenticeship experiences that differ from formal education provide students with preparation for certain jobs involving practices that are not part of formal education (Heath et al., 2020).

Analysis of extracurricular activity found that teachers, adults, and/or peers function as brokers assisting students to address certain weaknesses. They can provide individualized feedback through video recordings or commentary instead of remediation through worksheets or drilling practices (Hung et al., 2012). One limitation of remediation practices applied to all students in a classroom is that these practices may provide individual students with little help for addressing their unique weaknesses. In contrast, the brokers' feedback recognized how individual students were engaged in a particular context attempting to employ particular practices; for example, specific practices for preparing to deliver a speech.

Teachers can engage students in transferring their experiences in these ECAs for use in the classroom. For example, a teacher, Joe, drew on students' experiences of rap/hip-hop languaging actions from their local community to engage students in spoken-word performances (Fisher, 2005). Students' classroom performances involved valuing both performing as well as "listening for the words that incite and inspire" (p. 128). In this classroom,

> literacy was a practice; for example, the "read and feed" system in Joe's class depends on everyone making contributions by a) sharing their writing and b) actively listening in order to give constructive feedback to other members of the community.
>
> *p. 128*

By gaining certain practices from interacting with brokers for informal learning, students then employ those practices for use for formal learning in schools. For example, in a case-study analysis of a student, Nathan, who was having difficulty in his math classes, acquired practices for engaging in bowling competition based on support from his parents and other adults as brokers helping him develop practices to succeed in bowling (Hung et al., 2012). This included the use of an iPhone app to help Nathan identify certain issues in his bowling that resulted in what was framed as a "winning strategy" that he then applied to learn to comprehend and employ language for problem-solving in mathematics.

ACTIVITY: CONTEXTUALIZING THE ROLE OF BROKERS IN FOSTERING STUDENTS' PRACTICES

Students could discuss or write about certain practices acquired through their participation in ECAs to reflect on how they acquired those practices, and the value of doing so in terms of their development over time, through assistance from brokers. For example, students engaged in their school theater's production could describe practices associated with rehearsing and adopting different roles based on feedback from teachers or peers; for example, learning to employ a language register or dialect associated with their role as distinct from their own register or dialect.

They could then infer connections between practices involved in their ECAs and practices in the classes. For example, in their science classes, they

170 Students Co-Authoring Figured Worlds

> need to employ scientific language or, for argumentative writing, they need to adopt a formal register. Students could then reflect on the relationships between languaging and roles they adopt across different ECAs as well in different classes in their school.

Adhering to Norms Enacted Through Languaging Actions

Through participation in ECAs, students learn to adhere to certain shared *norms* through the use of languaging actions that often involve the specific use of unique "insider language" (Madsen et al., 2015). Adolescents participating in arts/theater groups were encouraged to take risks related to employing innovative practices. Taking these risks involved an awareness of the need to adhere to norms and deviate from norms perceived as limiting their performances (Heath & Soep, 1998).

Students in my study also developed specific languaging to share perceptions of practices or ideas associated with adhering to their ECA's norms. Students in the band employed "insider language" reflecting adherence to norms, words such as "band, left hace," "horn angles" and "projection"; on the dance team, "triple coupé" and "flying saucer." Student members of the school's DECA club, designed to prepare them for future careers in marketing and finance, used words such as "'channel of distribution,' 'vertical integration,' or 'cost allocation'" (see discussion of DECA later in this chapter).

Jennifer noted how members of the band used "insider language":

> In marching band, we use many different words that one might not hear on a regular basis. The main word used, that confuses people not in marching band, is chops. Mostly only brass players say the word, because they are the ones who can wear out their chops. Chops is another way of saying embouchure. An embouchure is a way in which a player applies the mouth to the mouthpiece of a brass or wind instrument. We usually say the word chops, when we can't physically play anymore. We say, "My chops are dead."
>
> Our band director will often tell us before a show to not wear our chops out. We band kids, of course, all know what this means, but when the audience hears this they are confused. Another phrase marching band kids say is "horn angles." When the marching band is practicing, we always try and focus on getting our horn angles parallel with the ground. It is hard for trombones to sometimes keep their horn angles parallel because the instrument is so long. Since I am the head trombone, I am often shouting "horn angles," to the trombones while we practice.

Consistent with the notion of "cultural modeling" (Lee, 2007), teaching languaging actions requires that teachers are willing to honor the norms underlying the specific languaging actions associated with spoken word/hiphop. For example, in one English class, one student employed the words "'they bodies' and 'they families.'" (p. 127). The teacher noted how these words involved the use of "Bronxonics to describe the words and styles of Bronx-based English, not unlike Ebonics, that many of his students use in their neighborhoods and families from all ethnic backgrounds" (p. 127). In acknowledging and valuing this use of a local dialect, "students always smile and laugh knowingly … Increasingly over the semester, students began to point out Bronxonics among each other" (p. 127). Because he believed students' use of Bronxonics "'to be real' and considered the language students spoke in their respective neighborhoods to be a dialect [the teacher supported sharing] information being transmitted all the time in other Englishes" (p. 127).

Norms Constituting Languaging Embodied Actions

Adolescents also learn to adhere to certain norms constituting use of practices in ECA events often based on shared embodied actions; for example, the ability to employ specific dance moves or cheers for use in judging a dance or cheerleading competition or effective speech delivery in speech contests. Students then receive specific feedback regarding their use of certain practices; for example, in delivering their speech, the extent to which they state their overall position on an issue in a coherent manner. Having a clear sense of these norms may differ from their classroom experience, in which a teacher's criteria may not be clearly defined or may be applied in different ways across different students.

In describing her participation on the school's dance team, Susan identified several practices associated with languaging embodied actions for coordinating dance moves with other members of her team.

> We all just share this really deep passion for dance, and when you're dancing with people, you're in close proximity all the time, because we dance so close to one another, and there're moves that you're just in each other's spaces. You just get used to it. Then, at that point, we're all just a big family.

She described this coordination in terms of how "we dance in such close proximity and go through so much together we might as well be a hive mind. We have our own language, not just as dancers but as teams. We pretty much always match (usually on purpose because we are nerds)" (Beach & Aukerman, 2019, p. 63). The language employed to describe these moves is often in French.

> If our coach told us to do six a la seconds into a triple coupé, we need to know what that means in order to execute it. Every leap or jump has a name, and some of them are pretty weird. For example, a flying saucer is not just a spaceship, but a turning leap. High kick move names get even more

interesting. With nearly everything reduced to keywords, dancers can easily learn and perform anything our coach throws at us. We also count. A lot. Every move we do needs to be in perfect unison, so numbers frequent our vocabulary.

Beach & Aukerman, 2019, pp. 63–64

She noted the importance of using embodied actions that require "stamina, strength, and power to do such difficult routines with an easy smile on our face. We need to be aware of every muscle in our bodies, down to the position of our fingers." This includes the ability to engage in mirroring other members based on the need to "count the music and make sure we are all in exactly the right formation. We need to execute every move at the right time and do all this while performing with our entire bodies and faces."

She values engaging in embodied actions as

a release for me and I feel best after an intense workout. I have developed a determination and passion that fuels me in everything. I know what it's like to be a part of a team, and the true meaning of that. Nothing can compare to the bonds I have made. The girls I dance with will always be my family.

Beach & Aukerman, 2019, pp. 64

I just think that it's affected who I am a lot, being a part of a team, and being a dancer, knowing how to move my body a lot different and how to feel emotion in things, really quickly, or just how to ... I don't know. It's just become a part of me. I've just always really enjoyed dancing and now I have a love of exercising, working out and doing yoga and things like that, and just moving.

Norms Constituting Languaging Emotions

Students also described how they employ languaging emotions in giving speeches in their speech-club competitions. Sandy values how in giving her speeches she engages in languaging actions of emotions, given how through her delivery

I made them cry. You made them feel the emotion. That was awesome. That's a huge accomplishment no matter how big or small it was, you got celebrated for it. You got positive feedback for it. Like no matter where you were or if like somebody who's always in finals and I was never in finals, they still complimented you.

Even if they didn't agree with my message, they could still see the beauty and the art behind the delivery of the message. And so, they still supported me even if they disagreed with my own personal opinions, because that didn't matter in the speech team; it was all about speech.

Co-Authoring Extracurricular Worlds **173**

She perceives languaging emotions are particularly important for moving her audience,

> for when I make the crowd cry that means I moved them with my words and I had delivered the emotion perfectly. This way of talking that can move people to tears makes our team unique. Every practice, we work on showing emotion through our words.

Marlene wrote about her experience on the school's two cheerleading teams, with one team being a competitive cheer team that competes on a national level and the other team being a "sideline" cheer team for participation during the school's sports events. Central to participation on the competitive team is the use of a "stunt": a "stunt is when there are three girls holding one girl up and doing flips and twists that look very cool and complex when done correctly." In participating in a national competition (her school's team has won two national championships at their school level), the team employs a routine consisting of a stunt sequence, tumbling, cheer, dance, jumps, and a pyramid.

> It is only allowed to be three or less minutes which is very difficult. This means that everything you do in a routine has to be perfectly thought out and put to counts which allows the girls to make it through the routine with all of the requirements.
>
> Participation on the team over a three-year period taught me the true meaning of friendship; which is honesty, trust, and happiness. It showed me different experiences, such as, responsibility, accountability, and discipline. It also helped me see what is a good decision to make and a poor decision to make. It has taught me how to approach a person you have a conflict with or even approach a person that is new and you want or need to talk to them.

Marlene perceives how her experience prepares her for a career in medicine to interact with people who when "in pain and are hurt … normally are not happy and don't wanna be nice. I have learned the correct way to approach a person that is difficult to be around or difficult to talk to." This will transfer to her "going into a hospital with sick, hurting people where I need to be able to set aside my personal life in order to better help my patients."

These students' descriptions of their participation in the school band, cheerleading, and dance teams focused on acquiring practices involving coordination of embodied actions between members of the band or teams. Susan's metaphor of how dancers are cognitively connected as a "hive mind" (Beach & Aukerman, 2019, p. 63) for coordinating dance moves reflects how they value bonding through their physical actions to coordinate movements with others.

ACTIVITY: CONTEXTUALIZING PRACTICES FOR ADHERING TO NORMS IN ECAS

Students could discuss or write about learning to adhere to norms constituting effective coordinated actions in their ECA events. They could note how to adopt these norms by recognizing the value of working collaboratively with peers based on shared "hive mind" thinking. They may also note how they employ an "insider language" to identify specific embodied actions to achieve their collaborative coordination with peers.

Students may also identify instances in which members of an ECA may have not been aware of these norms or violated certain norms, leading to their recognizing the need to acquire knowledge of those norms.

Adopting Identities in ECAs

Students also engage in the practice of adopting identities through participation in ECAs as members of a band, speech team, theater group, etc., contributing to their ECA. Jennifer described how participation in her band

> changed me, and ultimately me in the future. In the future, because of marching band, I will be looking to continue my music career at college. In the future, I think I will be more confident because of marching band. Marching band has forced me to be more confident in myself. I had to be confident in my entrances, in marching on the field, and in my solo. Confidence has been something I have struggled with my whole life.
>
> Marching band has helped me gain some much-needed confidence. I am positive that in my future, I will be a much more confident person. I've gotten so many friends from being in there. Now they're in my other classes, so I can pretend like I'm talking in front of the marching band if I have a couple of people in there.

Students' participation in friendship networks through ECAs in over 100 schools indicated that ECAs supported adolescents' school-based friendships and promotion of new friendships to a greater degree for high school than for middle-school students (Schaefer et al., 2011). One reason for this difference is that high school students have increased autonomy to select activities/friends, as well as that high schools provide more activity choices than do middle schools. Students were also more likely to participate in activities when their friends were engaged in the same activities.

Adolescents' participation as "student historians" in the New-York Historical Society Museum enhanced their sense of agency associated with the experience of autonomous actions leading to a sense of competency, belongingness with peers, and learning for future development (Frosini, 2017). In addition, students experienced a sense of purpose in helping their peers understand the history associated with museum exhibits.

Acquiring Leadership Roles in ECAs

Students also acquire leadership roles associated with mentoring or assisting peers. Analysis of ninth-graders' engagement in extracurricular activities found that, of six extracurricular domains, only student leadership and volunteering were associated with positive effects such as having a sense of purpose in life, autonomy, and self-esteem (Burdick, 2011). Arianna noted how "being in leadership positions in the group has helped me open up if I have to talk in front of people or smaller groups. It helps me to talk in front of bigger groups in school for single events or stuff like that."

In her band, Martha assumed the role of a "band librarian who works hard to make millions of copies of all our marching band tunes and organize them between all the instruments." Other roles include that of property manager, who organizes equipment, and "uni," who determines the needed sizes of uniforms for individual players.

Ken identified different roles students assume in the band based on a social hierarchy related to assuming authority in the band.

> At the top of the command is the drum major. This person is in charge of the whole band. Their job ranges anywhere from setting up practices to arranging halftime shows. Under them are the section leaders. These people are in charge of one group of instruments. The final level of power belongs to the Lieutenants. Each Lieutenant is in charge of a group of eight marchers. They teach their rank how to march, they make sure people are attending practices, they write up movement directions in shows, and many more jobs.

He assumed the role of lieutenant equivalent to "being the boss of a company; I have to keep my members happy, while also making sure they get their work done. Band has allowed me to practice those skills, while also doing an activity I enjoyed." He also valued how he learned to "play my instrument in a big ensemble, and how to make my playing stands out from the rest. I learned a lot about the capabilities of my instrument, and how to make use of them."

A number of students in the study were members of the school's DECA club, designed to prepare "emerging leaders and entrepreneurs in marketing, finance, hospitality and management in high schools and colleges" (*deca.org*). A primary activity for DECA members involves participation in local, national, and international competition events. These events involve engaging in a role-play in which members receive a prompt from a judge, who may be the CFO of a company who has hired the participants to address a certain situation or problem within the

176 Students Co-Authoring Figured Worlds

company. Participants then prepare for ten minutes to give a ten-minute presentation, including a poster or Google Slides.

Through their participation in clubs/organizations, students assumed leadership roles in ways that enhanced their sense of agency. A central aspect of Cassie's life is her four-year participation in DECA, resulting in her becoming president of the club in her senior year. She noted that an important aspect of the role-play presentations involves the use of "insider language" (Madsen et al., 2015) related to finance and business; for example, words such as "'channel of distribution,' 'vertical integration,' or 'cost allocation.' However, come competition time we throw those types of words around like we know what they mean (we usually don't)." She cited the example of being in a competition as a ninth-grader who has to address the problem of "'channels of use distribution' and I didn't really know what that meant that much, but you have to use a lot of context clues to kind of piece it together and then like give the best presentation on it."

She also noted the value of embodied languaging actions associated with "standing tall, firm handshake, maintaining eye contact; these are all things that become a part of our speaking during competition." Finally, she reflected on how in her initial competitions "I was very unsure and everything I did and talking to judges, that was very clear that I was uncertain. But now in like my fourth year of DECE, I'm much more confident by being more assertive and confrontational."

She perceived her local DECA school club as her "family" based on attending weekly meetings. In her initial meetings as a ninth-grader, she rarely spoke, but, over time, she developed an increasing sense of self-confidence, through participation in the competition, in her speaking ability. As she noted, "nothing cures the fear of public speaking like forcing yourself to do it repeatedly for three years, and nothing beats looking back and seeing your growth." Her enhanced speaking ability "has helped me so much in many other parts of my life, including school, job interviews, my job itself, college interviews, and more."

Cassie also acquired interviewing skills through participation in the competitions, given her interactions with judges. She noted how "so it's going to be someone who works like in the finance industry is like just a volunteer too but they're judging and so it's talking to an adult and being able to articulate your ideas and be confident."

She also perceived a connection between a focus on finance and her academic interest in math and data analytics. She noted how "you can take it a lot of different routes like biology or you can do something in the business sector, which is kind of what I'm thinking of doing is doing data analytics and then taking a marketing route or finance."

As president, she assumed several roles in her school, including working with another student to run the school store as well as prepare club members—40 members in Fall, 2019 (Beach & Beauchemin, 2019)—for participation in the competitions. This included helping members determine "what different events are, what you do, what people I like the best fit for, what events are then going to be like, so helping people on an individual basis."

Engaging in these mentoring practices includes the ability to build trust with new members by conveying

> that more experienced members do not necessarily know more. When new people join DECA they are usually hesitant because of the fear that they will not be good enough and because they do not know a lot about business. This establishes trust because it relieves the anxieties of new members and increases their self-confidence.

Engaging in these leadership languaging actions has bolstered her self-confidence "so that I find it much easier to interact with other people. I am much more comfortable talking to people, especially people I don't know." These experiences also help her envision future identities related to assuming

> leadership responsibilities within the company that I work for, as I believe this will make me more dedicated and rewarding. I plan to go into data science/math and tie it into the business world. To become a leader, I will work hard during college and seek internships and other experiences that will give me a leg up in the job market and help me to be the best version of myself that I can be, and to present myself as such.

Assuming these leadership identities enhanced students' sense of agency related to perceiving themselves as contributing to their ECA's overall success. The fact that DECA members rehearsed speeches for peers and family members meant that students received positive feedback related to their display of competence (Csikszentmihalyi & Larson, 1984).

Another member of the DECA club, Harry, also valued participating in the international DECA competition in Orlando where "I was able to meet kids from Spain who were able to give me so much insight on what their lives are like. I also learned many different leadership techniques that I was able to use this year in running the school store." In his work in managing the school store, he conducts surveys of students to make decisions about which products to include or not include in the store.

Because he wants to become an airline pilot and has no interest in going into business, he perceives DECA as "much more than just a business club. It's a place to practice social skills that will be essential later in life. For example, DECA has taught me how to act at a job interview and how to talk about my strengths without sounding like I'm bragging." He also "finds DECA to be more engaging than a classroom, merely because it's a subject I'm a bit more interested in."

178 Students Co-Authoring Figured Worlds

Envisioning Future Possible Selves through Participation in ECAs

Through participation in ECAs, students also adopt identities associated with envisioning future possible selves related to education or career options (Stevenson & Clegg, 2011). Jennifer reflected on how playing in the band as a "family; a community, gives people a place to belong when they feel left out." Her four years of playing in the band has "given me guidance on having to be a responsible person because I need to memorize music. It has helped me to become a leader because I had to direct my rank on and off the field. Band has also given me a sense of direction and a better future."

Analysis of British college students' participation in extracurricular/workplace activities indicated the value of these activities in helping imagine future possible selves. It was also important that students thought about "present selves" in their current time in college as well as the extent to which the students' colleges fostered students' reflection about the value of their extracurricular/workplace activities (Stevenson & Clegg, 2011).

At the same time, differences in students' race, class, and gender may have shaped the extent to which they were entertaining positive possible selves through participation in ECAs. Students participating in an after-school program for court-involved youths indicated that, in their urban schools, their experience with restrictions, rules, and detentions often limited the extent to which they could participate in extracurricular activities (Vasudevan et al., 2014). However, engagement in arts/multimodal media production within the program itself served to foster students' use of cosmopolitan literacies associated with experiencing a sense of belonging in the program.

ACTIVITY: DESCRIBING ENACTMENT OF IDENTITIES IN ECAS

How might you foster students' portrayal and reflection on their use of certain practices to enact their identities? Students could discuss or write about how they adopt certain identities through participation in ECAs associated with the use of certain practices for experiencing agency, enacting relations with others, or assuming leadership roles. They may then describe how they perceived the nature and responsibilities associated with adopting a certain role based on shared categories defining roles, as well as how they were socialized to acquire the practices specific to those roles.

For example, new members of the school's debate team may note how they learned to prepare for researching the debate topic from veteran members of the debate team. Members of a student theater production could describe how they learned to adopt certain characters' roles by

Co-Authoring Extracurricular Worlds **179**

> knowing how to interact with other characters. Students who assumed leadership roles could note how they acquired practices of formulating purposes or mentoring new members from observing previous leaders' practices.

Enacting Discourses Constituting the Value of Participation in ECAs

Students in my study voiced discourses for justifying engagement in ECAs based on the value of students learning to formulate goals or mentor as described in the book's introductory chapter. Related to her participation on the school's speech team, Sandy values how her participation fosters her sense of self-confidence for communicating with audiences. When asked in an interview about the value of participation in ECAs, she noted that students can choose to

> be a part of that and choose to learn and be better at that club. A lot of, like, our English class, that's assigned to us: you must take this English class no matter what and for a teenager that automatically puts them off, puts us off, because we don't like being told what to do. We're trying to explore ourselves, not the mold that you want me to fit into and so I feel like ... kids learn a lot more at a club because they choose it and they find a different part of themselves in that club and they make friends. They [are] like their own little-small family where they can just be themselves and they choose to be there.

She also values how she is assessed for her presentation not primarily on her topic or stance but rather on the quality of her delivery related to "the volume in your voice, the clearness in your words, run-on sentences, random subjects that you threw in there to ramble and make your speech a little bit longer."

Sandy perceives how giving speeches represents how ECAs foster the development of a sense of agency based on the need

> to be understood. Everybody strives to find someone that understands them, or a guy or a girl that they could attach themselves to that understands them on a deeper level than other people do. I feel like we're afraid to do public speaking because it's a way of showing ourselves, because it's hard not to put your emotions into your work.
>
> It exposes us, but also makes a sense of fear of not getting across what we want to. We all just want to be accepted and understood. Speeches really throw yourself out there to, like, please understand me. I guess that's why people are afraid of public speaking because it exposes so much of themselves.

180 Students Co-Authoring Figured Worlds

ACTIVITY: CONTEXTUALIZING DISCOURSES CONSTITUTING THE VALUE OF PARTICIPATING IN ECAS

Students could discuss or write about their experiences as members of ECAs involving uses of discourses constituting the value of their participation in an ECA related to their developing a sense of agency. For example, students in a school club focused on addressing environmental issues/climate change may justify the value of their participation based on the need to make changes in society, through collecting data about climate change effects in their community, related to the regulation of emissions in their community.

Employing Genres for Engaging in ECAs

Students in the study also learned to employ certain *genres* associated with participation in ECAs. Harry noted how members of the band employ genres of shared commands for engaging in certain movements during their performances.

> In order to make such a massive band move in unison, we use a lot of spoken commands. For instance, to make everyone in the band turn left, the drum major will yell "band, left hace!" As the band executes the command on the beat, we yell back "up one two three!" When we yell up, our left leg comes up in a high step. On one, we plant our left foot back down and pivot ninety degrees to the left simultaneously. The command is finished by bringing the left leg up and back down while yelling "two three!"

He describe how these commands "are effective at unifying the band in its movements, and to an outside observer, the unison movements look impressive."

> Some of the other language we use as a band relates to the music we play and how things should be played. Some of the terms we use are "horn angles" and "projection". When we say horn angles, we are referring at what angle our horn is to the ground. If we play correctly, the instrument should be held parallel to the ground. These angles directly relate to the next term, "projection". This term relates to how well an instrument's sound can cut through the sound of the band.

He also described his use of the genre of making presentations at the international DECA conference associated with the use of

> economics terms … to add a bit of "spice" to our presentations. For example, last year I made a presentation about a cutting board company

called *Epicurean*. The Judge asked me why I thought *Epicurean* should merge with a small Japanese cutting board company, and I promptly told him that we would achieve a high level of corporate synergy. I myself was only vaguely sure of what that word means, but it was enough to impress the judge, and secure a spot in the finals.

He contrasts this use of a more formal register with interactions with peers outside of the competition in which "we just have a very relaxed, normal way of talking to each other. We don't go around talking like entitled Wall Street bankers. We just talk the same way as any other group of teenagers. It gives us a way to bond with fellow chapter members."

He also noted how engaging in the competition role-play activities involving certain genres

> taught me to overcome that fear using the "Mother Bird Method." That can be described as throwing someone into something they're being afraid of and hoping they will learn how to get over it. It's done wonders, and just by doing many role-plays, I've learned how to get over my fear.

He recalled an example of a role-playing assignment in which, as a hotel manager, he had to convince a local high school to hold their prom at his hotel, requiring knowledge of argumentative genres.

ACTIVITY: CONTEXTUALIZING GENRES FOR ENACTING PRACTICES IN ECAS

Students could discuss their use of certain genres for enacting practices in ECAs; for example, the use of genres for delivering speeches or engaging in debates. They could identify how certain genre conventions serve to achieve certain uptakes; for example, how beginning a speech with a personal anecdote gains audience identification with their persona. Students could also note how they acquired these genres through observing others using genres or through mentors providing instruction in or modeling use of these genres.

Drawing on ECA Practices for Use in School Worlds

Teachers can draw on students' use of practices employed in ECAs for students to display competence in their classroom activities. In some cases, as with participation on the speech team or engagement in theater productions, the uses of speeches or drama activities are already employed in English language arts classrooms. For example, students participated in spoken-word performances in "open-mic" public events (Fisher, 2005). In these events, students experience how "'everyone has something important to say'" (p. 127).

Students could then transfer their use of languaging in these spoken-word performances to performances in the classroom. Schools themselves can promote transfer between ECAs and academic success by sponsoring ECAs to provide students with alternative opportunities to find an ECA that engages them. When these students are then successful in those ECAs, there may be opportunities for them to experience an enhanced sense of belonging with their school (Bradley & Conway, 2016).

Summary

In this chapter, I described how students employ certain practices through their participation in ECAs in ways that enhance their sense of agency and belonging. Through their participation in performing in a band or giving speeches, they are able to display competence to others in ways that bolster their identities.

References

Beach, R., & Aukerman, M. (2019). Portraying and enacting trust through writing in a high school classroom. In R. Beach & D. Bloome (Eds.), *Languaging relations for transforming the literacy and language arts classroom* (pp. 49–68). Routledge.

Beach, R., & Beauchemin, F. (2019). *Teaching language as action in the ELA classroom.* Routledge.

Blomfield, C. J., & Barber, B. L. (2011). Developmental experiences during extracurricular activities and Australian adolescents' self-concept: Particularly important for youth from disadvantaged schools. *Journal of Youth and Adolescence, 40,* 582–594. doi:10.1007/s10964-010-9563-0

Bradley, J. L., & Conway, P. F. (2016). A dual step transfer model: Sport and non-sport extra-curricular activities and the enhancement of academic achievement. *British Educational Research Journal, 42*(4), 703–728.

Brown, B. B., & Larson, J. (2009). Peer relationships in adolescence. In R. M. Lerner & L. Steinberg (Eds.), *Handbook of adolescent psychology: Contextual influences on adolescent development* (pp. 74–103). John Wiley.

Burdick, C. (2011). *Old broken crayons: Adolescent artists with autism in art education.* [Unpublished doctoral dissertation], Syracuse University. https://surface.syr.edu/tl_etd/234

Chapin, L., Deans, C., & Fabris, (2018). "After film club, I actually got better at everything": School engagement and the impact of an after-school film club. *Children and Youth Services Review, 98,* 10–16. doi:10.1016/j.childyouth.2018.11.057

Csikszentmihalyi, M., & Larson, R. (1984). *Being adolescent: Conflict and growth in the teenage years.* Basic Books.

Dell'Antonia, K. J. (2019, May 18). How high school ruined leisure. *New York Times,* Section SR, 8. Retrieved from http://t.ly/fEkI

Dworkin, J. B., Larson, R., & Hansen, D. (2003). Adolescents' accounts of growth experiences in youth activities. *Journal of Youth and Adolescence, 32*(1), 17–26.

Fisher, M. T. (2005). From the coffee house to the school house: The promise and potential of spoken word poetry in school contexts. *English Education, 37*(2), 115–131.

Frosini, C. (2017). An "I" in teen?: Perceived agency in a youth development program. *Afterschool Matters, 25,* 29–37.

Heath, S., Bellino, M. J., & Winn, M. (2020). Adaptive learning across the life span. In N. S. Nasir, C. D. Lee, R. Pea, & M. M. de Royston (Eds.), *Handbook of the cultural foundations of learning* (pp. 247–250). Routledge.

Heath, S. B. & Soep, E. (1998). Youth development and the arts in nonschool hours. *Grantmakers in the Arts Newsletter, 9*(1). www.giarts.org/article/youth-development-and-arts-nonschool-hours

Hung, D., Shu-Shing, L. & Lim, K. (2012). Teachers as brokers: Bridging formal and informal learning in the 21st century. *KEDI Journal of Educational Policy, 9,* 69–87.

Intrator, S. M., & Siegel, D. (2014). *The quest for mastery: Positive youth development through out-of-school programs.* Harvard Education Press.

Kuntz, T. L, (2011). High school students' participation in music activities beyond the school day. *Update, 30*(1), 23–31.

Lee, C. D. (2007). *Culture, literacy & learning: Taking bloom in the midst of the whirlwind.* Teachers College Press.

Madsen, J. M., Moller, J. S., & Karrebaek, M. S. (2015). *Everyday languaging: Collaborative research on the language use of children and youth.* De Gruyter.

Mancha, S. A., & Ahmad, A. (2016, October 31 & November 1). *Co-curricular activities and its effect on social skills.* [Conference presentation]. International Conference on Education and Regional Development 2016, Bandung, Indonesia (pp. 774–781).

Mehta, J. & Fine, S. (2019, March 30). High school doesn't have to be boring. *The New York Times.* Retrieved from http://t.ly/Lvol

Olson Beal, H. K., Burrow, L E., & Cross, C. (2019). The potential to empower youth and build community with out-of-school writing program strategies. *Voices from the Middle, 26*(4), 45–49.

Oyserman, D., Terry, K., & Bybee, D. (2002). A possible selves intervention to enhance school involvement. *Journal of Adolescence, 25*(3), 313–326. https://doi.org/10.1006/jado.2002.0474

Raffo, C., & Forbes, C. (2021). A critical examination of the educational policy discourse on/for school extracurricular activities—A Deweyan perspective. *Oxford Review of Education, 47*(3), 301–315.

Schaefer, D., Simpkins, S., Vest, A., & Price, C. (2011). The contribution of extracurricular activities to adolescent friendships: New insights through social network analysis. *Developmental Psychology, 47*(4), 1141–1152. doi:10.1037/a0024091.

Shernoff, D. J., & Vandell, D. L. (2008). Youth engagement and quality of experience in after-school programs. *Afterschool Matters, Occasional Paper Series, 9,* 1–11.

Shulruf, B. (2010). Do extracurricular activities in schools improve educational outcomes? A critical review and meta-analysis of the literature. *International Review of Education, 56*(5), 591–612. doi:10.1007/s11159-010-9180-x

Stevenson, J., & Clegg, C. (2011). Possible selves: Students orientating themselves towards the future through extracurricular activity. *British Educational Research Association, 37*(2), 231–246.

Vasudevan, L, Kerr, R. K, Hibbert, M., Fernandez, E., & Park, A. (2014). Cosmopolitan literacies of belonging in an after-school program with court-involved youths. *Journal of Adolescent & Adult Literacy, 57*(7), 538–548.

9

CO-AUTHORING SPORTS WORLDS

This chapter describes adolescents' use of practices for engaging in sports worlds. Adolescents infer certain purposes related to the benefits of participating in sports associated with enhanced sense of identity and development of a work ethic. Students also experience the need to adhere to norms and discourses for the use of certain practices, such as building supportive relations with team members and knowing how to cope with conflicts during games or matches. Students acquire practices related to assuming leadership identities on their teams. They also acquire use of certain genres for interacting with other team members and coaches; for example, use of charts/graphs for planning plays. Students can also engage in critical media literacy practices for responding to media sports broadcasts of professional sports.

Many of the students in my study played on one of the many teams at their high school. In doing so, they noted how they acquired a range of practices related to developing a sense of agency as well as the ability to work collaboratively with other members of their team. They also learned how to employ practices consistent with the purposes, norms, and discourses constituting their team; for example, how to play based on the rules operating in a particular sport. At the same time, they also recognized some of the limitations associated with a discourse of competition related to "winning is everything" through their own participation on teams and in viewing professional sports.

Purposes: Associated Benefits From Participation in Sports

The students perceived *purposes* for playing sports in terms of benefits from their participation in sports as contributing to their development over time (Nasir & Cooks, 2009). One study compared students who participated in sports only,

DOI: 10.4324/9781003246886-11

sports and other activities, school-based activities, and/or religious youth groups (Linver et al., 2009). The study found that students who participated only in sports had more positive relations with academic ability, self-confidence, connections with peers, character, and prosocial behaviors than students with low activity participation, particularly in developing self-confidence. In another study, participation in playing soccer enhanced adolescents' ability to connect with other players, cope with adversity, and imagine future opportunities in their life (Lee et al., 2017).

Adolescents who engage in sports also report a stronger sense of identity and work orientation than those not engaged in sports (Lee et al., 2018). A student in my study, Paul, noted how given that "school is supposed to be your main job, joining track on top of going to school, having a job, balancing my social and family life, has given me an image of what it is like to be a grown adult." Doing so requires "time management, to organize my affairs, and get my priorities in order for future, major steps in my life."

Analysis of 12,849 12th-grade student data from the Minnesota Student Survey found small, positive effect sizes on the value of participation in school sports based on opportunities to interact with peers and coaches (Van Boekel et al., 2016). By interacting with other team members, adolescents are learning to enact peer relations, as described in Chapter 7, for working collaboratively with others.

It may also be the case that certain students are more attracted to certain types of sports according to race, class, and gender differences. Some sports may entail more expense, resulting in students in middle or upper-middle-class families engaging in those sports. On the other hand, students from low-income families are likely to experience positive benefits of sports. Low-income adolescents participating in a sports program increased their social and physical competence and self-worth (Ullrich-French et al., 2013). Students from schools with a lower socioeconomic status (SES) actually have more positive experiences of success and identity development through sports than do students from higher SES schools. The former have fewer opportunities for success in their schools and other social arenas (Blomfield & Barber, 2011).

Students noted that a primary purpose for playing sports involved developing a sense of agency. A participant in a study of a track team, Octavia, developed an increasing sense of commitment related to her role, relations, and goals in improving her performance as a hurdler on the team (Nasir & Cooks, 2009). In the beginning of the season, she formulated the need to "'become a better hurdler,' which was quite general as compared to the goals of other team members who had run track longer—they had more specific goals" (p. 52).

Over time, she developed increasing confidence in her ability based on "instruction on ways to think, move, and feel like a hurdler. Octavia actively chose to take up this instruction … That is, she became more connected to the practice of track" (p. 52). She also developed more social relations with other team members, particularly with three members of her relay team, in which she perceived herself to be "'the mama of the team'… responsible for and responsive to the needs of others" (p. 53).

Students wrote about their development of agency through participation in sports based on achieving certain *purposes* (Ferrer-Wreder & Kroger, 2020). As a tenth-grade African-American new to the school, Kathy was doubtful about making the basketball team, given that "I was the new kid and the only person of color on the basketball team. I knew what I wanted to do in life would never be handed to me, so this was my chance to go out and get it."

After she impressed the coaches with her shooting ability, she made the team.

> This moment made me realize that I can go out and be the smallest person on the team, but my dedication and drive for the sport is what really makes me an athlete. I also learned that my skin color, my size, or my status was not the obstacle. It was myself.

Roberto described how through participation on his cross-country team he has

> learned what hard work really meant after running thousands of miles and hundreds of hours in the hope of dropping my time by a matter of seconds. I believe that I am also much more patient and tolerant than I would have been if I had not run cross-country which is important when dealing with the real world which I will begin to experience more and more as I go to college and beyond.

Anna reflected on how as captain of her volleyball team

> I became a much more confident and much louder person after spending the entire season with all of my crazy teammates. Without volleyball, I am certain that I would have a much different and much duller personality. I am grateful for all of the ways that my teammates and coaches have affected me and made me into an individual, rather than someone that is just like everybody else.

These students were identifying how they acquired certain *discourses* through their participation in sports that transferred to other aspects of their lives; for example, the need to cope with challenges. They also inferred how their beliefs/values were shaped by larger discourses constituting the world of sports; for example, recognizing that the need to win isn't necessarily of utmost importance in their lives.

Languaging Emotions/Embodied Actions in Sports Worlds

Students experience emotions of enjoyment and intrinsic satisfaction from participating in sports as opposed to engaging in sports for pragmatic reasons

(Inoue et al., 2015). They noted how they experienced a sense of "flow" associated with high levels of engagement through their "display of competence" (Csikszentmihalyi, 1991).

Having these positive experiences depends on the extent to which adolescents experience caring, supportive relations with team members and coaches (McLaren & Spink, 2018). For example, adolescents who perceived their soccer teams as providing a caring climate reported higher levels of enjoyment, positive attitudes towards teammates/coaches, and stronger commitment to soccer than students who reported lower levels of caring climates (Fry & Gano-Overway, 2010).

Marvin described how members of his soccer team often use language that matches our intimacy for each other: "The phrases 'I love you' and 'you are my sunshine' are commonplace on the team. Although these might seem out of place in a regular conversation, they are accepted and even desired on the soccer team."

Adolescents' languaging emotions were also related to their sensory experience of heightened embodied actions during games or matches. Kathy noted how, for members of her basketball team during a game,

> screaming and howling is how we communicate unless it's a firm smack on the back to say good job or nice shot. Trying to explain to anyone the feeling that rushes through our bodies as we run up and down the court is like trying to explain music through words, or a painting through text. We could give you a feeling of what it would be like to be us, be we can't recreate that magic that takes place on the hardwood.

Adolescents also highlighted the importance of trust as contributing to a team's sense of shared cohesion. For example, in his narrative portraying of playing in a finals' tennis match in a national tournament, Evan describes how his languaging actions shaped his perceptions of self-confidence as enacted through his inner speech: "'Yeah, I can do this,' I thought. But little did I know the maelstrom of emotions with which I was about to involve myself."

In his first match, he is losing zero to five games, resulting in "self-doubt rearing its ugly head, but there was no way I would let it show." After he loses the match, he perceives himself as "such a FAILURE. You had such a good first half of the match, but because you suck at tennis, you can't execute the win! You will NEVER win a match at Nationals."

While his peers and father provide him with positive comments to "ingrain in me that it's about effort, and not all about winning, I still didn't believe. I was slipping into the cold, deep waters of unrelenting negativity. I was set on my goal, and I was determined to reach it." His father tells him, "'Trust the process, Evan. It will come, I know it. I believe you can accomplish it, but you must believe it too.' Those words reverberated through my brain like a tennis ball being thrown into an empty court."

188 Students Co-Authoring Figured Worlds

For his next match, Evan noted that "something was different, though. I felt a calming confidence within. I don't know why, but the words 'Trust the process ... You must believe it too' continued to bounce in my head." In playing in another tie-break series of back-and-forth points that would decide the match, he notices his father and that "there was something about the way he stood so stolid, with a sense of underlying belief and courage." When he finally won the tiebreaker,

> emotions ran onto my face as my teammates surrounded me with high fives. What reverberated through my mind was my dad and his wisdom. It changed me. When you are emotional is when you are not at your most rational, but I felt as if I was seeing the match more clearly than ever ... I trusted the process, committed to perseverance, and frankly, refused to lose.

In this narrative, Evan portrays how languaging as emotion in the form of "external dialogue" with his peers and father shapes his "internal dialogue" (Zittoun, 2006) or "inner speech" (Fernyhough, 2016), to enact supportive relations with others and his self-doubts. Through writing his narrative, he understood how languaging emotions can pose difficulties while, at the same time, leading to his success.

ACTIVITY: CONTEXTUALIZING LANGUAGING EMOTIONS OR EMBODIED ACTION IN PLAYING SPORTS

Students can discuss or write about their languaging emotions or embodied actions constituting their relations with others in playing sports. They could identify a particular type of emotion, for example, their expression of joy or exuberance versus anger or disgust, or display of a certain embodied action related to their responses to a particular event in a game or match. They could also note others' responses to their emotion or embodied action and how those responses shaped their judgment of expressing that emotion or embodied action. Finally, they could also reflect on how they acquire use of particular embodied actions to coordinate interactions with other team members over time.

Building Supportive Relations with Team Members

Students also employ languaging actions to enact supportive, caring relations with team members as they interact with other team members. This includes providing verbal praise of others' embodied actions as well as sharing expressions of emotions about their team successes (MacPherson et al., 2016). Analysis of 8-to-15-year-old soccer players' interactions indicated that they engaged in discussions about strategies, modeling, and adhering to peer norms/values (Hwang et al., 2017). Kathy noted how, as a new member of her basketball team,

> I cared for these girls within the first couple of weeks of being together, and I trusted them to pick me up when I was down. We formed a family. A family that depends on each other to get the job done each and every game day, and no matter what the outcome was, win or lose, we were still a family.

Dennis valued how

> the brotherhood we embody off the football field is what makes us unique because we all are around each other a lot off the field as well as on the field. We laugh with each other which I believe is very important in building trust and friendship with others. Overall, I think we have so much fun together that it is really something that we hold as a value of our group; it is what makes football so fun.

Building these relations with other members bolsters their personhood and self-confidence. In their writing, students noted the importance of using languaging actions to enact positive relations with others. Michael describes the importance of how members of his lacrosse team

> talk with one another in our group to create a community that overall is very positive. This is why we have such a positive and fun time with one another in our group. The unique language that the group uses acts as a connection to help make the process of sharing our lives easier.

He notes how the group's languaging is based on how members are "interested in what others are doing, which increases the trust within the group. It is obvious that we trust one another to an extent where we will even tell them things that are happening in our lives outside of lacrosse." Susan describes how taking part in performances on her dance team fosters her "passion that fuels me in everything I know; I can always count on laughing with my teammates. Having so much fun every day makes any bad day worth it. The girls I dance with will always be my family."

Students also wrote about the practice of bonding with other team members through the languaging actions of complimenting, praising, promoting, or congratulating other players regarding their practices that enhanced their team's performance (MacPherson et al., 2016).

Jim noted the value of other members of his tennis team engaging in

> picking you up when you're down and lifting you up higher when you're up. This wonderful sport has taught me many things, but specifically how

190 Students Co-Authoring Figured Worlds

to never give up and to take ownership of failures, virtues I will have for the rest of my life. Tennis is as much of a mental sport as it is physical. Like other sports, the key is to never give up, even when the odds are against you.

Jim is recognizing the importance of adopting a psychological perspective on his play as necessary for persisting in his play.

ACTIVITY: CONTEXTUALIZING THE BENEFITS OF PARTICIPATING IN SPORTS

Students could discuss or write about the benefits derived from their experiences playing sports related to the development of practices associated with constructing identities and relations with others. For example, they could describe how they set specific purposes for improving their play over time, relating to their growth as a player.

They can also describe their use of languaging actions for building supportive relations with other team members. These actions include praising others for a specific play or performance, complimenting others regarding their abilities or strengths, or noting their contributions to their team's overall success. Students can note how others responded to their actions for building these relations and how their actions contributed to their team's sense of cohesion and trust. They can also note how they draw on or transfer these actions to other worlds, such as their interactions in their peer group worlds.

Adhering to Norms in Games or Matches

Through this participation in sports, students recognized the need to adhere to a specific set of rules governing their play in games and matches constituting *norms* shaping their practices in a game or match. They described conflicts involving referees or umpires during games in which they were perceived as violating certain rules. During a basketball game, Kathy was called for what she perceived as an unfair foul in an interaction with an opponent she had had previous conflicts with. After the call, she mumbled

that the ref was stupid and it was because I was Black. The whistle was blown and he slammed his hands into a "T" like form, indicating that I had gotten a technical foul. To make matters worse, I kicked my chair over and refused to sit down when my coach was trying to talk to me.

Later in the game, after she was called for another foul on what she believed was a block by an opponent whom she dislikes, but which was called as a charge,

Co-Authoring Sports Worlds **191**

she expressed her anger again and was called for another technical foul, resulting in her being ejected from the game.

In reflecting on her languaging actions, she noted that

> although we won the game by a buzzer-beater, I still felt as if I let my anger get the best of me and I let my entire team down. I realize that in situations that don't only involve me, I should make decisions that benefit us instead of hurting us, and that night I made a selfish move. I learned that feelings are temporary so don't make permanent decisions that could affect me in the long run.

In this event, Kathy portrays how she attempts to make sense of her own and the referee's actions as an "inner dialogue" (Shotter, 2012, p. 85) regarding her languaging actions of objecting to the referee's calls. In reflecting on the event, she noted that "in situations that don't only involve me, I should make decisions that benefit us instead of hurting us, and that night I made a selfish move."

Morgan portrayed an event during a close baseball game in which he was standing in the batter's box when a teammate was running home and the catcher had to retrieve an overthrown ball from the outfield. While he backed out of the way, knowing that he might be called for interference, the catcher objected to the umpire that he should be called for interference, to which the umpire agreed.

> After that, I was pretty mad that I got called out for something so dumb and that we lost the runs. I was also sad at the same time because it was my fault for letting my team down and not being able to potentially take the lead. When I was at first warming up by throwing grounders to the other infielders my coach approached me and said, "would you mind telling me what happened there?" I just shook my head and said, "I'm sorry coach it won't happen again."

These students identified how their languaging actions of failing to communicate effectively or voicing objections resulted in conflicts, even when they believed that their objections were justified. They were recognizing the limitations of these languaging actions and the need to experience caution in engaging in conflicts with others.

ACTIVITY: CONTEXTUALIZING ADHERING TO NORMS IN SPORTS EVENTS

Students can discuss or write about adhering to norms related to following or violating rules in a sports event. In some cases, these violations involve conflicts with other team members or referees/umpires based on identifying languaging actions constituting those conflicts. Students could contextualize

192 Students Co-Authoring Figured Worlds

these events based on the circumstances leading to the conflicts associated with their past and current relations with others in the event and on knowledge of certain norms. They could also reflect on further use of practices to rectify or resolve their conflicts; for example, through debriefing reasons for the conflicts with others or apologizing for their actions. They could also identify adhering to norms that serve to unify their team around a common sense of purpose associated with achieving success.

Discourses Constituting the Value of Practices in Sports Worlds

Underlying the use of practices constituting a sports world are certain *discourses* constituting the value of these practices in the world of sports. These discourses function to define how students formulate rationales for the value of participating in sports.

One primary discourse constituting the world of sports is reflected in a "winning is everything" discourse of competition. In contrast, students may assume that participating in sports has its benefits regardless of whether their team wins or loses a game or match. Players or coaches may employ languaging actions to emphasize or promote the value of winning a game or match by predicting how doing so leads to championship playoffs.

This discourse of competition reifies a discourse of individualism related to "achievement," as is the case in school worlds (Caraballo, 2019). Students may value participation in sports primarily for building a portfolio of achievements instead of recognizing the value of learning to engage in relations with others. This discourse of competition is most evident when students experience loss of games/matches or breakdowns. They may then blame themselves or their opponents instead of perceiving these matters as learning opportunities to improve in their play.

At the same time, students may also voice the value of learning from not always winning to apply to all aspects of one's life. Tanya described how she copes with the experience of how on her cross-country team

> sometimes you have a good race, sometimes you don't. Sometimes it's hot; sometimes it's cold. Some days you have a hard workout; some days it's a relaxing recovery run. The balance between the two highs and lows is a much-needed balance and allows for me to love the good days even more.
>
> Running has also taught me the importance of patience, effort, and perseverance. I often incorporate these lessons into my academics. I put effort into my school work; if I don't understand something, I am patient; and if I fail, I persevere.

Identifying the benefits of "patience, effort, and perseverance" in her running leads her to perceive similar benefits for use in her schoolwork.

Donald reflected on how he become overly obsessed with his mistakes in his play as center defenseman on his soccer team who was responsible for "keeping everyone on the field organized and directing my teammates on where, when, and how to pressure the other team."

> I became so focused on the "best play" that I couldn't let the past go. Every mistake in a game I carried with me unable to forget it, unable to move past mistakes, I made more mistakes, this started a vicious cycle. I focused so much on what I did wrong that even when we won games, I always felt like I had let my team down. I went down a slippery slope of delegating responsibility and blaming others for my mistakes.
>
> This was my wake-up call. I finally looked at my problems, confronting them and eventually getting rid of them altogether. Through this I've learned how to leave the past behind me, learning from it but not dwelling on it. I've learned to embrace my mistakes because messing up is the only way to learn and get better.

Through his reflection on the limitations of his negative self-perceptions, Donald recognized the need to no longer dwell on his problems but rather perceived them as opportunities to develop a more positive stance on his play in games.

ACTIVITY: CONTEXTUALIZING ADOPTION OF DISCOURSES SHAPING PARTICIPATION IN SPORTS

Students could discuss or write about the discourses related to their beliefs/values associated with their participation in sports; for example, the importance of acquiring a sense of agency regarding their ability to succeed in sports or the belief that "winning is everything." They may reflect on where and how they acquired these discourses—from their peers, coaches, parents, or sports media commentators. They may also compare their adherence to certain discourses; for example, how the discourses of competition/winning need not be of paramount importance as compared to the experience of acquiring relations with others through participation in sports.

Enacting Identities in Sports Worlds

Within the figured world of sports teams, students employ languaging actions to enact certain *identities* associated with the position(s) they are playing on a team, for example, guard, forward, or center on a basketball team, as well as leadership

194 Students Co-Authoring Figured Worlds

identities. David identified several different identities adopted by members of his lacrosse team, including his own role as "our group's comedian." He described how players adopt identities related to their designated physical abilities:

> Attack, which is usually shorter, faster kids. Middies, which usually are people with more strength and better endurance than attack, and finally, Defense. When most people think of defensemen, they think of protein powder-eating meatheads who are looking to kill someone. With me being the size I am, I am the group's meathead. My job is to toss around my body and to knock kids over.

Thomas noted how members of his football team have their own role or are a part of a group that has a role.

> Whether it's the captains and seniors and their role in leadership and guidance or the sophomores' role in moral support, every person has a job. Some of the various roles are things such as the jokester, the person who messes with everyone, and adds a little fun to the grind when things are getting rough. There is also the tough guy, the person who always acts like they are big and strong and invincible to pain and injuries. Often times there is a person on the team who is seen as the silent leader or someone that leads by example.

Students also described how their teams' uniforms themselves serve to convey certain meanings constituting their team's identity. Steve noted how his hockey team's uniforms serve to mark his team's identity. "The clothing we wear is used to show our pride in our school and our sport. We show that we are part of a select few that were chosen to play hockey on a varsity level, and that we are proud of it."

Assuming Leadership Identities

Students also described assuming leadership roles as team captains through languaging actions associated with modeling desired practices for others. Ken noted how as "the only returning starting defenseman, in games and practices, I was able to lead by my hard work and play. Since I am not the most vocal person, I have learned that if I want to fully succeed as a leader I have to be able to yell commands from the defensive position." He also helped coach younger students, noting the experience of having "trouble with one kid and I was able to encourage him by staying positive and trying to make it seem more fun and not as much work. At the end of the clinics, the kids in my group ended up having a great time and loving the sport."

Anna recalled how, as captain of her volleyball team, she was "forced to learn how to work with many different types of people and to bring them together

Co-Authoring Sports Worlds 195

to work as a team. I learned to respect the actions and decisions of the people in charge, even if I did not always agree with them."

Use of "Insider Language" for Enacting Identities

Adolescents also employ languaging actions through "insider language" (Madsen et al., 2015) to enact these identities through the unique use of words. They used words describing players or plays that outsiders may not understand and had the ability to employ both constructive and negative criticisms of other team members. Analysis of interactions by members of a youth soccer team found that positive comments had the highest relationship with social cohesion, while acceptance and support comments had the highest relationship with task cohesion (McLaren & Spink, 2018).

Students portrayed how they employed insider language for interacting with other team members. For interacting with each other on her dance team, as previously cited in Chapter 8, Susan noted how

> we dance in such close proximity and go through so much together, we might as well be a hive mind. We have our own language, not just as dancers but as teams. We pretty much always match (usually on purpose because we are nerds).
>
> *Beach & Aukerman, 2019, p. 63*

Thomas described how members of his football team used insider language, for example,

> "What a musclehead", "Odell it", "that's a big body", "you a little body". A musclehead is someone who is just built and strong but does not have the most brains. Odelling is the act of one hand catching a pass or making an amazing catch. Calling someone a little body or a big body can either be a dig at someone as a joke, or it is often used when someone makes a big play. For example, if someone gets a big hit saying "That's a big body" would be in order.

Roberto noted that his

> cross country team has the most expansive vocabulary of any sport. Words like "deplorable" and "indubitably" make daily appearances and are words I am sure have never been spoken by another Jefferson sports team. One might correctly make the comparison of the cross country team to a group of walking thesauruses.

Students also described how they employed insider language to enact their teams' sense of exclusivity related to outsiders not understanding or knowing

196 Students Co-Authoring Figured Worlds

actions or strategies familiar only to team members. Jim described how members of his tennis team have "specific ways of talking in this group that creates an esoteric or special inclusive feeling because of inside jokes only members of the group would understand. To others, they are meaningless." Steve identified how "to an outsider, the words dangle, snipe, and celly, may have no meaning to them, and may actually confuse them." Kathy noted how, for her basketball team,

> people outside of our group would not understand the way we talk. When we yell or say things in a certain tone only we would understand, people on the outside would think we hated each other. Often in the sport, we used code words to call plays to disguise what our next move is. For example, if we wanted to run a four across and one in the middle play we wouldn't scream those exact words, instead, we would think of a name that indicated that exact play.

David identified how

> with nicknames like "Pookie," no one knows who or what we are talking about. All of us have our own different language towards others. With nicknames like "Pookie" and "Black King," I'd say most people have no clue who or what we are talking about.

Students' use of insider language represents the use of languaging for enacting a sense of inclusivity within their teams for describing specific practices and roles unique to their teams. Students are using languaging to create their own unique sports team world whose meaning for actions are familiar only to their members in ways that, as is the case with secret cults, serve to bolster members' allegiance to the team.

ACTIVITY: CONTEXTUALIZING ACQUIRING IDENTITIES IN SPORTS WORLDS

Students can discuss or write about acquiring certain identities on their sports team related to how they employ languaging actions to enact their roles/identities associated with specific practices/tasks they assume on their teams. They can then reflect on their portrayals or descriptions in response to questions; for example: "How do you use certain words to describe the particular actions you assume in adopting roles/identities on your team? How do you perceive yourself in assuming these roles/identities contributing to your team's success? What are the particular languaging actions that team captains employ for providing leadership of their team?"

> Students can also identify examples of insider language used by team members to then reflect on how and why members employ their insider language in ways that others outside of their team may not understand. They can then reflect on the derivation of these words or phrases through team members inventing these words or phrases.

Employing Genres for Interacting with Team Members and Fans

Adolescents also employ *genres* for interacting with team members and their fans through the use of cheers, chants, or sayings designed to inspire players. Gloria noted the value of "the show" as a set of genre practices for members of her synchronized swim team to

> perform our routines without any judges and no other competitors. We get to show off to friends and family all the hard work we've done throughout the season, before going to sections. The show is always important to the girls because it's a stress-free way of practicing our performances, and most girls are excited because there's always food after.

Students also employed music as a genre for engaging in embodied actions. Anna described how members of her volleyball team

> sang and danced to explicit music at the highest possible volume on our speaker to warm ourselves up. We also played a game called Wa, where you got out if you lost the rhythm. Our last ritual before we left the locker room was to have a Moshpit right by the door. Everyone got in a circle and then screamed, "Mosh mosh mosh!" to the beat of the song "Shots" by LMFAO. After that, we ran down the stairs and into the gym. We quickly got into a huddle to anger scream together, and then we began our warmups.

Genres for Celebrating Team Successes

Students also wrote about events that included certain genre practices designed to celebrate their team's success. Thomas describes how for his football team

> the pregame meals are the time where you really get closer to the people on the team and get to be more comfortable around them. It is a time where you all sit down and just talk and have a good time, everything else that is going on at the time becomes irrelevant except the people there at that moment.

198 Students Co-Authoring Figured Worlds

He also notes the value of post-games dinners as "one of the most memorable experiences of football. The fun and discussions that are had after games are like no other; some of the best memories players remember come from post-game meals."

Team members, then, perceive these practices as established traditions associated with participation on their team. Students cited examples of the tradition of an annual end-of-season banquet to celebrate a season or award team letters. Roberto described a dinner to celebrate his cross-country team's season.

> The parents kick off the banquet with a special slideshow. This slideshow's purpose is seemingly to capture every runner at their absolute worst during a race. Expressions of pain and agony grace the projector screen for about ten minutes while the audience has a good laugh. Next on the agenda is the meal. This is a time for teammates and coaches to share memories and have conversations for possibly the last time while enjoying sub-par food. The senior speeches are well-prepared but also extremely heartfelt and emotional. They reflect on the best of memories along with lessons they've learned along the way.

As they employ these practices over time, they become established familiar traditions constituting their participation on their sports team. They then draw on these traditions for their own use as well as for socialization with new members of their team.

Genres for Interaction with Coaches

Coaches assume an important role during time-outs, huddles, or interactions on the sidelines, to identify relevant plays or strategies by contextualizing a particular situation or challenge facing their team during a game or match. Students also identified genres constituting these practices in their interactions with coaches. These practices included languaging actions of "instructing," "organizing," "confirming understanding," "praising," "getting attention," "requesting action," "requesting information," "criticizing," "encouraging," "responding to questions or statements," "showing gratitude," "informing," and "defining terms" (Masterson et al., 2006, p. 43).

Engaging in these interactions requires that both players and coaches draw on their shared prior knowledge of genres defining how their use of certain plays or strategies in the past were most relevant for addressing their current situations or challenges. One study found that coaches focused primarily on the use of certain plays or strategies instead of criticizing players or telling them what not to do; they also engaged more in praising and rewarding during games and more requesting during practices (Masterson et al., 2006).

Students also benefit from support from their coaches. Females from low-income, urban homes in Boston who participated in a rowing club often limited to adolescents from elite private schools were exposed to a different socioeconomic world (Sadowski, 2020). They also experienced positive support in their relations with coaches in ways that enhanced their development of agency. One rower described her relationship with her coach: "'She's in my face .... She's on my butt every day .... She has my back and I never question that. I don't want to let her down in the race by not giving it everything I have.'" (n.p.).

Coaches also interact with team members to enhance player enjoyment and relax players and correct players; they were also willing to act on players' suggestions (Harrist & Witt, 2015). In describing her track team's coaches' languaging actions, Gabby noted that

> every morning before a meet, my coaches gathered the team for a quick informational meeting. Numbers for our events were passed out and team goals were discussed. It was our way of getting pumped and excited for a long, exhausting day we had in front of us. "The strength of the team is each individual member. The strength of each member is the team," my coach would say. He always had a motivational speech before every track meet.

Adolescents also contrasted their coaches' language with their own as a reflection of the difference in their identities. Jim described how his tennis coach

> would speak differently as a result of maturity and position than I or anyone else on the team would. I would be more inclined to start a casual conversation, and he might be more likely to start a serious one. Typically, when he would walk onto the courts, I would strike up a conversation asking how his day has been, or how his kids are doing, while he would be the one to start a serious conversation about upcoming matches, strategies, and how I am holding up physically.

Students noted how they benefited from their interactions with coaches who provided them with support and assistance in ways that enhanced their plays. Michael noted how his coaches would draw on players' language to "use it at times they see fit and that helps us grow our relationships with one another. This also leads to creating a positive perception of our group." These students perceived their coaches as assuming important roles in their lives for mentoring use of practices contributing to their success as team members.

ACTIVITY: CONTEXTUALIZING USE OF GENRES FOR INTERACTING WITH COACHES

Students could discuss or write about their use of genres involving languaging actions for interacting with their coaches related to how their interactions served to bolster their performance over time. In addition, they could identify coaches' use of specific actions that enhanced their play; for example, the use of compliments regarding their specific strategies or techniques. They may also compare differences in language style or register of their coaches versus their own style or register related to how they may begin to incorporate their coaches' style or register in their language use.

Use of Media/Literature Associated with Participation in Sports

Adolescents and coaches employ digital/visual *media* through the use of charts or diagrams to visually represent certain plays or strategies (Rifenburg, 2014). Analysis of one chart of a defensive play, "'Cov. 4 play action,'" by Auburn University's football team depicts moves by four defensive backs ("dbs") and three linebackers ("lbs").

> While the lbs are trained to cover offensive players, the four dbs are trained to be responsible for covering particular "zones" of the field—four zones in a Cov. 4 defensive scheme—and any offensive player who may enter their particular zone. The phrase "play action" refers to the predicted offensive play, in this case, a play action, which the defense believes the offense will run. During a play action, the QB receives the ball and has been trained to fake a handoff to the TB with the halfback running ahead to block the defense. Ideally, the defense has been tricked by the fake hand-off and is rushing toward the TB, leaving the offensive receivers open to catch the ball.
>
> The QB, still in possession of the ball, runs out to either side of the field looking to throw the ball to an open receiver. To counter the play action, the defense needs to "read" the fake handoff. Once they have successfully identified the fake handoff, the defensive players have been trained to cover the receivers. For this text, the defensive coach believes the offense is preparing to run a play action, thus the title of this play: "Cov. 4 play action."
>
> *Rifenburg, 2014, n.p.*

This multimodal representation of plays employs the use of specific words such as "dbs" and "lbs" as well as visual portrayals of players' moves based on arrows. Mason described play-calling on his football team as involving the use of "different random words and hand signals. For instance, on any given defense play, everyone may be yelling bama, jag, trojan, or raven to signify the coverage we are in."

Larry notes how his lacrosse team "has a saying, Hay-Da-Lay. This saying can mean whatever you want it to mean. It is so important to our team that we have Hay-Da-Lay on the back of our helmets and have a team award … So as it has no real meaning; for me, the saying means to just continue to work hard and push through the adversity." Students also noted instances of the use of video replays to analyze their play. Larry described how viewing these videos led to reflections on what

we did well and what we did badly. It is a time when we can learn from our mistakes and our mistakes can teach the whole team so that we can be ready the next time. One specific time that happened to me is when I played too aggressively and my guy ended up scoring. When watching my mistakes in the film, I was called out by our coach. Although it was embarrassing, my mistake was able to teach the team, so next time that would not happen.

Use of Broadcast/Social Media for Viewing Practices for Participation in Sports Worlds

Students also described how their engagement with media broadcasts of professional sports contributed to team members' collaborative engagement in a particular sport. By viewing television broadcasts of professional sports, students learn about the effective use of certain practices from commentators and players describing their use of practices students may then want to emulate. Bill perceived his hockey team as having a shared "interest in hockey and anything related to hockey. Whether this is following the National Hockey League on TV, or partaking in a hockey fantasy league with friends, our conversations and life revolve around hockey."

Students also engage in social media interactions as fans, sharing responses to games/matches with peers. Students noted how they drew on social media memes for sharing perceptions of their play. Roberto described how members of his cross-country team

love memes, which have become deeply ingrained in our culture and are used to make light of many happenings of the team. These memes make an appearance in the team's Snapchat group chat called "OC." In this group chat, no one is safe from the memes' wrath. For example, just once I jumped the gun on a race and I have yet to hear the end of it. Our team now has an Instagram page dedicated to sharing memes with other cross-country teams across the state.

At the same time, these broadcasts often focus on the commercial/corporate branding of a team's image to maintain high viewer ratings, rather than portray individual players' own unique experiences/perceptions in a way that was similar to students' own focus on their individual experiences (Beach & Caraballo, 2021). The success of professional sports teams also stems from how those teams achieve positive media coverage, given that most of a team's revenues come from media outlets (Birkner & Nolleke, 2016).

Commentators often frame games or matches based on the need to achieve high viewer ratings, given a commercial agenda to please advertisers and expand a team's fan base (Birkner & Nolleke, 2016; Musto et al., 2017). Commentators adopt a discourse of high-stakes competition between teams related to the belief that every game "counts" in terms of teams making or not making playoffs. If a game no longer "counts" for making playoffs, then attendance and viewership may decline.

This suggests the need for teachers to have students adopt a critical stance on sports broadcasts. For example, students may identify certain broadcast practices as branding promotions for teams or leagues instead of focusing on individual players' skills (Beach & Caraballo, 2021).

Responding to Young-Adult Literature about Sports

Students could also respond to literary portrayals of adolescent athletes in young-adult novels about sports. Two novels that portray adolescent athletes employing practices related to their identity include *The Hate U Give* (Thomas, 2017) and *Mexican Whiteboy* (de la Peña, 2008) (Fredricksen et al., 2019). *The Hate U Give* portrays a 16-year-old female Black basketball player, Starr Carter, coping with the trauma of witnessing a police officer shooting her friend.

Starr describes how her basketball play with two of her peers is consistently in synch in the novel: "'No matter what's going on, when Hailey, Maya, and I play together, it's rhythm, chemistry, and skill rolled into a ball of amazingness' (p. 109)." (Fredricksen et al., 2019, p. 60). At the same time, she and her two peers do not experience the same synergy off the court, given how "'one day you realize there's a leader among you and your friends and it's not you' (p. 108)" (p. 60).

In *Mexican Whiteboy* (de la Peña, 2008), the main character, Danny Lopez, is a mixed-race adolescent pitcher on his baseball team. As does Starr, he is consistently reflecting on his competing, multiple perspectives shaping his play and tensions within his family and community related to defining his identity.

The *Crossover* series by Kwame Alexander includes three novels all written in verse about adolescents playing sports. *The Crossover* (2014) (graphic novel version, 2019) portrays two brothers who are basketball stars in their junior high and experience love for the same female. *Rebound* (2018) portrays the two boys' father as a basketball star and the boys' coach in *The Crossover*. *Booked* (2019) features a 12-year-old soccer player coping with learning the sport. (For other young-adult novels about sports, see Jensen (2019), *bookriot.com/ya-books-about-sports*; for analysis of young-adult novels' portrayal of race, see Domínguez & Domínguez, 2020).

Students in a sports literature classroom read *Season of Life: A Football Star, a Boy, a Journey to Manhood* (Marx, 2003), which portrays a football coach working with his players to challenge how traditional discourses of masculinity and manhood are adversely related to economic success, playing ability, and sex appeal (Rodesiler, 2021). Their teacher encouraged the students to challenge the individualist focus of a "false masculinity" so that his students "'would reflect on how they see themselves, how they present themselves. And maybe it would open their eyes [to another vision of masculinity].'" (p. 349).

Students conducted research on topics related to the book, leading to their critiquing discourses shaping sports. One female student noted that "'I thought it was important that guys in my class read it … Even going to school here you see [false masculinity] all the time and I think it's important that people understand those aren't the only things that matter'" (p. 348).

ACTIVITY: CONTEXTUALIZING USE OF MEDIA/ LITERATURE FOR PARTICIPATION IN SPORTS

Students can discuss or write about how they contextualize the use of media/ literature related to their participation in sports. They may share visual examples of charts or diagrams for planning strategies or plays or video replays to analyze their play. They may also describe how they respond to media broadcasts of certain professional teams and/or players as perceived role models for their engagement in sports. They may also compare responses to portrayals of sports in young-adult literature to their own experiences playing sports.

At the same time, students could critique how media broadcasts of sports reified certain discourses of corporate ownership related to the branding of the team as opposed to a focus on portrayals of individual players' personal identities (Beach & Caraballo, 2021).

Summary

In this chapter, I described adolescents' use of practices for engaging in sports worlds. These practices are shaped by certain purposes related to the benefits of participating in sports. Students also experienced the need to adhere to norms and discourses for the use of certain practices such as building supportive relations with team members and knowing how to cope with conflicts during games or matches. Students also enacted certain identities on their teams, including leadership roles and practices for engaging fans and interacting with coaches, practices they may acquire through viewing media sports broadcasts.

References

Alexander, K. (2014). *The crossover*. Houghton Mifflin.
Alexander, K. (2019). *The crossover* (graphic novel). Houghton Mifflin.

Alexander, K. (2018). *Rebound*. Houghton Mifflin.

Alexander, K. (2019). *Booked*. Houghton Mifflin.

Beach, R., & Caraballo, L. (2021). Languaging actions in sports media and students' writing about sports. In K. Garland, K. S. Dredger, C. L. Beach, & C. Leogrande (Eds.), *Critical literacy in media production, consumption, and dissemination* (pp. 145–170). Lexington Books.

Birkner, T., & Nolleke, D. (2016). Soccer players and their media-related behavior: A contribution on the mediatization of sports. *Communication & Sport, 4*(4), 367–384.

Blomfield, C., & Barber, B. (2011). Developmental experiences during extracurricular activities and Australian adolescents' self-concept: Particularly important for youth from disadvantaged schools. *Journal of Youth and Adolescence, 40*, 582–594. doi:10.1007/s10964-010-9563-0

Caraballo, L. (2019). Being "loud": Identities-in-practice in a figured world of achievement. *American Educational Research Journal, 56*(4), 1281–1317.

Csikszentmihalyi, M. (1991). *Flow: The psychology of optimal experience*. Harper Perennial.

de la Peña, M. (2008). *Mexican whiteboy*. Ember.

Domínguez, M. & Domínguez, A. (2020). Playing past racial silence: Cultivating conversations on racial identity through sports-related young adult literature. *Study and Scrutiny: Research on Young Adult Literature, 4*(2), 1–30.

Fernyhough, C. (2016). *The voices within: The history and science of how we talk to ourselves*. Basic Books.

Ferrer-Wreder, L., & Kroger, J. (2020). *Identity in adolescence: The balance between self and other* (4th ed.). Routledge.

Fredricksen, J. E., Thornberry, J. M., & Gritter, K. (2019). Censored young adult sports novels: Entry points for understanding issues of identities and equity. *The ALAN Review*, Winter 2019, 58–64.

Fry, M. D., & Gano-Overway, L. A. (2010). Exploring the contribution of the caring climate to the youth sport experience. *Journal of Applied Sport Psychology, 22*(3), 294–304. doi:10.1080/10413201003776352

Harrist, C., & Witt, P. (2015). Calling the screens: Self-reported developmental outcomes in competitive basketball. *Journal of Adolescent Research, 30*, 751–778. doi:10.1177/0743558414561293

Hwang. S., Choi, Y., & Machicda, M. (2017). The effect of peer interaction on sport confidence and achievement goal orientation in youth sport. *Social Behavior and Personality: An International Journal, 45*(6), 1007–1018. doi:10.2224/sbp.6149

Inoue, Y., Wegner, C. E., Jordan, J. S., &. Funk, D. C. (2015). Relationships between self-determined motivation and developmental outcomes in sport-based positive youth development. *Journal of Applied Sport Psychology, 27*(4), 371–383.

Jensen, K. (2019, May 6). Swish, swing, sashay, and score: 50+ must-read YA books about sports. [Weblog post]. Retrieved from https://bookriot.com/ya-books-about-sports

Lee, E. C, Fragala, M. S., Kavouras, S. A., Queen, R. M., Pryor, J. L, Casa, D. J. (2017). Biomarkers in sports and exercise: Tracking health, performance, and recovery in athletes. *Journal of Strength and Conditioning Research, 31*(10), 2920–2937. doi:10.1519/JSC.0000000000002122

Lee, J. E., Pope, Z., & Gao, Z. (2018). The role of youth sports in promoting children's physical activity and preventing pediatric obesity: A systematic review. *Behavioral Medicine, 44*(1), 62–76. doi:10.1080/08964289.2016.1193462

Linver, M. R., Roth, J. L. & Brooks-Gunn, J. (2009). Patterns of adolescents' participation in organized activities: Are sports best when combined with other activities? *Developmental Psychology, 45*(2), 354–367. doi:10.1037/a0014133

Madsen, L. M., Moller, J. S., & Karrabaek, M. S. (2015). *Everyday languaging: Collaborative research on the language use of children and youth*. De Gruyter.

Masterson, J. J., Davies, L. K., & Masterson, G. L. (2006). Coach talk: Linguistic demands inherent in youth sports. *Language, Speech, and Hearing Services in Schools*, 37(1), 39–49.

MacPherson, E., Kerr, G., & Stirling, A. (2016). The influence of peer groups in organized sport on female adolescents' identity development. *Psychology of Sport and Exercise, 23*, 73–81. https://doi.org/10.1016/j.psychsport.2015.10.002

Marx, J. (2003). *Season of life: A football star, a boy, a journey to manhood*. Simon and Schuster.

McLaren, C. D. & Spink, K. S. (2018). Team member communication and perceived cohesion in youth soccer. *Communication & Sport, 6*(1), 111–125.

Musto, M., Cooky, C., & Messner, M. A. (2017). "From fizzle to sizzle!" Televised sports news and the production of gender-bland sexism. *Gender & Society, 31*(5). doi:10.1177/0891243217726056

Nasir, N. S., & Cooks, J. (2009). Becoming a hurdler: How learning settings afford identities. *Anthropology & Education Quarterly, 40*(1), 41–61.

Rifenburg, J. M. (2014). Writing as embodied, college football plays as embodied: Extracurricular multimodal composing. *Composition Forum, 29*. Retrieved from http://compositionforum.com/issue/29/

Rodesiler, L. (2021). Focusing on sociopolitical issues in a secondary sports literature class: Opportunities and experiences. *English Teaching: Practice & Critique, 20*(3), 341–353.

Sadowski, M. (2020). *Adolescents at school: Perspectives on youth, identity, and education* (3rd ed.). Harvard Education Press.

Shotter, J. (2012). Ontological social constructionism in the context of a social ecology: The importance of our living bodies. In A. Lock & T. Strong (Eds.), *Discursive perspectives in therapeutic practice* (pp. 83–105). Oxford University Press.

Thomas, A. (2017). *The hate u give*. Harper Collins.

Ullrich-French, S., Cox, A., & Bumpus, M. (2013). Physical activity motivation and behavior across the transition to university. *Sport, Exercise, and Performance Psychology, 2*(90). doi:10.1037/a0030632

Van Boekel, M., Bulut, O., Stanke, L., Palma Zamora, J. R., Jang, Y., Kang, Y., & Nickodem, K. (2016). Effects of participation in school sports on academic and social functioning. *Journal of Applied Developmental Psychology, 46*, 31–40.

Zittoun, T. (2006). *Transitions: Development through symbolic resources*. Information Age Publishers.

10

CO-AUTHORING FAMILY FIGURED WORLDS

This chapter describes contextualizing practices in family worlds related to purposes associated with the need for family members to collaboratively support each other. Family members also learn family practices related to employing discourses, norms, identities, genres, and media/literature. Central to these practices is how parents socialize adolescents in terms of certain norms/discourses for interacting with other family members. Within a family world, adolescents develop identities related to achieving their own independence or autonomy from their parents (Grotevant, 2011). They also acquire use of certain genres for interacting with family members as well as acquiring knowledge of family practices through responding to portrayals of family worlds in media/literature.

Students and their parents engage in co-authoring family worlds in which adolescents acquire certain family literacy practices that may or may not be consistent with practices operating in other worlds. Students, particularly during childhood, spend a large amount of their time acquiring practices in their family worlds as central to their identity's development and sense of agency. It is also the case that, in contrast to practices employed in other worlds that often have relatively short-term consequences for relations, practices employed in family worlds can have high-stakes consequences that can impact members for a lifetime. For example, experiencing a divorce in their family has long-term impacts on students' lives (Scabini & Manzi, 2011).

Family Members Adhering to Purposes for the Use of Supportive Practices

Given the basic *purpose* of family members to provide support for other family members, adolescents need a sense of assurance that they can rely on these other

DOI: 10.4324/9781003246886-12

family members to provide this support for enacting trusting relations over time. As a result, family members who adopt supportive family practices enact trusting, cohesive family relations, while families that experience tensions in their relations suffer distress and poor health within their families (Scabini & Manzi, 2011).

Engaging in supportive practices is particularly relevant when members face certain challenges or difficulties in their lives (Beveridge & Berg, 2007). For example, Joseph described engaging in practices of being baptized and confirmed in his local church based on being an active member of that church:

> I come from a religious family. While we did not go to church every Sunday, but it was always a part of our family. When my older sister and I were babies, we were baptized, and we both had our first communion. The next step for both of us was being confirmed. My sister was confirmed when she was around thirteen years old, and at that time I was about ten.

Joseph describes his experience as a twelve-year-old engaging in what he described as a "coming out" experience in disclosing to his highly religious parents that he was an atheist after waiting several years to do so. In conducting research on atheism, he

> had read stories during my research about kids who, upon telling their parents they were atheist, were kicked out of their house, or sent away to church camps. I knew my parents weren't like that, but I was still afraid to tell them.

When his grandparents visited his family, during a visit to their local church, his grandfather sensed that he was "being disrespectful, and afterward, planned on having a not-so-pleasant talk with me about it," leading him to realize the need to talk with his parents.

> They didn't completely understand my position because they too had little exposure to people who held no religious beliefs. However, they were very accepting and understanding of it. I told them about my fears of being kicked out or sent away, and they were shocked that I thought they could or would do that. Despite not understanding at first, now my parents are very understanding and we've been able to have some very good, deep talks about what exactly I "believe in," what I think about life after death, and so on.

From this experience, he recognizes that the experience of "coming out" as an atheist or as an LGBTQ person within highly religious families would be highly difficult for some adolescents. He realized that "I was lucky enough to have a very understanding family, but many people aren't as lucky."

208 Students Co-Authoring Figured Worlds

In an interview, he asserted the importance of the fact that he could trust his parents,

> that they would have a good reaction to it, which they did. I wasn't surprised that they did, because they're very understanding, accepting people. I had read the stories of the people who did trust their parents enough to tell them, and it went terribly wrong.

Students also described instances in which parents provided support when they were coping with debilitating emotions. As she was engaged in a championship pool game tournament, Sharon recalls her father talking to her before her match.

> "I want you to know, I am PROUD of YOU no matter the outcome of your next match."
> "So, if I play the best I can and lose, you will not be disappointed?"
> "Sharon, all I can ask for is that you try your hardest. Of course, I would not be disappointed."
> "Well, either way, she isn't going to beat me. So here we go." I finished off.
> "No matter what, I am so proud of you."
> These words will forever ring in my head. My father had never said this before a match in my life. He knows how much words of encouragement like that mean to me and he knew how much that match meant to me. He knew that if I heard those words come out of his mouth, I was going to win that match. I will forever and always remember that moment because that is what won me the most important match of my life.

Sharon recognizes how her father's languaging of support served to bolster her self-confidence in ways that led to her being successful in winning her pool game.

ACTIVITY: CONTEXTUALIZING PURPOSES FOR PROVIDING SUPPORTIVE PRACTICES IN FAMILY WORLDS

Students could discuss or write about events in which other family members provided them with support for coping with an issue or challenge in their lives. They can note how the person assisting them employed certain practices through languaging actions; for example, voicing reassurance, valuing their beliefs or perspectives, bolstering their self-confidence, proposing solutions to their issues, sharing their coping mechanisms, etc. They can also note how the other conveys a caring stance through their embodied actions.

> They could also draw a circle map portraying relations between themselves and other family members by placing themselves at the center of the map with other members surrounding them in a circle. They then draw lines between themselves and other members and insert adjectives describing the nature of their relations; for example, supportive, tense, loving, distant, emotional, controlling, etc.

Families Providing Adolescents with Social Capital for Engaging in Different Worlds

Another primary *purpose* for families involves providing adolescents with social capital for successfully employing practices in their different worlds (Weiss, 2012). Providing social capital involves modeling effective use of practices through sharing their own experiences using these practices and noting instances of benefits of using these practices. For example, parents provide adolescents with practices associated with languaging interactions in constructive ways to interact with teachers or coaches in school/extracurricular worlds, such as learning to assert oneself in negotiating with adults in these worlds.

Adolescents' acceptance of parents' social capital depends on their willingness to accept their parents' modeling or advice, given that "adolescents should not just be viewed as sponges passively absorbing parental values" (Weiss, 2012, p. 21). At the same time, intergenerational relationships with relatives, neighbors, and peers can also influence acquiring social capital, regardless of adolescents' relations with parents.

However, parents of non-dominant families may lack social capital related to knowledge of academic literacies for modeling or providing advice on the use of practices for success in schools, particularly if those literacies clash with their own cultural practices (Tikkanen, 2016). For example, parents provide adolescents with assistance for completing school homework assignments and for engaging in college admissions and/or seeking employment opportunities, but parents who did not attend college may not be familiar with the practices involved in the college admissions process.

The extent to which parents can provide social capital may also vary according to race or social class differences. These differences often depend on how much time parents have to invest in or devote to interactions with adolescents and whether they have the knowledge or experience to provide that social capital. Students in higher SES homes may be more engaged in addressing societal issues, given that their parents themselves may be more actively involved in addressing societal issues to model their engagement practices (Wanders et al., 2020).

Students in schools with higher concentrations of the same race or ethnicity may experience more social capital related to academic engagement, while

210 Students Co-Authoring Figured Worlds

non-White students often receive less social capital support in schools with a smaller range of different races related to their family backgrounds (Parcel et al., 2010). For example, an analysis of Latinx adolescents perceived their parents as lacking social capital for bridging connections with schooling practices such as college application practices (Raymond-Flesch et al., 2017).

Adolescents' expectations regarding the likelihood of their attending college may also be related to their parents' social class status. For example, when students from low-income families are given favorable funding opportunities to attend college, they may still assume that attending college is not a viable option. They may also assume that their lack of social capital as low-income students limits their sense of future possibilities associated with attending college (Moses & Wiley, 2020).

ACTIVITY: CONTEXTUALIZING PARENTS' SOCIAL CAPITAL FOR PROVIDING PRACTICES

Students could discuss or write about how they did or did not acquire social capital from their parent(s) or grandparent(s) related to their ability to employ certain practices. For example, they may note how they acquired the ability to assert their own beliefs about an issue in a productive conversation by witnessing their grandparent(s) or parent(s) engage in debate with others who may have espoused alternative beliefs about an issue.

Students may also note instances in which they acquired social capital that benefited them in certain worlds, but not other worlds. For example, they may experience social capital in their peer group and sports team worlds, given their sense of agency as a leader in their peer group. In contrast, they may lack social capital for participating in their workplace world given their lack of knowledge about the practices valued in their workplace. Students could then reflect on these differences in their social capital across worlds in terms of determining how they acquire social capital from their families.

Changes in Family Structures Over Time Related to Providing Social Capital

Family members' ability to provide social capital has shifted over time, given changes in family structures. Prior to the 1950s, families were largely extended families, as evident in different generations living in the same house with a relatively large number of children (Brooks, 2020). These intergenerational, extended families could provide social capital through socializing adolescents to address challenges in their lives.

Starting in the 1950s, there began a shift to smaller nuclear families that involved fewer children and a focus more on valuing individual versus family needs (Brooks, 2020). One advantage of this shift is that family members were less dependent on conforming to family norms, resulting in their developing their sense of identity. However, women were still limited to household tasks without job opportunities outside the home.

One disadvantage of this shift to smaller families involved economic declines in wages and job options beginning in the 1970s, particularly for low-income families. The resulting income inequality related to class increased divorce and single-parent parenting. There was an increase in the number of single-parent families, from 13% of all families in 1960 to 28% of all families in 2018, families who often have fewer financial resources than families with married parents, resulting in income inequality between married versus single parents. Brooks notes that "Andrew Cherlin, a sociologist at Johns Hopkins University, once put it, 'It is the privileged Americans who are marrying, and marrying helps them stay privileged'" (p. 60). Brooks notes how this shift to smaller, nuclear families has resulted in making life freer for individuals and more unstable for families.

> We've made life better for adults but worse for children. We've moved from big interconnected, and extended families, which helped protect the most vulnerable people in society from the shocks of life, to smaller, detached nuclear families (a married couple and their children), which give the most privileged people in society room to maximize their talents and expand their options.
>
> *p. 56*

Given these shifts in family structures, students may examine how their grandparents' childhood experiences of family practices differed from the practices of students' parents as children, which in turn differ from students' own experiences. They may find differences in the degree to which parents required adolescents to be obedient versus providing adolescents with some degree of autonomy.

ACTIVITY: CONTEXTUALIZING HISTORICAL SHIFTS IN FAMILY WORLDS RELATED TO PROVIDING SOCIAL CAPITAL

Students could discuss or write about the historical development of the family unit itself over time in terms of shifts in family structures, functions, size, and roles within their own or other families related to having the social capital to provide supportive practices. For example, they may note how, in the past,

212 Students Co-Authoring Figured Worlds

> families were larger, given the need for children to perform work needed to support their family; for example, working on a family farm. In comparison, families today are relatively smaller, with a higher percentage of those families headed by single parents. Students may also note shifts in gender roles, with fathers in the past functioning as the primary breadwinner and mothers assuming domestic roles, compared with current families in which both parents may be employed.

Languaging Emotions in Family Relations

Related to providing supportive practices is the extent to which adolescents experience the practice of languaging emotions in their interactions with family members (Kim, et al., 2001). In voicing their emotions of fear, anger, envy, love, etc., they then experience specific responses or uptakes from other family members for enacting supportive relations with family members.

The extent to which students are comfortable disclosing certain emotions with parents depends on their assumptions about how their parents would respond to those disclosures in a supportive, caring, or dismissive manner (Kerr & Stattin, 2000). Parents may vary in terms of knowing how to invite adolescents to voice emotions when and if they sense that they are uneasy or reluctant to disclose those emotions.

Cassie describes how, as a senior, she experienced tensions with her parents, given their propensity not to value her "free time, where we can relax, relieve stress, and just have fun and enjoy being teenagers." She cites the example of her mother asking her to submit an additional scholarship application to the college to which she was admitted, an application that required her to write three essays. She rejected her mother's request, noting she already had a number of scholarships, as well as the fact that she was busy with schoolwork. "My mother did not understand ... that to me my time is valuable and [her] adding on too many additional things to fill it completely up is not worth it and is taxing."

In another similar encounter, her father was angry with her for not completing a part of her college application, resulting in her shutting down their conversation. Later, at her father's request, she and her parents met

> to talk about all the things that we weren't each of us, like, weren't happy or were having issues with at the moment. So we talked for a really long time. And I had, you know, a whole list of things I was mad about and my dad was mad about things and my mom was sitting there trying to be the mediator.
>
> And then we just have been in a very tense situation and while we were, like, mad in the moment. You wanted to be dynamic and stuff; we realized that, like, it wasn't worth it. So we let ourselves have, like, [a] half-hour to be mad and then we're, like, okay, we need to actually talk it out now.

Cassie's experience demonstrates how languaging emotions can influence family relations. In her meeting with her parents, she cites the value of identifying the different emotions shaping her relations with her father associated with the need "to be dynamic and stuff" as counterproductive to thoughtful reconciliation.

Cassie also recognized how languaging development itself shapes her ability to articulate her emotions, noting that

> when you're six, you don't know as many words that you don't know exactly, like, how to communicate, how you're feeling. But I would say now I just learned much better how to talk to people like my parents. So I would say we've grown in that sense.

Students also wrote about their emotions related to coping with death in their families. When she learned about the death of her brother who lived in another city, Karin described how

> I was so sad at that moment and at that moment, I was mad at the world and the only thing crossing my mind was how everyone around me was so happy and I was in so much pain and I had so much sadness. The train ride back to the house was miserable and full of sadness.

Because she could not afford to go to her brother's funeral,

> I was even sadder. I didn't go to school for three days. I didn't want to see anyone, but eventually, I went to school and it seemed like nothing happened. I learned to manage how I felt. And learned to live every day knowing that a piece of my family was gone.

In reflecting on her narrative, she recalls her close relationship with her brother:

> We used to hang out at each other's houses every single day and we use to play basketball with each other and video games and just have fun all the time. Adam was a really nice person who loved to joke around a lot and just have fun. Adam meant so much to me as a person and when I learned that he passed away, it was really heartbreaking.

She noted that coping with her brother's death led to her building a closer relationship with her sister, as well as the fact that "sometimes unexpected, emotional things that you can't believe happen in life and you have to be ready."

In portraying the emotions of anger, resentment, envy, love, and grief shaping their relations with family members, students are recognizing the need to acknowledge and cope with these emotions through interactions with family members.

214 Students Co-Authoring Figured Worlds

ACTIVITY: CONTEXTUALIZING LANGUAGING EMOTIONS IN FAMILY WORLDS

Students could discuss or write about their experiences with languaging as emotions constituting their relations with other family members, including experiences of anger, resentment, envy, love, grief, etc., as well as reactions and uptake from other family members. They could reflect on how these emotions as actions served to enact certain "in-between" meanings in their relations, such as how their expression of anger led to a fractured relationship with a parent. They could also portray how they then attempted to reconcile breakdowns in their relations due to expressions of emotions; for example, engaging in a "cooling off" phase leading to sharing alternative emotions or apologies.

Adhering to Norms of Constituting Practices in Family Worlds

Students wrote about the challenge of adhering to the *norms* of constituting practices in family worlds, particularly in terms of norms constituting family relations. In writing about growing up in a Somali family, Assad noted how the practice of communicating with adults required her use of particular types of languaging actions consistent with Somali cultural norms.

> I saw first-hand how speech was such an important aspect of being in this group. How speaking to any elder, we were supposed to call them aunt and uncle no matter what, and calling them by their first name was seen as an act of utter disrespect. How in speaking to our parents, we were never allowed to call them by their first name. Even though it was never actually told to us, it was yet again seen as an act of disrespect. The only names for our parents were "Aabo and hooya" the Somali words for father and mother. Yet speaking to elders was one language, while speaking to our peers was a whole other thing.
>
> I always remember how my friends and I would always change our dialogue right when our parents would come, and how hard it was to keep one language in the house and another outside. When I say this, I don't mean English and Somali, but a dialogue using them both. Somali kids who are first-generation know that the way we speak to our friends will never be allowed at home with our parents. When our parents had come to this country, they came with the thought of education and making a better life, so finding her kids speaking in anything that isn't respectful dialogue is seen as a disgrace.
>
> Being in this group gives a feeling of belonging. Having respect for myself and growing to be someone worthwhile. Being in this kind of group has made me the woman I am today and hope one day can evolve to be something greater than that.

Assad perceives how specific languaging actions for interacting with her family based on Somali cultural norms differ from her interactions with her peers, a sense of how languaging constitutes a "feeling of belonging" within her family.

In writing about issues of adhering to norms related to acknowledging family problems or maintaining trusting relations in their families, students recognized the importance of practices for using languaging actions for sharing honest perceptions of issues facing families (Pahl, 2004).

ACTIVITY: CONTEXTUALIZING ADHERING TO NORMS CONSTITUTING FAMILY WORLDS

Students could discuss or write about their experience with parents or siblings to establish *norms* for engaging in certain practices within their family and the extent to which family members adhere to or resist adhering to these norms. For example, students may describe how their parent(s) value the importance of voicing their own opinions or ideas without concern for whether those opinions or ideas will be rejected. They may note how creating space for exchanging competing opinions/ideas requires a sense of trust that others will be open to instead of dismissive of those opinions/ideas. In some cases, students may also note instances in which their parents perceive voicing opinions or stances challenging parents as problematic.

Students may also discuss or write about norms related to their being responsible for completing certain tasks or chores when they fail to complete those tasks or chores. The degree to which those issues occur may reflect the overall sense of family cohesion associated with the need for individual members to contribute to supporting their family.

Adhering to Discourses Constituting Practices of Parenting

Students can also contextualize family practices based on *discourses* constituting parenting practices. Some parents may subscribe to a "strict-father" discourse by requiring their children to comply with a father's authoritative dictates or experience repercussions (Lakoff, 2002). Other parents may subscribe to a "nurturing parent" discourse in which parents focus on providing support for their children (Lakoff, 2002).

In her college admissions essay, Marla portrayed how she initially subscribed to her parents' conservative political perspectives, reflecting a "strict-father" discourse related to not challenging her parents' beliefs. However, when she experienced challenges of those perspectives in high school, she recognized the need

> to form opinions for myself based on a plethora of information gathered. I began to research controversial topics and the cases held by each political

party. Much to my initial dismay, I continued to agree more with the Democratic perspectives.

This led her to note that by challenging her parents' conservative perspectives

I never want to feel stuck in my way of thinking again. With the wisdom gained from the trials of my political and moral beliefs, it is clear to me that keeping an open mind is of utmost importance for any kind of growth.

In her written reflections on her essay, she noted that she was applying to colleges that "are all liberal. They are adamant about having … a wide variety of people with different backgrounds. So I wanted to show that I was open-minded and interested in other people's opinions." She noted how, in her essay, she portrayed how she had "been stuck in a mindset that being close-minded was good and how I escaped that way of thinking. I tried to explain how I wanted to continue to take different people's opinions into consideration in addition to research." This included descriptions of

how unsettling it was when I started to try and think on my own. I was told how to think my entire life and I was scared to go against that. I feel much more confident now and more comfortable to make mistakes and learn from them.

Students also wrote about how coping with a "strict-father" stance (Lakoff, 2002) can result in problematic relations. For example, Detra described how her parents, who had migrated from Nigeria to the United States, were coping with continuous reports of their relatives losing their lives due to a war in Nigeria. When her family learned of another death, her parents scolded her for not responding appropriately when she responded sarcastically. This leads to further tensions when, contrary to the mandate that she must attend church on Sundays, she stopped attending, claiming she needed to work on her homework. This led to her father, as the minister, critiquing her decision and triggering her depression.

Given her depression, her mother then interacted with her to state that members of their family

don't go thinking that this is depression, because it's not. We in the Jibunor family do not get depressed, we are *uke ike* (strong). Depression is not a Nigerian thing too. We will beat it out of you. I don't know what they're feeding you in your school; you better go and pray it out of you, if not I will beat it out of you.

She then described how she continued to struggle in school in May at the end of the school year. At the end of May, she further alienated her sister and her close friend. After oral surgery at the beginning of June,

I was in pain from the surgery and my heart hurt. I let all my sorrow out with that cry. I stayed in the corner and cried, and my mom walks in and hugs me and stayed with me till I pulled myself together.

In reflecting on her narrative, she noted that:

People couldn't tell that I wasn't myself because I grew perfect at hiding behind a wall. I knew that I wasn't myself at all. There was a lot of tension between my mother and me. It was resolved at the end of the day and me and my mom grew closer. Language creates a connection between people. My mom used a language I was familiar with (pigeon) and used a firm tone with me to set me straight and put me on the right path. I learned that I'm human, and it is normal for me to go through human things. Life isn't all sunshine and rainbows. I learned that when I'm going through things I have to talk to people.

Detra's portrayal of tensions with her parents reflects the influence of larger cultural discourses shaping her parents' conceptions of parental roles and stances. She posits how her parents "are really" traditional given their adoption of a relatively "strict-father" cultural model of parenting related to assuming that Detra should be obedient and compliant (Lakoff, 2002). Adopting this authoritative stance led to her parents' failure to recognize Detra's psychological experience of depression, requiring a more supportive, compassionate parental stance.

Parents also socialize students to adopt certain discourses related to adolescents' race, gender, and class identity. For example, in writing a "racial autobiography" in Corinth Matera's 12th-grade English class at South High in Minneapolis, Mary Miranda described her experience as a member of a Mexican-Jamaican American family (Beach & Beauchemin, 2019).

My mother is Mexican and my father is Jamaican. My siblings were born in Mexico; their father stayed in Mexico when my mother got a divorce from him. A few years after my mother immigrated to the United States, my mother and father met. When my mother told him she was pregnant, he claimed that I wasn't his daughter and left her to raise me on her own.

p. 137

At age eight, she recounts being labeled as a "Black girl," which she assumed had a negative connotation, based on her mother's stereotypical notions that "'Black people just tend to be aggressive and obnoxious when you talk to them; I wouldn't want you to end up that way'" (p. 137). Then, at age 16, she and her mother attended a Social Justice Fellows (SJF) program at South High School that sponsored discussions of ways to foster positive self-images for Black youth. Through her participation, her mother recognized the need for Mary to enact

218 Students Co-Authoring Figured Worlds

an Afro-Latino identity: "She finally realized, stripping me of my blackness didn't protect me, but made me drown in my own denial," resulting in her perceiving herself as "not two separate entities; I'm not Mexican or Jamaican. I am both worlds and much more" (p. 138).

ACTIVITY: CONTEXTUALIZING ADOPTION OF DISCOURSES SHAPING FAMILY WORLDS

Students could discuss or write about how their parents' adoption of certain discourses constituting family practices shaped their interactions and relations with them. As reflected in the above examples, adolescents may experience concerns about their parent(s) actions being problematic, leading to a loss of a sense of trust and breakdown in relations with those parent(s). In reflecting on reasons for loss of trust, students may note the difficulty of revising their assumptions that they could previously trust a parent, while now no longer being able to experience that trust as central to family connections.

Enacting Identities in Family Worlds

Students enact certain *identities* within family worlds. In doing so, they may experience tensions in enacting their family identities versus their school "Educational Selves" identities, given differences in norms and discourses valued by families versus norms and discourses in school worlds (Heath, 1982), differences evident in studies of families' funds of knowledge in those families or communities based on racial or class differences (González et al., 2005). In one study, family literacies were embedded in family life in a middle-class community through, for example, bedtime stories, consistent with school-based literacies (Heath, 1982). In contrast, family literacies in White working-class and Black working-class communities were taught more by imitation in ways that differed from school literacy instruction (Heath, 1982). This suggests the need for a "culturally sustaining pedagogy" to recognize and draw on differences in families' literacy practices to support positive family practices in the classroom (Paris & Alim, 2014, p. 85).

Drawing on family practices for use in school worlds also involves working with parents and students to co-author/design a curriculum that provides students with social capital consistent with family needs and aspirations (Ishimaru, 2019). Analysis of parent-teacher conferences regarding their students' ability to enact a successful identity noted that

> Parents and teachers are ambivalent partners: they can be both allied and competitors in producing, making explicit and modulating representations of the student. Academic assessment is used not only to define the

characteristics of "good" and "poor" students but also to suggest a connotation of the person's Self. These processes involve of course different power dynamics: teachers/students; teachers/parents; parents/students.

González et al., 2005, p. 51

Given a student experiencing a lack of engagement in school, in a parent/teacher conference, parent(s) and a teacher may discuss ways to support students' defining certain purposes for school so that they may then value their work in school.

In this hypothetic situation, there is the student producing an I-position "I-as-demotivated-student", who listens to other voices that promote like "You-as-person-with-potential", "We-support-you", etc. The different voices also imply power relationships that frame the meaning-making process. This condition has the potential to generate new meanings to be negotiated through the student's Educational Self.

González et al., 2005, p. 55

Parents also assume an important role in helping adolescents cope with challenges. For example, a 15-year-old student in Brazil wanted to attend a specific university, but needed to pass an exam to be admitted to the university (González et al., 2005). When she did not pass the exam as she expected, she noted that her parents "'encouraged me a lot, [they said] that [the first fail] was the first obstacle; that I didn't pass, but I had more shots, and I would succeed later [entering the school], encouraged me a lot'" (p. 58). This support helped her project a positive future self, based on the notion "'that if I had studied a lot and got a better score, I would get it the second time and, as I was young, and that I had the chance to pass'" (p. 58).

Adopting Identities Related to Achieving Autonomy/ Independence From Parents

Within family social worlds, adolescents experience close attachments with parent(s) while also experiencing the need for separation to develop one's sense of identity (Ferrer-Wreder & Kroger, 2020; Mattanah et al., 2011). Adolescents have natural, developmental needs to assert their autonomy to become less dependent on their parents (Scabini & Manzi, 2011). However, parents may seek to continue to exert some control over adolescents' lives (Beveridge & Berg, 2007).

At the same time, adolescents still require an emotional connection with parents associated with a sense of belongingness and intimacy with their parents (Scabini & Manzi, 2011). The degree to which students experience positive attachment/separation experiences depends on how parents create spaces for adolescents to experiment with enacting their sense of identity (Ponappa et al., 2014). Parent(s) foster this connection through the practice of inviting adolescents' self-disclosures about their experiences with parents (Jiang et al., 2017), which includes parents voicing their "blessings" of adolescents' assertions of their independence in specific events (Ferrer-Wreder & Kroger, 2020).

As a result of the need for autonomy and connection, adolescents may also experience ambiguous, momentary positioning with other family members, resulting in shifts in love/hate relations that can challenge adolescents' sense of trust in other family members. Parents may experience anxiety over adolescents leaving home, which poses difficulties associated with adolescents' separation from parents (Kins et al., 2011). At the same time, the consistency of long-term love relations in a family typically mitigates any short-term tensions in family relations.

Achieving autonomy/independence involves challenging or pushing again certain parental boundaries, often resulting in tensions between adolescents and parents. In these interactions, both parents and adolescents may reference certain beliefs/discourses associated with their right to challenge or defend certain status-quo family practices. For example, an adolescent may note that "'My mother/ father allows me to decide things for myself' or 'My mother/father insists upon doing things her/his way (reverse coded)'" or "'My mother/father pushes me to think independently.'" (Kins et al., 2011, p. 576). This may include the extent to which family members allow adolescents to make their own decisions or spend time on their own.

Parents, therefore, need to provide adolescents with some autonomy, while adolescents still need to value parental support (Beveridge & Berg, 2007). Adolescents and parents can collaboratively address this need for autonomy in a supportive manner through engaging in shared decision-making as well as honoring each of their perspectives.

In writing about his parents' divorce as a "real-life game of tug of war," John describes how his parents "had two different philosophies on how they thought to raise a child. One being as lenient as possible, treating me as their best friend. The other being a locked prison cell of rules and regulations." The challenge he faced was that both parents attempted to have him favor one parent over the other, with the result that

> I was taught to hate the other parent simply because they didn't "provide." As I continued to grow up, I began realizing most of the things I was told weren't true, which only made me question everything. I went through a stage in my life when everything seemed pointless, and the stress of constantly being in the middle of arguments only made me want to shut everything and everyone out. However, my mood changed when I realized that I could make a point out of it all and think for myself. I was set on being my own person letting no one stop me.

Co-Authoring Family Figured Worlds **221**

In an interview, he characterized the languaging actions in family interactions as mostly argumentative.

> That's what put me in the middle of that. If it was talking to me about one another, it was always a play on words to get me to be on their side mostly. The tug of war was mostly just them wanting me to be on their side; rather than choosing a specific side that I wanted to be on, [I wanted] more to not care about any of the sides as much and balance between the two. Instead of it being a pull between the two, not letting either of the sides try to get me either way.

John then changed his perspective when he perceived the need to transcend his parents' positioning his identity to enact his own identity through success in school. He focused on improving his schoolwork, with the result that his "grades changed drastically giving me some clear ideas on where I wanted to go with my life." He identifies his long-term career goal as "becoming a Child Advocate Lawyer. I had already learned the pre-skills on what it takes by competing on my high school's debate and speech team and that only made me more interested."

Given the issues with his parents, John established a supportive relationship with his grandfather, who

> filled in the role as the father figure in my life. He taught me a lot of the things that my dad would have, but he just wasn't there until later when I moved to his house. Going to church, volunteering even at his age, just doing small things around the community like picking up other people's trash and stuff like that. Respecting others.

In asserting their independence from their parents, adolescents face the risk of alienating these parents, particularly in families based on rigid hierarchical relations in which adolescents are positioned through languaging as needing to "know their place" within that hierarchy.

ACTIVITY: CONTEXTUALIZING ACHIEVING AUTONOMY/ INDEPENDENCE FROM PARENTS

Students could discuss or write about their own or a peer's/character's experiences in developing a sense of autonomy in their relations with parent(s) through certain practices, while at the same time maintaining their connections with parent(s) through other practices. They may portray specific events in which they engaged in a certain practice that involved asserting their sense of autonomy/independence. For example, they may portray disagreements with their parent(s)' ideas or request to engage in an action. They could also portray how they may have framed this challenge in a manner that preserved their connection with their parent(s) so as not to alienate their parent(s).

Acquiring Family Practices Through Genres

Students experience *genres* for acquiring family practices, including *genres* of shared autobiographical narratives, messages, or cards for celebrating holidays, birthdays, graduations, etc. (Cigoli & Scabini, 2006). In a middle-school ELA classroom, students interviewed family members, caregivers, or older adults about their childhood memories and conducted research about the place and time associated with these events related to their memories to write a narrative for inclusion in a book (Landay & Heath, 2021).

Students then wrote their narratives from the first-person perspective of the parent or adult featured in their narratives. Based on reading each other's narratives in the book, students learned that families adopted different norms constituting what they valued or celebrated in family events. Students then received positive comments from family members who read their book.

In their narratives, they portrayed how their use of certain genre practices served to enact bonds between family members. In writing about her Vietnamese family in my study, Ngo described how her family experienced a shared interest in the genre of television comedy:

> One thing that we all enjoy to do together is watching comedies. It is not a rare thing to see us gather around in the living room and watching Vietnamese comedy on YouTube. Different from American comedy, Vietnamese comedy is about life lessons, criticizing the human vices in the most hilarious ways. Our sense of humor is so mordant and caustic. We will search the comedy video that had posted on YouTube from our favorite comedians. They do it by acting out in a play based on their daily life situations. We laugh all the time, even the hard person like my dad has to crack up laughing. These comedies are really meaningful, not only by bringing back the memories of our home country but also it is a great way to bring us along after a hard week.

Ngo also describes how her family's experience of the Tet Holiday as the Vietnamese Lunar New Year involves enacting certain shared genre practices.

> On this day, we clean and decorate our house with shiny bronze Chinese coins and metallic colorful ornaments because my father believes in Feng

Shui. Freshen up the house with lively pinkish, yellowish lily flowers that we put on the altar in our home as we also pray for our lives and hope that ancestors and God will help us in our new year. My mom will try to search all the Asian markets to buy mango, coconut, custard-apple, and papaya and place them on the big plate and place it on the table. The reason for that is because in Vietnamese, those names of fruits, if you say their names in euphemism, it will sound like "pray enough just to spend" that was just translated to English. After the tradition, we usually share amazing meals with others with Vietnamese traditional food and play cards afterward. We have a lot of fun. It is a great opportunity for family members to gather around and spend time to remember and appreciate our roots.

Students also can collect narratives from other family members about the practices valued in their family worlds, as reflected in the narratives about families in this chapter. Members of five African-American families participated in the Dig-A-Fam: Families' Digital Storytelling Project in which they created digital stories about events in their lives (Ellison, 2016). One mother created a story about raising her son, who was autistic, while she was a graduate school student. Another mother created a story about her family's genealogy to preserve memories of her mother, who had recently died.

ACTIVITY: CONTEXTUALIZING USE OF GENRES FOR PORTRAYING FAMILY WORLDS

Students could employ genres for portraying family worlds; for example, engaging in a family history project. In these projects, students acquire information about families across different generations; for example, how a family may value the importance of engaging in certain annual family celebrations/events. Students could trace their ancestors across time using free resources such as WorldGenWeb, *worldgenweb.org*; FamilySearch, *familysearch.org/en*; RootsWeb, *home.rootsweb.com*; or OliveTreeGenealogy, *olivetreegenealogy.com/index.shtml.* They can also collect letters or documents about how practices valued in previous generations were passed on to later generations.

Students could also interview their parents or grandparents about their own upbringing experiences based on their sharing autobiographical narratives as well as having parents or grandparents then reflect on what practices they acquired from these experiences. Students could reflect on the benefits of certain acquired practices, as did Ngo in noting how the celebration of the Tet Holiday "is a great opportunity for family members to gather around and spend time to remember and appreciate our roots."

224 Students Co-Authoring Figured Worlds

Responding to Representations of Family Worlds in Media/literature

Students acquire knowledge of practices constituting family worlds from *media/literature*. For example, students could view movies/television shows or read examples of novels or biographies that portray these practices related to how a person's or character's family upbringing or previous generations influenced their development over time.

In Ms. E's class, students responded to portrayals of families in literary texts. For example, they responded to portrayals of conflicts between Calvin and Beth as husband and wife portrayed in *Ordinary People* (Guest, 2015), given their difficulty coping with the death of their son and their other son's suicide attempt. Cassie noted how parents' difficulty in acknowledging or attending to each other's or their children's emotions creates tensions within families.

> Calvin in particular neglects Beth's emotional needs. Calvin makes Beth feel unvalued and misunderstood. He does this through his lack of an effort to check on her as he does with his son, his objectification of her, and dishonesty regarding his feelings on Conrad's suicide attempt and his drinking habits. This objectification would create issues in any relationship, especially one where the death of a child is involved. The entire Jarrett family, including Beth, needs emotional support.

Jodi attributes Beth's difficulty in interacting with Conrad, particularly about his suicide attempt, as due to her being a

> perfectionist. She wants her family to be run perfectly; no arguments or disagreements .... She believes that Conrad attempted suicide just to spite her. The way Beth feels about her son's attempted suicide directly affected how Conrad acted towards her.

Responding to characters' languaging of emotions leads students to reflect on how these emotions serve to enact conflicts in characters' relations.

ACTIVITY: CONTEXTUALIZING PORTRAYALS OF FAMILY PRACTICES IN MEDIA/LITERATURE

In responding to portrayals of family practices in media/literature, students could compare these portrayals with their family practices in terms of differences related to their family's norms, discourses, and identity relations. For example, in comparing the conflicts portrayed in *Ordinary People*, students may identify certain positive practices that serve to enact supportive relations in their family. Students could also critique media representations of families on television shows or in movies that dramatize family conflicts in unrealistic ways.

Summary

This chapter describes contextualizing family practices related to purposes, discourses, norms, identities, genres, and media/literature. Central to these practices is how parents socialize adolescents in terms of certain norms/discourses and how adolescents in developing their identities may seek to achieve their own independence from their parents. Students also acquire use of certain genres for interacting with family members as well as acquiring knowledge of family practices through responding to media/literature.

References

Beach, R., & Beauchemin, F. (2019). *Teaching language as action in the ELA classroom.* Routledge.

Beveridge, R. M., & Berg, C. A. (2007). Parent–adolescent collaboration: An interpersonal model for understanding optimal interactions. *Clinical Child and Family Psychology Review, 10*(1), 25–52. doi:10.1007/s10567-006-0015-z

Brooks, D. (2020, March 1). The nuclear family was a mistake. *The Atlantic.* https://infoweb-newsbank.com

Cigoli, V., & Scabini, E. (2006). *Family identity: Ties, symbols, and transitions.* Lawrence Erlbaum.

Ellison, T. L. (2016). Artifacts as stories: Understanding families, digital literacies, and storied lives. *Journal of Adolescent & Adult Literacy, 59*(5), 511–513.

Ferrer-Wreder, L., & Kroger, J. (2020). *Identity in adolescents: The balance between self and other* (4th ed.). Routledge.

González, N., Moll, L. C., & Amanti, C. (Eds.). (2005). *Funds of knowledge: Theorizing practices in households, communities, and classrooms.* Erlbaum.

Grotevant, H. D. (2011). Autonomy or connections: Identities as intergenerational projects. In C. Cooper (Ed.), *Bridging multiple worlds: Cultures, pathways, and bridges to college* (pp. 33–46). Oxford University Press.

Guest, J. (2015). *Ordinary people.* Penguin Books.

Heath, S. B. (1982). What no bedtime story means: Narrative skills at home and school. *Language in Society, 11*(1), 49–76. https://doi.org/10.1017/S0047404500009039

Ishimaru, A. (2019). *Just schools: Building equitable collaborations with families and communities.* Teachers College Press.

Jiang, L. C., Yang, I. M., & Wang, C. (2017). Self-disclosure to parents in emerging adulthood: Examining the roles of perceived parental responsiveness and separation-individuation. *Journal of Social and Personal Relationships, 34*(4), 425–445.

Kerr, M., & Stattin, H. (2000). What parents know, how they know it, and several forms of adolescent adjustment: Further support for a reinterpretation of monitoring. *Developmental Psychology, 36*(3), 366–380.

Kim, K. J., Conger, R. D., Lorenz, F. O., & Elder, G. H., Jr. (2001). Parent–adolescent reciprocity in negative affect and its relation to early adult social development. *Developmental Psychology, 37*(6), 775–790.

Kins, E., Soenens, B., & Beyers, W. (2011). "Why do they have to grow up so fast?" Parental separation anxiety and emerging adults' pathology of separation-individuation. *Journal of Clinical Psychology, 67,* 647–664.

Lakoff, G. (2002). *Moral politics: How liberals and conservatives think.* University of Chicago Press.

Landay, E., & Heath, S. B. (2021). "Hard-won joy": Equity through collaboration. *Theory Into Practice, 60*(1), 103–112.

Mattanah, J. F., Lopez, F. G., & Govern, J. M. (2011). The contributions of parental attachment bonds to college student development and adjustment: A meta-analytic review. *Journal of Counseling Psychology, 58*(4), 565–596.

Moses, M. S., & Wiley, K. E. (2020). Social context matters: Bridging philosophy and sociology to strengthen conceptual foundation for college access research. *American Educational Research Journal, 57*(4), 1665–1687.

Parcel, T. L., Dufur, M. J., & Zito, R. C. (2010). Capital at home and at school: A review and synthesis. *Journal of Marriage and Family, 72*(4), 828–846. doi:10.1111/j.1741-3737.2010.00733.x

Pahl, K. (2004). Narratives, artifacts and cultural identities: An ethnographic study of communicative practices in homes. *Linguistics and Education, 15*(4), 339–358. https://doi.org/10.1016/j.linged.2005.07.002

Paris, D., & Alim, H. S. (2014). What are we seeking to sustain through culturally sustaining pedagogy? A loving critique forward. *Harvard Educational Review, 84*(1), 85–100. https://doi.org/10.17763/haer.84.1.982l873k2ht16m77

Ponappa, S., Bartle-Haring, S., & Day, R. (2014). Connection of parents and healthy separation during adolescence: A longitudinal perspective. *Journal of Adolescence, 37*(5), 555–566.

Raymond-Flesch, M., Auerswald, C., McGlone, L., Comfort, M. & Minnis, A. (2017). Building social capital to promote adolescent wellbeing: a qualitative study with teens in a Latino agricultural community. *BMC Public Health, 17*(1), pp. 177–179.

Scabini, E., & Manzi, C. (2011). Family processes and identity. In S. J. Schwartz, K. Luyckx & V. L. Vignoles (Eds.), *Handbook of identity theory and research* (pp. 565–584). Springer.

Tikkanen, J. (2016). Concern or confidence? Adolescents' identity capital and future worry in different school contexts. *Journal of Adolescence, 46,* 14–24. doi:10.1016/j.adolescence.2015.10.011

Wanders, F. H. K., Dijkstra, A. B., Maslowski, R., & van der Veenc, I. (2020). The effect of teacher-student and student-student relationships on the societal involvement of students. *Research Papers in Education, 35*(3), 266–286. https://doi.org/10.1080/02671522.2019.1568529

Weiss, H. E. (2012). The intergenerational transmission of social capital: A developmental approach to adolescent social capital formation. *Sociological Inquiry, 82*(2), 212–235. doi:10.1111/j.1475-682X.2012.00414.x

11
CO-AUTHORING WORKPLACE FIGURED WORLDS

This chapter describes students acquiring practices constituting their jobs in workplace worlds. Students perceived their purposes for languaging actions involved establishing positive relations with customers. Students associated these practices with use of certain languaging actions with customers as consistent with norms and discourses based on corporate branding agendas defining the need to please customers. Students perceived some of their workplace experiences as useful for acquiring practices constituting their present and future identities. At the same time, they critiqued certain discourses related to race, class, and gender as shaping practices in workplaces. Students also identified use of certain genres constituting interactions with customers and co-workers. They can also respond to portrayals of workplace practices in media and literature for inferring connections to their own workplace practices.

Several students in my study were employed after school in workplace worlds such as coffee shops, restaurants, and retail stores. Through their participation in these workplaces, they acquired certain practices associated with being successful in these workplaces through learning to contextualize the purposes, norms, discourses, identities, and genres in workplaces (Dochy et al., 2021). At the same time, they also critiqued how certain corporate discourses served to define how they should interact with customers as well as shaping the meaning of consumer practices in their workplaces.

Risks and Benefits of Adolescents Engaged in Workplaces

A common concern about adolescents working is whether their working will be detrimental to their schoolwork or participation in extracurricular activities. Adolescents who spend an average of or less than 20 hours a week working do

DOI: 10.4324/9781003246886-13

228 Students Co-Authoring Figured Worlds

not devote less time to schoolwork or extracurricular activities (Keister & Hall, 2010; Staff & Schulenberg, 2010). At the same time, there may be detrimental effects for adolescents who work more than 20 hours a week (Staff & Mortimer 2007). Analysis of 14-year-olds from 20 different countries related a high amount of time spent working and academic achievement found that work negatively affects achievement in most countries (Post & Pong, 2009). This is particularly the case when students assume that acquiring certain practices will contribute to their success in their workplace, which may often not be the case.

Adolescents benefit from their work experience through acquiring time-management practices and developing agency/responsibility (Mortimer, 2003; Staff & Mortimer, 2007). However, these benefits may vary given the nature, quality, and pay levels of their work across different types of jobs, with stressful, demanding work having negative effects on mental health (Mortimer, 2003). For example, 12th-graders perceived work in fast-food restaurants as having the highest stress levels and interference with school/peers/family and not providing them with preparation for future careers (Staff & Schulenberg, 2010). Adolescents working as store clerks or in sales also had similar negative ratings related to stress, low job skills, interference with schools/peers/family, and career training; fast-food and store clerk/sales jobs accounted for 39% of all jobs. In contrast, 12th-graders rated office/clerical jobs as having low stress, supportive co-workers, little interference with school/peers/family, and high career-potential training.

The benefits or risks of adolescents working may also vary according to race, class, and gender. For example, adolescents working in fast-food restaurants in low-income neighborhoods benefit from connections to older adults in their community. However, employment opportunities vary by race. White students are twice as likely to be employed as Black or Hispanic students, given opportunities related to family social capital, or proximity to suburban shopping malls that hire adolescents (Aud et al., 2011).

It may be assumed that student employment within schools might be beneficial for adolescents, given that their work is in a school context. However, contrary to expectations, a study of 22,183 12th-graders with school-related jobs found that these jobs were no more beneficial and somewhat detrimental to schooling than jobs not related to school. Black students reported that they were twice as likely to have school-related jobs than Whites (Hamilton & Sumner, 2017), suggesting the need to enhance the quality and support for school-related jobs.

ACTIVITY: CONTEXTUALIZING WORKPLACE PRACTICES RELATED TO BENEFITS AND RISKS

Students could discuss or write about their general experiences in after-school and in-school jobs related to benefits and risks. They may note how differences in the number of hours/days and the nature of their work shape

> their perceptions of how they value their work and connections with school worlds. Students could then compare their overall experiences with their peers, including peers who are not working, related to their assessments of the benefits and drawbacks of their work. Students may discover that there is such a wide variation in work and relationships with their academic success that it is difficult to generalize any overall relationships between work and academic success.

Acquiring Purposes for Employing Practices in Workplace Worlds

Through engaging in their workplace jobs, students in our study wrote about their *purposes* for employing certain practices in their workplace worlds. They consistently noted how identifying these practices involves the need to please customers. Maintaining these positive relations with customers requires that they minimize any potential friction or conflict with customers that would undermine achieving positive uptake. Gina noted that "'our main mission is to make sure that the customers are satisfied because at the end of the day the customers are the people who supply my paycheck and tips.'"

In writing about her work at Starbucks, Hilary described her motivation or desire to please her customers at a Starbucks coffee shop through

> conversations with the customer to create a positive encounter. For instance, they'll say "what are you going to do today?" This engages the customer and employee. This is my favorite part of the job because I get to create bonds with regular customers.

Hilary perceives her practices as driven by Starbucks's larger corporate purpose of pleasing their customers through the use of languaging actions; for example, asking "'What are you going to do today?' This engages the customer and employee."

These practices constituting interactions with customers are often based on business management/corporate *norms* and *discourses*. Gaudio (2003) critiques Starbucks' branding with their promotion of "'coffeetalk,' [as] commercialized mutual infiltration of public and private spheres in the contemporary United States" (p. 674). He documents how Starbucks promoted their brand as providing a commodified public space for engaging in languaging equated with enacting middle-class values in ways that mesh differences between perceptions of different forms of talk in private versus public spaces. People may equate certain kinds of talk with work versus talk associated with casual interaction related to engaging in eating, drinking, shopping, or exercising.

230 Students Co-Authoring Figured Worlds

Part of Starbucks' corporate branding includes promoting the idea of equating engaging in this casual conversation, as opposed to work-related talk, with being a customer in a Starbucks, as evident in this promotional language:

> Your Starbucks experience is so much more than just coffees. It's the conversation you have with a friend, a moment of solitude at the end of the day, a quick stop on the way to the movies. And in the tradition of the coffeehouse, it's also the chance to immerse yourself in eclectic and enduring music while you sip your favorite coffee.
>
> *Starbucks, 2000, n.p.*

Gaudio also notes how Starbucks' branding equates their spaces with middle-class, suburban values, portraying Starbucks as "safe, comfortable and non-threatening [by] comparing Starbucks stores to other potential venues of social interaction that are by implication unsafe, uncomfortable, and threatening" (p. 677).

For their interactions with customers or shoppers, adolescent workers are trained to employ scripted languaging related to greeting, taking orders, and determining customer needs to achieve a positive uptake from those customers. It is also the case that these interactions are typically highly truncated and limited to brief question/answer languaging actions, minimizing any extended talk or sharing of personal experiences/information associated with interactions in peer or family worlds. Gina described her work as a barista at Starbucks and noted that "baristas have to work super hard and very fast. We want to serve our customers as fast as we can." Sandy noted how

> this job has taught me many things like how to multitask, to work fast and efficiently, and use communication skills. Multitasking and a strong work ethic will really help me in my future when I get a different job. This job has also taught me time management. I have to perfectly time things when I make something or do dishes.

Gina noted the importance of engaging in positive interactions with customers given that "I was told to prioritize talking to customers more than like making the drink fast. And so I'm, I'm talking to people constantly. I'm making drinks and I'm ringing up people on the register."

These students contextualize the practices for interacting with customers as consistent with purposes defined by Starbucks' corporate norms and discourses based on pleasing customers. At the same time, they noted that they draw on these practices for interacting with others in their other worlds.

> ## ACTIVITY: CONTEXTUALIZING PURPOSES FOR EMPLOYING PRACTICES IN WORKPLACE WORLDS
>
> Students could discuss or write about their use of practices in their workplace worlds related to achieving purposes as framed by their corporate workplace owners, particularly related to practices for languaging in their interacting with customers. They could reflect on how they acquired use of these practices through training or observing mentors, as well as instances in which their languaging served to enact positive relations with customers/clients. They could also critique the limitations of these corporate norms and discourses related to how they shape the authenticity of their interactions with customers.

Acquiring Practices Constituted by Norms in Workplaces

Students also described and wrote about their experiences learning to acquire certain *norms* within the workplace constituting practices based on those norms. John described his use of languaging in his job in a Gap store in which

> how we communicate with each other is very laid back; we're all fairly close. It's small talk, but at the same time, we're always together so we're pretty close. Then it's the opposite with customers where we have to be completely fake, in a way, by pretending we're really nice and interested.

To enact a trusting relationship with his customers, he noted the importance of adhering to norms related to

> the tone of your voice and how responsive you are. If you seem like you know what you're talking about, if you seem like you know the answers to the questions that they have, then they're more prone to listen to you and want to come back to the store. That's what we've always learned. Always trying to make the customer feel like they're welcome. You just always want to be a lot happier than they are. That tends to work. You need to be able to talk to people and seem confident and not super awkward.

He acquired these practices through

> greeting people and talking to them because you have to do it ....You don't want the customer to think that you're super awkward or you don't know what you're talking about because that's gonna make them not want to come back.

232 Students Co-Authoring Figured Worlds

Rachel noted the importance of wearing red shirts and blue jeans, given that "we all have a sense of uniformity," for her work at Target, as well as the "basic white, oval pin with Target written across the top in red bold letters." She noted how, in her clothing department, she interacts with co-workers in

> huddles, which is when we all meet at one place to talk and eat snacks. At this huddle, we call ourselves one of two things, blood clots, but we also call each other the target fambam. We all speak to each other with a lot of sarcasm and are constantly laughing.

She reflected on how this work

> has taught me how to make new friends outside of school. It also taught me how to calmly talk to people when they made me mad, and extremely frustrated. I want to be a nurse one day, so I need to be able to interact with people. So I think that's going to carry with me throughout my whole life.

Cassie also worked in a local Target store, in which she was responsible for training co-workers in the beauty section. In some cases, these co-workers "are older than I am. Just because I don't want to sound condescending towards them," in her interactions with her co-workers, she employs informal language.

She contrasted these more informal languaging interactions at Target with norms involved in working as a secretary in a summer job in a more formal setting, in which she adopted what "was definitely a more professional look, formal and everything so that how I communicated in talking to my bosses [was different]." At the same time, Cassie noted that, in interacting with her bosses, she recognized the importance of contextualizing the situation to vary her languaging, given that

> sometimes they're a little bit more casual. So when they're casual, I can be casual. Like sometimes we'll sit and have a conversation about life and where I'm going to college so then I can be more casual. But I kind of just try and follow their cues on how they do that.

In reflecting on her contextualizing social situations, she notes:

> How I speak depends mostly on the formality of the situation. For example, talking with teachers or my boss is a formal situation where I want to be professional, whereas talking with my classmates or co-workers is informal, so I use a more casual voice and slang. I think a big part of this is the power structure of the conversation, as a teacher or boss both are in a way "in

Co-Authoring Workplace Figured Worlds 233

charge" of me, so I want to represent myself as best as possible, whereas that is not needed with a classmate or co-worker as there is no power imbalance.

Students also wrote about acquiring norms for working with senior adults and children. Patricia described working in a senior retirement complex in which she serves meals to residents. She noted how "the residents grew up in a completely different era with different traditions and views of world issues. Some of the things that we say as teenagers, that seem normal and harmless, can be offensive to the residents." This included addressing a group of males and females at a table as "guys" or use of the words "no problem" as implying that "doing a favor for them was not a problem for you, or you did not go out of your way to help them. A better term would be 'you're welcome' or 'my pleasure.'"

She noted that co-workers interact with each other in daily huddles where they engage in the practice/activity of talking

> about work expectations and use real-life scenarios to help team members better connect and understand the views and goals of Lifespace Communities. The huddles are different each day. They consist of quotes and news that relate to the community and the message of the huddle.

Central to her relations with her co-workers is the need for a sense of trust: "trust and helping each other out when needed are huge values used at my job. Without it, nothing would get done, and no one would get along."

In her work, she described how she learned the need to interact with others based on coping with how

> not everyone's the same and … people handle situations differently. Some residents are very patient, while others are not. I learned that the customer is always right. Because of this, I have grown to be a more patient and understanding person.

Having to interact with "new people of all different ages [was] intimidating and nerve-wracking to me. A situation like this brings out my shyness and awkwardness. I would have kept to myself if it wasn't for the positive and joyful attitudes of my co-workers."

In writing about her experience as a gymnastics coach of young children, Laura noted how, in her own experience in gymnastics beginning when she was four,

> I was a pain to the coaches. I had an attitude and didn't know how much work they really were putting into our time at the gym. I didn't understand their side of being a coach until I was offered a job there and got to experience that side.

234 Students Co-Authoring Figured Worlds

When she was offered a job as a coach at age 14, she

> was clueless on how to handle children. I didn't really know how to talk
> to people. I was really bad at it. It made me super anxious. I tried to keep
> it as short as I could and I didn't do a lot of explaining and stuff like that.
> When I had to communicate with the other coaches, I would just assume
> that I was doing something, and I wouldn't talk to figure out if it was okay
> if I did something.

In talking with her supervisor,

> she told me some other ways to say things. She helped me a little bit with
> that. Also, I just listened to other coaches talking to parents, and I found out
> what they said, and if I had a parent ask me a similar question, I would try to
> respond similarly. But then I learned later that talking to parents, they don't
> want a short, simple answer. They want an explanation typically.

Through this experience over a four-year period, Laura learned how to interact
with parents in ways that were consistent with their needs.

> I learned how to deal with all different types of people, from all different
> ages. There's situations where I need a quick-fix in planning, or I've
> needed to compromise with the other teams at the gym. The gym has
> a schedule that it follows, and depending on when I was at work and at
> school, I had to make time for all my other activities like homework and
> friends.

These students acquired knowledge of the norms constituting needed practices
in their workplaces through training and simply observing and emulating their
co-workers' use of these practices.

ACTIVITY: CONTEXTUALIZING ACQUIRING NORMS FOR ENGAGING IN WORKPLACES

Students could discuss or write about acquiring certain norms for employing
practices in workplaces. They could identify those practices they perceive
to be most effective in their interactions based on norms valued in certain
workplaces. They could also note how they are valued for acquiring these
norms. For example, they may receive positive uptake/responses from others
for their use of certain practices; for example, responses from senior adults
about how they value students' support.

> They could also infer what they perceive to be norms constituting how they interact with customers based on valuing customers' expectations, needs, and concerns. At the same time, students could also adopt a critical stance on these norms related to how a focus on "bottom-line" profits in a workplace associated with a business-management discourse can limit a focus on authentic, human interactions in a workplace.

Analyzing Race, Gender, and Class Discourses Shaping Workplace Practices

Students could describe how *discourses* of race, gender, and class, as well as an overall focus on consumerism, shaped the meaning of practices in their workplaces.

Discourses of Race

Students also described how beliefs/values/discourses related to race shaped their perceptions of retail workplaces. Detra described her several visits to a barbershop run by Black males who serve customers of different races. She noted the importance of conversations between barbers and customers in ways that constitute the barbershop as "a community center where people go to connect and converse about things that are important in society today. They are supposed to make their clients or whoever walks in there comfortable. Their conversations are inclusive and relatable." She noted how the barbers consistently employ certain practices/ genres to spark conversations with customers:

> A., a barber there, talked about family, specifically his. It seemed like a conversation starter that got people, mostly the adults, interested in what he was saying. They make sure to respectfully use the appropriate language in a way that wouldn't offend the customers. They honestly don't act differently when a client shows up except when the clients are kids so they can set a good example for the younger ones.

Based on her experience, as a Black person, Detra interrogates her presuppositions regarding the notion that

> there are people in the Black community who think that being rude is a personality trait, and they stay this way in order to push people away. Prior to my haircut, I was nervous to go to an all-Black men's barbering studio. It was more like I felt insecure due to the behaviors of "moralized/cultured" close-minded adults. I understand and believe that not everyone is the same, and it is also wrong to generalize an entire group of people based on the

236 Students Co-Authoring Figured Worlds

actions of one and what I've been told. This experiment has taught me to be less judgmental and more open-minded.

Through her writing, Detra is reflecting on how her discourses of race shaped her perceptions of practices valued within the barbershop as a valued space for people to engage in languaging about their daily lives.

Discourses of Class

Students also examined how beliefs/values/discourses of class shaped perceptions of retail workplaces. Tanya wrote about her observations of what she perceived to be the largely White, middle-class customers frequenting a local North Face store that features outdoor clothing. She noted how the branding of North Face was linked to their support of "expeditions to the coldest and most untouched corners of the globe. More than fifty years after The North Face's grand opening, the store offers an extensive line of performance apparel, equipment and footwear."

She critiqued this practice as a reflection of customers' need for attention and approval by "someone else that might know something more than they do and this person is often an employee." She also characterized the customers as adhering to a materialist culture, given that the customers are overly focused on purchasing certain brands as a status symbol.

> Most people that walk into the store aren't much focused on buying a coat for a specific activity. They want to have it because it's a popular brand and can be stylish. Also, I often see people, including myself, wear an expensive North Face backpack. They get it for school, not because they are going on a crazy cool expedition. Overall, I think people are materialistic because possessing an item that people want makes them feel cool and stylish.

In writing an ethnography of a local art gallery that included art/jewelry by local artists, Cassie noted that the shoppers were largely "older, upper-middle-class white women," as well as how the prices for items were "ridiculously expensive. Seriously, $60 for a pair of minimalist earrings, [although the shoppers] are apparently not concerned with price, which is fitting with the upper-middle-class demographic." She observed that:

> The customers express that they are impressed by the fact that all of the gifts are handmade, and the employees utilize that as a selling point if customers do not bring it up first. They also remark that they enjoy purchasing unique gifts rather than items that have been mass-produced, as they feel that their gift is more special. When asked about why they chose to shop at the gallery,

the majority of the customers answered that they preferred to shop in niche places and enjoyed the creativity of the atmosphere.

She perceived these shoppers as openly displaying their analysis of items and purchasing decisions as not conforming to a majority opinion or stance. She noted how the visitors

> were praising themselves for choosing to shop there, instead of going to their local department store, like Target or Macy's or something for their shopping. So it just shows how unique they felt that they were choosing such unique things at the gallery.

Cassie critiqued the irony in their display of presumed individuality in how "the theme of uniqueness is prominent," given that the shoppers'

> love for the unique actually reveals a ubiquitous human instinct, starkly commonplace in contrast. The customers believe that they are different than other people because they chose to shop at a one-of-a-kind gallery instead of a large department store. But, in reality, they are in the gallery surrounded by other people of the same demographics who also shop there for the purpose of feeling unique.

In resisting "mainstream" shopping, she perceived, these "same people try to reject norms and things deemed 'basic,' and consequently by doing so become even more mainstream because their desire to feel unique is in every human."

Chris observed customers at an IKEA store featuring furniture made in Sweden, promoted as follows: "There's so much to know about IKEA beyond our low-price furniture. From our sustainable sourcing of cotton and wood to our stance on human rights; what it's like to work for IKEA, to our democratic design approach" ("This is IKEA" (IKEA, 2012)). He described the customers as largely White and "upper-to-middle class who have money to spend on this furniture," with a prototypical customer being "middle income, white, female in her early thirties with her friends or boyfriend."

As did Cassie, he critiqued what he perceived as IKEA's branding appeal to customers as reifying customers as experiencing an exclusive space so that they "stay in [their] comfort zone and only talk to people that [they] know like … friends and family."

Students also wrote about their observations of how workers employed practices related to marketing products for retail stores. Harry visited a warehouse where workers created marketing ads for products sold at Target stores. He described this workplace as "a hidden wonderland of imagination, a place where ingenuity and panache run wild; a place that has the tools to create anything one

238 Students Co-Authoring Figured Worlds

could imagine; a place full of people, each playing an important role in making sure the magic stays alive."

He identified "three different categories of people who were at the warehouse"—builders; prop managers; and photographers, editors, and seamstresses. He perceived the builders and prop managers as largely White and lower-middle class. In contrast, he perceived the photographers, editors, and seamstresses as "young professionals dressed in very fashionable outfits" and having more racial diversity.

He was consistently impressed with the collaboration between employees to "work together to creatively make ads to ensure people will be shopping at Target for many years to come." He noted that in working with each other to build a

> countertop for a kitchen scene. The way they talked to each other was very technical, and all about the stuff I did not understand. One guy asked another for a piece of oversized laminate to be cut on a bandsaw. He could've been speaking Greek, and I would have understood him the same amount.

At the same time, Harry was critical of the overall focus of this work related to advertising commercial products as opposed to addressing the

> countless problems every day, from insignificant problems like running out of milk, to large earth-shattering problems like global warming. It seems that any time we run into a problem as a society, we argue so much about our own opinions, we forget to actually solve the problem. Frankly, it makes humans look like a bunch of idiots who are too concerned with the self to actually get anything done.

Discourses of Gender

As described in Chapter 4, in writing about her visit to an auto body shop, Renee noted how her gender expectations regarding males working in an auto body shop were challenged through her observations, given how, as previously noted people may presupposed that the works are "rude men and how awkward the place can be" (p. 94).

Renee noted that, while all of the people working in the shop were males, she perceived how the workers valued the importance of knowing about each other given

> I believe that humans are and can be familiar. The word familiar origins from the French word famelier, meaning intimate and friendly. I heard some of the men ask each other about their kids and how their families were. The

other guy would respond, and I saw the other one listen closely to what his friend had to say. It was honestly very humorous to me because people say that some men are always so careless but not those men. They were all overall nice men who were respectful of one another and were simply trying to get their job done in a nice orderly manner.

In an interview with one of the workers about what he enjoyed about his work, he stated that

he loved his job because he got to hang out with some of his best friends every day and that sometimes it didn't seem like a job. It leads me to think that when a person truly loves what they do, it becomes a passion, not a job.

She then reflected on her gender assumptions to infer, as noted in Chapter 4, "that there's always more than the eyes see."

In her analysis of parents' interactions with their children at a LEGO store, "Toy Gendering in the LEGO Store," Yolanda described the store as a gendered space. She noted that some sections of the store were designed to appeal to boys, while only one section is "directed for girls; it gleams pink and purple colors."

Humans are still treating LEGOs as a boy toy. Both times I visited the LEGO store play area, I saw only boys. Tradition, the tradition of boys building and girls with babies. The minute anyone walks into the store they can see how this idea is pushed. The store is designed for boys. They provided one section that is for "girl" LEGO's. It is a section with princess LEGOs and LEGO "friends." The other sections are filled with dark colors and are targeted for boys. Anyone can see how parents' traditions help this seem normal. The gendering of kids' toys is making our society move backward, not forward.

These students' analyses led to recognizing how people may avoid employing stereotypical gender discourses as in the body shop as well as how those discourses can limit practice, as in the LEGO store.

These students adopted critical stances on these workplaces, given their recognition of how race, class, and gender, as well as consumerism, served as institutional, systemic forces shaping power hierarchies within workplaces. They also noted employees employing languaging actions for promoting products as gendered and class markers reflecting a discourse of consumerism constituting roles/identities. This discourse of consumerism is evident in retail store advertisements that celebrate the activity of shopping itself as a valued, engaging practice associated with, for example, advertising slogans such as "getting a great deal," or "finding just the right dress for you."

240 Students Co-Authoring Figured Worlds

ACTIVITY: CONTEXTUALIZING PRACTICES CONSTITUTED BY RACE, CLASS, AND GENDER DISCOURSES

Students could discuss or write about their experiences as employees or customers/observers of retail stores in terms of how factors related to gender, race, and/or class shape workplace practices. For example, they may identify demographic information about the type of customer who frequents a store related to how that store markets their products related to gender, race, and class. They may also critique how a discourse of consumerism influences customers' activity of engaging in shopping itself as a valued practice in their lives.

They may also describe instances of breakdowns in these interactions, given differences in gender, race, and/or class involving employees failing to provide relevant information to inform a customer's choices, resulting in a customer choosing not to purchase a product.

Adopting Identities in Workplace Worlds

Students also engaged in practices associated with the adoption of certain *identities* in workplace worlds as, for example, "waiters/waitresses," "baristas," or "clerks." They noted how they needed to assume identities distinct from identities adopted in other worlds. In talking with co-workers, John assumes the identity of "who I want to be and just talk about other customers that have annoyed me." However,

> if I were to talk to a customer, I'd have to get rid of my entire personality and act in a formal manner so then my opinions don't matter in this situation, and I need to go by only what my customer is doing.

Adopting these workplace identities involves languaging actions consistent with adhering to management norms in ways that limit the expression of students' personal beliefs/attitudes or attributes. For example, if they are having difficulty interacting with a customer, they know that they should not reference those difficulties, given the potential uptake of displeasing the customers. They also know that they need to be perceived by managers as valued contributors to their workplace through their ability to learn to work collaboratively with others (Billett, 2006).

Through assuming these vocational identities, they may acquire a sense of agency associated with their success within a workplace, ways of being, or personhood that differs from enacting agency in other figured worlds. At the same time, they may experience tensions between their vocational identities and other aspects of their personhood. In describing herself as an introvert, Sandy noted "that being social makes me very tired. I can only do that for so long, a short period of time until I'm tired and I just want to be alone, and I have to recharge."

Rachel also observed customers at a coffee shop, noting that most customers were primarily engaged in being on their computers working on their own projects for school or work.

> The majority of people as well also had headphones or AirPods in listening to music trying to drown out the noise that was given off by other people. Many people were hunched over their laptops draining away into the electronic screen looking frustrated at the fact that the amount of work that they had to do.

She also noted how customers being on their devices resulted in little verbal interaction

> between random people because they were too busy looking at their personal devices. The people observed seem to be very ignorant of one another, and were pretty selfish about their surroundings, taking up all of the room in the booth, as well as taking up a whole table for only one person. The human characteristic that I observed was that humans are very self-absorbed in their own life. These people take comfort in the privacy of their own lives rather than explore the unknown.

Roberto wrote a description about "Being Wholesome at the Deli," based on his visit to a local deli that features organic foods "with wholesome ingredients" (Deli Management, Inc., n.d.). He observed that the customers are all "white. I am the most diverse person I have ever seen in there, and I am only a quarter Mexican, as well as middle class, interested in getting a bargain and making the most of the complementary sides which is made clear in the reviews such as, '... all for under $10.'" He also noted that

> politics is among the favorite topics of conversation among the elderly and, while, in many situations, it might quickly get heated and out of hand, is very agreeable. On the other end of the age spectrum, the younger crowd likes to talk about world issues that they think they can solve by reposting a story on their Instagram.

Roberto posits that this focus on consuming organic foods fulfills the need for people to feel "good about themselves. At the deli, they act in a way that helps them feel good inside and satisfied. If they can make others feel good, it makes them feel good."

Amanda wrote about her observation of workers at a Target store at which she was a previous employee. She observed how cashiers at the check-out counters would greet customers by saying "'How are you doing today'" as they walked through the checkout lane. Others would tidy up items in their lanes and help

242 Students Co-Authoring Figured Worlds

customers who are searching for items. The language and tone used by the employees was very professional and polite."

Betsy conducted her observations of customers at a Trader Joe's, noting that she "was surprised to find that its people, environment, atmosphere, and employees were vastly different than that of other stores, and other places in general." She perceived the customers as cheerful or content in being there.

> I heard from my English teacher that once at Trader Joe's, everyone broke out into song, dance, or both when music came on. This sort of occurrence would never happen at another grocery store such as Target or WalMart, which attests to the unique and cheerful mood of Trader Joe's and its shoppers.

She also noted how the employees reinforced the positive atmosphere.

> While walking around, one employee wearing a Hawaiian shirt came up and nicely asked, "Is there anything I can help you with?" Her tone was helpful and open, and her offer seemed genuine, not just a formality that other employees may have utilized.

Betsy, therefore, framed Trader Joe's as

> a community of people who can bond over food, and this community is hard to recreate because of how unique it is. What brings shoppers to Trader Joe's is the atmosphere and the feeling that they are special and valued there. People like to feel special because there are many other places and times where they are not treated any differently from anyone else.

Employing Languaging Actions to Enact Workplace Identities

Students also wrote about employing languaging actions constituting their workplace identities; for example, learning to identify different types of coffee drinks as "insider language" (Madsen et al., 2015). Betsy described how "we have a very different lingo that we use that is sometimes hard to understand." She described specific language associated with

> the lingo of the barista. One of the most important terms we use are for the names for the cups. Like our "kid-size" is called short; small is tall; medium is "grande"; large is "venti"; and extra-large is a "trenta". Knowing the names of the cups by heart is super important for my job because obviously if we want someone to get the right size, we must know what Starbucks calls the size.

Larry wrote about his experience working as a "busser" in a Mexican restaurant. He described the importance of languaging actions to coordinate movements and interactions with co-workers

> when moving around in a tight space. When it gets hectic around the kitchen and in the dining room, the word we say to each other is "behind!" or "Right behind!" Some people even say, "Coming through!" We do this so the person in front can easily move out of the way when I am walking back to the dishwasher to put dirty dishware away, or a host is grabbing menus and/or silverware, or a dishwasher, or a server with a tray of food is walking through the kitchen. This communication between us is also a way of keeping accidents from happening, like dropping something or colliding with each other.

Through these interactions, he developed "a sense of trust with others in my group because they work just as hard as I do in extreme circumstances, and if anyone falls short of speed, then we can count on each other to pick each other up."

He noted from his work experience that he has learned that "being confident and arrogant isn't always a good thing, and it can distract you from the task at hand, and mistakes can easily be made." He perceives that the "career I plan on pursuing in the future will require a lot of group-orientated activities related to my future career. So this job has been very important in teaching me how to communicate with others in a timely and fast manner."

Assuming Leadership Roles in Workplace Worlds

Students also wrote about how they assumed identities related to leadership roles in their workplace worlds through the use of certain practices. Sandy described how one of her goals in improving her work in her coffee shop involves "becoming a leader. I am surrounded by co-workers who continue to step up and demonstrate leadership. Whether it's taking someone's shift or resolving an issue with a customer, it is my goal to make sacrifices that manifest my leadership."

After graduating from high school, Sandy was employed in a full-time job as a barista at Starbucks in Hawaii, rather than going to college. In this position, she was responsible for not only taking orders and preparing drinks, but also responding to customer questions, as well as cleaning machines and serving areas.

She describes how, when she is working at the counter, she is expected to "prioritize talking to customers more than like making the drink fast." Sandy needed to assume some degree of deference based on norms such as "the customer comes first." She cites the example of an exchange in which, after six months in this position, she was promoted to being a "shift supervisor" so that she became responsible for managing other baristas during her shift. She noted the importance of developing her self-confidence as a shift supervisor for interacting with co-workers. She learned that she needed "to have the confidence in myself and my own decisions. I have to show that confidence with my other workers so that they can have confidence in me as well. It's a huge display of confidence for everybody else that makes other people feel better."

Forecasting Future Identities for Participation in Workplace Worlds

Adolescents may not have a clear sense of how their current work is predictive of assuming future identities in workplace worlds (Johnson & Monserud, 2010). As a result, they may also make premature decisions about their college major or career options related to those projected identities. For example, they may assume that they want to be a marine biologist. They may then select a college or college major based on that focus, only to later discover that they have alternative interests, leading them to abandon their interest in marine biology.

When adolescents have difficulty projecting future identities related to their long-term academic/career options, they may assume that their after-school work in, for example, a Starbucks, has little relevance to making decisions about future career options. However, they may not appreciate how they may have acquired certain practices and social capital for interacting with others. Through their workplace experiences, they acquire extraversion, conscientiousness, agreeableness, emotional stability, or openness to experience (Baay et al., 2014). An analysis of 685 Dutch vocational training graduates found that both social capital and personality traits such as extraversion and emotional stability were related to their success in obtaining jobs after graduation, although these factors operated independently of each other (Baay et al., 2014).

Adolescents also face the challenge of having advanced degrees/academic preparation related to a limited number of job prospects, resulting in their having to accept jobs such as working in a coffee shop (Goldhill, 2014). As a result:

> Thanks to two decades of praise and affirmation, Generation Y entered the workforce with self-confidence bordering on narcissism. Research by a University of New Hampshire professor found that the latest generation of employees are the most entitled yet, with an "inflated view of oneself" and "resistance to anything that doesn't involve praise and rewards." The jobs available—which, for many, include working in a coffee shop—may not be meaningful or lucrative, but the blow to self-esteem could save overly-plumped egos from being entirely insufferable.
>
> *n.p.*

Students may therefore need to be open to adopting certain workplace identities that may not be consistent with their aspirational identities.

ACTIVITY: CONTEXTUALIZING ENACTING WORKPLACE IDENTITIES

Students could discuss their use of practices for enacting identities related to interacting with customers or clients based on the need to enact positive relations with them. If students assumed leadership roles in their workplaces, they could describe acquiring certain management practices for interactions with co-workers based on adherence to norms operating in a workplace.

Students may also reflect on how their sense of competency in the use of these practices constituting their identities related to taking certain courses in high school or college or selecting certain programs/majors to prepare them for future vocational/career options. Given their interest in certain potential vocational/career choices, students could interview adults/teachers about their vocations/careers. From these interviews, they may acquire knowledge of relevant practices needed for certain vocations/careers, as well as the challenges they perceive in their work and in making career choice decisions.

Acquiring Genres for Use in Workplace Worlds

Students benefit from acquiring *genres* for use in workplace worlds. Students participating in the After School Matters apprenticeship program for low-income students in Chicago (Alexander & Hirsch, 2012) acquired use of the genre of interviews for engaging in mock job interviews by interviewers who rated the students' success in these interviews. Students who demonstrated higher performance in these interviews had participated in programs that focused on languaging supporting collaborative interaction/teamwork, voicing opinions, and opportunities for students to assume leadership roles. Instructors in those programs employed positive feedback and encouragement.

In contrast, students who were rated as not performing well in the interviews were from programs that employed more negative communication practices and problematic criticism of students. This study suggests the importance of students having experiences in apprenticeship or workplace spaces that involve supportive languaging actions and opportunities to assume leadership roles.

Some students in my study participated in school activities that involved the use of genres for interacting with others based on the shared use of certain machine tools associated with gaining expertise in the workplace. Marcus described participation as president of the school's robotics club, associated with members having to build a robot over a four-month period to then compete in a competition, as involving the ability to employ languaging genres associated with displaying competence to judges and peers. To compete, members discussed whether to build a

246 Students Co-Authoring Figured Worlds

"general strobe that can do everything or … to have a specialist robot that can do one thing, just do it really, really, really well."

He also described how members enjoyed interacting with other members based on the use of certain shared languaging genres. "We just had fun talking robotics," given the need to collaboratively figure "out how to solve this problem" based on having a specific goal to do well in the competitions. He also noted how members did not perceive their participation as a means of self-promotion, given how members "didn't want their name on the robot because a lot of them were shy. They didn't want to be noticed they wanted to do something that was just cool."

ACTIVITY: CONTEXTUALIZING USE OF GENRES IN WORKPLACE WORLDS

Students could identify what they perceive to be genres associated with practices in their current and future workplace worlds. This includes valuable practices associated with their work experience related to how they may build on these practices/genres for future vocational/career choices. At the same time, they could also note how difficulties employing certain practices suggest that they may not want to pursue vocational/career choices associated with the use of these practices/genres.

Responding to Portrayals of Workplace Worlds in Media/ Literature

Students could respond to portrayals of workplace worlds in media/literature. In some cases, movies and television shows include realistic portrayals of hospital workplaces, as in *Grey's Anatomy, The Resident,* or *The Good Doctor,* as well as stereotyped portrayals. Analysis of high school students' responses to portrayals of nurses in movies or television found that, while they perceived portrayals of nurses as caring as positive, they also inferred that nursing was more of a vocation than a profession and involved low-level tasks related to being subservient to physicians, perceptions that are problematic, given students' lack of interest in pursuing nursing as a career and the shortage of nurses (Murray, 2002).

Students could view movies portraying adolescents engaged in other kinds of work. For example, the movie *Lean on Pete* (Haigh, 2018) portrays an adolescent taking care of an aging racehorse only to discover that the horse may be killed, resulting in his leaving his state to go West with the horse.

They could also view video clips from television series such as *The Baby-sitters Club* (Aniello et al., 2020), about early-adolescent females organizing a baby-sitting organization for working as baby-sitters.

They could also read young-adult novels portraying adolescents engaged in workplaces (Anclade, 2016). The main character in the young-adult novel *Wesley James Ruined My Life* (Honeybourn, 2017) portrays an adolescent female working in an upscale restaurant related to the challenges of working with a difficult co-worker. *The Education of Margot Sanchez* (Rivera, 2018) describes the main character working in her family's grocery store during the summer, struggling to pay off some debts for purchasing expensive clothes associated with being a student at a private school.

Students could also read short stories in an anthology portraying adolescents at work providing realistic portrayals of jobs in often difficult working conditions; for example, working on a late shift in a Taco Bell or in a dirty factory (Mazer, 1997).

The adult novel *Last Night at the Lobster* (O'Nan, 2007) portrays the challenges of the main character, the manager, running a Red Lobster that is shutting down, with disgruntled employees who work at minimum wages as well as unhappy customers.

ACTIVITY: CONTEXTUALIZING PORTRAYALS OF WORKPLACE WORLDS IN MEDIA/LITERATURE

Students can discuss or write about portrayals of workplace worlds in media/literature related to their own experiences in those worlds. They may identify how characters learned certain practices associated with their jobs as compared with their own job training experiences. They may also describe characters' difficulties in coping with the challenges of their jobs related to physical/health impacts or conflicts with managers, customers, or co-workers with comparisons to their own experiences. They may also reflect on the benefits of learning to employ certain practices in their workplaces related to the use of those practices in other worlds.

Summary

In this chapter, I describe students acquiring practices constituting their jobs in workplace worlds. Students associated practices with certain corporate branding agendas defining how they employed certain languaging actions with customers. They also critiqued certain discourses related to race, class, and gender shaping practices in their workplaces. At the same time, they perceived some of their workplace experiences as useful for acquiring practices constituting their present and future identities.

References

Alexander, K. P., & Hirsch, B. J. (2012). Marketable job skills for high school students: What we learned from an evaluation of After School Matters. *New Directions for Youth Development, 134*, 55–63. doi:10.1002/yd.20015

248 Students Co-Authoring Figured Worlds

Anclade, T. (2016, September 20). Working teens in young adult fiction. [Weblog post]. Retrieved from www.yalsa.ala.org/thehub/2016/09/20/working-teens-young-adult-fiction/

Aniello, L., Cucukov, N., De Luca, M., Kitada, L. W., & Shukert, R. (Executive Producers). (2020–2020). The baby-sitters club [TV series]. Netflix.

Aud, S., Ramani, A. K. & Frohlich, L. (2011). *America's youth: Transitions to adulthood.* National Center for Education Statistics. Retrieved from http://t.ly/Wct9

Baay, P. E., Van Aken, M. A. G., de Ridder, D. T. D., & Van der Lippe, T. (2014). Understanding the role of social capital in adolescents' Big Five personality effects on school-to-work transitions. *Journal of Adolescence, 37*(5), 739–748.

Billett, S. (2006). Work, subjectivity and learning. In S. Billett, T. Fenwick, & M. W. Somerville (Eds.), *Subjectivity and learning: Understanding learning through working life* (pp. 1–20). Springer.

Deli Management, Inc. (n.d.). *Jason's Deli.* Retrieved from www.jasonsdeli.com

Dochy, F., Gijbels, D., Segers, M., & Van den Bossche, P. (2021). *Theories of workplace learning in changing times.* Routledge.

Gaudio, R. P. (2003). Starbucks™ and the commercialization of casual conversation. *Language in Society, 32*(5), 659–691.

Goldhill, O. (2014, September 5). Why working as a barista could be the making of you. *The Telegraph.* Retrieved from https://tinyurl.com/y6yxtowk

Haigh, A. (Director) (2018). *Lean on Pete* [Film]. The Bureau.

Hamilton, S., & Sumner, R. (2017). High school students' jobs: Related and unrelated to school. *Peabody Journal of Education, 92,* 222–235.

Honeybourn, J. (2017). *Wesley James ruined my life.* Feiwel & Friends.

IKEA. (2021). *This Is IKEA.* Retrieved from www.ikea.com/us/en/this-is-ikea/

Johnson, M. K., & Monserud, M. A. (2010). Judgments about work and the features of young adults' jobs. *Work and Occupations, 37*(2) 194–224.

Keister, M., & Hall, J. (2010). High school employment and academic achievement: A note for educators. *Contemporary Issues in Education Research, 3*(1), 77–82.

Madsen, L. M., Moller, J. S., & Karrebaek, M. S. (2015). *Everyday languaging: Collaborative research on the language use of children and youth.* De Gruyter.

Mazer, A. (1997). *Working days: Short stories about teenagers at work.* Persea.

Mortimer, J. T. (2003). *Working and growing up in America.* Harvard University Press.

Murray, M. K. (2002). The impact of nurse characters in television and the movies on adolescent career choices. [Unpublished doctoral dissertation]. University of Kansas.

O'Nan, S. (2007). *Last night at the Lobster.* Viking

Post, D. & Pong, S. (2009). The academic effects of after-school paid and unpaid work among 14-year-old students in TIMSS countries. *Compare, 39*(6), 799–818. doi:10.1080/03057920802681804

Rivera, L. (2018). *The education of Margot Sanchez.* Simon & Schuster.

Staff, J., & Mortimer, J. (2007). Educational and work strategies from adolescence to early adulthood: Consequences for educational attainment. *Social Forces: A Scientific Medium of Social Study and Interpretation, 85*(3), 1169–1194. https://doi.org/10.1353/sof.2007.0057

Staff, J., & Schulenberg, J. E. (2010). Millennials and the world of work: Experiences in paid work during adolescence. *Journal of Business and Psychology,* 25(2), 247–255.

Starbucks. (2000). *About us.* Starbucks Coffee Company. Retrieved from www.starbucks.com/about-us

12

CO-AUTHORING SOCIAL/DIGITAL MEDIA WORLDS

This chapter describes adolescents' use of social/digital media for enacting identities and relations with others that involve both positive and problematic practices; for example, how use of social media emphasizes only celebratory presentations of the self. Students may benefit from engaging in connected learning activities that draw on the affordances of social/digital media for engaging students in classroom learning. Students also use video games and role-play for employing practices for co-authoring imagined versions of their worlds. Teachers can have students reflect on these experiences with social/digital media related to adhering to certain norms or enacting identities/relations, as well as critique how digital/media texts create both supportive and stereotypical representations based on race, class, and gender.

Adolescents devote considerable time to using social media, with 63% of adolescents in 2019 employing social media daily, by often accessing social media multiple times an hour (Rideout & Robb, 2019). This extensive use of social/digital media in their personal lives then raises questions about how and why adolescents are drawn to social/digital media as something they value in their lives. It also raises questions, as with any extensive use of media, about any adverse effects of social/digital media on their social identities and mental health. Further, teachers want to know how to draw on adolescents' use of social/digital media, given how "information, tools, and resources enter the spaces of virtual classrooms from multiple directions" (Bagga-Gupta & Dahlberg, 2019, p. 13).

Purposes for uses of Social/Digital Media

Adolescents' most frequently used social media platforms as of Fall 2020 were Snapchat (34%), TikTok (29%), and Instagram (25%), as opposed to Twitter (3%)

DOI: 10.4324/9781003246886-14

and Facebook (2%) (Statista, 2021), findings similar to the popularity of Snapchat (41%) and Instagram (22%) in 2018, with adolescents' preference for face-to-face communication versus social media declining from 49% in 2012 to 32% in 2018 (Rideout & Robb, 2018). Much of adolescents' time online involves the purpose of responding to social/digital media content instead of creating their own content, with only 10% enjoying creating digital art, music, games, etc. "a lot." (Rideout & Robb, 2019).

This increased use of screen time and digital social media has reduced their face-to-face interactions in their peer group worlds. For example, 12th-graders devoted less time to interacting with peers than they did as eighth-graders (Twenge, 2017). While 33% note that social media can help them engage in meaningful conversations with peers, 54% agree that social media can be distracting when interacting face-to-face with others.

Building Social Relations with Peers

At the same time, the use of social/digital media can also enhance increased opportunities to interact with friends across different locations (Sosik & Bazarova, 2014). 57% of adolescents indicated that they have met a new friend through social media and online gameplay, and 29% noted that they have made five new friends through online interactions (Lenhart, 2015). For example, participation in the Harry Potter Alliance, consisting of Harry Potter fans and young activists engaging in an online activity involved sharing responses to the novels and creating their own texts (Ito et al., 2012).

Given that she identifies more as an "outsider" in her peer relations, a student in my study, Doris, often prefers to use social media to texting others rather than engage in face-to-face interactions. "We don't have any special way of communicating. I personally find it hard to relate to everyone, so if I do want to communicate with someone, I just text them. I find our texts to be a lot more serious toned."

At the same time, she is critical of her peers' self-promotion using social media as

> a way to be like, hey, this is amazing about my life. Like I'm better than you. I am completely against it. I, yeah, I think relationship bias, the best relationships are like in front of you. Take the time to talk with them.

Lilly noted in an interview with me:

> It's kinda weird because it's like the whole point of it is social media and being connected with people, but you're caught up in it. I've fallen victim to it. I've been out with friends and still checked my phone. A lot of people say that they try not to go on their phone, but it's something that they do without maybe noticing it or they know but they try and say that they don't.

But yeah, I get that. I don't know … the lonely aspect: I can kinda see that sometimes.

Sometimes I'll be lying in bed not doing anything and I'm just on my phone. If I check something and I see friends are out together, but I'm just at home, so I guess I feel lonely from that. I don't know how other people feel lonely, but personally, to me, I guess that's how I feel lonely because it's like, oh all these people are out doing something fun and I'm just here in bed.

Beach & Beauchemin, 2019, p. 167

Limitations of Use of Social/Digital Media

Adolescents may also perceive the use of social/digital media as involving portrayals of only positive, celebratory aspects of their lives in order to obtain, for example, "likes" for their Facebook posts, as opposed to sharing difficulties or problems in their lives (Delahunty et al., 2014). They may be concerned about the lack of privacy in online spaces—what danah boyd (2010) defines as "context collapse," related to not having a clear sense of the context in which they are sharing information with online audiences. Finally, they may also falsely assume the need to be continually checking their devices to maintain interactions with others, based on "FOMO" (fear of missing out) (Holmes, 2015).

Researchers have also voiced concerns about the impact of social/digital media on enacting relations with peers. For example, one study found that 45% of adolescents posited that social/digital media has neither positive nor negative effects on their maintaining connections with others, given how 31% indicated that social/digital media has a mostly positive impact versus 24% indicating that it has a mostly negative effect (Anderson & Jiang, 2018). Students in my 2019 study were asked whether they agreed or disagreed with the statement, "being on social media is an essential requirement for creating and maintaining friendships with peers." 22.2% strongly disagreed, 33.3% disagreed, 18.5% were neutral, 24.1% agreed, and 1.9% strongly agreed. This suggests that a slight majority do not perceive social media as essential for enacting peer relations.

Other research indicates that social/digital media use correlates with increased physical activity, fewer sleep problems, and reduced family conflict (Feldstein-Ewing et al., 2018). It is also difficult to infer that social media use actually causes certain issues in adolescents' lives from correlations that separate out social media from other economic and societal factors shaping adolescents' lives (Dennis-Tiwary, 2018).

Impact of the Use of Social/Digital Media on Academic Work

There is also considerable debate regarding the positive versus negative effects of this increased screen time on adolescents' academic work. The increased use of social media may be related to a decline in reading books or magazines, from 60%

252 Students Co-Authoring Figured Worlds

in the late 1970s to 16% in 2016, which may also influence reading in their school worlds (Twenge et al., 2019). A study of 41,057 Canadian adolescents found that video game usage correlated negatively with academic achievement and physical activity and internet usage correlated negatively with self-esteem, while, at the same time, video game and internet usage had the same positive contributions to school connectedness (Fitzpatrick et al., 2019). One factor shaping these results is that screen time may detract from homework, peer interactions, sleep, and exercise, fostering social isolation.

Students and teachers may also express concerns that any focus on digital/social media in the classroom may conflict with what they assume to be traditional academic work, which, in turn, may have adverse effects on standardized test scores.

Adolescents also perceive disparities in their use of writing on social media to enact relations with others versus their writing in schools as driven primarily to obtain grades (Dredger et al., 2010). One student was concerned that students might argue, "'Oh well, I don't know how to write the essay because you didn't show me how to write an essay; you showed me how to make a video.'" (Mirra, 2019, p. 282).

A 2019 National Assessment of Educational Progress (NAEP) study found a decline in reading test scores from 2015 to 2019 for lower-performing male students and lower-performing public school students (NAEP, 2020). This included a decline in comprehension of literary texts for Black, Hispanic, and male 12th-grade students. It is also the case that 26% of 12th-graders indicated that they never read stories or novels outside of school, with low-performing students indicating that they never read literary texts outside of school. However, it may be difficult to assume a cause-and-effect relationship between time devoted to being online and students' reading comprehension ability, given that some of that time includes reading online texts.

Applying "Connected Learning" to Integrate Social Media into the Classroom

Students' extensive use of social/digital media raises the challenge of how to draw on their use of social/digital media in the ELA classroom. This suggests the need to draw on students' experiences in social/digital media worlds for learning in school worlds based on a "connected learning" model (Ito et al., 2012). A connected learning framework focuses on how social/digital tools foster connections with multiple audiences within and beyond the classroom (Mirra, 2019). For example, a student may compose a post on social media that receives extensive positive audience comments. She may then draw on that experience to enhance her engagement in writing for audiences in her school world.

In one study, three adolescents wrote about their use of digital and non-digital literacies as practices (Abrams et al., 2020). For example, one participant described how enacting social relations in her life was important to her. She perceived playing video games or participating on Instagram as limiting her engagement in social relations. She noted that "'I never really stopped to look around and enjoy the good life'" (p. 88). Another noted that "'I do not use my digital time for social media as much anymore. I still text my friends, but I usually do that for homework or when I am bored. I mainly use my phone for relaxing purposes'" (p. 89).

On the other hand, adolescents value how they can use social/digital media to interact with large audiences within and across different worlds through "relational mobilities," involving their acquiring practices based on "cosmopolitan literacies" (Hull & Stornaiuolo, 2014). For example, when an adolescent female posted a video on TikTok posing the question of whether math is based on any reality, she had 1.3 million viewers and millions more with reposting on Twitter (Haigney, 2020).

ACTIVITY: CONTEXTUALIZING PURPOSES FOR USES OF SOCIAL/DIGITAL MEDIA

Students can discuss or write about their purposes for using social/digital media practices related to how those practices serve to enhance or limit their relations with others. Students may posit the benefits or limitations of using social media versus face-to-face interactions to enact relations with others and how each may contribute to the other.

They may also describe the positive aspects of how social media allows them to maintain ongoing, continuous interactions with peers to maintain those relations over time. They may also describe how they post primarily positive aspects about their lives while at the same time expressing concerns about issues of privacy and confidentiality related to sharing information about themselves.

Co-Authoring Video Games/Role-Play Worlds

Adolescents also devote a considerable amount of time to playing video games. Ninety percent of adolescents ages 13–17 play video games on a computer, game console, or cellphone (Perrin, 2018). A study of British participants ages 5–15 found that 75% engage in online gaming, with early adolescents ages 12–15 averaging 13 hours and 48 minutes a week and males devoting over 16 hours a week compared to females devoting about nine hours a week (Sinclair, 2019). Puzzle/strategy games are the most popular, followed by adventure, shooter, role-playing, sport/racing, and simulation games (Kiss, 2020; Perrin, 2018).

In participating in video games, students are engaging in multimodal experiences for enacting "imaginative worlds … conjured for reader/players [through] … ways of telling stories and presenting challenges, with players taking an active role in

254 Students Co-Authoring Figured Worlds

bringing those stories into being and meeting those challenges" (Beavis, 2014, p. 435).

A model of "games as text/games as action" posits that "games as text" involves students' knowledge of games, the social world around playing games, the student as a game player, and how students learn through playing games (Beavis, 2014, p. 437). "Games as action" involves being in certain *situations* in games with other players, non-players, contexts, technologies, paratexts, etc.; certain *actions* with and against the computer involving multimodal literacies in certain virtual spaces; and *design* related to choosing actions, building avatars/objects, managing play, and reflection (p. 438).

Practices Involved in Games/Role-Play

Engaging in video games/role-play as "passionate affinity-based spaces" (Gee & Hayes, 2011, p. 69) involves a range of different practices related to different components for co-authoring worlds. Players are motivated to acquire these practices given the purpose of succeeding in a competitive space by outmaneuvering their opponents. Each team member needs to carefully coordinate their practices so that each member knows how to contribute to achieving success by tapping into others' "specialties enough to play as a team that is smarter and more powerful than any single play on the team" (Gee & Hayes, 2011, p. 81). This coordination involves collaborative problem-solving to address challenges while playing a game (Barab et al., 2010).

Engaging in these spontaneous actions in playing a game requires a willingness to be attending to others' actions to react with an alternative action based on what-if scenarios associated with an alternative sense of time, immediate feedback and assessment, and concrete embodiment of abstract concepts related to a game (Decker et al., 2017). Players employ "insider language" for identifying specific actions employed in video games. For example, a player employed certain words for describing his play as "inner speech" thinking as shaping his decision-making (Motobayashi et al., 2014).

In playing video games, students are also engaged in the practice of "systems thinking" for addressing global challenges associated with systems of energy, agriculture, economics, politics, etc. (Gee, 2013). For example, in playing Evoke, *www. urgentevoke.com*, players addressed issues of food shortages, power outages, water security, disaster relief, poverty, and pandemics (McGonigal, 2011). Players using the game Community PlanIt (CPI), *t.ly/8Jrg*, addressed issues of high school dropouts and the achievement gap in Boston schools (Gupta et al., 2012).

Using Video Games for Building Relations with Others

Students in my study wrote about the value of playing video games for learning how to build collaborative relations with others. Betsy described her experience

Co-Authoring Social/Digital Media Worlds **255**

playing Minecraft with peers as twelve-year-olds that included building "a whole town by ourselves over the course of a year, fully equipped with farms, homes, and shops" as well as going on virtual expeditions or engaging in fights with the "Ender Dragon." They employed "classic gaming slang" in their virtual interaction on Skype and in-game chat. "We all believed that the more lingo we used, the more professional we would sound. For example, someone who was doing something wrong or badly was a 'noob,' while an expert was called 'MLG,' which meant a major-league gamer."

Betsy noted how playing Minecraft

> helped me to make lifelong friends, but it also taught me how to better express myself, collaborate with others, and to not get discouraged when things don't work out. Additionally, I now understand that things that don't go well at first can still be worked out … I learned the importance of self-expression, cooperation, and persistence, and how to apply those values to my current and future life.

Larry plays the video game Dragon Ball FighterZ as a member of a community, The Teen Gohan Discord, which focuses their attention on one of the characters in the game, "Teen Gohan." Luke notes that playing the same game

> has allowed me to start thinking from the opponent's position more than I had before. When I'm not asking questions about the game, I'm able to acquire a glimpse of how people older than me behave since this community contains people of all ages and locations.

In thinking about his opponent's potential counter-moves "you have to constantly analyze what the opponent is doing in reaction to you. There's what's the opponent doing and what's the point of doing in reaction to you?" Learning to adopt his opponent's position transfers to perspective-taking "to see through another person's perspective easier than before. This skill is vital when dealing with other people in the real world."

Employing Video Games/Role-Plays in the Classroom

Students are often highly engaged when using video games or role-plays, whether on their own or related to topics in the classroom (Bell & Gresalfi, 2017). Games such as Minecraft that involve no set narrative or structures are appealing, given that students can then generate their own content (Checa-Romero & Pascual Gómez, 2018). For example, a 12th-grade English teacher, Paul Darvas (2014), has his students play the game Gone Home, *gonehome.com,* based on the daughter of a family arriving at her house to find a note on the front door from her sister and that there is no one in the house (see *t.ly/4n68*). Students must explore the house

256 Students Co-Authoring Figured Worlds

to find clues related to why no one is in the house. For Darvas's descriptions of his students playing the game related to learning certain literacy practices, see:

> Lesson 1: *t.ly/79SZ*
> Lesson 2: *t.ly/Ojs6*
> Lesson 3: *t.ly/m8fU*
> Lesson 4: *t.ly/Y9e4*
> Lessons 5 and 6: *t.ly/NwkO*
> Lessons 7 and 8: *t.ly/Ia55*

For creating online role-plays, teachers can employ a class blog or social media site so that students create fictional roles/avatars to formulate their arguments and counter-arguments in an online forum. To find stances on various issues, students can access sites such as Idebate, *idebate.org*; CreateDebate, *createdebate.com/teachers*; or Debategraph, *debategraph.org*.

To assist his students in playing role-playing games, Kevin Smith (2014) has students create "character sheets" to describe their character's background, narratives, relations, and game statistics. Students can use their character sheets to "construct, examine and discuss a representation of a character or characters—either fictional or actual characters and in some cases, I've asked the students to complete their own character sheet representing themselves" (p. 250).

ACTIVITY: CONTEXTUALIZING PRACTICES FOR USE IN VIDEO GAMES/ROLE-PLAYS

Students could discuss or write about learning to employ certain practices in playing video games/role-plays based on how they

- Acquired and employed certain practices for playing a game through assistance from others or online advice to advance in their play across different levels.
- Displayed competence to other players in the use of certain practices.
- Adhered to certain norms constituting the use of practices for moving up on different levels.
- Assumed certain identities as distinct from their own lived-world identity/identities.

Students may also instruct others or share their experiences playing video games by creating videos of their play. They may use the LetsPlay (*youtube.com/user/LetsPlay*) YouTube video site created by players describing their experiences playing games. (For a video on creating videos about playing Minecraft, see *t.ly/vDjR*.)

Using Social/Digital Media Based on Norms for Interacting with Others

Students also employ social/digital media based on *norms* constituting their "intra-actions" related to "the togetherness or in-betweenness of humans, materials, time, space and so forth mediated through the use of material resources/artifacts" (Kuby & Crawford, 2018, p. 22). Use of the word "intra-action" focuses on how the use of social/digital media serves to enact interaction with others (p. 22). For example, five adolescents created a digital book trailer to portray embodied "intra-actions" with peers and artifacts (Ehret et al., 2016).

Families and students often draw on YouTube tutorials to learn how to employ media/digital tools (Gutiérrez et al., 2019). For example, a fifth-grade participant created an origami video based on viewing YouTube tutorials, leading to mentors in the project recruiting him to share his work with other participants.

Teachers can use social/digital media tools for creating personal connections with students. For example, they can use the app Along, *www.along.org*, to share questions with students such as "What is something that you really value and why?" to answer the question in a text, video, or audio themselves. Students then respond with their text, video, or audio so that the teacher gains some sense of students' lives. (For resources on the use of apps for instruction, see *t.ly/FFZP* (Beach & O'Brien, 2015); TechScaffold, *techscaffold.com*, can be used for selecting apps related to teaching specific practices by grade level and topic.)

Adhering to norms for use of social/digital media allows students from different local and global worlds to interact with each other. Marvin noted that "on our phones, we share stories of things that have happened in school and outside of school which we find funny or interesting," interactions that shape "the way I act, look, and dress based on the relations I've made with these people."

As part of the Space2cre8 project, adolescents from around the world interacted with each other online to share their experiences of living in particular countries/cities. They then gained an awareness of how certain practices shape their identities and beliefs/attitudes (Hull & Stornaiuolo, 2014). A participant in this project, a male adolescent, was initially going to complete an analysis of the social norms constituting life in his Brooklyn neighborhood. After he interacted with a female adolescent in India, who shared challenges of coping with poverty in her neighborhood, he decided to alter his analysis to focus more on aspects of poverty in his neighborhood (Hull & Stornaiuolo, 2014). Through exposure to adolescents living in different community worlds, adolescents in this project acquired "cosmopolitan literacies" associated with an understanding of how different norms and beliefs/attitudes constitute participation in different figured worlds.

Students also employ social/digital tools to engage in activism in organizations. For example, students involved in the Gay-Straight Alliances (GSAs) to support LGBTQ youth shared videos online to educate others about LGBTQ experiences (Poteat et al., 2016).

258 Students Co-Authoring Figured Worlds

Adolescents also employ digital/media to engage in imaginative play based on open-ended norms of play. For example, students who created a digital comic for responding to *The Outsiders* (Hinton, 1967) were more focused on learning imaginative, creative literary responses than on creating their own digital comic (Wissman & Costello, 2014). Mary Lou notes how her group, the Horton Squad, shared their viewing of TV shows to create "the ragestas, an essential part of the Horton Squad. Ragestas are our secret, private Instagram accounts, and they function primarily as a humorous way to get things that have been upsetting us off our chests."

ACTIVITY: CONTEXTUALIZING NORMS CONSTITUTING SOCIAL/DIGITAL MEDIA PRACTICES

Students could discuss or write about their perceptions of norms constituting certain social/digital media practices. For example, they could note how they acquire and adhere to norms in their use of Snapchat, TikTok, and Instagram, as well as texting, for sharing experiences with and responding to peers to achieve uptake with audiences. They could also compare their adherence to norms for engaging in face-to-face verbal interactions with norms con- stituting their virtual interactions. They may note differences in the kinds of languaging they employ on social/digital sites related to enacting certain kinds of relations; for example, the extent to which they can express their emotions in those interactions.

Critiquing Discourses Constituting Use of Digital/Social Media

Adolescents base their digital/social media use on *discourses* regarding beliefs or attitudes about the validity and reliability of information shared on news and digital/social media platforms. In a 2020 survey, 88% of 20,000 Americans indicated that it is "critical" or "very important" for the news media to provide accurate reports; 83% perceive a "great deal" or "a fair amount" of political bias in coverage; and 74% perceive misinformation in the news as a "major problem" (Gallup & Knight, 2020). However, a study of 3,446 students across America found that they had difficulty responding critically to misinformation in the media and on websites (Breakstone et al., 2021). Their lack of critical response suggests the need for critical media literacy of both political and economic discourses shaping online misinformation. In political campaigns, politicians may generate misinformation about issues or their opponents, while corporations may create advertisements promoting problematic products, such as energy companies cri- tiquing the promotion of renewable energy options.

Students in my research also wrote about concerns with misinformation shared on social media. Marcus wrote about how he discerned the validity of information on social media sites based on his trust in the validity of certain information regarding political topics. In discussing how he learned to trust online information, he noted that he applies a critical perspective based on determining whether someone is

> able to talk with authority. They talk as if they know what they're doing. So I trust news sources that I've been able to cross-check information they're giving. 50 years ago there were only three television stations. All of them ran news at a certain time, so it was very hard to avoid what was happening in the world. And because of those small organizations, there's a certain amount of trust between them.

Critiquing Discourses of Race, Class, and Gender

Students can critique discourses of race, class, and gender reflected in stereotypical media representations in television shows or movies through "restorying" related to "racebending" by creating alternative representations of race (Thomas & Stornaiuolo, 2016). Students could also use social/digital media for sharing their critiques of representations in literary texts. For example, preservice teachers interacted with students online about stereotypical portrayals of Asian Americans in the graphic novel *American Born Chinese* (Yang, 2008), including sharing YouTube videos (Schieble, 2011).

Students could also critique media representations of different groups or their schools. For example, in response to a TV news report on a fight in their school, Black students in an ELA class created a counter-narrative version of the event. They contradicted the report's stance that the fight was gang related and that students were not mistreated by police, and they argued that, given that only White students were interviewed, their perspectives were not represented (Kohnen & Lacy, 2018). They then wrote a letter to the local paper documenting their critique related to the larger issue of how their school is "gang-ridden" and how the media misrepresents their perspectives and lives.

Students could study how the local media portrays certain issues in their community, particularly given differences in partisan media outlets' coverage reflecting conservative versus liberal perspectives. One study of a small town in Kentucky found that residents experienced competing perspectives about events and policies shaping their town based on polarized media representations of rural America (Wenzel, 2018).

One limitation of media representations of communities is that the audiences' experiences involve a virtual instead of a physical experience of place. As a result, media representations on travel websites or advertisements glamorize the realities of a place or community based on imaginary versions of places (Gamesby, 2015). For example, visitors at the Disney parks in Florida, California, and France frame their experience based on their imagined experiences with Disney movies and

260 Students Co-Authoring Figured Worlds

products. "When at Euro Disney it is clear the castle lacks all of the authenticity of a real castle; it has a 'fake feel' to it. However, the castle is a symbol for the park and the Disney movies, and is representative of a holiday visit for millions of people" (Gamesby, 2015, n.p.).

Sharing Critiques of Discourses with Audiences

Students may also engage in critiquing discourses with peers through the use of online games involving formulating arguments such as The Persuasive Games, *persuasivegames.com*; Democracy, *positech.co.uk/democracy/faq.html*; or World Climate Simulation, *www.climateinteractive.org/tools/world-climate-simulation/*.

Students can also produce online texts addressing issues, reflecting how certain discourses impact their community. For example, students post content on the KQED Do Now site, *t.ly/hO1o*, to critique discourses in biased news reports (Turner & Reed, 2018). For example, they addressed the question "Should athletes use their public platforms to make political statements?" (p. 45). After listening to a discussion of teen suicide on Youth Voices, *www.youthvoices.live*, students created a public service announcement video to share with audiences (Turner & Reed, 2018). After the murder of George Floyd in Minneapolis, students in a Voices class at South High School, located near the site of the murder, worked with members of Minnesota Public Radio to create a series of podcast stories. These podcasts featured descriptions of activities involving responses to the murder and upkeep of the memorials at the site of the killing, *t.ly/nDOt*, involving a range of different topics, *t.ly/tjIm*.

Students can also engage in role-play activities to critique discourses. For example, students used role-play to address how immigration is related to discourses of racism as portrayed in the novel *Something About America* (Testa, 2005) (Enciso, 2014). In the novel, the town's mayor published a newspaper letter telling members of the Somali community that their additional family members would not be welcome to the town. In the role-play, students assumed the roles of news reporters investigating bigotry in a fictional town similar to the town portrayed in the novel. Enciso double-voiced a bigoted stance, with statements requiring students to voice their rebuttals; for example: "'This is my America.'" "'But people come to America for freedom.'" / "'Get out of my country.'" "'Maybe your ancestors were immigrants.'" / "'I am American.'" "'You have no right to say all of those mean things.'" (p. 186).

Students then created videos of peers describing their experiences with immigration and bigotry related to how they need to cope with issues of immigration for sharing with students in another class. As a result, "they were located in the same imagined world, with actual concerns for one another's histories and futures" (p. 185).

Students engaged in an online role-play to critique discourses of censorship of website access in their school (Doerr-Stevens et al., 2011). They responded

Co-Authoring Social/Digital Media Worlds **261**

to an actual event in which administrators blocked access to websites perceived as containing objectionable content while students needed access to information from those sites to write papers. In the role-play, students adopted different roles of administrators, teachers, parents, students, counselors, or school technology personnel arguing for and against blocking the sites. After completing the role-play, students met with the school administrators to share arguments related to problems with blocking the sites, which led to the administrators unblocking the sites. Students then reflected on how certain arguments were effective in achieving their goal of changing the school's policy.

Through participating in these role-plays, students benefit from stepping out of their roles to reflect on certain practices employed in the role-play. For example, after engaging students in role-play activities, Katherine Macro (2019) has her students respond to the questions, "'What did you notice?' 'What stood out to you?' How or what did you feel during the exercise?'" (p. 75). Students in a role-play about discourses of race reflected on how, in their roles, they adopted racist, stereotypical attitudes through their use of language (Seltzer, 2019). Students addressed the questions, "How does the way I communicate connect with my identity and who I am?" "How can language be used to open and close doors?" "How can I integrate multiple language practices and elements of voice into my schoolwork?" (p. 150). Through reflecting on how they were using languaging practices, students in this role-play recognized the importance of their languaging for enacting certain identities.

ACTIVITY: CONTEXTUALIZING DISCOURSES EMPLOYED IN MEDIA/DIGITAL TEXTS

Students can engage in critical responses to media/digital texts by drawing on questions developed by the National Association of Media Literacy Education (NAMLE) (2007) (Key Questions: *t.ly/TpRS*):

AUTHORSHIP: Who made this message?

PURPOSE: Why was this made? Who is the target audience (and how do you know)?

ECONOMICS: Who paid for this?

IMPACT: Who might benefit from this message? Who might be harmed by it? Why might this message matter to me?

RESPONSE: What kinds of actions might I take in response to this message?

CONTENT: What is this about (and what makes you think that)? What ideas, values, information, and/or points of view are overt? Implied? What is left out of this message that might be important to know?

n.p.

Students could also critique political and economic discourses shaping political campaigns and corporate promotions of problematic policies and products; for example, critiques of increasing taxes and policies related to increased support for low-income people or adoption of political discourses reflected in critiques of critical race theory or vaccination mandates.

To address issues of misinformation in social/digital media, students could play the *LAMBOOZLED!* game *www.lamboozled.com*, which includes the use of cards with fictional headlines, cards with background information related to the source of the headlines, evidence cards related to whether the headline cards are real or fake, and cards for what actions players can take to assess the headline cards (Literat et al., 2021).

Using Media/Digital Tools for Enacting Identities

Adolescents also employ media/digital tools as "funds of identity" (Esteban-Guitart et al., 2019) for portraying their *identities* in different worlds. When asked to identify types of symbolic resources that engaged them, students noted playing video games or reading manga with others (Zittoun, 2017). A 17-year-old, Ben, used Snapchat to portray and share his daily experiences, including his walk to school and participation in a playground with his sister (Wargo, 2015). Ben noted how sharing his Snaps involved

> "being with someone for that day. It is very intimate. When you see that snap, only a small group can see that snap. I get to feel like I am with them, even when I am not. People who I don't care about, or who I don't want to share that moment with, they don't get to know. It's a memory for a small collective, an experience we have together."
>
> *p. 56*

Using Media/Digital Tools to Create Multimodal Self-Portraits

Tenth-grade students created "digital self-portraits" (DSPs) to portray how they enact their identities through the use of media/digital resources (Canady et al., 2018, 2020). One Latino student portrayed the difficulties of coping with stereotypes of himself associated with his low-income neighborhood versus being successful in his school world (Canady et al., 2018).

Another student, Aubrey, created a digital comic portraying positive and negatives aspects of her use of social media. In her comic, the narrator holds up emoji masks indexing positive versus negative experiences using social media. She concludes her DSP by portraying herself as an avatar from the video game Skyrim, with the statement, "'I feel like when I'm in a game, it's like I want to be that person in the game, so I should be who I am.'" (Canady et al., 2020, n.p.).

Students participating in the Compose Our World project, *t.ly/tTsX*, created drawings/posters, artwork, and videos for display in a virtual museum as a means of sharing the results of their projects (Boardman et al., 2021). Students engaged in the Lens on Climate Change, *t.ly/E87c*, the Young Voices for the Planet, *youngvoicesfortheplanet.com*, or the Frontline Youth: Fighting for Climate Justice *ClimateJusticeAlliance.org/youth* project created videos about the need to address climate change. As part of the We Are All Connected project, *t.ly/vw5E*, students created the Something in Our Water documentary, *vimeo.com/345962549*, about the effects of coal mines on local water quality (Douglas et al., 2020).

Enacting Identities through Role-Plays

Students may also enact different identities through engaging in face-to-face role-playing games; for example, assuming the identity of a detective identifying clues associated with a murder. To adopt these identities, students draw on their knowledge of popular culture/fictional texts to frame their identities' collaborative/problem-solving practices within familiar narratives (Smith, 2014).

Beginning in sixth grade, Marcus began engaging in role-play games organized by his father in which different players create groups and compete against each other (Beach & Aukerman, 2019). His father assumes the role of Dungeon Master, who organizes the role-play based on formulating challenges and then rolling dice to determine which player will take their turn in engaging in certain actions. Marcus noted how "The dungeon master tells us here's what's happening. And then we say we're doing this. So it's a lot of oral. And then sometimes the master draws out a map and says, here's the area you're in. Where do you want to go?"

He describes the different roles players adopt, including that of the

> party leader. A prestigious position, you get to have the biggest voice in where the party goes, what the party does, and how the party does it. There is also a reserve leader that takes over in these situations. This is our second in command, who also takes over if the party leader is dead, or the person who is playing is not able to make it to the session. We also have a note-taker who records important information and interactions during each session.

To create their specific roles, players write "about a four-to-five-page story, which develops the character as far as, 'Here's my personality. Here's where I'm from related to what events happened to me that affect the way that I see the world.'"

Once Marcus begins assuming a role,

> I'm thinking, okay, how would, in any given situation, this character react? So, I'm going into a situation where I'm trying to get information from someone. So my friend and the other person in the party who's this big, hulking brute, he might just try to intimidate and beat the information out

264 Students Co-Authoring Figured Worlds

of someone, versus my character might try to coerce them to say, "oh, I can do something for you if you can do something for me."

He perceives the value of role-playing as

teaching me how to lead. In my old party, I was a party leader. And during my time in charge I had to deal with lots of high-stress situations. This taught me how to make decent decisions in a very short period of time.

He also noted that he learned to enact certain emotions. "I have found that when I play as a different person, I start to think and feel like that person. So if I feel like I'm going into a situation that could strain my emotions I try to put myself into this other mindset."

Through his participation in role-play activities over a seven-year period prior to college and then when he was in college organizing role-play with friends, he noted that he learns from the role-play, given how

my dad constantly puts us into situations that are so detached from reality. At no point in my life will I ever have to talk to a king. If that happens, I would be very, very surprised. But, in putting us in these ridiculous situations, he's preparing us for a lot more mundane ones. So, in situations where you're talking with someone who is like in the situation when I'm talking to a king, the closest I'll ever probably come to it is talking to the boss of my boss at a company or whatever.

Through his participation in role-play activities, Marcus has developed his identity through the use of practices for effectively building relations with others. As noted with the examples of online role-plays, teachers can create similar role-play activities by having students write narratives about the roles and provide specific problem-based situations in which they adopt their roles for addressing these problems.

ACTIVITY: CONTEXTUALIZING USES OF MEDIA/DIGITAL TOOLS FOR ENACTING IDENTITIES

Students could describe or write about their use of media/digital tools and material artifacts as "symbolic resources" for enacting their identities. Students could conduct media ethnographies to study their own or others' use of media related to how or why people are engaged in media (Garcia, 2016). (For methods of conducting media ethnographies, see *tinyurl.com/ t9ppmyf*.) For example, students could study participation in online fan-club

> sites to note reasons for the appeal of certain media texts and sites such as FanFiction, *www.fanfiction.net*, which includes remixes of literary texts. They may also interview participants regarding their responses to media texts; for example, asking them for their reasons for their preferences in certain TV shows, music, or movies.

Acquiring Genre Practices for Use in Social/Digital Media

Students acquire use of certain genre practices for engaging in social/digital media. These genre practices include multimodal practices through the use of "layout, typography, texture, images, including of course emojis, rather than intonation, voice quality, facial expression, gaze behaviour, gesture and posture—and this affects how the 'non-verbal' is expressed." (Jovanovic & Van Leeuwen, 2018, p. 685). Using social/digital media provide users "with new visual resources for realizing both initiating moves and responses, so making it possible to replace words and sentences with emoticons, stickers, and so on" (p. 687).

Students employ these multimodal digital practices as "spreadable media" (Jenkins et al., 2013) to achieve positive uptake from their audiences, who may be more likely to attend to images and/or videos than written text.

Many of the social/digital platforms and apps involve the use of genre practices related to remixes of photos or videos for conveying certain meanings. For example, an Instagram post may include an edited version of different clips of a child interacting with a pet dog to portray the development of the child's relationship with the dog over time. Students may also use images or videos as memes, as "remixed and iterated messages which are rapidly spread by members of participatory digital culture" (Wiggins & Bowers, 2014, p. 903). For example, students may take images of classical paintings and add certain titles or sayings to create a meme about an issue or topic.

> ## ACTIVITY: CONTEXTUALIZING USE OF MEDIA/DIGITAL GENRES
>
> Students may reflect on their use of and how they learned to employ multimodal media/digital genres to achieve positive uptake from their social media audiences. They may analyze responses to their use of these multimodal genres in terms of positive responses from audiences. They may also consider how people learn to infer the underlying shared meanings of certain images, such as emojis, related to certain shared social or cultural meanings.

Using Social/Digital Media to Respond to Media/Literature

Rather than have students only discuss or write about their response to media or literary texts, students can employ digital tools such as Flipgrid, Padlet, or Book Creator to create multimodal video responses for sharing their responses to texts (Burns, 2021). For example, in a free-reading program, students can use Flipgrid to share their book recommendations.

Greek adolescents took photos portraying their use of English, in which they assumed the role of photographers creating images for a youth magazine (Rothoni & Mitsikopoulou, 2019). They also portrayed how they employed digital tools and devices for using English words; for example, "@, PC, nice, Friend request, OK, LoL" or "'Nice', 'Party Girl', 'cinema', 'music', 'Let's tea party'" (p. 241). This suggests how

> It is a language which permeates teenagers' everyday life-words and which they use to do things connected to their personal interests, such as listen to songs, watch films, read magazines, visit online spaces and interact with other speakers.
>
> *p. 247*

Teachers can also have students respond to representations of adolescents using media/digital resources in young-adult literature, television, movies, or magazines (Dail et al., 2018; Rish, 2019). For example:

- *Yolo: The Internet Girls* (Myracle, 2015) portrays three adolescent females using digital tools for interacting with each other over a two-year period.
- *My Life Undecided* (Brody, 2012) portrays the main character creating blog posts seeking help from readers on how to address challenges in her life.
- *Girl Online* (Sugg, 2014) portrays how the main character's anonymous blog goes viral through social media.
- *Rob&Sara.com* (Petersen & Ruckman, 2006) portrays a relationship between Rob and Sara, who meet each other online.

ACTIVITY: CONTEXTUALIZING PORTRAYALS OF ADOLESCENTS' PRACTICES USING SOCIAL/DIGITAL MEDIA

Students can use social/digital media to respond to media/literature texts portraying adolescents' use of digital media in literature, television, movies, or magazines. Students could discuss or write about how characters' social/digital media shapes their development and relations and infer connections to similar issues in their digital tools/media (Rish, 2019).

Students may also critique how many portrayals of adolescents using digital media are often middle-class, White adolescents, with a lack of portrayals of non-dominant adolescent populations. Adolescents in one study critiqued the use of stereotypical representations of race, class, and/ or gender in the media and how news media broadcasts often foster fears, anger, or depression (Robb, 2017; *t.ly/fmlz*). To engage in critical inquiry about multimodal texts, students can pose the questions, " 'What's going on in this image?' or 'What emotions do you associate with this image?' 'What in the image made you think X?' or 'What's missing or left out of this picture?' " (Beach et al., 2010, p. 132). (For other resources on teaching critical media literacy, see *teachingmedialiteracy.pbworks.com*; Beach, 2007).

Summary

In this chapter, I described the use of social/digital media resources for adolescents engaging in practices for enacting identities and relations. Students employ digital tools/social media for interacting with peers involving the use of both positive and problematic practices. They also employ video games and role-play for employing practices for co-authoring fictional worlds. Teachers can have students reflect on these experiences related to adhering to certain norms or enacting identities/ relations and critique how digital/media texts create both supportive and stereo-typical representations based on race, class, and gender.

References

Abrams, S. S., Schaefer, M. B., & Ness, D. (2020). Adolescents' digital literacies in flux: Intersections of voice, empowerment, and practices. *Journal of Media Literacy Education, 11*(2), 79–94.

Anderson, M., & Jiang, J. (2018). Teens, social media & technology 2018. Pew Research Center. Retrieved from https://pewrsr.ch/2zImT64

Bagga-Gupta, S., & Dahlberg, G. M. (2019). On epistemological issues in technologically infused spaces: Notes on virtual sites for learning. In S. Bagga-Gupta, G. M. Dahlberg, & Y. Lindberg (Eds.), *Virtual sites as learnings spaces: Critical issues on languaging research in changing eduscapes* (pp. 2–25). Palgrave Macmillan.

Barab, S. A., Gresalfi, M., & Ingram-Goble. A. (2010). Transformational play: Using games to position person, content, and context. *Educational Researcher, 39*(7), 525–536. doi:10.3102/0013189X10386593

Beach, R. (2007). *Teaching medialiteracy.com.* Teachers College Press.

Beach, R., & Aukerman, M. (2019). Portraying and enacting trust through writing in a high school classroom. In R. Beach & D. Bloome (Eds.), *Languaging relations for transforming the literacy and language arts classroom* (pp. 49–58). Routledge.

Beach, R. & Beauchemin, F. (2019). *Teaching language as action in the ELA classroom.* Routledge.

Beach, R., Campano, G., Edmiston, B., & Borgmann, M. (2010). *Literacy tools in the classroom: Teaching through critical inquiry, grades 5–12*. National Writing Project/Teachers College Press.

Beach, R., & O'Brien, D. (2015). *Using apps for learning across the curriculum: A literacy-based framework and guide*. Routledge.

Beavis, C. (2014). Games as text, games as action: Video games in the English classroom. *Journal of Adolescent & Adult Literacy, 57*(6), 433–439. doi:10.1002/jaal.275

Bell, A., & Gresalfi, M. (2017). Teaching with videogames: How experience impacts classroom integration. *Technology Knowledge and Learning, 22,* 513–526. doi:10.1007/s10758-017-9306-3

Boardman, A. G., Garcia, A., Dalton, B., & Polman, J. L. (2021). *Compose our world: Project-based learning in secondary English language arts*. Teachers College Press.

boyd, d. (2010). Social network sites as networked publics: Affordances, dynamics, and implications. In Z. Papacharissi (Ed.), *A networked self: Identity, community, and culture on social network sites* (pp. 39–58). Routledge.

Breakstone, J., Smith, M., Wineburg, S., Rapaport, A., Carle, J., Garland, M., & Saavedra, A. (2021). Students' civic online reasoning: A national portrait. *Educational Researcher, 50*(8), 505–515. https://doi.org/10.3102/0013189X211017495

Brody, J. (2012). *My life undecided*. Square Fish.

Burns, M. (2021). Let's "hear" it for student learning. *Educational Leadership, 79*(1), 84–85.

Canady, F., Martin, K., & Scott, C. E. (2018). "Song of myself": A digital unit of study remix. In J. S. Dail, S. Witte, & S. T. Bickmore (Eds.), *Toward a more visual literacy: Shifting the paradigm with digital tools and young adult literature* (pp. 101–118). Rowman & Littlefield.

Canady, F., Scott, C. E. & Hicks, T. (2020). "Walking a thin line": Exploring the tensions between composition curriculum and students' lives as digital writers. *Journal of Language & Literacy Education, 16*(2). Retrieved from http://jolle.coe.uga.edu/volume-162

Checa-Romero, M., & Pascual Gómez, I. (2018). Minecraft and machinima in action: Development of creativity in the classroom. *Technology, Pedagogy and Education, 27*(5), 625–637. doi:10.1080/1475939X.2018.1537933

Dail, J. S., Witte, S., & Bickmore, S. T. (Eds.). (2018). *Young adult literature and the digital world*. Rowman & Littlefield.

Darvas, P. (2014, March 5). Prologue: A video game's epic-ish journey to a high school English class. [Weblog post]. www.ludiclearning.org/2014/03/05/gone-home-in-education/

Decker, A., Phelps, A., & Egert, C. A. (2017). Disappearing happy little sheep: Changing the culture of computing education by infusing the cultures of games and fine arts. *Educational Technology, 57*(2), 50–54.

Delahunty, J., Verenikina, L., & Jones, P. (2014). Socio-emotional connects: Identity, belonging and learning in online interactions. A literature review. *Technology, Pedagogy and Education, 23*(2), 243–265.

Dennis-Tiwary, T. A. (2018, July 14). Taking away the phones won't solve our teenagers' problems. *The New York Times*. Retrieved from www.nytimes.com/2018/07/14/opinion/sunday/smartphone-addiction-teenagers-stress.html

Doerr-Stevens, C., Beach, R., & Boeser, E. (2011). Using online role-play to promote collaborative argument and collective change. *English Journal, 100*(5), 33–39.

Douglas, D., Garcia, E., & Grueser, M. (2020). Connecting youth, eco-media and resilience in Appalachia. *Journal of Sustainability Education, 23*. Retrieved from http://t.ly/UYZW

Dredger, K., Woods, D., Beach, C., & Sagstetter, V. (2010). Engage me: Using new literacies to create third space classrooms that engage student writers. *Journal of Media Literacy Education, 2*(2), 85–101.

Ehret, C., Hollett, T., & Jocius, R. (2016). The matter of new media making: An intra-action analysis of adolescents making a digital book trailer. *Journal of Literacy Research, 48*(3), 346–377.

Eisenbach, B., Greathouse, P., & Farnham, J. (2018). Infusing young adult literature into the virtual classroom. In J. Dail, S. Witte, & S. T. Bickmore (Eds.), *Toward a more visual literacy: Shifting the paradigm with digital tools and young adult literature* (pp. 63–76). Rowman & Littlefield.

Enciso, P. E. (2014). Prolepsis and educational change through drama: Bringing the future forward. In S. Davis, H. G. Clemson, B. Ferholt, S-M. Jansson, & A. Marjanovic-Shane (Eds.), *Dramatic interactions in education: Vygotskian and sociocultural approaches to drama, education and research* (pp. 171–188). Bloomsbury Academic.

Esteban-Guitart, M., Lalueza, J. L., Zhang-Yu, C., & Llopart, M. (2019). Sustaining students' cultures and identities: A qualitative study based on the funds of knowledge and identity approaches. *Sustainability, 11*(12), 3400. https://doi.org/10.3390/su11123400

Feldstein Ewing, S. W., Chang, L., Cottler, L. B., Tapert, S. F., Dowling, G. J., & Brown S. A. (2018). Approaching retention within the ABCD Study. *Developmental Cognitive Neuroscience, 32*, 130–137.

Fitzpatrick, C., Burkhalterd, R., & Asbridge, M. (2019). Adolescent media use and its association to wellbeing in a Canadian national sample. *Preventive Medicine Reports, 14*. doi.org/10.1016/j.pmedr.2019.100867

Gallup Inc., & Knight Foundation (2020). American views 2020: Trust, media and democracy. https://knightfoundation.org/reports/american-views-2020-trust-media-and-democracy/

Gamesby, R. (2015). Categories of place. [Weblog post]. Retrieved from http://t.ly/qMML

Garcia, A. (2016). *Good reception: Teens, teachers, and mobile media in a Los Angeles high school.* MIT Press.

Gee, J. P. (2013). *Good video games and good learning: Collected essays on video games, learning, and literacy* (2nd ed.). Peter Lang.

Gee, J. P. & Hayes, E. R. (2011). *Language and learning in the digital age.* Routledge.

Gupta, J., Bouvier, J., & Gordon, E. (2012). *Exploring new modalities of public engagement: An evaluation of digital gaming platforms on civic capacity and collective action in the Boston public school district* [White paper]. Retrieved from http://t.ly/dogM

Gutiérrez, K. D., Higgs, J., Lizárraga, J. R., & Rivero, E. (2019). Learning as movement in social design-based experiments: Play as a leading activity. *Human Development, 62*, 66–82. doi:10.1159/000496239

Haigney, S. (2020, September 16). Do viral videos really tell you anything about today's teens? *The New York Times Magazine*, pp. 7–9.

Hinton, S. E. (1967). *The outsiders.* Viking.

Holmes, A. (2015, July 14). What are the consequences of our cultural obsession with newness? *The New York Times.* Retrieved from https://goo.gl/5CtWsR

Hull, G. A., & Stornaiuolo, A. (2014). Cosmopolitan literacies, social networks, and "proper distance": Striving to understand in a global world. *Curriculum Inquiry, 44*(1), 15–44.

Ito, M., Gutiérrez, K., Livingstone, S., Penuel, B., Rhodes, J., Salen, K., Schor, J. … Watkins, S.C. (2012). *Connected learning: An agenda for research and design.* Digital Media Literacy Research Hub.

Jenkins, H., Ford, S., & Green, J. (2013). *Spreadable media: Creating value and meaning in a networked culture.* New York University Press.

Jovanovic, D., & Van Leeuwen, T. (2018). Multimodal dialogue on social media. *Social Semiotics, 28*(5), 683–699. https://doi.org/10.1080/10350330.2018.1504732

Kiss, S. V. (2020, September 14). Video games in the English classroom. [Weblog post]. Retrieved from https://tinyurl.com/y655pg3c

Kohnen, A. M., & Lacy, A. (2018). "They don't see us otherwise": A discourse analysis of marginalized students critiquing the local news. *Linguistics & Education, 46*(2), 102–112.

Kuby, C. R. & Crawford, S. (2018). Intra-activity of humans and nonhumans in Writers' Studio:(re) imagining and (re) defining 'social'. *Literacy, 52*(1), 20–30.

Lenhart, A. (2015, April 9). *Teens, social media & technology overview 2015.* Pew Research Center. Retrieved from www.pewresearch.org/internet/2015/04/09/teens-social-media-technology-2015

Literat, I., Chang, Y. K., Eisman, J., & Gardner, J. (2021). LAMBOOZLED!: The design and development of a game-based approach to news literacy education. *Journal of Media Literacy Education, 13*(1), 56–66.

Macro, K. J. (2019). Integrating drama: An embodied pedagogy. In K. J. Macro & M. Zoss (Eds.), *A symphony of possibilities: A handbook for arts integration in secondary English language arts* (pp. 65–78). National Council of Teachers of English.

McGonigal, J. (2011). *Reality is broken: Why games make us better and how they can change the world.* Penguin.

Mirra, N. (2019). From connected learning to connected teaching: Reimagining digital literacy pedagogy in English teacher education. *English Education, 51*(3), 261–291.

Motobayashi, K., Swain, M., & Lapkin, S. (2014). Autobiographical episodes as languaging: Affective and cognitive changes in an older adult. *Language and Sociocultural Theory, 1*(1), 75–99.

Myracle, L. (2015). *Yolo: The Internet girls.* Amulet Press.

National Assessment of Educational Progress (2020). *Explore NAEP long-term trends in reading and mathematics.* Retrieved from www.nationsreportcard.gov/ltt

National Association of Media Literacy Education (2007). *Key questions to ask when analyzing media messages.* Retrieved from https://namle.net/resources/key-questions-for-analyzing-media

Perrin, A. (2018). *5 facts about Americans and video games.* Pew Research Center. Retrieved from https://tinyurl.com/y6ocvm89

Petersen, P. J. & Ruckman, I. (2006). *Rob&Sara.com.* Laurel Leaf.

Poteat, P., Heck, N. C., Yoshikawa, H., & Calzo, J. P. (2016). Greater engagement among members of gay-straight alliances: Individual and structural contributors. *American Educational Research Journal, 53*(6), 1732–1758.

Rideout, V., & Robb, M. B. (2018). *Social media, social life: Teens reveal their experiences, 2018.* Common Sense Media. Retrieved from www.commonsensemedia.org/research/social-media-social-life-2018

Rideout, V., & Robb, M. B. (2019). *The common sense census: Media use by tweens and teens, 2019.* Common Sense Media. Retrieved from http://t.ly/SI6K

Rish, R. M. (2019). Representation of media and technology in young adult literature. In R. Hobbs & P. Mihailidis. *The international encyclopedia of media literacy.* (pp. 1–9). Wiley.

Robb, M. B. (2017). *News and America's kids: How young people perceive and are impacted by the news.* Common Sense Media.

Rothoni, A., & Mitsikopoulou, B. (2019). Visual representations of English language learning and literacy in Greece. In S. Bagga-Gupta, A. Golden, L. Holm, H. P. Laursen,

& A. Pitkänen-Huhta (eds.), *Reconceptualizing connections between language, literacy and learning* (pp. 231–251). Springer Nature.

Schieble, M. (2011). A case for interruption in the virtual English classroom with the graphic novel *American Born Chinese*. *Australian Journal of Language and Literacy, 34*(2), 202–218.

Seltzer, K. (2019). Performing ideologies: Fostering raciolinguistic literacies through role-play in a high school English classroom. *Journal of Adolescent & Adult Literacy, 63*(2), 147–155.

Sinclair, B. (2019, January 31). Early teens gaming online more. [Weblog post]. Retrieved from https://tinyurl.com/y5tjwkpe

Smith, K. (2014). Critical hits & critical spaces: Roleplaying games and their potential in developing critical literacy and new literacy practices. In P. Paugh, T. Kress, & R. Lake (eds.), *Teaching towards democracy with postmodern and popular culture texts* (pp. 239–256). Sense Publishers.

Sosik, V. S., & Bazarova, N. N. (2014). Relational maintenance on social network sites: How Facebook communication predicts relational escalation. *Computers in Human Behavior, 35*, 124–131. https://doi.org/10.1016/j.chb.2014.02.044

Statista. (2021, January 28). Most popular social networks of teenagers in the United States from fall 2012 to fall 2020. [Weblog post]. Retrieved from www.statista.com/statistics/250172/social-network-usage-of-us-teens-and-young-adults/

Sugg, Z. (2014). *Girl online*. Atria/Keywords.

Testa, M. (2005). *Something about America*. Candlewick Press.

Thomas, E. E., & Stornaiuolo, A. (2016). Restorying the self: Bending toward textual justice. *Harvard Educational Review, 86*(3), 313–338.

Turner, K. H., & Reed, D. (2018). Responding to young adult literature through civic engagement. In J. S. Dail, S. Witte, & S. T. Bickmore (Eds.), *Toward a more visual literacy: Shifting the paradigm with digital tools and young adult literature* (pp. 41–52). Rowman & Littlefield.

Twenge, J. M. (2017). *iGen: Why today's super-connected kids are growing up less rebellious, more tolerant, less happy and completely unprepared for adulthood*. Atria.

Twenge, J. M., Martin, G. N., & Spitzberg, B. H. (2019). Trends in U.S. adolescents' media use, 1976–2016: The rise of digital media, the decline of TV, and the (near) demise of print. *Psychology of Popular Media Culture, 8*(4), 329–345.

Wargo, J. M. (2015). Spatial stories with nomadic narrators: Affect, Snapchat, and feeling embodiment in youth mobile composing. *Journal of Language & Literacy Education, 11*(1), 47–64.

Wenzel, A. (2018). Red state, purple town: Polarized communities and local journalism in rural and small-town Kentucky. *Journalism, 21*(4), 557–573. https://doi.org/10.1177/1464884918783949

Wiggins, B. E., & Bowers, G. B. (2014). Memes as genre: A structurational analysis of the memescape. *New Media & Society, 17*(11), 1886–1906.

Wissman, K. & Costello, S. (2014). Creating digital comics in response to literature: Aesthetic, aesthetic transactions, and meaning making. *Language Arts, 92*(2), 103–117.

Zittoun, T. (2017). Symbolic resources and sense-making in learning and instruction. *European Journal of Psychology in Education, 32*, 1–20. doi:10.1007/s10212-016-0310-0

Yang, G. L. (2008). *American born Chinese*. Square Fish.

PART III
Implications for Teaching

13

IMPLICATIONS FOR TEACHING

Bringing Students' Worlds into the ELA Classroom

The final chapter of the book formulates implications for teaching related to importing students' experiences of practices in different worlds into the classroom through having them discuss and write about how they are contextualizing the different components constituting their experiences. Students can also recontextualize these practices by critiquing discourses constituting status-quo practices for making changes in their identities in certain worlds, as well as enacting third-space alternative worlds (Tierney, 2020). Students also benefit from reflecting on their use of genres to examine their use of practices for enacting relations with others, leading to their growth over time. They can also respond critically to portrayals of different worlds in media/literature for inferring connections between characters' and their own practices.

As illustrated in this book, students drew on experiences in different worlds to write about and reflect on their practices in their worlds. This raises the question of how teachers can draw on their students' experiences for use in classroom activities, the focus of this final chapter.

Having Students Share Their Experiences in Figured Worlds

To draw on students' experiences in different figured worlds, it is important that students feel comfortable sharing those experiences in their lives outside of the classroom with teachers. Students are more likely to feel comfortable doing so when they have a positive relationship with their teacher, as was the case with the students' relationships with Ms. E, who frequently shared her own experiences with her students.

Students are more likely to share their experiences when they have some clear purpose for doing so based on their teachers' purposeful activities. For example,

DOI: 10.4324/9781003246886-16

276 Implications for Teaching

for studying ways of resolving family tensions in *Romeo and Juliet*, students may share their experiences with coping with tensions in their family worlds.

As demonstrated in the chapters about different worlds, as organized around components described in Chapter 2, students may contextualize:

- *Purposes* for sharing experiences to illustrate learning certain practices. Students may share their learning experiences to display competence with peers; for example, demonstrating their ability to engage audiences through their performance in a school play. They may then reflect on how displaying competence may apply to other worlds, contributing to their success in those worlds.
- *Norms* and *discourses* constituting students' use of practices in different worlds. Students may share their experiences of learning norms and discourses for playing sports or video games. Students may then reflect on how those norms or discourses apply to analyzing how characters adhere to certain norms or discourses in a novel or play.
- *Identities* related to acquiring practices for enacting identities in certain worlds; for example, how they learned practices constituting the identity of a leader of their extracurricular school club related to use of certain languaging actions. Students could then reflect on how learning those practices applies to enacting identities in other worlds. For example, they may reflect on how using languaging to support peers in their club relates to supporting peers in their peer group or co-workers in their workplace.
- *Genres* associated with learning consistent practices for employing languaging action. For example, they may reflect on how their use of genres to communicate about specific strategies or plays in a sports world relates to engaging in their classroom discussion in school worlds.
- *Media/literature* based on practices for using social media to identify their virtual audiences to connect with those audiences. Students could then reflect on how identifying their audiences connects with writing essays for the teacher or peer audiences.

ACTIVITY: CONTEXTUALIZING EXPERIENCES WITH PRACTICES IN DIFFERENT WORLDS FOR APPLICATION TO SCHOOL WORLDS

It is critical that students have opportunities to share their experiences in different worlds with their teachers. Students could describe or write about their experiences contextualizing certain practices in different worlds for sharing those experiences with their teachers, assuming that their teachers would draw on those experiences for planning classroom activities. For example, students could describe how, as leaders on their sports team, they engaged in socializing new team members about the use of certain practices. Based on their leadership in their sports world, they could identify similar practices for facilitating open-ended discussions in their small group discussions.

Fostering Reflections on Relationships Between Components

In addition to contextualizing different components constituting the meaning of practices, students also benefit from reflecting on relationships between these components. For example, enacting identities in a peer group world entails learning the norms or discourses constituting that peer group world.

Inferring these connections involves recognizing similarities and differences between their use of practices across different worlds. For example, in their workplace worlds, they acquire norms for positive interactions with customers based on the larger corporate or company discourses for enacting positive interactions—a norms/discourse connection.

They may then compare or contrast this use of languaging related to employing only positive interactions with customers to engaging in debate in their ECA club or in a classroom discussion in which they challenge or critique others' positions based on a different set of norms/discourses.

Students are also inferring connections between their identities and the use of certain genres or media/literature. Students may perceive themselves as adopting the identity of an effective group leader through formulating a set plan or agenda for an event or gathering. They may also define their identities according to their engagement in producing YouTube videos.

For reflecting on these connections between components, students learn to think about how they employ similar or different practices related to the use of components within and across different worlds. To then think about how they think about these connections, they employ "languaging thinking practices" (Kim & Bloome, in 2021).

Teachers can ask students, "How did you think about this?" to have them make explicit their thinking about their thinking. For example, for enacting the *purposes* of engaging audiences through their speeches or writing, students are thinking about how to position their *identity* as a certain persona to achieve identification with their audiences (Burke, 1969). In arguing for the need for her school to reduce the use of standardized testing as a means of labeling or assigning students, a student may describe how she adopts the deficit identity of a "struggling reader" based on her reading test scores, consistent with a discourse of "achievement" (Caraballo, 2019), even though she is an avid reader of young-adult novels.

278 Implications for Teaching

In thinking about how she thinks about adopting this identity as her persona, she may believe that using herself as someone who is penalized by the misuse of standardized testing may serve the rhetorical purpose of engaging her audiences.

ACTIVITY: MAPPING SIMILARITIES AND DIFFERENCES IN PRACTICES ACROSS DIFFERENT WORLDS

To have students reflect on how they are thinking about their use of practices within and across different worlds, students could create a map in which they list certain practices as languaging actions they employ in certain worlds. For each of the actions, they could underline actions that are similar across different worlds and add dotted lines for actions that are unique to or different from their other worlds. For example, in the illustrative map (see Figure 13.1), actions are listed for the worlds of school, work, soccer, and family where certain actions are similar across worlds ("listen and follow directions"), while others are unique to those worlds: for example, "write papers" in their school world.

Students could then reflect on how they draw on similar practices for use across different worlds—for example, how they use the practice of "listen and follow directions" across their worlds—while, in other worlds, they need to

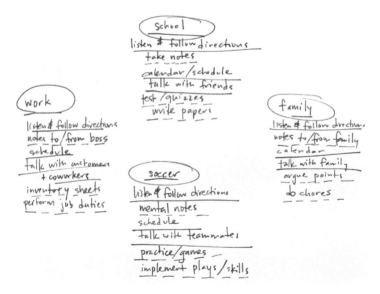

FIGURE 13.1 Students mapping languaging actions for participation in school, work, soccer, and family worlds

Bringing Students' Worlds into the Class **279**

> acquire practices unique to those worlds. They could also reflect on how to acquire these practices—from teachers, managers, coaches, parents, and/or peers, as well as how they improve in their use of these practices over time as they are engaged in their worlds.

Recontextualizing Practices to Adopt a Critical Perspective

How then do students change in their use of practices over time? Students recontextualize their use of practices from a critical perspective to recognize the limitations in their use of status-quo practices. They may recognize that, as a team captain, trying to tell players how they should enact certain plays is counterproductive, resulting in their perceiving a need to change or develop new practices. They may then switch to modeling or demonstrating the use of certain plays, which they then find to be more productive.

As described by Limarys Caraballo in Chapter 6, students engage in critical inquiry about the *norms* and *discourses* constituting practices in their worlds (Schieble et al., 2020). For example, in reflecting on local events such as the police killing of a Black person, adolescents may analyze the larger discourses of systemic racism shaping perceptions of these events. As a team captain, they may also critique the limitations of adopting a "winning is everything" set of norms and discourses associated with the need to acknowledge difficulties of their team members accepting and learning from instances in which their team loses.

Students can recontextualize their practices by critiquing race, class, and gender discourses for co-authoring across figured worlds leading to changing those practices.

Critiquing Discourses of Race on Practices in Worlds

Students may examine how institutional, systemic racism discourses shape people's enactment of agency within and across different worlds. For example, they may critique how Black and Latinx students are often assigned to lower-track/ability group classes, given their performance on standardized tests. They may also examine how their non-White peers may not be afforded the same opportunities or responsibilities as White peers in their workplaces or community organizations.

Given the recent focus of the Black Lives Matter movement, students may consider ways to challenge these institutionalized racist practices. They may identify the negative impacts of these practices on their peers' lives and propose changes in these practices. For example, they may challenge the use of the school tracking/ability grouping related to differences in students' race or language use (Kirkland, 2010).

Teachers can also have students write about or discuss issues or challenges in their lives related to adopting critical stances on these issues or challenges.

280 Implications for Teaching

Critiquing Effects of SES on Practices in Worlds

Students could also examine the effects of the SES of their community world related to the level of financial support for their school, extracurricular, and sports worlds. While the location of a school in a higher SES neighborhood was a predictor of students' academic success independent of school and family social capital, the school's educational expectations and drop-out rate mediated these SES effects (Roscigno et al., 2006).

Students' families' SES influences adolescents co-authoring practices in their school, extracurricular, and sports worlds, given how higher-income families can provide more social capital related to acquiring practices in those worlds than can lower-income families (Crosnoe, 2004). For example, students from higher-income homes may have fewer obligations related to providing support for their families so that they have more time to participate in extracurricular or sports worlds (Parcel et al., 2010). On the other hand, students from lower-income families often benefit more from participation in those worlds than students from higher-income families, given that the latter group already have acquired certain practices (Crosnoe, 2004).

Given disparities in wealth across different communities, considering how schools are funded based on property taxes, rural and inner-city communities may not have the tax base to invest in schools compared with suburban communities. In addition, rural or inner-city communities may also not perceive the need to invest in their schools, given that graduates are leaving those communities to work elsewhere (Roscigno et al., 2006).

Critiquing Effects of Gender on Practices in Worlds

Students may also examine how gender difference influences participation in different worlds. For example, students may note how male sports may receive more financial support and publicity in sports and school worlds, leading to analysis of the degree to which their school is adhering to Title IX compliance related to gender discrimination for sports participation. They may also examine differences in academic performance in their school world related to gender differences in which females generally outperform males, leading to consideration of factors shaping those differences.

ACTIVITY: ADOPTING CRITICAL STANCES FOR RECONTEXTUALIZING RACE, CLASS, AND/OR GENDER DISCOURSES SHAPING SCHOOL WORLDS

Students could adopt a critical stance to discuss or write about how discourses of race, class, and/or gender shape institutional practices in school worlds. For example, based on the YPAR Cyphers for Justice projects described in Chapter 6, students could study how their school practices related to ability grouping/tracking, testing, and disciplinary policies impact students according to students' racial or family SES differences. To do this, they may collect data on the demographic make-up of students in honors/AP classes or the number of school suspensions based on race and/or class. Students could also examine how teachers and students enact gender discourses through stereotypical language related to differences in females' versus males' abilities or assets.

Recontextualizing Practices to Create Third-Space Alternative Worlds

Recontextualizing practices also leads to students changing their status-quo practices to co-author new, alternative worlds as *third spaces*, as noted in Chapter 6 (Sojo, 1996; Moje & Ellison, 2016). Enacting third spaces involves students moving beyond practices in their status-quo worlds as *first spaces* by resisting traditional *second spaces* consisting of official, institutionalized contextualizations of practices in their school, organization, or workplace worlds. Students may challenge this traditional second-space framing constituted by norms and discourses of authority to enact new, alternative *third spaces* constituted by alternative norms and discourses (Gutiérrez, 2008). For example, adolescents who resided in disadvantaged neighborhoods employed social media as third spaces for sharing positive experiences in ways that transcend the challenges of living in those neighborhoods (Stevens et al., 2017).

Black students in a youth-offender program moved between their experience in their figured worlds of prison and college to enact a third-space world that was neither prison nor college through taking college courses while in prison (Urrieta et al., 2011). Through participation in this hybrid third space, students perceived themselves more positively as students with future selves through meshing experiences outside of school with school experiences (Gutiérrez, 2008).

Engaging in recontextualizing practices through critical inquiry involves:

- *Identifying a problem or issue in a world.* For example, in the Sustainable Democracy Project illustrating a community project in Chapter 5, students in a high school located in a Puerto Rican neighborhood contextualized a problem related to having a lack of access to stores with healthy food (Schultz, 2017).
- *Recontextualizing the problem in terms of reasons for the problem or issue.* Students then recontextualized the problem of lack of access to healthy food in terms of the larger systemic problem of living in a low-income community world as "food deserts" with a lack of access to stores with healthy food.

282 Implications for Teaching

- *Identifying solutions for addressing the problem.* Formulating reasons for the problem can then lead students to entertaining solutions for addressing the problem. One reason for the "food desert" problem was that, given that the neighborhood was an urban neighborhood, there were no gardens located relatively near any of the stores, leading to perceiving the need to create indoor gardens.
- *Engaging in making change.* Based on formulating solutions, students then assumed active identities related to making change. For example, students worked with local community members to participate in growing food in indoor gardens, resulting in enhanced access to healthy food.

Teachers associated with this project recognized how to draw on the students' engagement to apply similar critical inquiry in their classrooms. One teacher in the project who lived in the students' neighborhood noted how participation in the project served as

> a catalyst for students, teachers, and community members to become participants of a dynamic social transformation process together, developing problem-solving and critical thinking skills together, and sharing an ever-expanding amount of creativity … The students were being viewed as young intellectual activists who were needed and respected in the community … I loved creating a classroom where students schooled me, as it displaced the prevalent top-down learning dynamic.
>
> *Schultz, 2017, p. 81*

Critical Reflection on Genre Practices for Enacting Identities

Students also engage in critical inquiry about their use of *genre* practices for enacting *identities* as viable change agents. For example, a teacher discovered disparities between an online, original version of Liam O'Flaherty's story "The Sniper" versus a version in the school's textbook. She noted that references related to characters' references to religion, as when one character utters, "'Christ'" when he was shot, had been omitted from the textbook version (Gorlewski, 2008).

She then decided to, rather than herself, have her students compose letters to the textbook editors inquiring about reasons for these omissions as censorship. One editor did respond, noting that, for their textbook adoption in some districts or states, they needed to omit references to the use of "God's name, profanity, or references to the occult" (p. 29). The students were pleased about the sense of social agency that writing their letters to challenge status-quo practices gave them. As the teacher noted, "my working-class students, who tend to resist authority even as they accept the immutability of the status quo, had a sense of how to use language for empowerment" (p. 29).

Students could also reflect on their use of genre practices constituting certain languaging actions. In her ethnographic writing about genre practices in her peer group world, in responses to Ms. E's prompts, Marla reflected on genre practices she employs in her peer group world.

1. How would you describe how the specific ways of talking or communicating in your group served to create positive or negative relations with others in your group?

   The self-confidence I have gained from my group is not just from the evolution of my speaking skills and sense of belonging, it is also from the insults. It may sound backward, but when people who you care about and care about you mock parts of you, it's impossible to think of them as things to feel bad about. Things I was self-conscious about suddenly became something I feel comfortable to joke about.

2. How would you describe how the specific ways of talking or communicating in your group served to create positive or negative relations with peers outside this group?

   In previous years, my friends and I were, for the most part, friends in name only. I didn't feel like a part of the group and because of this I isolated myself and my self-confidence plummeted. I stopped interacting with people and really only spoke when spoken to. After I met my current friend group this changed. I felt like I was accepted as a part of the group and wasn't a nuisance to others. I started talking more and gained not only confidence but also speaking skills.

3. How would you describe the degree of ethical concern and/or trust in the group for others and/or others outside the group evident in people's interactions and the language you have already identified that the group uses?

   My friends and I make jokes about nearly everything, but when push comes to shove, we are here for each other. We don't often talk about serious things, but when we do, everyone comes together to either solve the problem or to comfort the distraught.

4. How do others perceive your group in your school or community? How would you describe how figures of authority and/or other groups trust your group more or less than other groups?

   Because of our backwards talk and obscure references, people outside the group have a hard time understanding what we are saying. Too many times people hear only parts of our conversations and are confused. It is not uncommon for someone to say something along the lines of "I wasn't paying attention and now you are talking about (fill in odd conversational topic or quote)."

5. What are some ways of talking or acting in your group that influence these other groups or people's perceptions of your group?

   It has become part of my character to try and make everything into a joke. Whether this is good or bad, I'm not quite sure. Even my way of thinking has changed somewhat. Instead of how much you know about someone, I feel that the amount of experiences and memories made with someone determines how close we are.

284 Implications for Teaching

Through reflecting on how she employs different genre practices, Marla notes how insults and jokes function as genres for enacting her identity and relations with peers, given how "experiences and memories made with someone determine how close we are."

Drawing on Students' Use of Media/Literature for Use in the Classroom

To engage students in critical inquiry about their practices in different worlds, teachers can also draw on students' responses to *media/literature* to have them infer connections between portrayals of practices in media/literature and their lived-world experiences with those practices. For example, Ms. E had students think critically about online privacy issues related to government or corporate access to personal information in responding to portrayals of Big Brother government control in *1984* (Orwell, 1960). She provided them with an example of how their school can track information on their Chromebooks.

> They're given a Chromebook, and the Chromebook tracks what they're doing. They can't really do work offline, so they have to do it through the school stuff, so they can't really do anything, like save a document that would incriminate them in some way because then it's saved in their Google Cloud that they signed in with their school stuff.
>
> I've had that happen before where kids were on a document and saying some pretty gross things. Someone at the district office called my room, and they were like, "I don't know what project you have kids working on right now," but there's a code in there about what they can't say, which involved sodomy. They were just joking back and forth. So I pulled them up, and I went into the history of the document, and I was like, "Anybody want to tell me why this is what you're spending your time on right now."
>
> They were shocked. Faces red; one kid was almost in tears because he hadn't come out to anybody else except for this other student, and here they just did it all over this document. So the district can track that stuff. I think they have a pretty good understanding about why some of these practices are related to our genetics and our thoughts; why that can be scary and a problem.

These surveillance practices are now commonly employed in schools throughout the United States. One surveillance company, Gaggle, daily monitors students' postings on school-issued Google and Microsoft accounts (Keierleber, 2021). Gaggle will notify school officials of any posting associated with self-harm or suicide, claiming that doing so has saved students' lives. However, the fact that students know that they are being monitored could be counterproductive in that they then do not disclose the need for assistance. There is also little empirical evidence about the efficacy of the surveillance; it raises legal questions about violation of student privacy, as well as potential liability claims for schools, and it may adversely impact students from non-dominant families (Fedders, 2019).

> ## ACTIVITY: ADOPTING CRITICAL STANCES IN RESPONDING TO MEDIA/LITERATURE
>
> Students can adopt critical stances for discussing or writing about their responses to media/literature by comparing their own practices in different worlds with characters' experiences. Ms. E had students compare their responses to portrayals of characters' deceptions and mistrust not only in *1984* but also in response to *Lord of the Flies* (Golding, 1997). Tanya connected Jack's failure to maintain the signal fire in *Lord of the Flies* contrary to his commitment to do so with Ralph with her own experience of her peers failing their obligations to their commitments: "I can relate to this because I've had instances in class where I'm working with a group/partner, and they don't follow through to do the thing they were supposed to do ... So I can relate to how Ralph feels when Jack didn't do his part." (Beach & Beauchemin, 2019, p. 109). In comparing their experiences, students could also formulate explanations for similarities and differences in the norms/discourses shaping practices in worlds of media/literature texts with the norms/discourses shaping practices in their worlds.

Engaging in Formative Assessment of Students' Work

As students engage in the activities included in this book, they benefit from teachers' formative assessment regarding their effectiveness in contextualizing their practices in different worlds in students' discussion, writing, or projects. Teachers can provide descriptive feedback to foster their reflection on what and how they learned about their practices through engaging in these activities. Through their reflection, students identify their success in using certain practices for portraying their experiences and practices on which they need to improve.

Consistent with using e-portfolios for formative assessment, students could collect and curate documents/writings or images/videos that illustrate their development across time to include in an e-portfolio. One adolescent, Ben, employed Snapchat and a mapping app to document his physical movements within his community across time and his interactions with his sister to share and reflect on his experiences in these events (Wargo, 2015).

> Feelings across this spacetime traversal, ones which pushed Ben to touch feeling and create experiences for his users, allows us to read the ways in

286 Implications for Teaching

which the digital screen is enfolded within spatio-temporal scales of composing. Snapchat allowed Ben the opportunity to be an experienced architect, one whose own processes of embodied composition facilitate the touching of time and the possibility as spatial storyteller.

p. 55

Snapchat allowed him to curate his "collective life" and document his ""consciousness." … For Ben, snapping is about curating an experience, collecting moments through visual frames to tell a moment, or perhaps to experience a rememory." (p. 56).

In another example of using digital tools for reflection, preservice English teachers created digital story videos documenting their literacy development over time within and across their diverse school, family, and community worlds (Marlatt, 2019). The teachers addressed questions such as "'What kinds of literacy practices and cultural traditions did you grow up with?' and 'How does your background shape the kind of writer and thinker you are?'" (n.p.).

One teacher noted how she wanted to share the importance of how her "'identity is shaped by Spanish customs. That's who I am. By sharing how proud I am, I think that will make students comfortable sharing who they are, especially kids from other backgrounds. Making the video helped me realize this'" (n.p.).

Another noted how her video could "'help bridge gaps' between what students know 'outside of school and in their classes' … 'I think videos could be a chance for me and my students to talk with one another about real stuff, rather than just me talking at them about class'" (n.p.).

Students may also reflect on how their practices with certain media/literature lead to their developing agency in using those practices. Marcus reflected on how his positive experiences in playing Legos led to his interest in becoming a civil engineer major in his school world.

> It was the first time that I really experienced something that I was good at. And initially, I had an actual sort of knack and desire to create things that it led into me constantly wanting to build things early on. I could think about, I'm going to build this house, and I could build it. And at the end of the day, I had a house that I had made. The entire process gave me a sort of drive to continue doing this. And that, of course, has led me to become a civil engineer.

Marcus also noted how experiences in interacting with others in his role-playing activities enhanced his interactions with others in his engineering courses and lab work. He noted how his role-play interactions involved "learning how to make sure that everybody's having fun, then that translated into making sure everybody's doing what they need to do that almost ironically translates really, really well."

ACTIVITY: CONTEXTUALIZING GROWTH IN PRACTICES OVER TIME

As illustrated by quotes from student interviews and writing in this book, students could use their e-portfolios to collect examples of writing about their participation in different worlds to reflect on their growth in practices over time in or across different worlds. For example, students could reflect on their development across time in their family world related to their ability to interact in constructive ways with their parent(s) and siblings to assume more responsibilities for supporting their families. They may describe how their parent(s) and/or siblings mentored them to employ these practices by sharing their own practices; for example, modeling ways to voice concerns in collaborative planning of family activities.

Summary

In this final chapter, I posited the need for students to adopt critical stances on their use of practices in different worlds, stances that may lead to their making changes in those practices in ways that lead to changes in their own identities and the practices within a world. I hope that teachers will perceive the value of Ms. E's activities in having students discuss and write about their experiences in different worlds, leading them to reflect on the value of those experiences as leading to their growth over time.

In conclusion, I recommend that, for additional links, activities, and readings for each of the chapters in this book, teachers go to the book's website, *adolescentsworlds. pbworks.com*.

References

Beach, R., & Beauchemin, F. (2019). *Teaching language as action in the ELA classroom.* Routledge.

Burke, K. (1969). *A grammar of motives.* University of California Press.

Caraballo, L. (2019). Being "loud": Identities-in-practice in a figured world of achievement. *American Educational Research Journal, 56*(4), 1281–1317. https://doi.org/10.3102/0002831218816059

Crosnoe, R. (2004). Social capital and the interplay of families and schools. *Journal of Marriage and Family, 66*(2), 267–280.

Fedders, B. (2019). The constant and expanding classroom: Surveillance in K-12 public schools. *North Carolina Law Review, 97*(6), 1673–1726.

Golding, W. (1997). *Lord of the flies.* Penguin.

Gorlewski, J. (2008). Christ and cleavage: Multiculturalism and censorship in a working-class, suburban high school. *The English Journal, 97*(3), 26–30.

Gutiérrez, K. D. (2008). Developing a sociocritical literacy in the third space. *Reading Research Quarterly, 43*(2), 148–164.

Keierleber, M. (2021, September 14). What Minneapolis Public Schools learned from six months of monitoring student communications: Inside and outside school hours. *MinnPost*. Retrieved from http://t.ly/hSp7

Kim, M-Y., & Bloome, D. P. (2021). When thinking becomes a topic of classroom conversations: Languaging thinking practices in a high school English classroom. *Research in the Teaching of English, 56*(2), 177–199.

Kirkland, D. E. (2010). English(es) in urban contexts: Politics, pluralism, and possibilities. *English Education, 43*(3), 293–306.

Marlatt, R. (2019). This is my story: Preservice English teachers create welcome videos to navigate the places and spaces of their literacy lives. *Contemporary Issues in Technology & Teacher Education, 19*(2). Retrieved from https://tinyurl.com/y8h2u7ze

Moje, E. B., & Ellison, T. L. (2016). Extended—and extending—literacies. *Journal of Education, 196*(3), 27–34.

Orwell, G. (1960). *1984*. Signet.

Parcel, T. L., Dufur, M. J., & Zito, R. C. (2010). Capital at home and at school: A review and synthesis. *Journal of Marriage and Family, 72*, 828–846. doi:10.1111/j.1741-3737.2010.00733.x

Roscigno, V. J., Tomaskovic-Devey, D., & Crowley, M. (2006). Education and the inequalities of place. *Social Forces, 84*(4), 2121–2145.

Schultz, B. D. (2017). *Teaching in the cracks: Openings and opportunities for student-centered, action-focused curriculum.* Teachers College Press.

Schieble, M., Vetter, A., & Martin, K. M. (2020). *Classroom talk for social change: Critical conversations in English language arts.* Teachers College Press.

Sojo, E. W. (1996). *Thirdspace: Journeys to Los Angeles and other real-and-imagined places.* Blackwell.

Stevens, R., Gilliard-Matthews, S., Dunaev, J., Woods, M. K., & Brawner, B. M. (2017). The digital hood: Social media use among youth in disadvantaged neighborhoods. *New Media & Society, 19*(6), 950–967.

Tierney, R. (2020). Reading our worlds. *Literacy Today, 38*(1), 6–7.

Urrieta, L., Martin, K. & Robinson, C. (2011). "I am in school!": African American male youth in a prison/college hybrid figured world. *Urban Review, 43*(4), 491–506.

Wargo, J. M. (2015). Spatial stories with nomadic narrators: Affect, Snapchat, and feeling embodiment in youth mobile composing. *Journal of Language and Literacy Education, 11*(1), 47–64. Retrieved from https://tinyurl.com/y22vbvo3

INDEX

academic success in school 63–64; academic language 74; deficit discourses of adolescents and 40, 58, 60, 80, 87, 96–97, 100, 109, 112, 277; impact of social/digital media use on 251–252; participation in ECAs and 166, 169, 182; social class discourses and disparities in achievement tests 58, 119–120; sports participation and 192; valuing of literary practices of non-dominant groups and 96–97, 135, 137

adolescentsworlds.pbworks.org 21

affirmative action programs 76, 98

African-American Vernacular English (AAVE) 13, 55, 105

agency 11; development and 60; from goal-setting 99; from leadership roles in extracurricular activities 176–178; from participating in community projects/social change 95, 107–109, 119, 136–137; from participation in extracurricular activities 166, 174, 179–180, 182; from performance in extracurricular activities 163–164, 166; positive discourses and 56–57; school belonging and 56–57, 60–62; from sports participation 185–186; through media/literature 86; through writing 81; undermining of by norms of "proper speech" 105; from working 243–244; Youth Participatory Action Research

(YPAR) as third space of 120–121, 124, 137

alternative instructional practices 11–14, 18, 53, 67, 76; "Body Map" activity 89; critiques of media/literature representations of discourses 111–112; different "Ways of Seeing" as 88; GripTape *(griptape.org)* project for learning outside school 99; interrelated research and activism/art in CFJ 129–131, *131*; open-ended questions and 75; Participatory Literacy Communities" (PLCs) as 96, 111; use of literacy practices from Black communities for 13, 96–97, 109

apprenticeships 50, 123, 245

arrests, disproportionate of Black youths 96, 133

authoring self 124

Baldridge, B. J. 100

barbershops 235–236

Barrio Writers ECA program 165

basketball, norms and engagement in 54

Beach, R. 21, 127, 131

belonging 59; from ECA participation 163, 166–167, 178, 182; enacting identities for 61–62, 64, 90; norms and 54; from peer group participation 143–145

Bertau, M.-C. 16

Between the World and Me (Coates) 86

Bhabha, H. 120

290 Index

Big Brother/Sister organization 99
BIPOC LGBTQ youth 131
Black communities 105, 109; African-American Vernacular English (AAVE) and 13, 55, 105; barbershop languaging practices 235–236; BIPOC LGBTQ youth 131; critique of local news/media representations of Black men 112; intricate literacy practices to draw on in classrooms 96–97; perception of workplace practices and 235–236; policing issues in 112–113, 133
Black students 13–14, 40, 79, 98, 112; CRT and 88–89; disproportionate disciplinary practices for *vs*. White students 109; hip-hop and social status of 150; impact of social/digital media use on reading/writing 252; peer groups and 147–148; risks and benefits of adolescent work and 228; socialization of identities of in school worlds 63
Bloome, D. 39
body image 36, 132–134
boundary-crossing practices 3, 21–22, 61, 102
break dancing 13–14
brokers, in ECAs 168–170
Bronxonics 171
Browning, R. 28
Bucholtz, M. 11, 39, 150–151
bullying 40

California 99
Caraballo, L. 21, 108
censorship, critiquing of 260–261
characters in media/literature: critical inquiry into 76; identification with 42–43, 72, 85–86, 89–91; *see also* media/literature; social/digital media worlds; young-adult literature
cheerleading 165–167
chosen spaces 96
classroom activities for contextualizing practices 9–10, 21; on addressing challenges in geographic community worlds 102; on benefits of sports participation 190; on challenges in learning practices 68; on conducting studies of participation in community worlds 108–109; on critical thinking practices 77; on critiquing media/literature representations of urban communities 112–113; on describing

identity enactment in ECAs 178–179; on discourses 37; on discourses on value of participation in ECAs 180; on discourses shaping sports participation 193; on employing genres for engaging in critical inquiry on community problems 110; on enacting identities and increased agency for belonging in school and 62; on enacting workplace identities 245; on examples of students in outside worlds 14; on experiences with different world practices for school 276–277; on formulating purposes for practices in ECAs 167–168; on genres for enacting practices in ECAs 181; on historical shifts in family capital provision 211–212; on identification with characters in media/literature 90–91; on identity development in sports 196–197; on incorporating youth-engaged research in classroom 136–137; on languaging actions as medium for enacting/co-authoring of different worlds activity 16; on languaging actions/embodied action in sports 188; on languaging emotions in families 213–214; on languaging for constituting community identities 105; on media/literature as "text worlds" 44–45; on media/literature use in sports participation 202–203; on norm acquisition for workplace engagement 234–235; on norm adherence in family worlds 215; on norm adherence in sports 191–192; on norms 55–56; on portrayals of adolescent social/digital media practices 266–267; on portrayals of workplace worlds in media/literature 247; on practices constituted by race, class and gender discourses 238–240; on practices for adhering to norms in ECAs 174; on practices for enactment of identities 40; on practices for moving across grade levels/school cultures 66; on practices for participating in peer groups 146–147; on practices in environmental worlds 104; on practices in media/literature portrayals of peer group conflicts 159; on practices related to norms/discourses in peer groups 149–150; on practices shaped by certain discourses 59; on practices in community youth organizations

101; on purposes constituting formal *vs.* informal learning and 53–54; on purposes for employing workplace practices 229–231; on purposes for social/digital media use 253–254; on purposes for supportive family practices 208–209; on recontextualization of student worlds thru responses to media/literature 89–90; on risks and benefits of adolescent work practices 228–229; on role of brokers in fostering student practices in ECAs 169–170; on role-playing activities 181; on social/digital media discourses/practices 258, 261–262; on social/digital media practices 258; on student participation in their figured worlds 9–10; on use of "insider language" in peer group relations 157–158; on use of external dialogue for acquiring internal dialogue 20; on use of genre for in workplace worlds 246; on use of genre for portraying family worlds 223; use of hip-hop 97; on use of languaging as emotions and embodied actions 18; on use of media/literature for enacting practices 43; on use of social/digital media genres 265; on use of video game/role play practices 256; on uses of social/digital media tools for identity enactment 264–265; on worlds based on genre knowledge 42; writing about peer group perceptions in a school 151–152

climate crisis 89–90, 96, 104; addressing of in video games 254; social/media tools for online activism on 263; youth organizations focusing on 103–104

co-learner, teachers as 52, 57, 136

Colley, M. 125

communities 9, 21, 50, 85, 134; as "communities of practice" 95–96; "Participatory Literacy Communities" (PLCs) 96, 109, 111; activities for addressing challenges in geographic community worlds 102; activities on practices in community youth organizations 101; agency and identity enactment from participating in community projects/change in 95, 107–109, 119, 136–137; challenges with community-based educational programs and 100; community agreements 54; community genre practices in school

109–110; community injustice 101; critical inquiries into community problems 101–102, 119; critical inquiries into US community discourses/Manifest Destiny 111–112; critique of local news/media representations of urban communities 112–113; ethnographic research for studying issues in 106–107; identity and "deep story" discourses and 112–113; identity practices enactment in 105, 112, 119; limitations of media representations of 259; norms in 96–98; online and face to face clubs 95; purpose and sense of community 95; research practices for studying issues in communities 106–110; student practices in community worlds 96–97; Trader Joe's as 242; youth organizations addressing racial injustice 98; youth organizations focusing on climate crisis and 103–104; youth organizations/clubs 97; *see also* 4-H organization; Black communities; extracurricular activities; Latinx communities; LGBTQ youth; non-dominant/low-income communities; social class discourses; Youth Participatory Action Research (YPAR)

comparison, limitations of 80–81

competence 38, 276; displaying for deeper learning 50; displaying for identity development 182; displaying in the workplace 243–245; displaying through languaging genres 245–246; displaying via ECA practices 164, 181–182

Compose Our World project *(composeourworld.org)* 72

Confessions of a Serial Kisser (Van Draanen) 91

conflict: languaging actions and 188–190; tension in family relations 202, 207, 212, 216–218, 220, 224, 276

connected learning 28; for integrating social/digital media into classroom 252–253; media/literature and 43, 72–74, 87–88, 91, 111

consumerism 236–237, 239–240

corporate discourses 229–231

cosmopolitan literacies 178, 253, 257

courtroom trials 41

COVID-19 pandemic 121, 135; change in instructional practices during 4–5, 11–12, 75; recovery from for educators

292 Index

and students 121–122; reduction of face-to-face interactions during 5, 17
cow judging 97–98
crime 133–135; critique of in media representations 112–113
critical thinking/inquiry: "Body Map" activity 89; "critical conversations" 76; activities on employing genres for engaging in on community problems 110; into community problems 101–102, 119; Critical Response Protocol 75; critical-thinking practices 56, 76–78, 85, 87; critique of local news/media representations of urban communities 112–113; on US community discourses/Manifest Destiny 111–112; on workplace practices 235–240; in YPAR/CFJ 122–124, 134–137
critical media pedagogy, need for 134, 136–137
Critical Race Theory (CRT) 34–35, 121; contextualizing media/literature from 88–89
Crossover series (Alexander) 202
cultural contexts 26–27, *27*, 58–59, 72, 85, 214; cultural modeling 13, 89, 109, 170; drawing on funds of identity derived from outside of school and 60–61; of practices and adolescent co-authoring of figured worlds 11–12, 39; in student's outside school *vs.* in school worlds and 21
culturally sustaining pedagogies (CSP) 32, 122, 127, 135, 137; family literacies and 218
customer is always right" discourse 42, 229–231, 243
Cyphers for Justice (CFJ) program 78–79, 119, 121–123; activism and 127–129; as figured world 124; interrelated research and activism/art in 129–131, *131*; knowledge and identity construction in 124–129, 135–137; youth research/ survey on body image and 132–134; *see also* Youth Participatory Action Research (YPAR)

dairy cow judging 97–98
"Danger of a Single Story" (Adiche) 111
DECA 178, 180
deep story discourses 112–113

deeper learning 8–10, 21–22, 26; displaying competence and 50; theater participation and 86; through culturally sustaining pedagogies 127; through relational pedagogy and purpose 50–52
deficit discourses of adolescents 40, 58, 60, 80, 87, 96–97, 100, 109, 112, 128, 277
Denver schools 97
Detroit schools 98
Dezuaani, M. 158
Diasgranados, A. 6
digital literacy 123, 129, 134, 137; *see also* social/digital media worlds
disciplinary practices 97; disproportionate for Black *vs.* White students 109
discourses 21, 26, 56, 68; "deep story" discourses in communities 112–113; "winning is everything" discourse 38, 184–186, 192; of 4-H organization 97–98; activities for contextualizing discourses 37–38, 149; in communities 96, 98, 105, 112–113; as component of contextualizing of practices 33–34, 78; contextualizing for student framing practices 49; contextualizing worlds based on genre knowledge and 42; corporate discourses on pleasing customers in the workplace 229–231; critical inquiries into US community discourses/Manifest Destiny 111–112; critiquing and sharing critiques of discourses on social/digital media worlds 258–261; critiquing of sports world discourses 202–203; deficit discourses of adolescents 40, 58, 60, 80, 87, 96–97, 100, 109, 112, 128, 277; discourse-world in response to media/literature responses and 44; of ecology/nature 37; enacting identities through 33–34; of gender and sexuality 36–37, 202–203; in geographically based community worlds 101; learning about adherence to from media/literature 86–87; of race 34–35; race discourses and need for redefining academic literacy and 57–58; of social class 35–36; social class and disparities in achievement discourses and 58; *see also* race discourses; social class discourses
discussions as genres 74–77; "critical conversations" in 76; online sites for discussion 75
Disney World, media representations of 259–260

divorce 206, 211, 217, 220
Dry (Shusterman) 90
dyslexia 66–67

ecological discourses 37–38, 42, 49
educational justice 133–134, 136–137
ELA teaching. *See* teaching ELA practices
elementary school 67; transition to middle school from 64
embodied actions: COVID-19 pandemic and 17; hugging in classroom and 53; languaging actions and 16–18, 22, 148–149, 187–188, 211–214; student engagement and 38
emotions 186; grief 213–214; languaging actions as emotions 16–18, 22, 148–149, 187–188, 211–214; voicing emotions as shaping peer relations 148–149
environmental worlds 104; *see also* climate crisis; ecological discourses
ethnographic writing and research 72–73; about adherence to norms and discourses 84–85; for portraying use of lived-world practices 80–84, 91; for studying issues in communities 106–107, 112–113; writing prompts on norms activity 55–56
explanation 78
external dialogue 187–188; exposure to and language acquisition 18–19; student reflection on for social interactions and support 19–20
extracurricular activities (ECAs) 163–182; acquiring leadership roles in 175–177; activities for describing identity enactment in 178–179; activities for formulating purposes for practices in 167–168; benefits of for adolescents from lower socioeconomic groups 166–167; deeper learning in 9; enacting discourses on value of participation in 179–180; envisioning of future possible selves 178; extrinsic *vs.* intrinsic purposes for participation in 165–166; flow experience in 86; genres employed with participation in 180–181; identity adoption in 174–175, 178–179; interacting with brokers in 168–169; languaging actions in 168–174, 176; need for schools to provide opportunities for engaging 182; participation for court-involved youths in urban communities 178; purposes

related to benefits of participation in 163–165
extrinsic *vs.* intrinsic purposes 165–166

face-to-face interactions: identity enactment through role-plays 263; limitations of social media *vs.* 253; reduction of during COVID-19 pandemic 5; *vs.* screen time 250; *see also* peer groups; social/digital media worlds
Facing History and Ourselves Project *(www.facinghistory.org)* 111
family figured worlds 206–225; discourse adherence on parenting practices and 215–218; enacting identity in 218–219; independent/autonomous identity adoption in 219–222; languaging emotions in family relations 211–215; narrative writing on family practices 222–223; need to respect family *vs.* school-based literacies 218–219; responding to family portrayals in media/literature and 224–225; social capital provision and historical shifts in families and 209–212, 218; supportive practices in 206–209, 212, 219; tension in family relations 202, 207, 212, 216–218, 220, 224, 276
FanFiction 265
Faust, S. 39
feminist critical perspective 76
figured worlds, adolescent co-authoring of: constitutions of 3, 6–7, 120; informal learning as deeper learning in 8–10, 22; informal learning of different practices in different worlds and 21–22, 26, 45, 127; relational pedagogy and agency and sense of ability to co-author 51; figured worlds: Youth Participatory Action Research (YPAR) as a 120–121
Fine, S. 6, 9, 50, 167
Fisher, M. T. 96
Fletcher, J. 41
flow experience 86, 166
Floyd, G. 260
fossil fuel industry 112
Four-H organization 97, 98
free-reading programs 159–160
friendship. *See* peer groups
"From where do you read the world?" 20–21
funds of identity 60–61, 262
future possible selves, envisioning of 178

"games as text/games as action" model 254
Garcia, A. 11
Gay-Straight Alliances (GSAs) 97
Gee, J. P. 7–8, 11, 27
gender discourses 36–37, 58, 85, 87, 124, 212; activities for contextualizing 37–38; body image and 36, 132–134; impact of on perception of workplace practices and 238–240; on masculinity in YA literature on sports participation 202–203; on parenting practices 215–218; in peer groups 147–151; in peer groups based on race, class, and gender 147–148; redefining academic literacy for non-dominant communities and 57; in sports worlds 185, 192–193; student contextualization of for learning in school 276; in Texas *vs.* German schools 59; on value of participation in ECAS 179–180; writings about adherence to 84–85; YPAR activism promoting awareness of problematic 128; *see also* discourses
genre: acquiring genre practices for use in social/digital media 265; contextualizing worlds based on genre knowledge 41–42; contextualizing use of as social action for enacting practices 41; in ECAs participation 180–181; fostering discussions as genre in school worlds 74–76; narrative writing on family practices 222–223; for portraying use of lived-world practices in school worlds 91; reconceptualization practices from different genres to school worlds and 72–74, *73*; research practices as genres for studying figure worlds 78–80; in sports worlds 197–200; student contextualization of for learning in school 276; use of community genre practices in school 13, 109–110; use of for enacting peer relations 158–159; in workplace figured worlds 245–246
gentrification 102, 112
Germany, gender in 59
global perspective adoption, need for 102
Google Docs 85
grief 213–214
GripTape (*griptape.org*) project 99
grounded theory 126
GroupMe chat app 85

Hate U Give, The (Thomas) 202
Hawaiian ecological proverbs 37
Hawkins, K. L. 37
Hedgaard, M. 52
helicopter teaching discourses 56–57
high school: high school dropouts 101; peer groups in 64–65, 174
Hochschild, A. R. 112
Hodge, T. 111
hospital workplaces 246
House on Mango Street, The (Cisneros) 72, 87
hugging 53
Hunley, Andrea 5

identities 26, 68, 105; "deep story" discourses in communities 112–113; "good student" identities and 59–60, 219; activities for contextualizing practices for enactment of 40; community member identity 96; contextualizing personhood according to norms 39–40; drawing on funds of identity and 60–61, 262; in ECAs 174–175, 179; enacting identities constituting personhood 39; enacting identities for school belonging 61–62, 64, 90; in family worlds 218–219; identification with characters in media/ literature 42–43, 72, 85–86, 90–91, 96, 119; identity construction in Cyphers for Justice 120–121, 124–129, 135–137; identity development from elementary- middle-high school-college 64–65; identity enactment from participating in community projects/social change 95, 107–109, 119, 136–137; independent/ autonomous identity adoption in families 219–222; insider language for enactment of 170, 174, 176, 195–197, 242, 254; multiple identities and literacies of nondominant groups 119–123, 137; narrative writing and 42, 136; outsider identities in school 60; in peer groups 143, **150**, 150–155; social/digital tool use for enacting 262–264; socialization of students' 63–64; sociocultural contexts of 60–61, 124–125, 262; in sports worlds 193–197; student contextualization of for learning in school 276; student learning to contextualize for framing practices 49; symbolic resources and 42–43, 61, 72,

90–91, 264; teacher as co-learners with students 52; in the workplace 240–245; in the workplace *vs.* future aspirational 244–245
IKEA 237
"In the Good Old U.S.A" (poem, Villablongo) 112
in-between" relations/meanings, languaging actions and 17–18
individual education plans (IEPs) 66
inequality and income inequality 14, 85, 98–99
informal learning 8–10, 21–22, 26, 169
inner dialogue 19–20, 187–188, 192; languaging actions and 18–19
insider language: in ECAs 170, 174, 176; in peer group relations 154–158; in sports worlds 195–197; in video games 254–255; in the workplace 242
Instagram 253, 265; *see also* social/digital media worlds
integrative thinking 13–14
IRE genre (initiate, react, evaluate) 75

"A Jelly-Fish, A" (poem, Moore) 44
job interviews 245; *see also* workplace figured worlds

Klu Klux Klan (KKK) 89

Lang, J. M. 28
languaging actions: "language thinking practices" 76–78, 277; African-American Vernacular English (AAVE) and 13, 55, 105; Appalachian English *vs.* Standard 105; barbershop languaging practices 235–236; based on Somali cultural norms 214–215; Bronxonics 170–171; in CFJ 127, 137; contextualizing practices as 15; in ECAs 168–174, 176; as emotions and embodied actions 16–18, 22, 148–149, 187–188, 211–214; enacting personhood and 39; external and inner dialogue looping and 18–20; in family worlds 207–209, 211–215; genre and 41–42; hip-hop as 13, 40, 125; as identity practices enactment in communities 105, 137; insider language 170, 174, 176, 195–197, 254–255; languaging thinking 28; learning to use different genres of across different worlds 74; as medium for enacting practices/co-authoring worlds with

others and 15–16, 22; norms of prescriptive *vs.* descriptive 54–55; obesity and 36; in peer relations/groups 19–20, 22, 142–145, 148–149, 160, 186–190; in role-playing 261; in sports worlds 186–192, 195–197; student research on 80; supportive languaging 143–145, 186–190, 207–209, 212, 245; teenspeak 87; Text World Theory and 44; in the workplace 229–233, 240, 242–243; youth culture and media/ literature in PLCs and 96; *see also* discourses
Latinx communities 12, 60–61, 87, 101, 105, 112; BIPOC LGBTQ youth 131; impact of social/digital media use on reading/writing 252
leadership identity enactment: in ECAs 175–177; in sports worlds 194–195, 277; in the workplace 243–244
learning: informal learning as deeper 8–10, 21–22, 26; learning challenges 66–68; relational learning 7–8; *see also* academic success in school; alternative instructional practices; classroom activities; connected learning; deeper learning; teaching ELA practice
Lee, C. 89, 109
LGBTQ youth 97, 101, 131, 148, 207–208, 257
Linked Learning Alliance *(linkedlearning. org)* 99
literacy, redefining academic 57
literature. *See* media/literature; young-adult literature
Lord of the Flies (Goldman) 158–159
Louisiana 112

Manifest Destiny discourse 111
marching band participation 164–166, 174, 180
masculinity discourses in sports 202–203
math 18, 62, 169
Meaningful Writing Project *(meaningfulwritingproject.net)* 81
media/literature 26; "deep story" discourses and identities in communities 112–113; analysis of language norms in movies and 55; CFJ research on female body image in 132–133; connected learning and 43, 72–74, 87, 91; critical inquiries into US media/lit representations of Manifest Destiny 111–112; from Critical

Race Theory (CRT) 88–89; critique of local news/media representations of urban communities 112–113; critiquing and sharing of discourses on 258–261; cultural modeling in responses to 89; global, multicultural perspectives through 102; impact of social/digital media use on reading/writing 252; learning about norm/discourse adherence from 86–87; limitations of community representations in 259–260; minimum wage activism in 99; misinformation in 258–259; need for critical media pedagogy 134; norms of language in media use and 87; peer group conflict in 158–159; in PLCs 96; purposeful engagement with at school 86; race and gender discourses and 87; recognition practices 87–88; reconceptualization practices from different to school worlds and 73, 73–74; recontextualization of student worlds thru responses to 89–90; recontextualization practices 87–88; responding to family portrayals in 224–225; responding to peer group portrayals in 142; responding to portrayal of workplace worlds in 246–247; responses to as enacting "text worlds" 43–45; social and narrative imagination practices and 87–88; student contextualization of for learning in school 276; as symbolic resources for identity development 42–43, 72–74, 85–86, 90–91, 264; use of by "Participatory Literacy Communities" 111; use of for enacting peer relations 158–159; use of in sports worlds 200–203; use of social/digital media tools for responding to 266–267; YPAR activism promoting awareness of problematic discourses in 128; *see also* social/digital media worlds; young-adult literature

Mehta, J. 6, 9, 50, 167

mentoring: brokers in ECAs 168–170; in community worlds 98–99

meritocracy 35–36

Metz, M. 55

Mexican Whiteboy (de la Peña) 202

Michigan Youth Policy Fellows (MYPF) 98

middle school 67, 101, 174; peer groups in 64–65; transition to from elementary school 64–66

military 74

minimum wage increases 99

misinformation 258–259; critiquing of 261–262

Moore, M. 44

"Mother Bird Method" 181

Ms. E (ELA teacher in Beach research study) 21, 158; purposeful use of relational pedagogy by 52–53, 57; survey of on norms and discourses in peer groups 150–151; writing prompts for contextualizing norms activity of 55–56; *see also* teaching ELA practices

Ms. Nelson (teacher) 88

multicultural perspectives 102

multimodal self-portraits 262–263

Murphy, K. 17

Myers-Lipton, S. 99

narrative writing 72–73; about adherence to norms and discourses 84–85; on family practices 222; identities and 42; narrative imagination practices 87–88; for portraying/reflecting use of lived-world practices 80–84, 91; use of role-playing for 264; writing prompts for contextualizing norms activity 55–56

National Writing Project workshops 12

Native Americans 111–112

news: critique of local news/media representations of urban communities 112–113; misinformation in 258–259; newspapers 86, 90; *see also* media/literature; social/digital media worlds

Noguera, P. 121

non-dominant/low-income communities 97, 99, 112; apprenticeship programs for 245; culturally sustaining pedagogy for 218; disciplinary practices impacting in Denver schools and 97; disparities in achievement tests and 58, 119–120; employment pathways and 99, 245; impact of social/digital media use on reading/writing 252; importance of valuing of in school worlds 96; lack of portrayals of in social media 267; media representations of crime in 112; multiple identities and literacies of 119–123, 137; need for valuing of academic/literacy practices of 96–97,

135, 137; non-dominant peer groups 150; peer group membership and 148; problematic "remediation" discourses in community-based youth programs for 100; social capital provision by families and 209–212

norms 21, 26–27, 27; "good student" identities and 59–60; of 4-H 97–98; acquiring practices in the workplace by 231–235; activities for contextualizing practices related to norms in peer groups 149; adherence to through languaging actions in ECAs and 170–174, 176; adherence to through languaging actions in family worlds 214–215; adherence to through languaging actions in sports worlds 190–192; adhering to as component of contextualizing of practices 32–33; adhering to in peer groups 147; in communities 96–98, 101; contextualizing personhood according to norms 39–40; corporate norms on pleasing customers in the workplace 229–231; learning about adherence to from media/literature 86–87; prescriptive vs. descriptive language use and 54–55; in school worlds 54, 68, 84–85; Standard English as 80, 105; student contextualization of for learning in school 276; student engagement and belonging and 54; student learning to contextualize for framing practices 49; survey on norms in peer groups 150–151; in video games/role-playing worlds 256–258; writing prompts for contextualizing norms activity 55–56; writings about adherence to 84–85

nursing 246

O'Connor, C. 54
obesity, languaging around 36
open-ended questions 75
"open-mic" spoken word performances 14, 130, 169; as ECA practice for displaying competence in classroom 181–182

PACHS (Chicago High School) 101, 110
Packer, G. 35
Padres y Jóvenes Unidos project (Denver) 97
parent-teacher conferences 218–219
"Participatory Literacy Communities" (PLCs) 96, 109, 111

"passing theories" 75
"passionate affinity-based spaces" 7, 96; informal out-of-school learning and 8; video games/role-play as 254
peer groups 52; activities for contextualizing practices for participating in 146–147; activities for contextualizing practices related to norms/discourses in 149–150; adherence to norms and discourses in 147–148; Australian Voice Crackers as 3–4, 12, 14, 28–29, 52, 143; conflict in 146, 148–149, 158–159; in ECAs 166, 174; exclusion from 145–146; group identity in 147–148; importance of in middle and high school 64–65; limitations of social media interactions/relationships in 251, 253; peer support 13–14, 158; practices of for teaching ELA 159–160; recognizing peers' unique traits and perspectives in 145–146; reflection on own/peer group external dialogue for social interactions 19–20; relational agency and pedagogy and 51; relational agency from ECAs and 166; self-explanation in 78; social media interactions/relationships in 250–253; in sports worlds 185, 187–190; survey of on norms and discourses in peer groups 150–151; trust in 144–145, 159; use of genre and media/literature for enacting peer relations 158–159; voicing emotions as shaping peer relations 148–149; see also face-to-face peer interactions
performance, in CFJ 130–131
personhood 39–40, 91
Photovoice projects 98, 129–130
playful language 74
police, community relations of 112, 133
popularity in school 150, **150**, 150–151
positionality 124–125
power relations 86–87, 99, 111; YPAR and 120–121
practices, adolescent co-authoring of figured worlds and: acquiring practices as ways of doing/acting 10–11, 26; boundary-crossing and integrative thinking for learning in classroom and 13–14, 22; contextualizing as languaging actions 15; languaging actions as medium for enacting/co-authoring of different worlds 15–16; learning to

298 Index

contextualize 26–27, *27*; practice theory 125; practices defined 10–11; social and cultural contexts in figured worlds and 11–12, 39; using knowledge of past practices to contextualize present/future practices 27–28; wobble experiences in and alternative instructional practices 12–13; *see also* classroom activities for contextualizing practices; discourses; genre; languaging actions; purpose

purpose 21, 26–27, *27*, 45, 68; in community-based youth programs 95–98, 100; contextualizing for student learning and engagement in schools 49–50, 78, 276; deep learning through relational pedagogy and 50–52; defining as component of contextualizing of practices 28–32; for employing corporate discourses on pleasing customers 229–231; extrinsic *vs.* intrinsic purposes for ECA participation 165–166; in family worlds 206–212; group identity and engagement from shared sense of 143, 146–147; media/ literature engagement at school and 86; purposeful use of relational pedagogy by Ms. E 52–53; reflection on constituting formal *vs.* informal learning of 53–54; from sports participation 184–186

Qatar 85
questions, posing 75, 79

race discourses 34–35, 65, 76–77, 79, 87, 89, 98, 100–101; activities for contextualizing 37–38; Critical Race Theory (CRT) 88–89; critiquing and sharing critique of stereotypical media/ social media representations 87, 112, 260–261; peer groups and 147–148; perception of workplace practices and 235–236; prescriptive language use and 55; redefining academic literacy and 57–58; risks and benefits of adolescent work and 228; role-playing activities for critiquing 260–261; sports participation and 185–186; in YPAR seminars 133–134

racial justice/injustice 13–14, 79, 88–89, 96, 100, 109, 135; youth organizations addressing 98; youth theater productions exploring 112

Radesky, J. 5

"rape culture" 128
reading 56–57; impact of social/digital media use on 251–252
Real Women Have Curves (Lopez) 86
"The Red Wheelbarrow" (poem, Williams) 44
relational agency 12–14; peer groups from ECAs and 166; reflection on external dialogue for 19–20; through relational pedagogy and student-to-student interactions 51
"relational mobilities" 253
relational pedagogy 50–54, 57, 68
religion in families 206–207
remote instruction 4–5, 75, 121; online sites for discussion 75
research practices 85, 95, 102, 119; apprenticeship in social research in CFJYPAR program 123, 125, 129–131, *131*, 132–133; GripTape project and 99; research for studying issues in communities 106–110; research practices as genres for studying figure worlds 78–80; *see also* ethnographic writing and research; Youth Participatory Action Research (YPAR)
right-wing deep story discourses 112
risk taking 170
robotics clubs 245–246
role-playing activities 181; for critiquing racial discourses and censorship 260–261; use of for enacting identity 263–264
Romeo and Juliet (movie) 86
rural schools 102; Appalachian English *vs.* Standard 105

Schatzki, T. R. 10
school culture 43, 65–66, 85, 89
school-to-prison pipeline 133–134
screen time 42, 250; *see also* social/digital media worlds
self-explanation 78
self-in-practice 124–125
Servant of Two Masters (play, Goldoni) 86
sexuality discourses 36–37; *see also* LGBTQ youth
Sir Mashalot: Mind-Blowing SIX Country Song Mashup" (YouTube video) 41
skiing 80
small group discussion 75
Small Teaching (Lang) 28
soccer 78

social capital provision 209–210; historical shifts in families and 210–212

social change 99, 165; addressing challenges of in video games 254; educational justice 133–134, 136–137; social/media tools for online activism for 263; students in CFJ/YPAR programs as agents of 123–131, 136–137; in wake of COVID-19 pandemic 32, 122

social class discourses 35–36, 76, 85, 95–96, 100; activities for contextualizing 37–38; benefits of ECAs for adolescents from lower socioeconomic groups 166–167; disparities in achievement tests/discourses 58, 119–120; gender and popular girl discourses 37; impact of on perception of retail practices 236–238; peer groups and 147–148, **150**, 150–151; prescriptive language use and 55; redefining academic literacy for non-dominant communities and 57; social capital provision by families and 209–212; sports participation and 185–186

social imagination practices 87–88

social justice 101, 104, 108

social/digital media worlds 134, 144; as "funds of identity" 262; acquiring genre practices for use in 265; adverse effects of 249; for connecting with large audiences 253; critiquing and sharing of discourses on 258–261; digital literacies 123, 129, 134, 137; face-to-face interactions *vs.* screen time 250; impact of on academics 251–252; integrating into classroom practices 252–253; limitations of community representations in 259–260; limitations of for social relations in peer groups 251, 253; misinformation in 258–261; most used platforms as of Fall 2020 (Snapchat, TikTok, Instagram) 249–250; multimodal self-portraits creation in 262–263; norms and sites for interacting with others 257–258; for social relations in peer groups 250–252; in sports worlds 201–202; student contextualization of for learning in school 276; usage time of for adolescents 249–250; use of for enacting identity 262–264; use of tools of for responding to media/literary texts 266–267; YA literature on use of 266; *see also* video games/role playing worlds

Somali cultural norms 214–215, 260

sports worlds 38, 78, 85; "winning is everything" discourse 38, 184, 192; benefits and purpose from participation in 184–186, 190, 192–193; embodied emotions in 186–188; flow experience in 86; genres for celebrating team success 197–198; genres for interaction with coaches 198–200; genres for team member interaction 197; identity enactment in 193–197; languaging actions in 186–188, 190–192; leadership identity enactment in 194–195, 277; norm adherence in games/matches 190–192; social and broadcasting media in 201–203; supportive and caring team member relations in 188–190; YA lit on 202–203

Standardized English 80, 105

Starbucks 229–230, 243

STEM, gender discourses and 58

stereotypes 55, 76, 87, 148, 258–259

student engagement 59; contextualizing purpose for 50, 131; display of competence for 38; enactment of identities and 40, 64; norms in informal and formal learning and 54; outside school experiences and perspectives and 4–6, 8–9, 11–14, 20–22, 57, 135; outsider identities and 60; parent-teacher conferences and 219; situating in specific social and cultural contexts and 11–12, 57; survey on during COVID pandemic 4–5; teacher practices for 11–13

suburban schools 98

Sustainable Democracy Project (SDP) 101

Swift, T. 28

symbolic resources, media and literature as 42–43, 72–74, 85–86, 90–91, 264

systems thinking 254

Target 237, 242

teaching ELA practice 21, 275–287; analysis of language norms in movies and 55; building text-words 44; on climate crisis 89–90; courtroom trials 41; critical-thinking practices 56, 76–78; discourses' impact on 56–57, 61; deficit discourses of adolescents and 40, 58, 60, 80, 87, 96–97, 100, 109, 112, 277; ECA practices for displaying competence in classroom 181–182; employing video games/role playing worlds 255–256;

300 Index

ethnographic/narrative writing for portraying use of lived-world practices 80–84, 91; ethnographic/narrative writing for studying community issues 106–107; formulating explanations and self-explanations and 78; hip-hop pedagogy 169; impact of social/digital media use on reading/writing 251–252; need to know and use students lived-world/outside school practices and 26–27, *27*, 57, 72–73, 78, 96–97, 134–135, 218–219, 275–287; need for support for gay adolescents 148; need to respect family *vs.* school-based literacies 218; norms in school worlds and 54; online sites for discussion 75; peer group practices to draw from in 159–160; reconceptualization practices from different to school worlds *73*, 73–74; relational pedagogy and purpose in 50–52, 54; research practices for studying figured worlds 78–80; social/digital tools for connecting with students 257–258; for student engagement 11–13; supporting alternative perspectives 76; teachers as co-learners and 52, 57, 136; use of role-playing for narrative writing 264; use of social/digital media tools for responding to media/literary texts 266–267; writing prompts for contextualizing norms activity 55–56; *see also* alternative instructional practices; classroom activities for contextualizing practices; Ms. E (ELA teacher in Beach research study); student engagement
teenspeak 87
Texas, gender in 59
"text worlds" 43–45
text-speak 87
theater participation 9, 50, 86, 164, 168–169, 181; deeper learning and 9, 86; identity development and 90; on racial injustice 112
Things Fall Apart (Achebe) 88
Thompson, I. 19
Thunberg, G. 103
TikTok 253
time limits 40
Titanic (movie) 86
Trader Joe's 242
trust: in families 207–208, 215, 218, 220; in peers and peers' groups and 144–145, 159–160; in sports 187

video games/role playing worlds 253–255; "systems thinking" for addressing global challenges and 254; employing in the classroom 255–256; norms and sites for interacting with others 256–258; role-playing activities for critiquing racial discourses and censorship 260–261; use of for enacting identity 263–264; *see also* social/digital media worlds
Villablongo, J. A. 112

White privilege 34, 76, 88–89, 98, 135; academic white privilege 96; consumerism and 236–237; disproportionate disciplinary practices and 109
White students 79, 98; as "preppies" 150; Appalachian English *vs.* Standard and 105; disproportionate disciplinary practices for Black *vs.* White students 109; peer groups and 147–148; risks and benefits of adolescent work and 228
Williams, W. C. 44
Wilner, A. 13
"winning is everything" discourse 38, 184–186, 192
Wittek, L. 19
wobble experiences 12–13
work ethic, from sports participation 184–185, 192–193
workplace figured worlds 227–247; acquiring genres for use in 245–246; acquiring norms for employing practices in 231–235; gender discourses' impact of on perception of workplace practices and 238–240; identity adoption in 240–242; leadership identity enactment in 243–244; openness to adoption of workplace *vs.* future aspirational identity and 244–245; purposes for employing corporate norms and discourses on pleasing customers 229–231; race discourses' impact on perception of retail 235–236; responding to portrayal of in media/literature 246–247; risks and benefits of adolescent working 227–229; social class discourses' impact on perception of retail 236–238
writing: impact of social/digital media use on 251–252; inner and external dialogue looping and 19; Meaningful Writing Project *(meaningfulwritingproject. net)* 81; *see also* classroom activities for

contextualizing practices; ethnographic writing and research; narrative writing

YMCA/YWCA 97
young-adult literature: on sports worlds 202–203; on use of social/digital media 266; on work and workplaces 247
youth culture 43, 96, 123
youth oppression 127

Youth Participatory Action Research (YPAR) 78–80, 119–125; race discourses in YPAR seminars 133; youth research/survey on body image and 132–134
YouthTruth project 2
YouTube 41, 257

Zittoun, T. 73, 85

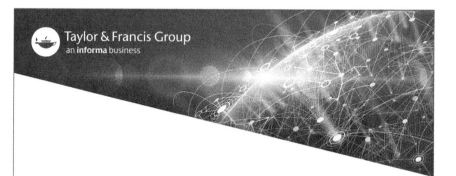

Taylor & Francis eBooks

www.taylorfrancis.com

A single destination for eBooks from Taylor & Francis with increased functionality and an improved user experience to meet the needs of our customers.

90,000+ eBooks of award-winning academic content in Humanities, Social Science, Science, Technology, Engineering, and Medical written by a global network of editors and authors.

TAYLOR & FRANCIS EBOOKS OFFERS:

A streamlined experience for our library customers

A single point of discovery for all of our eBook content

Improved search and discovery of content at both book and chapter level

REQUEST A FREE TRIAL
support@taylorfrancis.com